Red and Black in Harlem and Jamaica

"This astonishing compendium is a valuable corrective to parochial conceptions of the 'black radical tradition'. It places the prolific work of Wilfred A. Domingo back in the center of the history of anticolonial politics."

—Paul Gilroy, Emeritus Professor of Humanities, University College London

"A wonderfully lucid introduction to the life and work of Wilfred A. Domingo, with the 'red and black threads' in his writings edited magnificently by Peter Hulme and Leslie James."

—Catherine Hall, chair of the Centre for the Study of the Legacies of British Slavery at UCL

"An outstanding contribution. Hulme and James have rendered invaluable service by providing the most authoritative and detailed biographical portrait capturing the brilliance of W. A. Domingo. One of Harlem's leading 'New Negro' radicals of the 1920s, Domingo was also a combative antiracist and anti-colonial intellectual and a relentless and distinguished fighter for Jamaica's independence."

—Winston James, Professor of History at the University of California, Irvine

"A magnificent interpretation of Caribbean decolonization, seen through the lens of the Jamaican, W. A. Domingo, whose stunning writings make up half the book. It's a Harlem story as much as it is Caribbean: a glorious narrative, bringing the displacements of the Caribbean back to life."

—Bill Schwarz, Professor at Queen Mary University of London

"This brilliant collection pulls W. A. Domingo from decades of misunderstanding, and returns him as one of the most central thinkers of the Caribbean intellectual tradition. The deep background research of Hulme and James forces scholars of black radicalism to reconsider this quiet, 'unforgettable man' whose dedication to true and full freedom in Jamaica carries eternal lessons."

—Matthew J. Smith, University College London, author of *Red and Black in Haiti*

"Fascinating exploration of a controversial figure. Friend of Garvey in the early days, a thought-provoking critic of Garvey later on. W. A. Domingo was not a federalist. An independent thinker. Jamaican nationalist. Thought-provoking perspectives on what would now be called a Caribbean story. An informative and important read."

—Merle Collins, poet and novelist, author of *Ocean Stirrings*

Black Critique

Series editors: Anthony Bogues and Bedour Alagraa

Throughout the twentieth century and until today, anti-racist, radical decolonisation struggles attempted to create new forms of thought. Figures from Ida B. Wells to W. E. B. Du Bois and Steve Biko, from Claudia Jones to Walter Rodney and Amílcar Cabral produced work which drew from the historical experiences of Africa and the African diaspora. They drew inspiration from the Haitian revolution, radical black abolitionist thought and practice, and other currents that marked the contours of a black radical intellectual and political tradition.

The Black Critique series operates squarely within this tradition of ideas and political struggles. It includes books which foreground this rich and complex history. At a time when there is a deep desire for change, black radicalism is one of the most underexplored traditions that can drive emancipatory change today. This series highlights these critical ideas from anywhere in the black world, creating a new history of radical thought for our times.

Also available:

Against Racial Capitalism:
Selected Writings
Neville Alexander
Edited by Salim Vally and Enver Motala

Ere Roosevelt Came:
The Adventures of the Man in the Cloak – A Pan-African Novel of the Global 1930s
Dusé Mohamed Ali
Edited by Marina Bilbija and Alex Lubin

Moving Against the System:
The 1968 Congress of Black Writers and the Making of Global Consciousness
Edited and with an Introduction by David Austin

Revolutionary Movements in Africa:
An Untold Story
Edited by Pascal Bianchini, Ndongo Samba Sylla and Leo Zeilig

Anarchism and the Black Revolution:
The Definitive Edition
Lorenzo Kom'boa Ervin

After the Postcolonial Caribbean:
Memory, Imagination, Hope
Brian Meeks

A Certain Amount of Madness:
The Life, Politics and Legacies of Thomas Sankara
Edited by Amber Murrey

Of Black Study
Joshua Myers

Become Ungovernable:
An Abolition Feminist Ethic for Democratic Living
H. L. T. Quan

On Racial Capitalism, Black Internationalism, and Cultures of Resistance
Cedric J. Robinson
Edited by H. L. T. Quan

Black Minded:
The Political Philosophy of Malcolm X
Michael Sawyer

Red International and Black Caribbean Communists in New York City, Mexico and the West Indies, 1919–1939
Margaret Stevens

The Point is to Change the World:
Selected Writings of Andaiye
Edited by Alissa Trotz

Red and Black in Harlem and Jamaica

The Revolutionary Life and Selected Writings of W. A. Domingo

Edited by
Peter Hulme and Leslie James

PLUTO PRESS

First published 2025 by Pluto Press
New Wing, Somerset House, Strand, London WC2R 1LA
and Pluto Press, Inc.
1930 Village Center Circle, 3-834, Las Vegas, NV 89134

www.plutobooks.com

British Library Cataloguing in Publication Data
A catalogue record for this book is available from the British Library

ISBN 978 0 7453 4857 5 Paperback
ISBN 978 0 7453 4859 9 PDF
ISBN 978 0 7453 4858 2 EPUB

Typeset by Stanford DTP Services, Northampton, England

Simultaneously printed in the United Kingdom and United States of America

EU GPSR Authorised Representative
LOGOS EUROPE, 9 rue Nicolas Poussin, 17000, LA ROCHELLE, France
Email: Contact@logoseurope.eu

W. A. Domingo in 1926. (Courtesy of the Hubert H. Harrison Papers, Series VI: Photographs, Box 15, folder 3, Rare Book and Manuscript Library, Columbia University, New York)

Contents

Figures

Note on the Texts

Obvious errors and misprints have been corrected. Spelling, punctuation, capitalisation, and italicisation have been silently regularised, with the exception of the US spelling used in the pieces first published in the USA. Minor grammatical adjustments have been made where necessary to clarify sense. In the case of texts originally published in newspapers, some paragraphs have been consolidated. Editorial additions appear in square brackets. The titles of pieces are as they were given at first publication unless otherwise noted. Numbered footnotes are the editors' additions. References to the texts included in this collection take the form [#o].

Abbreviations

AACC	Anglo American Caribbean Commission
AACE	American Association for Caribbean Advancement
ABB	African Blood Brotherhood for African Liberation and Redemption
ACWIF	American Committee for West Indian Federation
AFL	American Federation of Labor
AJGP	Amy Jacques Garvey Papers, Box 1, file 7, Fisk University, Nashville, TN
ALP	Alain Locke Papers, Coll. 164, Box 25, folder 28, Moorland-Spingarn Research Center, Howard University, Washington, DC
APL	American Protective League
AWIACA	American West Indian Association on Caribbean Affairs
BI	Bureau of Investigation (until 1935, when it became the FBI)
BITU	Bustamante Industrial Trade Union
BLI	British Library of Information
CB	Cathy Bergin, ed., *African American Anti-Colonial Thought, 1917–1937*, Edinburgh, UK: Edinburgh University Press, 2016
CID	Criminal Investigation Department
CLC	Caribbean Labour Congress
CO	Colonial Office papers (in The National Archives, London)
CPUSA	Communist Party of America
CUC	Closer Union Commission
DLP	Democratic Labour Party
EEBP	Egbert Ethelred Brown Papers, 1914–1956, Sc MS87, Schomburg Center for Research in Black Culture, Manuscripts, Archives, and Rare Books Division, New York Public Library
FBI	Federal Bureau of Investigation (from 1935, previously Bureau of Investigation)
FBIWAD	Federal Bureau of Investigation (Wilfred Adophus Domingo). Documents released under FOIPA (Freedom of Information/Privacy Acts) request number 1213480-002. Courtesy of Jacob Zumoff
FCA	Federation of Citizens' Associations (Jamaica)
FDRP	Franklin D. Roosevelt, Papers as President: The President Secretary's File (PSF), 1933–1945, Franklin D. Roosevelt Presidential Library & Museum, Hyde Park, NY

IWW	Industrial Workers of the World
JDP	Jamaica Democratic Party
JLP	Jamaica Labour Party
JPL	Jamaica Progressive League
JPL(K)	Jamaica Progressive League (Kingston)
JPL(NY)	Jamaica Progressive League (New York)
MGP	*The Marcus Garvey and Universal Negro Improvement Association Papers*, ed. Robert A. Hill, Berkeley, CA: University of California Press/Durham, NC: Duke University Press, 13 vols, 1983–2016
MID	Military Intelligence Division (US)
NAACP	National Association for the Advancement of Colored People
NAACPACWIF	NAACP 1940–55. General office file. Leagues—American Committee for West Indian Federation, 1945–48
NAACPRDPS	NAACP Racial discrimination and political sovereignty in the British West Indies Folder 001432-002-0252 Found in Papers of the NAACP, Part 13 NAACP and Labor, Series A Subject Files on Labor Conditions and Employment Discrimination
NARA	US National Archives and Records Administration, Washington, DC
NMP	Norman Manley Papers, Jamaica Archives and Records Department, Spanish Town, Jamaica
NYPL	New York Public Library
PNP	People's National Party (Jamaica)
RAHC	Robert A. Hill Collection, 1890–2014, Box PS9, Domingo, Wilfred A., Duke University
RBMP	Richard B. Moore Papers, Sc MG 397, Schomburg Center for Research in Black Culture, Manuscripts, Archives and Rare Books Division, New York Public Library
SCAC	Standing Closer Association Committee (British)
SCRBC	Schomburg Center for Research in Black Culture, Manuscripts, Archives and Rare Books Division, New York Public Library
SIS	Secret Intelligence Service (British)
SPA	Socialist Party of America
TNA	The National Archives (London)
TUAC	Trade Union Advisory Council (Jamaica)
UNIA	Universal Negro Improvement Association and African Communities League
WARA	W. Adolphe Roberts Archive (MS 353), National Library of Jamaica
WIFA	West Indian Federation of America (New York)

WIFLP	West Indian Federal Labour Party
WINC	West Indies National Council (previously WINEC)
WINCC	West Indies National Council Collection, Sc MG 665 Box 1, Schomburg Center for Research in Black Culture, Manuscripts, Archives and Rare Books Division, New York Public Library
WINEC	West Indies National Emergency Committee (became WINC in November 1940)
WIR	*West Indian Review* (Jamaica)

Acknowledgements

For generously sharing materials and for discussions about Domingo, warm thanks to Cathy Bergin, Rafe Dalleo, David Featherstone, Susan Gillman, Catherine Hall, Bobby Hill, Christian Högsberg, Winston James, Kesewa John, Rupert Lewis, Saje Mathieu, Ernest Mitchell, Chris Ouma, Louis J. Parascandola, Jak Peake, Caryl Phillips, Alan Rice, Kim Robinson-Walcott, David Scott, Bill Schwarz, Margaret Stevens, Birte Timm, Cornel West, and Jacob Zumoff. Thanks to Deanna Lyncook for research assistance.

Thanks to the librarians and archivists at the Rubinstein Rare Book & Manuscript Library at Duke University, Durham, NC; Senate House Library at the University of London; National Library of Jamaica; Jamaica Archives and Records Department, Spanish Town, Jamaica; Harvard University Library; John Hope and Aurelia E. Franklin Library at Fisk University, Nashville, TN; Stuart A. Rose Manuscript, Archives, and Rare Book Library, Emory University, Atlanta, GA; New York Public Library at 42nd Street; Schomburg Center for Research in Black Culture, New York Public Library; Moorland-Spingarn Research Center at Howard University, Washington, DC; The National Archives (London); University of California Berkeley Library.

Invaluable digital resources include HathiTrust Digital Library, newspaper archive.com and Ancestry Library®.

Thanks to Sarah Manley for permission to quote from the letters to her grandfather, Norman Manley.

Peter Hulme undertook research for this book while Stuart Hall Fellow at the Du Bois Institute in the Hutchins Center for African & African American Research at Harvard University: he thanks the director, Henry Louis Gates, Jr, the Center staff, and the other visiting fellows for their collegial support. Leslie James undertook research for this book while a Leverhulme Early Career Fellow at the University of Birmingham Department of African Studies and Anthropology (DASA): she thanks the Leverhulme Trust for their financial support, and colleagues in DASA, especially Kate Skinner, for facilitating the time and space to travel for research. Financial support for research at the National Archives of Jamaica and the National Library of Jamaica was provided by the School of History, Queen Mary University of London.

Some of the biographical information about Domingo was previously published in Peter Hulme, "Wilfred Domingo under Investigation: The 'Negro Menace' of 1919", in *Revolutionary Lives of the Red and Black Atlantic since 1917*, ed. Christian Hogsbjerg, David Featherstone, and Alan Rice, Manchester, UK: Manchester University Press, 2022, pp. 55–71.

Introduction
A Dedicated Man

I was born in Kingston, Jamaica, B.W.I., on November 26th, 1889. After attending the elementary public schools, I graduated from "The Board School" where high school instruction was given. I worked as a book keeper for a short while after leaving school and emigrated to the United States in August 1910.

Though a notoriously quiet man, W. A. Domingo made the headlines on two very different occasions. In June 1919, at the height of the Red Scare, the *New York Times* reported "a startling plan for the organization of the negroes into radical units" written by one W. A. Domingo.[1] Then, on Domingo's return to Jamaica in 1941, the British authorities locked him up for nearly two years as a threat to national security: his case was debated in the British House of Commons and he was named at the London Subject Peoples' Conference in a protest against political imprisonment. When he was finally released, he couldn't get back to New York for several years because, asked for its opinion, the FBI reported that Domingo was "one of the chief trouble-makers among the negroes".[2] These two moments begin to suggest the range of Domingo's interests: socialism, race, Jamaican self-government. When one considers that Domingo was also the first editor of Marcus Garvey's newspaper, *Negro World*, a contributor to Alain Locke's landmark collection, *The New Negro: An Interpretation*, and one of the most powerful critics of the idea of a West Indian federation, it is perhaps surprising that he's remained such a shadowy figure, frequently mentioned but rarely studied. The present volume brings Domingo out of the shadows by collecting together a substantial number of his writings—essays, letters, pamphlets—and providing a contextual background to illuminate his life and activities over the middle decades of the twentieth century.

* * *

Wilfred Adolphus Domingo (1889–1968) belonged to that extraordinary generation of black Jamaicans born in the 1880s who had such an influence on New

1. "Moves to Close the Rand School", *New York Times*, 28 June 1919, p. 1.
2. "Memorandum for Mr Ladd Re. W. A. Domingo, Visa Applicant", 8 July 1943; FBIWAD [FBIWAD = Federal Bureau of Investigation (Wilfred Adophus Domingo). Documents released under FOIPA (Freedom of Information/Privacy Acts) request number 1213480-002. Courtesy of Jacob Zumoff].

York and the Caribbean—and indeed beyond—in the first half of the twentieth century. He was just two months younger than the poet Claude McKay and two years younger than the black activist Marcus Garvey, with whom he had a teenage friendship on the island. In New York these three were joined by many others, including Joel A. Rogers, a prodigious researcher and writer, James S. Watson, who became the city's first black judge, Lucien M. Brown, prominent Harlem doctor, and E. Ethelred Brown, Unitarian minister. Arrival in New York broadened Domingo's friendships and associations, chiefly with other Caribbean immigrants such as Hubert Harrison, Richard B. Moore, Cyril Briggs, Frank Crosswaith, Otto Huiswoud, Martin Luther Campbell, Hope Stevens, and James O'Meally, but also with some prominent African-American radicals such as A. Philip Randolph, Chandler Owen, George Schuyler, and Grace P. Campbell. Re-engagement with the island of his birth in the 1930s brought new Jamaican friends: Walter Adolphe Roberts, Richard Hart, William Seivright, Norman Manley, and Edna Manley.

Generation and location both matter. The Jamaican historian David Scott has subtly probed these ideas in his reflection on the interviews he's conducted with members of the generation immediately previous to his. Domingo belonged to the previous generation to that and, in terms of the Caribbean intellectual tradition, he belonged to the part of it located in New York rather than in the Caribbean. It's perhaps a universal tendency for one generation to have its achievements downplayed or even forgotten by the following generation. In Domingo's case that tendency was exacerbated since the following generation in Jamaica was looking back on a predecessor located in Harlem, and the following generation in Harlem was looking back on a Jamaican whose chief focus, at least in the second half of his life, had been on the land of his birth. That is perhaps why Domingo has tended to fall out of, or be seen as peripheral to, several established narratives, such as those of African-American radicalism or Jamaican independence.[3]

3. Domingo's significance as a writer and activist has not gone completely unrecognised. He features prominently in Winston James's landmark study of Caribbean radicalism in the USA and again, if more equivocally, in a recent study by Margaret Stevens. Arnold Bertram recognises Domingo's relevance to the "making of modern Jamaica". Ken Post pays attention to Domingo and the Jamaica Progressive League in his valuable book, recently superseded with respect to Domingo by Birte Timm's exhaustive study; as do Minkah Makalani and Clifton C. Hawkins. Important anthologies of Caribbean writers in Harlem by Louis J. Parascandola and of African-American anti-colonial thought by Cathy Bergin reproduce some of Domingo's essays. Winston James, *Holding Aloft the Banner of Ethiopia: Caribbean Radicalism in Early Twentieth-Century America*, London: Verso, 1998; Margaret Stevens, "The Early Political History of Wilfred A. Domingo, 1919–39", in *Caribbean Political Activism: Essays in Honour of Richard Hart*, ed. Rupert Lewis, Kingston, Jamaica: Ian Randle Publishers, 2012, pp. 118–143; Arnold Bertram, *N. W. Manley and the Making of Modern Jamaica*, Kingston, Jamaica: Arawak, 2016; Ken Post, *Arise Ye Starvelings: The Jamaican Labour Rebellion of 1938 and Its Aftermath*, The Hague, the Netherlands: Martinus Nijhoff, 1978; Birte Timm, *Nationalists Abroad: The Jamaica Progressive League and the Foundations of Jamaican Independence*, Kingston, Jamaica: Ian Randle, 2016, and "Caribbean Leaven in the American Loaf: Wilfred A. Domingo, the Jamaica

Of his contemporaries, Domingo is closest in profile to the slightly older Hubert Harrison, both in background—Harrison came to the USA from St Croix as an impoverished 17-year-old orphan in 1900—and in politics: socialist but highly race-conscious, aware of the attraction of Marcus Garvey's ideas but impatient with the man's vanity and incompetence. Domingo was radicalised by Harrison and always admired him. Like Harrison, "he had no long-term, sustaining and identifying relationship with any organization or institution, and so lacked the recognition and support that would have come with such a tie".[4] But unlike with Harrison, there is no trove of papers and diaries and scrapbooks of the kind that enabled Jeffrey Perry to write a more than 1,500-page biography. And unlike Harrison, Domingo seems to have shunned the limelight: there are very few photographs of him, even though he was active on public platforms.

* * *

Reliable biographical information on Domingo is sparse. In September 1925 Domingo sent Alain Locke a brief biographical note; he wrote another brief one in the Jamaican newspaper *Public Opinion* in 1946; and he was interviewed in 1958 by Theodore Draper in connection with the historian's research into US radicalism.[5] After Domingo's death, Robert A. Hill interviewed some family members, including both of Domingo's wives, producing information from which he constructed the main biographical sketch, drawn upon by almost everyone else who writes about Domingo.[6] There are also short entries in biographical dictionaries and a piece written by Lionel M. Yard for an 1976 Association for the

Progressive League, and the Founding of a Decolonization Movement for Jamaica", *GHI Bulletin Supplement*, 5 (2008), pp. 81–97; Minkah Makalani, *In the Cause of Freedom: Radical Black Internationalism from Harlem to London, 1917–1939*, Chapel Hill, NC: University of North Carolina Press, 2011; Clifton C. Hawkins, *"Race First Versus Class First": An Intellectual History of Afro-American Radicalism, 1911–1928*, PhD thesis, University of California Davis, 2000; *"Look for Me All Around You": Anglophone Caribbean Immigrants in the Harlem Renaissance*, ed. Louis J. Parascandola, Detroit, MI: Wayne State University Press, 2005, pp. 163–183; and *African American Anti-Colonial Thought, 1917–1937*, ed. Cathy Bergin, Edinburgh, UK: Edinburgh University Press, 2016, pp. 28–30, 31–34, 39, 88–90, 97–100, and 163–168 [=CB].

4. These are Jeffrey B. Perry's words about Harrison: *Hubert Harrison: The Voice of Harlem Radicalism, 1883–1918*, New York: Columbia University Press, 2008, p. 13.

5. See Letter from W. A. Domingo to Alain Locke (21 September 1925), ALP [ALP = Alain Locke Papers, Box 25, folder 28, Moorland-Spingard Research Center, Howard University, Washington, DC]; W. A. Domingo, "Sparks from My Anvil", *Public Opinion*, 3 May 1946, p. 3; "Theodore Draper, Interview with W.A. Domingo" (18 January 1958), Theodore Draper research files, 1919–1990, MS coll. 579, Stuart A. Rose Manuscript, Archives, and Rare Book Library, Emory University, Atlanta, GA.

6. "W. A. Domingo", *MGP* [*MGP* = *The Marcus Garvey and Universal Negro Improvement Association Papers*, ed. Robert A. Hill, Berkeley, CA: University of California Press/Durham, NC: Duke University Press, 13 vols, 1983–2016], 1, pp. 527–531. See also Hill's notes of these interviews in RAHC [RAHC = Robert A. Hill Collection, 1890–2014, Duke University, Durham, NC, Box PS9, Domingo, Wilford A.].

Advancement of Caribbean Education memorial symposium, held in Brooklyn, of which few copies survive, perhaps only one. Yard also spoke to people who knew Domingo, notably his second wife, Mabel.[7] Beyond this, the documentary record provides only a few details about Domingo's family background and occasional illumination of his activities in New York. His FBI file is quite substantial but unreliable with regard to personal details. As a result of this sparsity, errors about Domingo's life abound: indeed several commentators even manage to get his name wrong.[8]

What we offer here and in the introductions to each section, alongside the biographical information we've been able to retrieve, is a sense of the intellectual milieux that Domingo inhabited, with a view to enabling fresh interpretations and analyses of his work. These selected writings show a thinker who defied any single categorisation but whose ideas animated debates about socialism, anti-imperialism, nationalism, internationalism, anti-racism, and anti-fascism. He celebrated African achievements and contributions to humanity. His was a steady and consistent voice against colonialism and its dependent psychology, and in favour of social and racial justice. Unlike some of his contemporaries, Domingo had no inclination to blow his own trumpet. This book finds in his words a tune worth hearing.

* * *

In 1889, the year of W. A. Domingo's birth, the future of Jamaica was becoming a subject for discussion on and off the island. Less than 25 years earlier, Governor Edward Eyre's brutal suppression of the rebellion at Morant Bay, followed by the trial and execution of George William Gordon, Paul Bogle, and 14 others, had resulted in the island's return to Crown Colony status, slightly modified in 1884. In 1887 the historian and imperial ideologue James Anthony Froude had

7. Greg Robinson, "Domingo, W. A.", *Encyclopedia of African-American Culture and History*, Encyclopedia.com (1996); J. A. Zumoff, "Domingo, Wilfred Adolphus", in *Harlem Renaissance Lives*, ed. Henry Louis Gates, Jr and Evelyn Brooks Higginbotham, New York: Oxford University Press, 2009, pp. 159–160; Philip Howard, "Domingo, Wilfred Adolphus", in *Dictionary of Caribbean and Afro-Latin American Biography*, Oxford: Oxford University Press, 2016, https://doi.org/10.1093/acref/9780195301731.013.73820, (accessed 4 September 2024); Lionel M. Yard [W. A. Domingo], Association for the Advancement of Caribbean Education—Report on the Symposium Honoring Wilfred Domingo, 20 June 1976, pp. 1–20, in RAHC.

8. He appears as "William H." in a Bureau of Investigation report (see below, p. 29, n. 59); Wilford in Yard [W. A. Domingo], p. ii; and in the Robert A. Hill Collection (see n. 6 above); Warner, in Theodore G. Vincent, *Black Power and the Garvey Movement*, San Francisco, CA: Ramparts Press, 1972, p. 268; and Oscar Berland, "The Emergence of the Communist Perspective on the 'Negro Question' in America: 1919–1931 (Part One)", *Science and Society*, 63, no. 4 (Winter 1999), pp. 411–432, at 413; and Walter in Gordon K. Lewis, *The Growth of the Modern West Indies*, New York: Monthly Review Press, 1968, p. 182, and Ewart Walters, *We Come from Jamaica: The National Movement 1937–1962*, Ottawa, Canada: Boyd McRubie Communications, 2014, p. 69.

visited Jamaica and written a damning account of the island, pushing the case for a return to direct rule by Britain and condemning the black population as an "inferior race" who should have no say in the island's future.[9] There were immediate local responses in the West Indies from Trinidadian journalist J. J. Thomas and C. S. Salmon—an Englishman but with experience as president of Nevis and with local knowledge and sympathies. Thomas's *Froudacity* was published precisely in 1889 and has been called the starting point of nationalist protest in the region.[10] Salmon's title (*The Caribbean Confederation*) introduced a term whose implications would run through Domingo's life: was nationalism to be Jamaican or West Indian, island or federation?[11] Domingo was born, therefore, right on cue, though in personal circumstances that were less than propitious.

The biographical sketch of Domingo in the *Marcus Garvey Papers* states:

> Born in Kingston, Jamaica, Domingo was the youngest child of Francisco and Alice Domingo. His father, who was Spanish, owned and operated a large fleet of hansom cabs in Kingston. His mother was from St Thomas parish in eastern Jamaica. Domingo and his elder brother and sister were orphaned at an early age and were brought up by their mother's brother, Adolphus Grant, a master butcher in St Ann's Bay.[12]

The Jamaican documentary record and Domingo's own words somewhat complicate this picture. In fact, Wilfred Domingo was born illegitimate in Kingston on 26 November 1889 to the second family of Francisco Domingo.[13] Interviewed by Robert Hill, Domingo's first wife Eulalie probably provided a rose-tinted version of the Domingo family background, including the detail about his father running a fleet of hansom cabs, a respectably middle-class occupation. The father may have been Spanish, although—since there were very few, if any, black Spaniards in Jamaica at the time—it's more likely that he was Cuban; but he certainly wasn't prosperous or respectable.[14] The "fleet of hansom cabs" turns out to have been

9. James Anthony Froude, *The English in the West Indies, or The Bow of Ulysses* [1888], London: Longmans, Green, 1909, p. 286.

10. J. J. Thomas, *Froudacity*, London: T. Fisher Unwin, 1889; Denis M. Benn, *The Caribbean: An Intellectual History, 1774–2003*, Kingston, Jamaica: Ian Randle, 2004, p. 69. See Faith Smith, *Creole Recitations: John Jacob Thomas and Colonial Formations in the Late Nineteenth-Century Caribbean*, Charlottesville, VA: University of Virginia Press, 2002. John Jacob Thomas (1841–1889) was a Trinidadian linguist and writer.

11. C. S. Salmon, *The Caribbean Confederation*, London: Cassell, 1888.

12. "W. A. Domingo", *MGP*, 1, p. 527.

13. On Kingston in the years of Domingo's childhood, see *"Squalid Kingston", 1890–1920 : How the Poor Lived, Moved and Had Their Being*, ed. Brian L. Moore and Michele A. Johnson, Kingston, Jamaica: Social History Project, Department of History, University of the West Indies, 2000.

14. Domingo notes that his paternal grandfather was an immigrant (Domingo, "Sparks from My Anvil"). Many Cubans found refuge in Jamaica at the beginning of the first Cuban war of independence in 1868.

one horse and a trap, a horse he was prosecuted for mistreating, among several other offences against the local hackney carriage regulations.[15] And Domingo's mother, Alice Maud Grant (1863–1892), a laundress, was not married to Francisco Domingo. Francisco had a wife and six children; but also, and overlapping in time, a second household and four children with Alice Grant.[16] Not exactly unusual in Kingston at that time, where illegitimate births outnumbered legitimate ones, but not really respectable. Domingo never knew his mother, who died when he was three, and may have never known his father: he was certainly brought up by his mother's brother, Adolphus Emanuel Grant (1871–1949), who may have kept him out of his father's orbit: Francisco Domingo's last appearance in the records has him being fined for disorderly conduct and trespass.[17] West Indian immigrants into the USA came from many different backgrounds, but it's striking that whereas the family story gives Domingo a respectable middle-class background not dissimilar to those of Marcus Garvey, Joel Rogers, Claude McKay, and James Watson, the real story of illegitimacy and orphanhood is a relatively unusual one out of which a black Jamaican should attain some moderate success and prosperity in the USA, as Domingo eventually did.[18]

The reference to St Ann's Bay in the *Marcus Garvey Papers* is intriguing since Garvey himself and Joel Rogers both grew up there at approximately the same time. Although it's possible that Domingo's uncle, Adolphus Grant, was "a master butcher in St Ann's Bay", it seems unlikely: the Grant family connections were with St Thomas, and Domingo never mentions St Ann's Bay: he always writes about growing up in Kingston. Marcus Garvey does speak of the two of them as "friends from boyhood", but that must refer to the period in the capital where Garvey moved when he was 17.[19] Later in life Domingo suggested that he and Garvey

15. He was "sentenced to pay the heaviest fine the law allows, £3, or in default of payment to be imprisoned for 60 days with hard labor, for driving a horse all covered with dung" (*The Gleaner*, 17 September 1879, p. 2). Further infractions of the hackney carriage regulations were reported in the paper on 16 December 1891, p. 2 (fined 2s 6d) and 19 December 1894, p. 7 (fined 5s or seven days in prison).

16. Francisco Domingo married Agnes Elizabeth Robertson and had six children with her between 1880 and 1895; he had four children with Alice Grant between 1884 and 1889; and he had at least three children with other women. On the birth certificates of Alice Grant's children, no father is named, but the children all carry the last name of Domingo.

17. *The Gleaner*, 8 August 1895, p. 6. He was fined, respectively 1s and 6s 6d costs and 1s and 8s 6d costs.

18. Domingo probably had a less advantageous background than any of the examples in Patrick Bryan's chapter on "The Black Intelligentsia", *The Jamaican People, 1880–1902: Race, Class, and Social Control*, London: Macmillan Caribbean, 1991, pp. 239–265. The best study of the background of West Indian immigrants into the USA is Winston James, "Explaining Afro-Caribbean Social Mobility in the United States: Beyond the Sowell Thesis", *Comparative Studies in Society and History*, 44, no. 2 (2002), pp. 218–262.

19. Marcus Garvey, "Why the Black Star Line Failed", in *Marcus Garvey and the Vision of Africa*, ed. John Henrik Clarke, with the assistance of Amy Jacques Garvey, New York: Vintage Books, 1974, pp. 139–149, at 140.

became close in Kingston as teenagers.[20] And his words in 1946 clearly state: "I was born in Kingston and lived there until I was twenty years of age." He adds: "My contacts were with all classes except the ruling element. I attended school here, went to church and Sunday school, played, made love, fought, engaged in pranks like any other healthy boy. My life and career were typically Jamaican."

In the 1925 biographical note provided for Alain Locke, Domingo wrote simply: "I was born in Kingston, Jamaica, B.W.I., on November 26th, 1889. After attending the elementary public schools, I graduated from 'The Board School' where high school instruction was given. I worked as a book keeper for a short while after leaving school and emigrated to the United States in August 1910."[21] A little more detail is possible. The "Board School" was a relatively new institution established in Kingston in the 1890s. An Englishman, J. G. Peet, arrived in 1897 to become headmaster.[22] The school was called the Manual Training School, which indicates its priorities. When Domingo attended, it occupied the premises at 82 Hanover Street formerly occupied by Mico College. During his time as a book keeper Domingo was drawn to S. A. G. Cox's National Club, a political movement which shook up the colonial status quo for a couple of years. Garvey served as assistant secretary, and together—it seems—Garvey and Domingo wrote a pamphlet called *The Struggling Mass*, no copy of which has survived.[23] So Domingo's political interests and priorities were established early, at least by his twentieth year.

* * *

In 1895 the number of elected members in the Jamaican Legislative Council was raised from nine to 14 and the franchise extended by lowering the property qualifications and removing the literacy restriction. Voter registration consequently rose from 2,000 in 1884 to 43,266 in 1894–95.[24] These modifications had been optimistically read in Jamaica as indicative of a British inclination to grant gradual progress towards self-government, but Joseph Chamberlain's appointment to the

20. "When we met, he was a stranger to Kingston" [#47]. Throughout, these numbers in square brackets refer to the entries in this volume.

21. Letter from W. A. Domingo to Alain Locke, 21 September 1925, ALP.

22. Peet left the post and the island in 1925.

23. The pamphlet was published in Jamaica under Marcus Garvey's name, but Domingo later said that he had co-written it. See "Report of a Pamphlet by Marcus Garvey: 'Mr Marcus Garvey has issued a pamphlet in which he upholds the policy of Mr Cox and deals severely with the Press which he declares is now the enemy of the people'" (*Jamaican Times Supplement*, Saturday 28 May 1910, in *MGP*, 11, p. 3). Domingo's recollection was of "a pamphlet which, in a sense, we both wrote in Kingston and he [Garvey] published" [#47].

24. Graham Knox, "Political Change in Jamaica (1866–1906) and the Local Reaction to the Policies of the Crown Colony Government", in *The Caribbean in Transition: Papers in Political, Social, and Economic Development*, ed. F. M. Andric and T. G. Mathews, Rio Piedras, Puerto Rico: Institute of Caribbean Studies, University of Puerto Rico, 1965, pp. 141–162, at 144.

Colonial Office saw a sharp about-turn. In a March 1897 speech, Chamberlain announced the third stage of British imperial history: a "new imperialism" based on a clear distinction between the colonies in which a sense of possession had given way to a sense of kinship—Canada, Australia, South Africa—and the tropical colonies marked by a sense of obligation, where majority black populations were in need of firm white hands on the tiller.[25] An imperial ideology was indeed still widely supported in Jamaica, as would have been witnessed by Domingo in the huge public demonstrations in honour of Queen Victoria's diamond jubilee in 1897.[26]

But at the same time Chamberlain's *racialised* conception of Empire ran counter to a slowly growing national consciousness in Jamaica. For example, around the time of Domingo's birth, an emergent black elite was offering some early and tentative imaginings of a different future for the island, at least in the subtitle of the collection of essays called *Jamaica's Jubilee; or, What We Are and What We Hope to Be*, published in 1888 by a group of ministers and lay preachers. In that first-person plural could be seen a sense of an island identity other than the imperial one that had been taken for granted by the island's white elite, whether British or creole. For the most part the essays struck a positive note, intended as they were to demonstrate how successful Emancipation had been. Looking to the future, the keywords were unity, industry, and Godliness. Of greater significance was the act of publication in itself. In the preface Robert Dingwall wrote that "we venture to ask permission to speak for ourselves!", although of course they were actually speaking *without* asking permission.[27] Most openly critical of the essayists was J. H. Reid, who spoke of white Jamaicans as "the least Jamaican of everything pertaining to the country". The native Englishmen want to go home, he wrote; those born in Jamaica still want to visit England; some few have become identified with Jamaica—but more with the Jamaican soil than the Jamaican people.[28] So, as Dingwall put it in the final essay, "Outlook for Jamaica and Her People", attention should be turned "to what we emphatically call 'our race'"; and it should

25. Joseph Chamberlain, "The True Conception of Empire", in *Mr Chamberlain's Speeches*, ed. Charles W. Boyd, London: Constable, 1914, 2, pp. 1–6. According to Chamberlain, the first stage had been when colonies were viewed solely as source of profit; the second when, no longer obviously profitable, they were seen as eminently disposable.

26. See Anne Spry Rush, *Bonds of Empire: West Indians and Britishness from Victoria to Decolonization*, Oxford, UK: Oxford University Press, 2011, pp. 51–55; and more generally, *Making Imperial Mentalities: Socialisation and British Imperialism*, ed. J. A. Mangan, Manchester, UK: Manchester University Press, 1990.

27. *Jamaica's Jubilee; or, What We Are and What We Hope to Be*, London: S. W. Partridge, 1888, p. 7. For background on the authors, see "Five Dreamers", in C. A. Wilson, *Men of Vision: A Series of Biographical Sketches of Men Who Have Made Their Mark upon Our Time*, Kingston, Jamaica: Gleaner, 1929, pp. 87–126. See also Deborah A. Thomas, *Modern Blackness: Nationalism, Globalization, and the Politics of Culture in Jamaica*, Durham, NC: Duke University Press, 2004, pp. 33–48.

28. J. H. Reid, "The People of Jamaica Described", *Jamaica's Jubilee*, pp. 85–102, at 86 and 87.

be appropriate to do so because "we form the bulk by far of Jamaica's people. Jamaica is emphatically ours".[29]

Another straw in the wind from Domingo's teenage years was the conversation the English visitor John Henderson reports having with a black Jamaican he met on a road just outside Spanish Town who was "prepared to make Jamaica the horizon of his political outlook". "We black people outnumber you whites by at least forty to one," he said to Henderson, "is it rational that we should always submit to your despotic government? … Since the population is black let the government be black." His complaint was that, politically, Jamaicans were still bound: not permitted to govern themselves as they would like. "I would have Jamaica governed as England is governed," he stated vehemently: "The people of this island have every moral right to govern themselves, to frame their own laws and to administer those laws. We are no longer barbarians; we are an educated people with ambitions, and the strength to attain our ambitions. We recognise that it is a fine thing to be a part of the great Empire of Britain, but we recognise, even more clearly, that it is a finer thing to be a free, unfettered nation."[30]

On the whole, the first 15 years of Domingo's life belong firmly to what Faith Smith characterises as a "quiet period", yet, as she recognises, it's often possible to glimpse signs of disturbance just below placid surfaces, and there were indeed riots and social upheavals while Domingo was growing up, notably at Montego Bay in April 1902.[31] And then there was J. Robert Love (1839–1914), the most important black intellectual on the island at this time. Born in the Bahamas, Love, a medical doctor, had lived in the USA and Haiti before coming to Jamaica in 1889.[32] He founded a newspaper, promoted voter registration, and helped to cement an electoral alliance of black and coloured politicians to contest the island

29. R. Dingwall, "Outlook for Jamaica and Her People", *Jamaica's Jubilee*, pp. 103–128, at 111.

30. John Henderson, *The West Indies*, London: A. & C. Black, 1905, pp. 146–147. On this period, see Bryan, *The Jamaican People, 1880–1902*; the essays in *Victorian Jamaica*, ed. Tim Barringer and Wayne Modest, Durham, NC: Duke University Press, 2018; the essays in *Neither Led Nor Driven: Contesting British Cultural Imperialism in Jamaica, 1865–1920*, ed. Brian L. Moore and Michele A. Johnson, Kingston, Jamaica: University of the West Indies Press, 2004, especially Joy Lumsden, "A Forgotten Generation: Black Politicians in Jamaica, 1864–1914", pp. 112–222; and more particularly on the political developments, Joy Lumsden, "Jamaican Constitutional and Political Developments 1866–1920" (1999), https://jamaica-history.weebly.com/jamaican-politics-1866-1920.html (accessed 11 November 2020).

31. Faith Smith, *Strolling in the Ruins: The Caribbean's Non-Sovereign Modern in the Early Twentieth Century*, Durham, NC: Duke University Press, 2023, p. 2. See Bryan, *The Jamaican People*, pp. 266–277. O. Nigel Bolland notes "at least 16 serious disturbances … between 1884 and 1905" in the British West Indies, "most of them in Jamaica" (*On the March: Labour Rebellions in the British Caribbean, 1934–39*, Kingston, Jamaica: Ian Randle/London: James Currey, 1995, p. 7).

32. See Joyce Mary Lumsden, "Robert Love and Jamaican Politics", PhD thesis, University of the West Indies, 1987; Robert A. Hill, "Joseph Robert Love", *MGP*, 1, pp. 532–536; W. Adolphe Roberts, "Robert Love", in his *Six Great Jamaicans: Biographical Sketches*, Kingston, Jamaica: Pioneer Press, 1951, pp. 70–85.

elections of 1896 under the new extended franchise. Love was elected to the Kingston City Council in 1898, the year he established the People's Convention to commemorate the fiftieth anniversary of full emancipation. Alexander Dixon, a black cabinet-maker, was elected chairman and in 1899 became the first black man to win a seat on the Jamaican Legislative Council; Love himself was elected in 1906. He was also involved in the short-lived Jamaican branch of the Pan-African Association, formed in March 1901 after an island visit by its founder, Henry Sylvester Williams.[33] Domingo recalled having heard Love speak [#39]. Another influential Jamaican was Theophilus Scholes, whose magnum opus, *Glimpses of the Ages*, Domingo remembered getting the Institute of Jamaica to purchase from London [#35]. These two volumes would have provided him with a good grounding in anti-colonial thinking.

Other timely elements in Domingo's earliest years included the introduction of free elementary education in 1892 and the arrival on the island of the English art historian Frank Cundall in 1891 as secretary and librarian to the Institute of Jamaica (founded in 1879), where, as Domingo later remembered, he read practically every book they had "dealing with the Negro" [#47]. He especially recalls Edward Blyden's *Christianity, Islam, and the Negro Race*. Under Cundall's tenure, which lasted until 1937, the West India Reference Library was established in 1894 as a repository of materials for the study of Jamaica and Jamaican culture—despite Cundall's own unreconstructed views as to the superiority of all things English. His article "The Story of the Life of Columbus and the Discovery of Jamaica", published in the *Journal of the Institute of Jamaica* in 1894, was an early indication of the recognition of a Jamaica that existed before the British conquest, and he also continued and developed the writing of island history with *Studies in Jamaica History* (1900) and *Historic Jamaica* (1915).[34] In 1914, shortly after

33. Williams introduced the idea at a well-attended meeting in Kingston on 28 March 1901, notable for a lengthy introduction by the governor, Sydney Olivier, which attempted to undermine the very idea of a pan-African association before Williams even got to open his mouth ("The Pan-African Association", *The Gleaner*, 30 March 1901, p. 9).

34. Frank Cundall (1858–1937). The West India Reference Library became the nucleus of the National Library of Jamaica, formed in 1979. *Studies in Jamaica History*, London: Institute of Jamaica, 1900; *Historic Jamaica*, London: published for the Institute of Jamaica by the West India Committee, 1915. Commissioned by the Institute of Jamaica, Irene Wright undertook research in the Archivo de Indias in Seville which resulted in the important volumes: Frank Cundall and Joseph L. Pietersz, *Jamaica under the Spaniards, Abstracted from the Archives of Seville*, Kingston, Jamaica: Institute of Jamaica, 1919; and Irene A. Wright, ed., *The English Conquest of Jamaica*, Camden Miscellany, 13, no. 5, London: Offices of the Royal Historical Society, 1923. Cundall also drew up a list of historic sites and buildings at the request of Governor Sydney Olivier, an early move to preserve what would later be regarded as Jamaican built heritage. For background, see Howard Johnson, "Historiography of Jamaica", in *General History of the Caribbean, Volume 6: Methodology and Historiography of the Caribbean*, ed. B. W. Higman, New York: Palgrave Macmillan, 2003, pp. 478–530, at 484–485; and Brian L. Moore and Michele A. Johnson, *"They Do as They Please": The Jamaican Struggle for Cultural Freedom after Morant Bay*, Kingston, Jamaica: University of the West Indies Press, 2011, pp. 110–117.

Domingo left for Boston, the first edition of *The Gleaner Geography and History of Jamaica* appeared. In multiple editions, this would remain for the rest of the century the standard school and popular history of the island.

All this testifies to what Gordon Lewis calls "the slow, tortuous growth over the centuries of a powerful local sentiment, of a Jamaican sense of being".[35] This local sentiment found its strongest expression during Domingo's youth in the establishment of the National Club, founded at a public meeting held on Wednesday 3 March 1909 by Gilbert Cox (often known as Sandy).[36] Black members of the club included Alexander Dixon, the club's second vice-president.[37] The key demand was "to secure for the inhabitants of this island self-government".[38] Cox's newspaper, *Our Own*, advocated "self-government within the empire", similar to the self-determination given to Australia and New Zealand.[39] Domingo remembered acting as an assistant secretary despite, according to the club's rules, being too young to join.[40] At the meeting on 19 August 1909, Cox announced that the club had nearly 500 members.[41] Marcus Garvey was elected one of the club's secretaries on 20 April 1910.[42]

Cox got under the skin of the colonial establishment sufficiently to provoke *The Gleaner*, now edited by Herbert G. de Lisser, and for one of its correspondents to attach a letter from the *Daily Mail Overseas Edition*, simply signed "Imperialist", which, noting the National Club's aims, announced that "Self-government would, I think, inevitably tend to make Jamaica more of a negro land than it is even now, with a preponderance of blacks over whites; and things have not gone so well in

35. Gordon K. Lewis, "The Emergence of National Society: Jamaica", in his *The Growth of the Modern West Indies*, pp. 167–196, at p. 169.

36. Solomon Alexander Gilbert Cox (1873–1922). The club's president was Hubert Ashton Laselve Simpson (1872–1938), a "Jamaican white" solicitor, but Cox, first vice-president, a "high-coloured" barrister who could pass for white, was obviously the driving force. Simpson later stood for election unsuccessfully on behalf of Marcus Garvey's People's Political Party in the 1930 general election. He had several spells as mayor of Kingston.

37. Love, now in poor health, was not involved. On the National Club, see Glen Richards, "Race, Class and Labour Politics in Colonial Jamaica, 1900–1934", in *Jamaica in Slavery and Freedom: History, Heritage, and Culture*, ed. Kathleen E. A. Monteith and Glen Richards, Kingston, Jamaica: University of the West Indies Press, 2002, pp. 340–362; and the notes in *MGP*, 1, pp. 21–22.

38. "Forming Club. The Political Platform of Mr S. A. G. Cox", *The Gleaner*, 4 March 1909, p. 3; and the longer account of the initial meeting in "Formation of Political Club. Meeting of Mr Cox on Wednesday Night", *The Gleaner*, 5 March 1909, p. 9. Cox's own account, including the sentence "The object of this club is to procure self-government for this colony", is in "National Club", *The Gleaner*, 14 April 1909, p. 7.

39. *Our Own*, 15 August 1910, cited in Richard Hart, *From Occupation to Independence: A Short History of the Peoples of the English-Speaking Caribbean*, London: Pluto Press, 1998, p. 103.

40. W. A. Domingo, "The Self-Government Movement", *The Gleaner*, 26 April 1955, p. 8. But he certainly did not, as Philip Howard suggests, in "Domingo, Wilfred Adolphus", "establish" the National Club alongside Gilbert Cox and Marcus Garvey.

41. "Box and Cox Go Hand-in-Hand", *The Gleaner*, 21 August 1909, p. 3.

42. "Tumultuous Meeting", *The Gleaner*, 22 April 1910, p. 4.

Figure 1 S. A. G. Cox.
(*The Gleaner*, 13 October 1909, p. 1)

Hayti this last century that one could look with equanimity on such a change in a British Colony."[43] Thinking expansively, in a letter to *The Gleaner* in November 1909 Cox announced his plan to form a National League of the West Indies, whose members would be pledged to secure self-government for each island—in other words, a West Indian league leading to independent islands, not to a federation.[44]

In October 1909 Cox was elected to the Legislative Council as the member for St Thomas. He was briefly suspended in May 1910, re-elected in January 1911, and then immediately removed entirely by dint of a challenge under the 1895 Kerr-Sharp amendment, which required legislative representatives either to have twelve months' residence in the parish they wished to represent, prior to elec-

43. "National Club. How Mr Cox's Club Is Regarded Abroad", *The Gleaner*, 24 April 1909, p. 9. One of the most prominent Jamaican journalists and authors of the twentieth century, Herbert George de Lisser (1878–1944) became editor of *The Gleaner* when he was 26, a position he occupied until his death. He wrote many books of fiction and non-fiction, worked for the Jamaican sugar industry, was general secretary of the Jamaica Imperial Association, honorary president of the Jamaica Press Association, and chairman of the West Indian section of the Empire Press Union. He was a consistently conservative and pro-British voice in the first half of the century, though broad-minded enough to publish pro-nationalist articles and letters by Domingo and his colleagues.

44. "Plans League. Hon. S. A. G. Cox Going Farther Afield", *The Gleaner*, 13 November 1909, p. 17.

tion, or possession of a property in the parish yielding a net income of £150 per annum, an amendment crafted precisely to exclude politically ambitious—read, black and coloured—candidates.[45] Disgusted by his treatment at the hands of the colonial establishment, Cox left the island in October 1911, ostensibly going to Panama and Costa Rica to raise funds for his newspaper, although he never returned, instead migrating to Boston, where he practised as an attorney, dying in 1922, aged 49.[46]

The National Club may have been short-lived but it was the subject of lively controversy during the last year before Domingo left the island and undoubtedly had a significant impact on his ideas. In 1943, shortly after being released from internment in Kingston, Domingo wrote a piece for *The African*, published in New York, about the ongoing struggle in Jamaica. He recalled the National Club as the first attempt to effect change, noting that Cox had no clear-cut plan but modelled his organisation on Sinn Fein: he was a nationalist, Domingo underlined.[47] Typically, he doesn't mention his own involvement. Then in 1960 Domingo wrote to *The Gleaner* to contest the opinion voiced by a correspondent that Marcus Garvey was the greatest Jamaican in history [#46]. The names that came to his mind, Domingo wrote, were Richard Hill, George William Gordon, Norman Manley ... and S. A. G. Cox. Not many Jamaicans would have remembered Gilbert Cox in 1960, so the remark is indicative of the formative experience of Domingo's twenty-first year, the last before he left for the USA.

* * *

We present Domingo's writings in chronological order. They stretch from 1917 to 1964 with two clear spikes of activity. We've identified over 900 pieces of writing, totalling nearly two million words and ranging from a few long essays such as "Socialism Imperilled" and the two critiques of Federation (all running at just under 9000 words) to short(ish) letters to newspapers. Our selection is therefore only indicative. With an element of arbitrariness, we divide the writings into three parts. "A New Day: Harlem, 1917–1935" includes the first spurt of writing in the late 1910s and early 1920s when Domingo took a full part in the radical movements of the time, founding his own newspaper and beginning a life-long campaign to set the record straight with respect to his relationship with Marcus Garvey. From 1926 onwards he seems to have written hardly anything until the late 1930s, but we choose to begin the next part, "Seeking Freedom: Jamaica, 1936–1947", in the year that marks his re-engagement with the island of his birth,

45. "Public Meeting. The Kerr-Sharp Resolution Being Condemned", *The Gleaner*, 5 September 1911, p. 3. See Lumsden, "Jamaican Constitutional and Political Developments".

46. See Robert Hill, *MGP*, 11, p. 3, n. 2.

47. W. A. Domingo, "Jamaica Fights for Freedom", *The African*, 2 (October 1943), pp. 5 and 16, and (November 1943), pp. 5 and 12.

manifest in his part in founding the Jamaica Progressive League in New York. This period includes the second and most sustained burst of writing when he was closely involved in the newspapers *Public Opinion* and *New Negro Voice* in Jamaica from 1943 to 1947. After his return to New York his writing in the final phase ("Securing Independence: New York, 1948–1964") is almost exclusively confined to the two issues of Federation and Marcus Garvey. A brief Conclusion offers a summary assessment of Domingo's importance.

PART I

A New Day: Harlem, 1917–1935

When I was actively opposing Mr Garvey I did so openly and publicly, both on the platform and through the press. I never concealed my views for I was not afraid to speak my mind.

On 22 August 1910 Domingo arrived in Everett, Massachusetts, just north of Boston, to stay with his aunt, Jennie Mason, and sister Alberta (Bertha), who was three years older than Wilfred. The family story is that his uncle had agreed to finance his study of medicine. Domingo attended night school before moving to New York in early 1912, where he worked in a variety of menial jobs, including elevator operator, while establishing an import business: his first surviving letterhead notes "W. A. Domingo. General Selling Agent. Importer of Alligator Pears, Mangoes, Preserves & Tropical Produce. 115 West 135th Street".[1] On the New York state census for 1915 his occupation is listed as "fruit merchant".[2] In December 1917 he wrote to the Chamber of Commerce in Miami seeking farmers who could supply him with 200 bushels of pigeon peas.[3] At that point he was living at 127 West 135th Street, in the heart of Harlem, lodging with his friend Martin Luther Campbell, a tailor.[4] In the biographical note written in 1925 for Alain Locke, Domingo said that on account of the war he had to suspend his business activities, during which time he worked in the Post Office.[5] At the end of his political career, in a brochure produced in 1964 by the Jamaica Progressive League (New York) to celebrate the second anniversary of Jamaican independence, W. A. Domingo has an advert for his imported goods firm, based at 615 East 168th Street.[6] So, from the time of his arrival in New York until the end of his life, Domingo was primarily a businessman. He was only ever close to being a full-time writer-activist for two shortish periods: first in Harlem between 1917

1. W. A. Domingo, Letter to Secretary of State for the Colonies, 22 December 1914, CO 137/707, TNA [TNA = The National Archives (London)]. The letter concerned the importing of scrap rubber from Jamaica to New York.
2. New York, USA, State Census, 1915, AD 21, ED 20. He appears as Adolphos Domingo, lodging at 135 West 135th Street, New York.
3. "Wants Some Farmer to Raise Lots of Peas", *The Miami News*, 24 December 1917, p. 2.
4. Martin Luther Campbell (1888–1947). Campbell returned to Jamaica during the 1930s.
5. W. A. Domingo, Letter to Alain Locke, 21 September 1925, ALP.
6. *Souvenir Journal: 2nd Anniversary Celebration of Jamaica Independence*, New York: Jamaica Progressive League (of New York), 1964, p. 15.

and 1921 when working as an editor on various newspapers, including the one he founded, and then in Jamaica between 1941 and 1947 when he was initially paid by the People's National Party and, after his release from prison, unable to get a visa to return to New York.

On 5 June 1917 Domingo, as required, completed his registration card for the draft, claiming exemption for "religious reasons", although evidence of religiosity in his life is entirely lacking and, in any case, as a resident alien he couldn't have been drafted into the US Army. However, later that year the British Army, desperate for reinforcements, put aside its opposition to having black soldiers in its ranks and decided to recruit among the large number of British citizens—most of them black West Indians–who were living on the east coast of the USA and Canada. As the need for troops increased, so the pace of recruitment stepped up. In July 1918 it was announced that British male subjects between the ages of 18 and 45 resident in the USA would have 60 days to enlist in the British Army. If they didn't do so, they would be drafted into the US Army.[7] Many years later, when Marcus Garvey accused him of being a draft dodger, Domingo claimed that he had visited the British and Canadian Recruitment Mission at 220 West 42nd Street and been given exemption on health grounds. He doesn't specify exactly what those grounds were, and no documentary evidence seems to survive. During this first period in New York, Domingo also started a family: on 3 April 1919 he married Eulalie Manhertz, a Jamaican classical pianist, and they went on to have two children.[8]

By the time of his marriage Domingo had a firm foothold in Harlem's political life. Reasonable assumptions are that he received his higher education in the orbit of Hubert Harrison, establishing friendships that would sustain him for many years. Arriving in New York in 1900 from St Croix (in the then Danish Virgin Islands) and relocating to Harlem in 1907, Harrison had rapidly acquired an encyclopaedic knowledge as well as an unequalled ability to speak cogently and compellingly in public on just about any subject: he attracted huge audiences all over Manhattan, from Wall Street to Lenox Avenue.[9] A committed radical, he was soon disillusioned by the endemic racism of the Socialist Party of America (SPA). Although not the first to use the term, Harrison became the embodiment of the radical "New Negro", offering to break with the accommodationism he associated with the established figures of Booker T. Washington and W. E. B. Du Bois.[10]

7. "Call British Subjects to Join the Army", *New York Times*, 29 July 1918, p. 7.

8. Eulalie Albriton Fogarty Manhertz (1898–1988). Karl Nikolai (1919–1992), born two months after the wedding, and Yolanda Alicia (1926–2002). Once they both had reputations to protect, the Domingos reported the marriage date as 3 April 1918: for example, *Who's Who in Colored America*, 3rd edn, New York: Thomas Yenser, 1933, p. 133.

9. Hubert Harrison (1883–1927). See Jeffrey B. Perry, *Hubert Harrison: The Voice of Harlem Radicalism, 1883–1918*, New York: Columbia University Press, 2008, and *Hubert Harrison: The Struggle for Equality, 1918–1927*, New York: Columbia University Press, 2021.

10. Booker Taliaferro Washington (1856–1915), educator and author, was the pre-eminent

Figure 2 Eulalie Manhertz Domingo. (*New Pittsburgh Courier*, 4 February 1928, p. 13)

The other "Caribbean crusaders" were already in New York when Domingo arrived.[11] Cyril Briggs, born in Nevis, reached New York in 1905 and was soon working as a journalist on the *New York Amsterdam News*. Richard B. Moore, born in Barbados, arrived in 1909, and Otto Huiswoud from Suriname in 1910.[12] It's unclear exactly how they met, but all four had an incipient political radicalism in common, as well as an interest in trade unions. They probably all felt Harrison's gravitational pull, but Domingo was also involved in the development of the Elevator Operators Union, of which he became the first president: most West Indian immigrants did their shifts in what they jokingly referred to as "internal aviation", so that would also be a possible meeting ground.[13]

Moore's daughter knew the "awesome foursome" as a child. "They had in common", she writes, "a seriousness imposed by the responsibility to support themselves, a sense of loss through separation or the death of one or both parents, a keen intellectual ability that sought answers to questions posed by society, a sensitivity to injustice, and a thirst for knowledge that was stimulated but severely unquenched by a grade school education." All of them "lacked the university education and degrees common among leaders of the existing civil rights organizations, but their excellent basic education provided in accordance with British and Dutch standards was superior to instruc-

figure in the African-American community from the late nineteenth century until his death. William Edward Burghardt Du Bois (1868–1963), sociologist, author, and civil rights activist, took over that position after 1915 and held it throughout Domingo's political career. Domingo always expressed the greatest admiration for Du Bois. The two met in Jamaica in 1945.

11. Joyce Moore Turner, *Caribbean Crusaders and the Harlem Renaissance*, Urbana, IL: University of Illinois Press, 2005.

12. Cyril Valentine Briggs (1888–1966); Richard Benjamin Moore (1893–1978); Otto Eduard Gerardus Majella Huiswoud (1893–1961).

13. On Moore, Huiswoud, and Briggs, see Minkah Makalani, *In the Cause of Freedom: Radical Black Internationalism from Harlem to London, 1917–1939*, Chapel Hill, NC: University of North Carolina Press, 2011, pp. 29–32. He notes that none of them had been politically active in the Caribbean. Domingo and Garvey had been, which perhaps suggests a more vibrant political scene in Jamaica in the opening decade of the twentieth century.

tion in most of the segregated schools of the United States". They were known "for their wit, keen sense of humor, integrity, and concern for others. Serious as they were, they had the ability to kid each other and laugh at themselves."[14]

Another key figure and good friend to Domingo, at least during these Harlem years, was E. Ethelred Brown. Born in Falmouth, on the north coast of Jamaica, Brown had trained as a civil servant and moved to Spanish Town, but lost his job in 1907. He enrolled in a Unitarian college in the USA and was ordained in 1912—the first black Unitarian minister. He tried working back in Jamaica in Montego Bay and Kingston, but eventually relocated to New York in 1920, founding a community church in Harlem.[15] Plagued by financial problems, he took other jobs, including as an elevator operator for nearly six years. In the founding congregation of his Harlem Community Church were figures such as Domingo, Moore, and Grace Campbell.[16] Brown's church was very much a forum for political debate: he chaired and encouraged heated discussions. Additionally, Brown became chairman of the British Jamaicans Benevolent Association and vice-president of the Federation of Jamaican Organizations. Other meeting places for this group were Harlem's 21st Assembly District Socialist Club and People's Educational Forum, where they studied Marx and Engels, Grace Campbell's house at 116 West 133rd Street and Martin Luther Campbell's tailor's shop, almost next door to the Harlem branch of the New York Public Library.

In late 1915 Domingo's teenage friend Marcus Garvey re-established contact, initially by letter from Jamaica. Garvey himself had also left the island in 1910, spending time in Central America and Europe before returning briefly to Jamaica, where he founded the Universal Negro Improvement Association (UNIA), which failed to thrive there. He arrived in New York in March 1916 and immediately called on Domingo, through whom he was accepted into the broad sphere of Hubert Harrison's world. Garvey's first speech, in the parish hall of St Mark's Church in Harlem in May 1916, was later remembered by Domingo as a fiasco, but Garvey soon honed his speaking skills on the step-ladders and soap-boxes of Harlem, and by July 1917 had established the New York branch of the UNIA.[17]

---

14. Moore Turner, *Caribbean Crusaders*, pp. 58, 37, 38, and 242.

15. E. Ethelred Brown (1875–1956). See Mark Morrison-Reed, "A Dream Aborted: Egbert Ethelred Brown in Jamaica and Harlem", in his *Black Pioneers in a White Denomination*, 3rd edn, Boston, MA: Skinner House, 1994, pp. 31–111; and Juan Marcial Floyd-Thomas, *The Origins of Black Humanism in America: Reverend Ethelred Brown and the Unitarian Church*, New York: Palgrave Macmillan, 2008. Brown was the author of the valuable study "Labor Conditions in Jamaica Prior to 1917", *Journal of Negro History*, 4, no. 4 (October 1919), pp. 349–360.

16. Grace Philomena Campbell (1883–1943) was born in Georgia and brought up in Washington, DC before moving to New York, but her father, William Alexander Lamb Campbell, was from Jamaica. See Lydia Lindsey, "Gendering the Black Radical Tradition: Grace P. Campbell's Role in the Formation of a Radical Feminist Tradition in African-American Intellectual Culture", in *Revolutionary Lives of the Red and Black Atlantic since 1917*, ed. David Featherstone, Christian Hogsbjerg, and Alan Rice, Manchester, UK: Manchester University Press, 2022, pp. 94–142.

17. "Account by W. A. Domingo of Marcus Garvey's St Mark's Church Hall Lecture", *MGP*, 1,

Domingo's own first major appearance as a political activist came on the evening of Tuesday 12 June 1917 in a 2,000-strong meeting at the imposing Bethel African Methodist Episcopal church at 52–60 West 132nd Street in Harlem, just off Lenox Avenue, to launch Harrison's Liberty League of Negro Americans and to raise money for *The Voice* to act as the League's journal. The charismatic Harrison had drawn together a richly diverse group, both socially and politically. Alongside young West Indians such as Domingo, Briggs, Garvey, and Anselmo Jackson (from St Croix) were established African-American figures such as Monroe Trotter, John E. Bruce, and Adam Clayton Powell, Sr, as well as Lovett Fort-Whiteman, recently returned from the experience of revolutionary Yucatan.[18] Radical and race-conscious, the Liberty League promised a great deal. As an organisation it soon fell apart, but it provided the seeds for much of the black radicalism that followed. Although *The Voice* was supposedly the official journal of the Liberty League, another newspaper called *The Clarion* appeared in August 1917, advertising a Liberty League meeting to discuss its constitution: Harrison is listed as president, Domingo as assistant secretary (appearing as "A. W. Domingo"). The following month's issue of *The Clarion* contained Domingo's first surviving piece of writing [#1], pointing out the hypocrisy of the white press, which, after many decades of spewing forth racial slurs and insults, was now moderating its tone because North and South were competing for black labour.[19]

Helped by dissension between Harrison and other Liberty Leaguers, Garvey soon began to compete with Harrison for followers and started his own newspaper, *Negro World*, produced by a printer to whom Domingo had introduced him, and for which he asked Domingo to write editorials: the first issue appeared on 3 August 1918.[20] Always inclined to spread his eggs between different baskets, and increasingly drawn by reports of the achievements of the Russian Revolution, Domingo also worked with Owen and Randolph in 1918 on the short-lived newspaper *Negro Worker*, as well as on their election campaign as Socialist Party candidates.[21] He also collaborated with Briggs on *The Crusader News Service* and

pp. 190–192. Having decided to stay in the USA, Garvey incorporated the UNIA in New York on 2 July 1918.

18. Perry, *Hubert Harrison: The Voice of Harlem Radicals*, pp. 281–327. Anselmo R. Jackson (1891–1965); William Monroe Trotter (1872–1934), Boston-based editor and radical activist (see #34); John E. Bruce (1856–1924), often known as Bruce Grit, journalist and pan-African nationalist, and in his last year a supporter of Marcus Garvey; Adam Clayton Powell, Sr (1865–1963), pastor of the Abyssinian Baptist Church in Harlem and one of the founders of the National Urban League; Lovett Huey Fort-Whiteman (1889–1939), writer and activist who died in a Soviet prison camp.

19. Domingo once referred to a series of articles he'd written during his early days in New York titled "Citizens or Subjects?", but no trace of these has been found ("A Beam in Our Eyes", *Public Opinion*, 27 May 1944, p. 3).

20. See Brian Kwoba, "Pebbles and Ripples: Hubert Harrison and the Rise of the Garvey Movement", *Journal of African American History*, 105, no. 3 (Summer 2020), pp. 396–423.

21. "Socialist Candidates Hold Big Meeting", *Chicago Defender*, 3 August 1918, p. 5. Chandler

then on the monthly publication *The Crusader*, which first appeared in September 1918 and ran for just over three years.

The Crusader was established by Briggs with the financial support of Dominica-born Anthony Crawford, who owned the Inter-Colonial Steamship and Trading Company.[22] *The Crusader* soon began to link colonisation and racial oppression to capitalism and, in response to increased racial tensions and violence against black people, the magazine took a more militaristic tone. Advocating the creation of a separate armed organisation of African Americans for self-defence, it reported in October the formation of the African Blood Brotherhood for African Liberation and Redemption (ABB). In June 1920 it announced itself as the official journal of the ABB and began to promote Communism as the solution to racial and economic inequality. That Briggs could advocate a paramilitary self-defence organisation at the same time as running a sheet music company (the Crusader Music Company) and a basketball team suggests the range of his interests.

It wasn't long before Domingo's socialist-leaning editorials in *Negro World* started upsetting Marcus Garvey. A leader on 14 June 1919, no copy of which has survived, is reported to have "openly counselled negroes" to turn to Lenin and the Bolsheviks for assistance against their real oppressors, such as Lloyd George, Woodrow Wilson, and Georges Clemenceau.[23] This piece may, Robert Hill surmises, have contributed to Garvey bringing Domingo before a disciplinary panel and trying to remove him as editor.[24] Unfortunately for Garvey, Domingo's contract clearly stated that he could write what he wanted, so the move was unsuccessful. In addition, Garvey's biographer, Colin Grant, claims that Garvey had found out that Domingo "was stubborn and wilful … over the matter of his remuneration for his work on the *Negro World*", evidenced in Amy Ashwood Garvey's recollection that Domingo had "a habit of demanding prompt payment upon production of his article". Grant reads this behaviour as running counter to Domingo's "Socialist ideals" because he was supposedly "constantly exercised by

---

Owen (1889–1967) was an African-American writer, editor, and early member of the SPA. He later moved to Chicago and established his own public relations company. Asa Philip Randolph (1889–1979) was a labour unionist and civil rights activist. Together they edited *The Messenger*, with which Domingo was also soon associated.

22. Anthony Crawford (1881–1936) was born in Dominica to a US father and French Madagascan mother. In 1907 he was president of the West India Trading and Development Company, importers and producers of tropical products (*New York Age*, 3 October 1907, p. 3). With his significant experience in the shipping business, Crawford was able to disclose to Briggs the extravagant price Marcus Garvey paid for the nearly unseaworthy *Yarmouth* (Mark I. Solomon, *The Cry Was Unity: Communists and African Americans, 1917–36*, Jackson, MS: University Press of Mississippi, 1998, p. 26).

23. As reported in a letter from Reginald Popham Lobb, Administrator of St Vincent, to George Basil Haddon-Smith, Governor of the Windward Islands, dated 6 August 1919, in *MGP*, 11, pp. 268–269.

24. Ibid., p. 270, n. 5.

the need for money to fund his various capitalist projects".[25] In fact, Garvey was doubtless annoyed that Domingo—who knew Garvey better than most at this time—should have decided that a written contract to be paid $5 for writing an editorial for *Negro World* should imply that he would actually be paid, unlike the many others who found that a UNIA "salary" actually meant an unacknowledged contribution to UNIA funds.

Domingo had never joined the UNIA, but by the summer of 1919 he decided to cut all ties to Garvey by resigning from *Negro World* to become a contributing editor on *The Messenger*, in the pages of which, on 1 September, he announced that severance:

> NOTICE Mr W. A. Domingo takes this opportunity of informing the public that he is no longer connected with The Negro World. He also wishes to disabuse the minds of many of his acquaintances and friends who have unconsciously identified him with the various business projects of the Universal Improvement Association.
>
> It is his intention shortly to publish a weekly newspaper of scientific radicalism and fearless opinion.[26]

As Richard B. Moore put it: "Domingo also reached the point where human dignity made it impossible for him to tolerate Garvey's overbearing manner any longer."[27]

* * *

The first half of 1919 had been a fraught time in New York which, with the fighting in Europe over, was—at least for the moment—a very inward-looking city. Things had started to come to a boil on May Day with vigilante attacks on socialist and radical targets in New York led by returning soldiers, the press whipping up anti-foreigner hysteria. The Rand School of Social Science was one of the targets, the fourth time it had been attacked since the Armistice.[28] The Rand School belonged to the American Socialist Society, running adult education and training classes as well as housing various organisations and individuals associated with the SPA, which was having its own fraught time in the summer of 1919. Elsewhere in the country racial violence flared, with several hundred black

25. Colin Grant, *Negro with a Hat: The Rise and Fall of Marcus Garvey*, London: Vintage, 2009, pp. 147–148.
26. In *The Messenger*, 2, no. 9 (September 1919), p. 32.
27. Richard B. Moore, "The Critics and Opponents of Marcus Garvey", in *Marcus Garvey and the Vision of Africa*, ed. John Henrik Clarke, with the assistance of Amy Jacques Garvey, New York: Vintage Books, 1974, pp. 210–235, at 229.
28. See "Rand School and Other Nests of Anarchy Are Wrecked by Mobs", *The Sun*, 2 May 1919, p. 1.

people killed in Chicago and Washington, DC and in rural Arkansas, leading James Weldon Johnson to call this the "Red Summer".[29]

The shadow war against internal subversion spawned a large intelligence community and a vast web of patriotic organisations with thousands of volunteer spies: the biggest was the American Protective League (APL) with a quarter of a million subscribed members, often helping the Military Intelligence Division (MID) in a semi-official capacity.[30] Efforts to decommission these groups after the Armistice were only partially successful, and many continued to operate at a local and unofficial level, sometimes with the connivance of officials. They looked for new targets: the anarchists, labour agitators, and radical socialists usually referred to in the round as Reds or Bolsheviki. Despite the Armistice, in 1919 the USA was still formally in a state of war with Germany (as it in fact remained until the summer of 1921), which meant that wartime legislation was still in force. It was also the case that many official and unofficial agents of the US state saw the Bolsheviki as German-inspired revolutionists, so that for them the campaigns of 1919 were just a continuation of the war with Germany.[31]

That was the case with Senator Lee S. Overman (North Carolina), whose Senate sub-committee had alleged that Germans controlled all Jewish businesses in the USA and that German-owned munition plants were supplying arms to radicals, as it was with Archibald Stevenson, a lawyer who during the war had worked in the MID's Bureau of Propaganda.[32] On 22 and 23 January 1919 Stevenson testified at the Overman Committee hearings, sharing his view that university campuses were centres of dangerous Bolshevik propaganda and providing a helpful list of

29. James Weldon Johnson, *Along This Way: The Autobiography*, New York: Viking Press, 1933, p. 341; and see Chad L. Williams, "The War at Home: African American Veterans and Violence in the Long 'Red Summer'", in his *Torchbearers of Democracy: African American Soldiers in the World War I Era*, Chapel Hill, NC: University of North Carolina Press, 2010, pp. 223–260. The "Red Summer" and the "Red Scare" are linked because the government blamed race riots—overwhelmingly started by non-radical whites ("lawless white men" as James Weldon Johnson called them)—on blacks stirred up by radical whites, thus getting it wrong twice over. The Johnson quotation is from his editorial "Views and Reviews", *New York Age*, 20 December 1919, p. 4.

30. Ann Hagedorn, *Savage Peace: Hope and Fear in America, 1919*, New York: Simon & Schuster, 2007, pp. 25–26. See also on this period Adam Hochschild: *American Midnight: The Great War, a Violent Peace, and Democracy's Forgotten Crisis*, New York: Mariner Books, 2022, and Roy Talbert, Jr, *Negative Intelligence: The Army and the American Left*, Jackson, MS: University Press of Mississippi, 1991, especially pp. 33–37.

31. The view that Lenin and Trotsky were German agents was based on documents smuggled out of Russia by the Committee of Public Information's agent Edward Sisson, and later shown to be forgeries: *The German-Bolshevik Conspiracy*, Washington, DC: Committee on Public Information (War Information Series, no. 20), 1918: see George F. Kennan, "The Sissons Documents" *Journal of Modern History*, 28, no. 2 (June 1956), pp. 130–154.

32. Regin Schmidt, *Red Scare: FBI and the Origins of Anticommunism in the United States, 1919–1943*, Copenhagen, Denmark: Museum Tusculanum Press, 2000, pp. 136–145. A vocal opponent of Reconstruction, Lee Slater Overman (1854–1930) would in 1922 lead the filibuster that defeated the Dyer Anti-Lynching Bill. Archibald Ewing Stevenson (1884–1961), lawyer and conservative public intellectual: see Talbert, *Negative Intelligence*, pp. 141–148.

names which included, even after the Committee had removed two-thirds of them, a good number of the great and the good, many of them academics, who took strenuous exception to seeing their names plastered across the front page of the *New York Times* as having engaged in un-American activities.[33] The Secretary of War, Newton Baker, tried to distance himself and the MID from Stevenson and from civilian watchdogs such as the APL, but was stymied when a general strike closed down Seattle, awakening public fears of Bolshevik influence and enabling Overman to extend his remit.

Stevenson had wanted to continue his work at federal level, but the US Senate refused him authorisation, so he held his own investigation of radicalism in New York City under the auspices of the private Union League Club, which then petitioned the State of New York to set up a Joint Legislative Committee Investigating Seditious Activities in the State of New York, chaired by junior State Senator Clayton R. Lusk—hence the Lusk Committee.[34] Stevenson offered himself as unpaid special counsel: he was basically an unelected zealot who was prepared to do the hard work and so allowed to drive the agenda. The Lusk Committee set up headquarters at the Prince George Hotel on Broadway. It employed no more than 50 people but, as it happened, Lusk's brother was the former head of the APL's New Jersey branch and therefore able to supply a whole slew of volunteers, who were given ID cards, guns, and press credentials by the New York police department, enabling them to set about breaking into and bugging suspects' homes and offices. The head of the Lusk Committee's investigative division was a former Bureau of Investigation (BI) agent, Rayme W. Finch, and the Military Intelligence chief for New York was wealthy New York socialite Captain John B. Trevor, Harvard graduate, member of the Union League Club, trustee of the American Museum of Natural History, and associate of the prominent scientific racist Madison Grant. Trevor wrote a memorandum on "Negro Agitation", warning that it aimed at Pan-Negroism and "has relations with the Irish, the Jews, and the Hindus".[35] Trevor became a counsel of the Lusk Committee.

On the afternoon of Saturday 21 June 1919 Lusk Committee agents raided the Rand School and seized a large quantity of papers suspected of encouraging sedi-

---

33. "I.W.W. Gaining Here, Senators Are Told", *New York Times*, 23 January 1919, p. 4; "Lists Americans as Pacifists", *New York Times*, 25 January 1919, p. 1.

34. *Revolutionary Radicalism: Its History, Purpose and Tactics …*, 4 vols, Albany, NY: J. B. Lyon, 1920, p. 1. See *The Truth About the Lusk Committee: A Report Prepared by the Legislative Committee of the People's Freedom Union*, New York: Nation Press, 1920; Julian F. Jaffe, *Crusade Against Radicalism: New York During the Red Scare, 1914–1924*, Port Washington, NY: Kennikat Press, 1972; Todd J. Pfannestiel, *Rethinking the Red Scare: The Lusk Committee and New York's Crusade against Radicalism, 1919–1923*, New York: Routledge, 2003; and William J. Maxwell, *F.B. Eyes: How J. Edgar Hoover's Ghostreaders Framed African American Literature*, Princeton, NJ: Princeton University Press, 2015.

35. Hagedorn, *Savage Peace*, p. 228, quoting Trevor to Director of Military Intelligence, 5 April 1919 and 2 May 1919, Military Intelligence 324-IO, New York, RG 165, NARA [NARA = US National Archives and Records Administration, Washington, DC].

tion. This was no targeted raid: basically they took away every piece of paper they could find and then proceeded to read through them all, looking for signs of subversion. The front page report in the *New York Times* on 22 June included the sub-heads: "Revolution Openly Urged" and "Bloodshed is Predicted in Change of Government".[36] Just a week later Stevenson was ready to make public what he called the "worst" of the evidence, which he did at a public hearing. This "worst" turned out to be, in Stevenson's words, a "startling plan for the organization of the negroes into radical units" written by W. A. Domingo, a name not previously on the radar either of the groups hunting subversives or of the mainstream New York press. The lengthy document was read out and, according to the *New York Times*, members of the committee "expressed amazement". As well they might, since this time the *New York Times* sub-heads included "Planned Negro Uprising".[37] Close reading was apparently not part of the skillset of the members of the Lusk Committee since nowhere in the piece in question did Domingo refer to anything that might be construed as a "planned Negro uprising". Domingo's name puzzled the press. Even the *New York Age* wondered "whether there actually exists such an individual as this alleged W. A. Domingo".[38]

For all its huffing and puffing, the Lusk Committee achieved nothing. Its report was, as Adam Hochschild puts it, "a monument of alarmist pseudoscholarship".[39] The following year Lusk himself wrote an account for the *Review of Reviews*, claiming that the radical movement had been begun "by paid agents of the Junker class in Germany as part of their programme of industrial and military world conquest".[40] There was, he claimed, "ample and convincing evidence" for this, none of which, in the event, was ever produced. Unsurprisingly—if illogically—the cause of all the problems was "unresticted immigration".[41] No prosecutions followed the inquiry, and the matter was quietly dropped. As David Brion Davis put it: "The years from 1917 to 1921 are probably unmatched in American history for popular hysteria, xenophobia, and paranoid suspicion."[42]

The "Negro problem"—or rather the SPA's problem with Negroes—had first been raised by Isaac Max Rubinow in twelve articles for the *International Socialist Review* between 1908 and 1910.[43] Then the idea of the Negro as a potential

36. "Raid Rand School, 'Left Wing,' and I.W.W. Offices", *New York Times*, 22 June 1919, p. 1.
37. "Moves to Close the Rand School", *New York Times*, 28 June 1919, pp. 1 and 3.
38. "A Curious Document", *New York Age*, 5 July 1919, p. 4.
39. Hochschild, *American Midnight*, p. 228.
40. Clayton R. Lusk, "Radicalism under Inquiry", *Review of Reviews*, 41, no. 2 (February 1920), pp. 167–171, at 167.
41. Ibid., p. 168.
42. David Brion Davis, in *The Fear of Conspiracy: Images of Un-American Subversion from the Revolution to the Present*, ed. with commentary by David Brion Davis, Ithaca, NY: Cornell University Press, 1971, p. 205.
43. Written under the pseudonym I. M. Robbins, "The Economic Aspects of the Negro Problem", *International Socialist Review*, 8, no. 8 (February 1908) to 10, no. 12 (June 1910). For background and context, see Philip S. Foner, *American Socialism and Black Americans: From the*

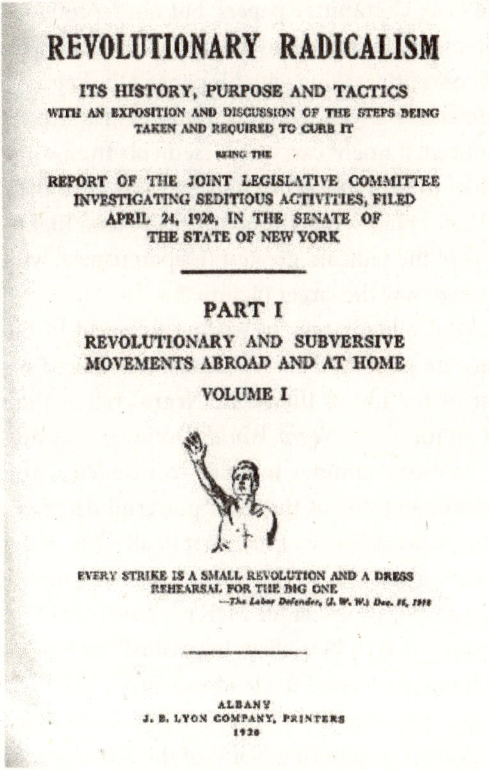

REVOLUTIONARY RADICALISM

ITS HISTORY, PURPOSE AND TACTICS

WITH AN EXPOSITION AND DISCUSSION OF THE STEPS BEING TAKEN AND REQUIRED TO CURB IT

BEING THE

REPORT OF THE JOINT LEGISLATIVE COMMITTEE INVESTIGATING SEDITIOUS ACTIVITIES, FILED APRIL 24, 1920, IN THE SENATE OF THE STATE OF NEW YORK

PART I

REVOLUTIONARY AND SUBVERSIVE MOVEMENTS ABROAD AND AT HOME

VOLUME I

EVERY STRIKE IS A SMALL REVOLUTION AND A DRESS REHEARSAL FOR THE BIG ONE

—*The Labor Defender*, (I. W. W.) [illegible]

ALBANY
J. B. LYON COMPANY, PRINTERS
1920

Figure 3 Title page of *Revolutionary Radicalism: Its History, Purpose and Tactics...*, 4 vols., Albany: J. B. Lyon Company, 1920, the report of the Lusk Committee.

menace to socialism was the subject of a Hubert Harrison essay in 1912.[44] The situation hadn't improved over the next seven years, and it was no accident that, just as Domingo was finishing his piece, the editors of *The Messenger* published an editorial in May 1919 called "The Negro—A Menace to Radicalism".[45] Randolph, Owen, and Domingo were—one can safely assume—on the same page because they'd already been in the same rooms discussing how to get the SPA to take matters of race seriously.[46]

Ironically, Domingo's paper, "Socialism Imperilled, or the Negro—A Potential Menace to American Radicalism" [#3], only survives at all because it was read into the evidence of the Lusk Committee and published in its findings. Written with some sophistication, both stylistic and political, the paper aimed at getting policy-makers in the SPA to think about the threat that the absence of black members might ultimately pose to the

Age of Jackson to World War II, Westport, CT: Greenwood Press, 1977, pp. 202–311. Local New York at least recognised that there was an issue, but it managed to alienate both Harrison and Du Bois, the very people it needed most for black recruitment, who left the party.

44. Hubert Harrison, "Socialism and the Negro", *International Socialist Review*, 13 (July 1912), pp. 65–68, reprinted in *A Hubert Harrison Reader*, ed. Jeffrey B. Perry, Middletown, CT: Wesleyan University Press, 2001, pp. 72-76, at 73; see also W. E. B. Du Bois, "Socialism and the Negro Problem", *The New Review*, 1, no. 5 (February 1913), pp. 138–141.

45. "The Negro—A Menace to Radicalism", *The Messenger*, May–June 1919, p. 20 (the magazine had extremely irregular numbering in its early years: this issue carried no number). On *The Messenger*, see Theodore Kornweibel, Jr, *No Crystal Stair: Black Life and the "Messenger," 1917–1928*, New York: Greenwood Press, 1976.

46. See Sally M. Miller, "The Socialist Party and the Negro, 1901–1920", *Journal of Negro History*, 56, no. 3 (1971), pp. 220–229. Domingo still urged support: "Socialism the Negroes' Hope", *The Messenger*, 2, no. 7 (July 1919), p. 22 [CB, pp. 28–31]; and "A New Negro and a New Day", *The Messenger*, 2, no. 10 (November 1920), pp. 43–44 [CB, pp.97–100].

socialist project.[47] Also among the Lusk Committee papers, but not reproduced in its four-volume report, is the letter that Domingo had sent to David Berenberg, editor of the Rand School editorial committee, along with his paper. One key as to why the document did not find immediate favour with the SPA lies in Domingo's suggestion that if it were to be produced, it might carry endorsements from some important figures. "For the pamphlet to be a success in rousing radicals to their danger," he wrote, "it is necessary that it reach Anarchists, Lefts, Centres, Rights, and even Liberals."[48] At the moment of the radicals' greatest fissiparousness, with the SPA about to break apart, Domingo saw the larger picture.[49]

Domingo was now on a roll: seven other pieces of writing followed in the second half of 1919. The first piece he published in *The Messenger* offered his well-informed argument in favour of the use of the term "Negro" rather than "colored".[50] On 26 July, in his last editorial for *Negro World*, Domingo—clearly responding to the terrible events of those summer months—concluded: "In a world of wolves one should go armed, and one of the most powerful defensive weapons within the reach of negroes is the practice of race first in all parts of the world" [#4]. In the same vein, a piece entitled "If We Must Die" appeared in *The Messenger* in September, Domingo paraphrasing Claude McKay's poem [#6].[51]

There was also a shorter companion piece to "Socialism Imperilled", addressed to his black readership, in which Domingo decried the tendency of US blacks to "cling to past and present economic ideals with the desperation of a dying man" and urged them to look at examples from around the world of the broadness of the socialist vision towards all oppressed humanity.[52] The red and black threads were being wound tightly together in Domingo's writing. In September 1919 *The Crusader* announced the formation of the African Blood Brotherhood: Domingo became a member alongside Briggs, Moore, Huiswoud, and Grace Campbell. In

47. See the account in Winston James, *Holding Aloft the Banner of Ethiopia: Caribbean Radicalism in Early Twentieth-Century America*, London: Verso, 1998, pp. 274–282.

48. Letter from W. A. Domingo to David P. Berenberg, 6 June 1919, Lusk Committee Papers, L0028, Box 1, folder 14, New York State Archives, Albany.

49. For general background, see Barbara Foley, *Spectres of 1919: Class and Nation in the Making of the New Negro*, Urbana, IL: University of Illinois Press, 2003; Theodore Kornweibel, Jr, *Seeing Red: Federal Campaigns Against Black Militancy, 1919–1925*, Bloomington, IN: Indiana University Press, 1998; and Solomon, *The Cry Was Unity*.

50. "What Are We, Negroes or Colored People?", *The Messenger*, 2, no. 6 (May–June) 1919, pp. 23–25.

51. According to federal surveillance, during one street-corner meeting Domingo reasserted black people's right to self-defence in forthright terms: "Our aim is to allow those who attack us to choose the weapons," he told listeners from his step-ladder; "if it be guns, we will reply with guns" (Makalani, *In the Cause*, p. 66, quoting Federal Surveillance Report, File 202600-2031-3, RG 65, NARA).

52. "Socialism the Negroes' Hope", *The Messenger*, 2, no. 7 (July 1919), p. 22 (in CB, pp. 28–30]. On Bolshevism's attraction to black radicals, see Winston James, "To the East Turn: The Russian Revolution and the Black Radical Imagination in the United States, 1917–1924", *American Historical Review*, 126, no. 3 (September 2021), pp. 1,001–1,045.

his late-life interview with Theodore Draper, Domingo was dismissive of the ABB as a paper outfit, and even suggested that he wasn't actually a member: "I was never an organization man."[53] While Briggs did probably exaggerate its membership numbers and importance, Domingo was clearly active in the ABB. His name features prominently in *The Crusader*'s July 1921 account of "A.B.B. Activities", making appeals for funds and speaking at public meetings.[54] One of Briggs's obsessions was the need for the different black organisations to have an overarching body that would co-ordinate their work. The ABB programme published in *The Crusader* proposed bringing "all Negro organizations [in the United States] together on a Federation basis" to build "a united, centralized Movement" as well as combining "all Negro organizations in each of the African countries into a worldwide Negro federation".[55] This remained a pipe-dream whose main obstacle was Marcus Garvey. Any US-based federation would need to include the UNIA, which had by far the biggest membership, but Garvey was uninterested in co-operation: he was, after all, president-in-waiting for the whole of Africa. Briggs's own plan for what was effectively a rival organisation to the UNIA, but organised on more democratic principles, then immediately swung into action and as quickly faded from view. In the background, Domingo perhaps noted that federations were more easily proposed than achieved.

There was a third strand to Domingo's thought running through 1919. A March editorial in *Negro World* showed that part of his attention was still on the West

53. Theodore Draper, Interview with W. A. Domingo (18 January 1958), Theodore Draper Research Files, Subseries 1.3, American Communist Party (1919–1929), 1915–1968, Box 21, folder 20, Stuart A. Rose Manuscript, Archives, and Rare Book Library, Emory University, Atlanta, GA. Domingo's self-image as somebody commenting from the outside of organisations has an element of truth, and it's important that he was never constrained as his friends Briggs, Moore, and Huiswoud were by membership of the Workers Party of America, the fledging Communist Party that they soon joined, but at different stages of his life he did belong to the SPA, the ABB, the Jamaica Progressive League, and the People's National Party.

54. "A. B. B. Activities", *The Crusader*, 4, no. 5 (July 1921), p. 13. In addition, the call for a National All-Race Assembly was signed by Domingo for the ABB and a publicity leaflet for the ABB listed Domingo as Director of Publicity and Propaganda (*American Communism and Black Americans: A Documentary History, 1919–1929*, ed. Philip S. Foner and James S. Allen, Philadelphia, PA: Temple University Press, 1987, pp. 38 and 39). On the ABB, see Robert A. Hill, "Introduction: Racial and Radical: Cyril V. Briggs, *The Crusader* Magazine, and the African Blood Brotherhood, 1918–1922", in *The Crusader: Facsimile of the Periodical*, 3 vols, with an introduction by Robert A. Hill (New York: Garland, 1987), I, pp. v–lxxiii; Jacob Zumoff, "The African Blood Brotherhood: From Caribbean Nationalism to Communism", *Journal of Caribbean History*, 41, no. 1 (2007), pp. 200–226; Makalani, "Liberating Negroes Everywhere: Cyril Briggs, the African Blood Brotherhood, and Radical Pan-Africanism", in his *In the Cause of Freedom*, pp. 45–69; Cathy Bergin, "'Unrest among the Negroes': The African Blood Brotherhood and the Politics of Resistance", *Race & Class*, 57, no. 3 (2016), pp. 45–58; and Jak Peake, "Cyril Briggs: Guns, Bombs, Spooks and Writing the Revolution", in *Revolutionary Lives of the Red and Black Atlantic since 1917*, ed. David Featherstone, Christian Hogsbjerg, and Alan Rice, Manchester, UK: Manchester University Press, 2022, pp. 72–93.

55. "Program of the A.B.B.," *The Crusader*, 5, no. 2 (October 1921), pp. 15–18, at 16.

Indies [#2]. The opportunity here lay in the notion of self-determination, initially outlined by Lenin in October 1916 and articulated by the new provisional government in Moscow—under the influence of the Bolshevik-controlled Petrograd soviet—in April 1917.[56] On the back foot, the Allies had started to adopt the same terminology. Woodrow Wilson's address to Congress on 11 February 1918 (the "Four Points" speech) was crystal clear: "In the coming settlement," he said, "national aspirations must be respected; people may be dominated and governed only by their own consent .... 'Self-determination' is not a mere phrase. It is an imperative principle of actions which statesmen will henceforth ignore at their peril."[57] However, when the crunch came, at the Paris Peace Conference in the winter of 1918–19, Wilson made it very clear that self-determination was going to be ignored when it came to European colonies. Domingo's response was a Leninist analysis of why colonies are essential to the maintenance of capitalism [#5].

Domingo's writing about colonialism did not go unnoticed. Given that a significant number of the black Reds in New York were West Indians, and therefore British citizens, the British Secret Intelligence Service (SIS) took a lively interest in their activities. An SIS office had been operative in New York since late 1915, originally concerned with German activity, but latterly with Irish and Indian revolutionaries in the city. Just before the raid on the Rand School, one of the Lusk Committee's Russian translators jumped ship and gave an interview in which he said that the driving force behind the Lusk Committee was actually an Englishman called Robert Nathan. Nathan was an SIS agent who previously had been the police commissioner in Dhaka, suppressing Bengali revolutionaries. His contact, it turns out, was Rayme W. Finch, the ex-BI agent working as a special investigator for the Lusk Committee, but also for Nathan—and therefore for the British SIS. It's therefore not surprising that the British were interested in a BI report by the African-American Walter Loving, a copy of which was sent by the SIS to London—where it was edited and sent back to the US State Department in October 1919. Major Loving, a talented cornetist, had had a distinguished career in military music, leading the Philippine Constabulary Band and playing at the inauguration parade of President Taft in 1909. Charged with investigating subversive activities by African-American leaders, he attended rallies in plain clothes and developed a network of agents, but was clearly known to—and to a degree respected by—at least some of those leaders: his reports are usually respectful and

56. V. I. Lenin, "The Socialist Revolution and the Right of Nations to Self-Determination" (1916), www.marxists.org/archive/lenin/works/1916/jan/x01.htm (accessed 20 June 2017); and see Erez Manela, *The Wilsonian Moment: Self-Determination and the International Origins of Anticolonial Nationalism*, New York: Oxford University Press, 2007, p. 37.

57. As "Only One Peace Possible", in *Americanism: Woodrow Wilson's Speeches on the War—Why He Made Them—and—What They Have Done*, ed. Oliver Marble Gale, Chicago, IL: Baldwin Syndicate, 1918, pp. 103–109, at 106. See Mark T. Gilderhus, *Pan American Visions: Woodrow Wilson in the Western Hemisphere 1913–1921*, Tucson, AZ: University of Arizona Press, 1986.

insightful. In this "Final Report" he wrote that Domingo was "a very able young man of West Indian birth. It was Mr Domingo who drafted the plan of campaign of the Socialist Party among Negroes." It is telling that the British version, while keeping the substance, left out the "very", left out the "Mr", and lowered the upper-case initial letter in "Negroes".[58] So, by the end of 1919, when the Attorney General submitted the BI report, Domingo's name was frequently invoked (even if he sometimes appeared as William H. Domingo).[59]

* * *

In March 1920 Domingo launched his own newspaper, *The Emancipator*, announced as "A paper with principle and purpose".[60] It was published by the New Negro Publishing Company, printed by Up-To-Date Printing of Canal Street, and its editorial office was at 2295 Seventh Avenue. The New Negro Publishing Company had been incorporated in September 1919 under the names of W. A. Doringo [Domingo], F. R. Crosswaith, and G. P. Campbell, at 116 West 133rd Street, Grace Campbell's home, where the ABB usually met.[61] British Military Intelligence took note of this in its report of 27 September 1919, which stated:

> The Negro Socialists of New York are waging a campaign for funds with which to publish a Negro Socialist weekly. A company has been formed and Thomas A. E. Potter, an active Socialist party member for the past 17 years, has been

58. W. H. Loving, "Final Report on Negro Subversion", New York, 6 August 1919, Military Intelligence Division File 10218-361, p. 3, RG 165, NARA; and "Unrest among the Negroes", British Special Report no. 10 to the US State Department (7 October 1919), Records of the Post Office Department, Office of the Solicitor, Reports and Exhibits Relating to Transmittal of Mail Violating 1917 Espionage Act, 1917–1921. Unarranged Box no. 53, file no. 398, RG 28, NARA. The latter is reproduced in W. F. Elkins, "'Unrest Among the Negroes': A British Document of 1919", *Science & Society*, 32, no. 1 (1968), pp. 66–79. Kornweibel (*Seeing Red*, p. 72) says that Special Report no. 10 was "actually penned by" Loving, but the cover note to the NARA copy only states that the report was "based entirely upon a statement made by" Loving. The British report itself says that "it is especially interesting to hear the views" of Loving and, although clearly *based* on Loving's report, the two are not identical. On Loving, see Wray R. Johnson, "Black American Radicalism and the First World War: The Secret Files of the Military Intelligence Division", *Armed Forces & Society*, 26, no. 1 (Fall 1999), pp. 27–53; and Talbert, *Negative Intelligence*, pp. 131–134.

59. "Radicalism and Sedition among the Negroes as Reflected in Their Publications", Exhibit 10 in [US Senate], *Investigation Activities of the Department of Justice, 66th Cong., 1st sess. Doc. 153.*, Washington, DC: GPO, 1919, pp. 161–187.

60. It seems as if *The Emancipator* was originally going to be named *The New Era*: an advertisement for the appearance of that title appeared in *The Crusader*, promising "fierce, uncompromising, and scientific editorials" by W. A. Domingo, supported by Anselmo Jackson, A. Philip Randolph, and Cyril Briggs; "Coming What?—'The New Era'", *The Crusader*, 2, no. 2 [October 1919], p. 28.

61. "New Incorporations", *New York Times*, 9 September 1919, p. 25.

Emancipator

"A Paper With Principle and Purpose"

VOL. I. No. 1. New York, Saturday, March 13, 1920.

COLOR LINE DISAPPEARING

Black Professor in Paris Condemns Associated Press

Advises Prejudiced News Service To Enlighten Europe About Lynchings and Burnings.

WILL AMERICAN NEGROES WAKE UP TO THIS PERIL?

Our Security Demands That We Fight Hurtful Propaganda With Counter Propaganda.

COLORED GIRL HEADS UNION

EDUCATIONAL FORUM CENTER OF LIGHT IN HARLEM

AFRICAN LEAGUE HOLDS MEETING

NEGRO WORKERS STRIKE IN PANAMA

Blacks and Whites Coming Together In South Africa

WELCOMED AS BROTHERS AND EQUALS BY SOCIALISTS.

BLACK WORKERS JAILED FOR STRIKING IN TRINIDAD

Figure 4 Front page of the first issue of *The Emancipator*.

> elected president. … The Negroes have sent out an appeal to all members of the Socialist Party for funds, which are to be sent to Thomas A. E. Potter, 2411 Seventh Ave.[62]

This seems to be the only reference to Potter's involvement. Domingo was editor-in-chief and treasurer, Frank Crosswaith secretary, and the contributing editors were Owen, Randolph, Moore, Briggs, and Jackson, indicating considerable crossover with both *The Messenger* and *The Crusader*. The opening editorial, unsigned but clearly written by Domingo, stressed the need for a newspaper with "the vision and comprehension of world events":

62. File 10218-364/7, RG165, NARA, quoted in *MGP*, 8, p. 40, n. 2. Thomas E. A. Potter (St Kitts, 1884–?) was a baker by occupation. After a spell in the navy, Frank Rudolph Crosswaith (St Croix, 1892–1965) became a lecturer at the Rand School, a correspondent for *The Messenger* and an organiser for the Brotherhood of Sleeping Car Porters and then for the International Ladies Garment Workers Union: see John H. Seabrook, *Black and White Unite: The Career of Frank R. Crosswaith*, PhD dissertation, Rutgers University, 1980, and Cornelius L. Bynum, "The New Negro and Social Democracy during the Harlem Renaissance, 1917–37", *Journal of the Gilded Age and Progressive Era*, 10, no. 1 (January 2011), pp. 89–112. In his speech to the May 1920 convention of the SPA at Finnish Hall in Harlem, requesting financial support for *The Messenger* and *The Emancipator*, Domingo recalled that his local branch of the SPA had realised the need for a weekly newspaper that would speak directly to a black readership and, having decided to organise such a paper, "we got Karlin to get things started" (Eighth National Convention of the Socialist Party, Socialist Party of America Papers, National Convention Proceedings, Folder 201901-076-1185 [11 May 1920], p. 129, Duke University Library, Durham, NC). William Karlin (1882–1944) was a Russian-born lawyer and Socialist politician.

> We launch out on the troubled waters of journalism with a principle and a purpose, a message and a mission. We shall uncompromisingly champion the cause of the oppressed of all lands; the right of workers everywhere to secure the full social value of the products of their toil; the prescriptive right of the native Africans to their ancestral domain. We shall vigorously battle against all the forces of international reaction which strive to reduce mankind, particularly the darker portions, to economic serfdom. Caring little for entrenched and legalized tyranny, and less for the mercenary myrmidons of might it will be our purpose to expose to the white light of public opinion the vile deeds of venal officials, the fallacies of uninformed leaders and the truckling subservience of corrupt contemporaries who sacrifice the race's interest upon the altar of Mammon.[63]

Hubert Harrison suggested—at least according to Jeffrey Perry's reading—that *The Emancipator* had been secretly subsidised by the SPA in an attempt to cut into black solidarity.[64] This seems unlikely given that Domingo spoke in May 1920 at the SPA convention in Finnish Hall requesting financial support for *The Emancipator*. His plea was greeted by "prolonged applause" and his request was referred to the Committee on Organization, Propaganda and Finance, but it seems that no support came forth.[65] Domingo struck back at Harrison, suggesting that he had been bought off by Garvey with the editorship of *Negro World*.[66] The following week *The Emancipator* challenged Harrison to publish his true opinion of Garvey—which by this point differed little, if at all, from Domingo's, but which Harrison was keeping to himself and his diary.[67] And a week later the paper suggested that Harrison ("not his Mr Hyde, H. H.") would make the best leader of the UNIA, given Garvey's "meagre mental attainments".[68]

The first issue of *The Emancipator* led on a story about South Africa, optimistically headed "Color Line Disappearing", with other front page stories featuring black workers striking in Panama, Trinidad, and Jamaica.[69] Page three noted the arrival in New York of E. Ethelred Brown and his family from Jamaica, and advertised the pianoforte teaching of Mrs W. A. Domingo.[70] Page four addressed the

63. "Our Reason for Being", *The Emancipator*, 13 March 1920, p. 4.
64. Harrison, "Race First versus Class First" (*Negro World*, 27 March 1920, reprinted in the *Hubert Harrison Reader*, pp. 107–109); Perry, *Hubert Harrison: The Struggle for Equality*, p. 153.
65. Eighth National Convention, pp. 130–131.
66. W. A. Domingo, "Marcus Garvey Challenged", *The Emancipator*, 3 April 1920, pp. 1–2.
67. "'H.H.' Challenged", *The Emancipator*, 10 April 1920, p. 2.
68. "Discard Ambition and Ignorance", *The Emancipator*, 17 April 1920, p. 3.
69. "Color Line Disappearing", "Negro Workers Strike in Panama", "Negro Workers Jailed for Striking in Trinidad", "Black Workers of Jamaica, B.W.I. Strike", *The Emancipator*, 13 March 1920, p. 1.
70. "Liberal Pastor Arrives from Jamaica", "Learn to Play the Pianoforte", *The Emancipator*, 13 March 1920, p. 3. Brown immediately started the Harlem Community Church with Domingo and several of his friends as charter members.

key issue of Bolshevism's take on race [#7]. It also cleared its throat with a general article about the danger of wild-cat business promotions, caught its breath in the second issue with a warning about get-rich-quick schemes which quickly crashed and burned, and then launched its third issue with a denunciation of the fraud of the Black Star Line, prompting an immediate $400,000 lawsuit from Marcus Garvey.[71] After a short period observing how Garvey operated, Domingo had formulated his view of him as an unscrupulous demagogue. Particularly galling to Domingo were Garvey's claims to business acumen—such as the Black Star Line being "the embodiment of the commercial sentiment of the Negro"—when Domingo was evidently himself the one with such acumen, which just as evidently Garvey lacked.[72]

The Emancipator was international in focus, even if the critique of Marcus Garvey's activities provided the most prominent strand.[73] Only two pieces appeared under Domingo's name, one being his first addressing of African issues [#8], although he probably wrote the vast majority of the editorial material, which would add another 18 or so pieces to the list of his writings. According to Domingo, *The Emancipator* "went out of business because of insufficient capital".[74] One essay of Domingo's from this period was taken by Claude Mackay to Russia and is only available in a back translation from the Russian translation [#9].

71. "An Era of 'Wild-Cat' Business Promotions", *The Emancipator*, 13 March 1920, p.4; "Bubbles", *The Emancipator*, 20 March 1920, p. 4; "Black Star Line Exposed", *The Emancipator*, 27 March 1920, p. 1; Anselmo R. Jackson, "An Analysis of the Black Star Line", *The Emancipator*, 27 March 1920, p. 2; 3 April 1920, p. 2; 10 April 1920, p. 2; 17 April 1920, p. 2; 24 April 1920, p. 2; "Garvey Sues Emancipator", *The Emancipator*, 3 April 1920, p. 1. The lawsuit was not pursued.

72. Black Star Line Flyer and Promotional Letter from Marcus Garvey, President of the Black Star Line, J. R. Ralph Casimir Papers, Sc MG 110 Box 2, folio 8, SCRBC [SCRBC = Schomburg Center for Research in Black Culture, Manuscripts, Archives, and Rare Books Division, New York Public Library]. The correspondence between Crawford and Casimir indicates that Casimir had taken umbrage at Domingo's criticism of Garvey in *The Emancipator* and that Domingo had showed Crawford Casimir's letter as an example of how West Indians of good faith were being duped. Crawford wrote to Casimir (they may have known each other from Dominica) to underline Domingo's credentials (21 May 1920), but Casimir was unpersuaded (17 June 1920), remaining an ardent Garveyite: see Kathy Casimir MacLean, *"Black Man Listen": The Life of Ralph Casimir*, London: Papillote Press, 2022. Crawford's business activities contradict claims that Garvey's black-owned shipping line had "little if any parallel in New World black history" (Tony Martin, *Race First: The Ideological and Organizational Struggles of Marcus Garvey and the Universal Negro Improvement Association*, Dover, MA: Majority Press, 1976, p. 152).

73. There are only seven *surviving* issues of *The Emancipator*, although Joyce Moore Turner refers to ten issues ("Richard B. Moore and His Works", in Richard B. Moore, *Caribbean Militant in Harlem: Collected Writings 1920–1972*, ed. W. Burghardt Turner and Joyce Moore Turner, Bloomington, IN: Indiana University Press, 1988, pp. 19–108, at 32), as does Domingo himself [#15]. Certainly Domingo was asking for funds to keep the newspaper going on 11 May, which would have been a strange thing to do if the final issue had been the last surviving one, on 27 April. And furthermore, Claude McKay reproduced an article by Domingo, seemingly from *The Emancipator* [#9], but which doesn't appear in any of the surviving issues.

74. W. A. Domingo, Letter to Alain Locke, 21 September 1925, ALP.

Harrison's opinion of Garvey quickly dipped once, as editor of *Negro World*, his contact got closer. By May 1920 he could comment in his diary that Garvey "is spiritually as well as intellectually a little man".[75] In effect, he came to the same view as Domingo, but almost a year later. Harrison then tried to revive the Liberty League as the Liberty Party when it seemed as if Garvey's bubble might have burst, but it lasted only about four months in late 1920.[76] He then tried—while Garvey was out of the country—to resurrect the Liberty League, with as little success, and to start an International Colored Unity League: ditto. All efforts were indicative of his desire to lead a mass movement. Writing of the original Liberty League in 1923, Harrison wrote that, "From that league Garvey appropriated every feature that was worth while in his movement."[77]

Garvey's apotheosis came on 1 August 1920 with a huge UNIA parade through the streets of Harlem. This was spectacle rather than argument, but it proved effective at galvanising support. As David Krasner suggests, "Garvey's parade provided a site for those who lacked identification with common social identity and national pride." He was reaching people even Harrison's oratory couldn't touch. The spectacle of the UNIA served as a focal point for a generalised black consciousness, void of specifics: "The visceral experience would supersede substance."[78] More interested in substance, Domingo had by now become Garvey's staunchest critic. Two more pieces followed in 1921: a forensic analysis of UNIA finances [#10] and a further letter to *The Gleaner* [#11]. It was around now, in the summer of 1921, that Domingo took two trips downtown for meetings of the black Reds organised by Hubert Harrison, the first at the office of *The Liberator* on East 14th Street, the second at the house of Rose Pastor Stokes on Ann Street in Greenwich Village. According to Claude McKay, the first meeting focused on the possibility of making the UNIA more class-conscious; according to Edgar Grey, the second involved Stokes trying to persuade Harrison to accept Communist backing for his Liberty League.[79] Both ended in failure.

* * *

From the heights of his popularity in the years between 1919 and 1921, Marcus Garvey's fortunes took a calamitous dive, culminating in his conviction on

75. Perry, *Hubert Harrison: The Struggle for Equality*, p. 147.
76. Ibid., p. 252.
77. Hubert Harrison, "Marcus Garvey at the Bar of United States Justice", Associated Negro Press, July 1923, reprinted in *Hubert Harrison Reader*, pp. 184–199, at 196–197.
78. David Krasner, "'In the Whirlwind and the Storm': Marcus Garvey and the Performance of Black Nationalism", in his *A Beautiful Pageant: African American Theatre, Drama, and Performance in the Harlem Renaissance, 1910–1927*, New York: Palgrave Macmillan, 2002, pp. 167–187, at 173.
79. Claude McKay, *A Long Way From Home* [1937], London: Pluto Press, 1985, p. 109; Perry, *Hubert Harrison: The Struggle for Equality*, pp. 338–339.

charges of mail fraud. Trouble had earlier been brewing behind the scenes. In May 1920 J. Edgar Hoover had submitted a brief to the Department of State about Garvey's activities in the USA. The annual UNIA convention in August 1921 had, in its closed sessions, debated charges against various UNIA executive officers with whom Garvey had fallen out. Then in December the BI requested that the Internal Revenue Service investigate Garvey and the UNIA. But 1922 was when things really started to deteriorate, beginning with Garvey's arrest on 12 January for fraudulent use of mails: he was held on a $2,500 bond pending presentation of his case to a federal grand jury. Meanwhile, in April the Black Star Line was dissolved due to financial failure. Thus far, it would have been possible for sympathisers, or even the neutral, to see state repression of radicalism, by whatever means, and the venality of employees as the reasons for Garvey's travails. But the meeting on Sunday 25 June 1922 in Atlanta with Edward Young Clarke was less easy to explain away.

Negro World reported a fairly mundane UNIA gathering in New York on that day, interrupted by the receipt of a telegram that was immediately read out:

> Chairman Liberty Hall, 120 West 133th street, New York: Have this day interviewed Edward Young Clark, acting Imperial Wizard Knights of the Ku Klux Klan. He denied any hostility toward the Negro as a race. He expresses sympathy for aims and objects of Universal Negro Improvement Association. He believes America to be a white man's country, and also states that the Negro should have a country of his own in Africa. He denied that his organization, since its re-organization, ever officially attacked the Negro. He has been invited to speak at forthcoming convention to further assure the race of the stand of the Klan. Interview will be published in Negro World. Best wishes to members and friends. Signed: Garvey.

The reading of the telegram was reportedly met with thunderous applause.[80]

As news leaked out and the criticisms began, Garvey provided his own more detailed account of the meeting in advance of the promised full transcript, but increasingly found himself on the defensive.[81] In the *New York Age* James Weldon

80. "Garvey Interviews Wizard of Ku Klux Klan", *Negro World*, 1 July 1922, p. 7.

81. "Imperial Wizard Has Conference with Mr Garvey", *Chicago Defender*, 8 July 1922, p. 2; "Hon. Marcus Garvey Tells of Interview with Ku Klux Klan", *Negro World*, 15 July 1922, pp. 7 and 12; "Hon. Marcus Garvey Defends His Position in Relation to Interview with Ku Klux Klan", *Negro World*, 22 July 1922, p. 7. No transcript was ever published. On Garvey's extensive relationships with a series of asinine white supremacists, see Tony Martin, "The Ku Klux Klan, White Supremacy, and Garvey: A Symbiotic Relationship", in his *Race First*, pp. 344–357. J. A. Rogers noted Garvey's "racial fascism" in "Marcus Garvey, Leader of the Back-to-Africa Movement", in his *World's Great Men of Color*, New York: J. A. Rogers, 1947, pp. 599–610, at 602. See also Paul Gilroy, *Against Race: Imagining Political Culture Beyond the Color Line*, Cambridge, MA: Belknap Press, 2000, pp. 231–237.

Johnson accused him of "an ingenuousness which is almost inconceivable".[82] The first big name to jump ship was William Pickens, previously sympathetic to the UNIA despite working for the National Association for the Advancement of Colored People (NAACP). Pickens received an invitation cum summons from Garvey to present himself at the forthcoming August UNIA convention in order to receive an honorary title from the hands of Gabriel Johnson of Monrovia, Liberia, "His Highness the Potentate of the Universal Negro Improvement Association". In response, Pickens took the opportunity to state that he wanted nothing to do with an organisation in alliance with the Ku Klux Klan—and for good measure leaked both letters to the press.[83]

Meetings denouncing Garvey began to proliferate in New York, Randolph and Chandler's Friends of Negro Freedom leading the way, usually with NAACP support.[84] In the circumstances it wasn't surprising that the third UNIA convention that August was a fraught affair.[85] James W. H. Eason, a prominent UNIA leader, spoke out against the Ku Klux Klan connection, severed his relationship with the UNIA, and was accused by Garvey of double-crossing him. The next month Eason established a rival organisation, the Universal Negro Alliance, and he was due to testify at Garvey's upcoming trial when he was murdered in early January 1923 in New Orleans by three Garveyites, possibly acting on Garvey's instructions or indications.[86] One of the killers, Esau Ramus, had been sent to New Orleans to organise a police and secret service for the local branch of the UNIA. Garvey established a defence fund for the accused.

In *The Messenger* Chandler Owen fired the opening shot in what soon turned into a "Garvey Must Go" campaign. Lambasting him as "a blustering West Indian demagogue", Chandler announced a campaign "to drive Garvey and Garveyism in all its sinister viciousness from the American soil".[87] The eight black signatories to a public letter to the US Attorney General on 15 January 1923 were referred to by Garvey in *Negro World* as "traitors" and "turncoats".[88] Domingo

82. James Weldon Johnson, "Views and Reviews", *New York Age*, 22 July 1922, p. 4.
83. "Marcus Garvey and Wm. Pickens Interesting Letters Are Exchanged", *Savannah Tribune*, 27 July 1922, pp. 1 and 8.
84. "Garvey Denounced at Negro Meeting", *New York Times*, 7 August 1922, p. 7; "2000 Negroes Hear Garvey Denounced", *New York Times*, 21 August 1922, p. 7.
85. "Garvey Fighting to Hold Followers", *New Journal and Guide* (Norfolk, VA), 26 August 1922, p. 1.
86. On the background to UNIA violence, see Thomas P. Lennon, "'Lower Types of Cranks, Crooks and Racial Bigots'? The Universal Negro Improvement Association and Black Political Violence in the United States, 1918–1930", *Radical Americas*, 5, no. 1 (2020), pp. 1–23.
87. [Chandler Owen], "Garvey, Black Eagle, Becomes Messenger Boy of Clarke, Ku Klux Kleagle", *The Messenger*, 4, no. 7 (July 1922), p. 437.
88. Marcus Garvey, "Eight 'Uncle Tom' Negroes Try to 'Tell' on Man Who Is Exposing Negro Crooks as Leaders", *Negro World*, 10 February 1923, p. 1. Presumably the headline should have read "Negro Leaders as Crooks".

had been one of Garvey's earliest and harshest critics—as Garvey would always remember—but Domingo's name was conspicuously absent from the "Garvey Must Go" campaign over the winter of 1922–23, for reasons that would become apparent when he took a principled stand against Randolph and Owen, his fellow editors on *The Messenger*. The disagreement had been brewing for several weeks. In the January *Messenger* there was an editorial, probably written by Owen, titled "A Supreme Negro Jamaican Jackass", which interpreted Garvey as a typical and representative Jamaican, as if that were an explanation for his crimes and shortcomings. Then on Sunday 25 February Owen gave a talk at the People's Educational Forum on "The Problem of the Relationship between the American and West Indian Negroes": there were three reasons for the friction, Owen said, and the West Indians were to blame for them all.[89] West Indians accept lower wages and then bring in all their friends and crowd out Americans. West Indians have an offensive sense of superiority inherited from their imperial masters. And West Indians refuse to naturalise and are therefore unable to help solve the problems they've created. While he was at it, Chandler threw in the charges of submissiveness and inclination to litigation. As a solution to the problem he suggested limiting immigration, to which Domingo—in the audience and with the figures to hand—pointed out that net immigration from the West Indies in the year to June 1922 was 156, a figure hardly amenable to significant restriction. Domingo then expanded on this point in his own presentation to the Forum on 1 April.[90] Owen was not present.

Domingo finally wrote to *The Messenger* in March to respond to the January editorial [#12], one of his most effective pieces of writing. While underlining his credentials as a critic of Garvey, Domingo took issue with the "national animus that finds a convenient vent in this particular subject". Having referred to Du Bois's view in his letter, Domingo wrote to *The Crisis* editor to check that his remarks had been accurate: "As I am a stickler for accuracy of statement I will be only too glad if you advise me if I have correctly interpreted your attitude on the Garvey question in so far as his nativity is concerned."[91]

Garvey's trial for mail fraud began on 18 May and lasted for 27 days: Domingo attended for 24, indicative of his investment in the fate of his former friend. After being found guilty, Garvey let fly an anti-semitic rant.[92] He was sentenced to

89. "West Indian and American Negroes", *New York Amsterdam News*, 28 February 1923, p. 2.
90. "'No West Indian Problem', Domingo", *New York Amsterdam News*, 4 April 1923, p. 1.
91. W. A. Domingo, Letter to W. E. B. Du Bois, 17 January 1923, W. E. B. Du Bois Papers, MS 312, Special Collections and University Archives, University of Massachusetts Amherst Libraries. Du Bois replied (18 January 1923) that he thoroughly agreed with Domingo's thesis that the subject of the attack should be Garvey's opinions and not the man or his birthplace.
92. According to Hubert Harrison, "when he was ordered to be taken to the tombs, [Garvey] broke out into an undignified tirade of foul abuse and low language describing both Judge and district attorney as 'damned dirty Jews'" ("Marcus Garvey at the Bar of United States Justice", *Associated Negro Press* (*c.* early July 1923), pp. 2–3, quoted in *A Hubert Harrison Reader*, pp. 194–

five years' imprisonment and a $1,000 fine, but released on bail in September pending his appeal against conviction. In February 1925 he lost his appeal and began serving his sentence in Atlanta Federal Penitentiary.

For Garvey, enemies and traitors were legion, but Domingo came in for some particularly harsh words. In 1923 Garvey lashed out in a pamphlet titled *Eight "Uncle Tom" Negroes*:

> A Barber Shop Philosopher. In reference to W. A. Domingo as an "intelligent" West Indian Negro of Jamaica who made an analysis of the Garvey membership, all those acquainted with the Universal Negro Improvement Association know that Domingo was a dismissed employee of the Association and that he represents no one but himself. He is what commonly is called a "barber shop rat", who talks the kind of philosophy indulged in by frequenters of the tonsorial artist. He also is a Socialist who has a desperate grudge against work and who has the dreamer's vision that one day all the rich people of the world will divide their wealth with the loafer, thereby bringing into existence the true reign of Socialism.[93]

Then in 1925, in his application to President Coolidge for executive clemency, Garvey referred to Domingo as "a red communist arch enemy and plotter against my liberty, who was dismissed from my employ as Editor of one of my newspapers, because of his dangerous communistic principles ...; Domingo being a draft evader, having renounced his application for citizenship during the pendency of the war, so as to be in non-draftable status".[94] And in 1930, when Garvey—now back in Jamaica after his deportation from the USA—began a long and self-pitying series of articles for the *Pittsburgh Courier*, complaining of "invisible influences ... operating against me all over the world" and "secret propaganda" spread by other blacks, his many enemies were listed, Domingo prominent among them, the parting of the ways now attributed to Domingo's jealousy and his Communism.[95] The virulence of Garvey's attacks is perhaps attributable to

200, at 195–96. In a later interview Garvey repeated the accusation: "When they wanted to get me, they had a Jewish judge try me, and a Jewish prosecutor. I would have been freed but two Jews on the jury held out against me ten hours and succeeded in convicting me, whereupon the Jewish judge gave me the maximum penalty" (*Seattle Jewish Transcript*, 12 October 1928, p. 6).

93. *Eight "Uncle Tom" Negroes and W. E. Burghardt Du Bois As A Hater of Dark People*, New York: Press of the UNIA, 1923; reproduced as "The Aptitude of the Negro to Disobey Orders Coming from Himself", in *The Philosophy and Opinions of Marcus Garvey*, 2, ed. Amy Jacques Garvey, New York: Universal Publishing House, 1925, pp. 333–348, at 346.

94. "Application for Executive Clemency for Marcus Garvey" [*c.* 13 June 1925], file 42-793, RG 204, NARA, in *MGP*, 6, pp. 171–195, at 171. Like many immigrants, Domingo took out "first papers" but didn't apply for citizenship. There is no evidence that he was thereby trying to evade the draft.

95. "We were friends from boyhood, but because of my success he became jealous of me and, being a Communist, while editing my paper he attempted to impress his Communist views

the fact that his usual rhetorical armoury for the dismissal of opponents was not available: Domingo was almost as black in complexion as Garvey himself, and Domingo had offered considerable assistance in getting the UNIA established in New York.[96] His actual charges are all demonstrably false: Domingo was not dismissed from the editorship, he evidently had no grudge against work, he didn't evade the draft, and he was never a member of a communist party.

Domingo allowed himself two further forays on Garvey in 1923. In a September letter to *The Forum* he responded to an article by William Pickens, contesting Pickens's suggestion that Garvey's ideas were essentially foreign imports that good native African-Americans had had to fight against. Pickens himself, as Domingo immediately points out, had eulogised Garvey only two years previously in articles in *The Nation* and *Negro World*. And again Domingo underlines that Garvey's main support came from African-Americans and that his most powerful detractors—and witnesses against him in his trial—were West Indians.[97] His other letter was to *The Gleaner*, in Jamaica, offering support to that paper's critical editorials on Garvey and adding his own twopenn'orth about the man's propensity for exaggeration and mendacity—this time about his Jamaican origins, which Domingo knew well.[98] Garvey's reputation and achievements would preoccupy Domingo in later life, but during Garvey's lifetime (he died in 1940) there was just one further published piece about him, a letter to the *Pittsburgh Courier* in 1930 following that newspaper's serialisation of Garvey's autobiography. Domingo wrote to take issue with Garvey's particular allegation that Domingo, along with S. A. Duncan, "wrote to various governments warning them against him", but Domingo also took the opportunity to point out Garvey's record of having to make abject apologies for the falsehoods he had propagated.[99]

* * *

Domingo's political views had not changed fundamentally, but the absence of any party membership probably meant that editors of prestigious journals now felt comfortable calling on Domingo as an authority—indeed, *the* authority—on

---

upon the readers and myself, even though he knew we had no inclinations toward Communism: we disagreed on policy and he left the paper", "'My Race Betrayed Me'—Garvey", *Pittsburgh Courier*, 29 March 1930, pp. 1–3, at 3.

96. As Stevens points out in "The Early Political History of Wilfred A. Domingo, 1919–39", in *Caribbean Political Activism: Essays in Honour of Richard Hart*, ed. Rupert Lewis, Kingston, Jamaica: Ian Randle Publishers, 2012, pp. 118–143, at 124.

97. W. A. Domingo, "More About Garvey", Letter in *The Forum*, 70, no. 2 (September 1923), pp. 1,949–1,950, responding to Pickens's article, "The Emperor of Africa: The Psychology of Garveyism", *The Forum*, 70, no. 1 (August 1923), pp. 1,790–1,799.

98. W. A. Domingo, "Garveyism: What It Means", Letter to *The Gleaner*, 8 October 1923, p. 9.

99. W. A. Domingo, "Domingo Scores Garvey", Letter to *Pittsburgh Courier*, 12 April 1930, 2d., pp. 1 and 13. Samuel Augustus Duncan, born St Kitts (1880–?), worked in real estate in New York.

West Indians in New York. Meanwhile, he would not have been human had he not taken some satisfaction in watching Marcus Garvey's reputation disintegrate, even if Domingo himself wasn't able to entirely escape the fallout.

The four most prestigious essays that Domingo ever wrote appeared in the mid-1920s and mark his recognition as the pre-eminent West Indian intellectual spokesman in New York. By 1924 Domingo had become an established figure, comfortable in New York circles, visible on public platforms, no longer—since leaving *The Messenger*—associated with a particular journal or position, not a member of a political party, and consistently critical of Marcus Garvey. His recognition came from two of the most powerful African-American cultural brokers of this decade, Charles S. Johnson and Alain Locke. Johnson was in the process of turning the National Urban League's magazine, *Opportunity*, into the leading black cultural journal of the day while Alain Locke, professor of philosophy at Howard University in Washington, DC, had been entrusted with putting together what would come to be seen as a landmark issue of the journal *Survey Graphic* entitled "Harlem: Mecca of the New York", quickly expanded into the anthology *The New Negro: An Interpretation.*[100]

The National Urban League had been founded at the same time as the NAACP, also with a civil rights mission, but its journal, *Opportunity: A Journal of Negro Life*, only started in January 1923 with the announced aim of presenting, objectively, the facts of Negro life in order to provide a basis for understanding and solving the social problems facing African-Americans. Domingo was an early reader. He wrote to the journal in the summer of 1923, warmly appreciative of (what else?) its article "After Garvey—What?" (written by Johnson), and also praising a piece by Eric Walrond and an unsigned review of an African art exhibit (which may have been written by Johnson).[101] Domingo says that he'd been introduced to *Opportunity* by his friend Arthur E. King, a Guyanese economist whose work *Opportunity* was already publishing.[102] Johnson would surely have come across Domingo's writing in *The Messenger* and certainly knew him personally since they'd worked together in 1923 on the Independent Lecture Committee of the 135th Street branch of the New York Public Library, so Domingo would have been a very likely person for Johnson to ask to write a commentary on the

100. "Harlem: Mecca of the New Negro", *Survey Graphic*, 53, no. 11 (March 1925); *The New Negro: An Interpretation*, ed. Alain Locke, New York: Albert and Charles Boni, 1925. Charles Spurgeon Johnson (1893–1956), sociologist, founding editor of *Opportunity* magazine, and first black president of Fisk University. Alain LeRoy Locke (1885–1954), writer and philosopher, and prominent figure within the Harlem Renaissance.

101. W. A. Domingo, "New York", *Opportunity*, 1, no. 9 (September 1923), p. 279; commenting on Charles S. Johnson, "After Garvey—What?"; Eric Walrond, "On Being a Domestic"; "The Creative Art of Negroes", *Opportunity*, 1, no. 8 (August 1923), pp. 231–233, 234, 240–245.

102. Arthur Ernest King (1891–1963?) had studied economics at McGill University in Toronto; he wrote extensively on politics, economics, and finance, including for *Negro World*. He had a Jamaican wife.

implications of the 1924 Immigration Act, which followed his earlier letter to the *Gleaner* on the subject [#13].[103] It was probably this piece in *Opportunity* that alerted Alain Locke to Domingo's analytic and rhetorical skills—certainly the brief exchanges that survive in Locke's papers don't suggest any prior acquaintance—and led him to invite Domingo to write about West Indians in New York for the special issue of *Survey Graphic* that he was compiling.

Increasingly, Domingo, like many others at the time, was having to navigate the choppy waters of nationalist thinking. His most formative experience in Jamaica—albeit brief—had been with the National Club, where the nation (in waiting) concerned was Jamaica. He'd lived through the disappointment of Woodrow Wilson's seeming embrace of the universal notion of self-determination turning out not to be so universal after all. He was still animated by the Leninist commitment to colonial liberation, although Lenin's death in early 1924 had cast a shadow. He'd witnessed and nearly himself become a victim of the rabid nationalism that had overcome sections of the USA in the war years and immediately afterwards, and that had been unthinkingly embraced by even his socialist friends in their "Garvey Must Go" campaign, calling not just for prosecution, but for deportation. At the same time he had completely rejected Garvey's own racially based nationalism, the nasty mirror-image of the white supremacist nationalism that was burning crosses and lynching blacks. As a reader of *The Crisis* and *Opportunity*, where he would have encountered Locke's writing as well as Du Bois's, Domingo would also have been aware of the tendency of this black intellectual mainstream to frame its own aim as an adjustment of the US narrative to include the various contributions—practical and cultural—that African-Americans brought to the national table.

It must therefore be telling that Domingo's essay "The Tropics of New York" [#14] immediately widens the angle in its opening sentence, in which speakers of English have to wait their turn, with six other languages accommodated before them. The tropical immigrants are on a "dogged, romantic pilgrimage", but unlike their counterparts from the US South, they carry with them memories of "palm fringed sea shores" and "murmuring streams", not shabby hovels and endless cotton fields, a contrast underlined by the reproduction at the bottom of the opening page of the essay of Claude McKay's poem "The Tropics in New York", whose title Domingo had borrowed. Despite the strenuous even-handedness that marks his essay, Domingo can't help ending on a note that must have grated with Locke. West Indians' outstanding contribution, he says, has been the introduction of an assertiveness into an environment marked by African-American servility

103. On the lecture committee, see Perry, *Hubert Harrison: The Struggle for Equality*, pp. 505–506. W. A. Domingo, "Restricted West Indian Immigration and the American Negro", *Opportunity*, 2 (October 1924), pp. 28–29.

and acquiescence, a spirit eloquently expressed by McKay's defiant lines from "If We Must Die" with which Domingo ends his piece.

When Locke compiled his anthology *The New Negro: An Interpretation*, Domingo's essay was carried over, substantially unchanged except that it had a new title, "Gift of the Black Tropics", and a new beginning:

> Almost unobserved, America plays her usual role in the meeting, mixing and welding of the colored peoples of the earth. A dusky tribe of destiny seekers, these brown and black and yellow folk, eyes filled with visions of an alien heritage—palm-fringed seashores, murmuring streams, luxuriant hills and vales—have made an epical march from the far corners of the earth to the Port of New York and America. They bring the gift of the black tropics to America and to their kinsmen. With them come vestiges of a quaint folk life, other social traditions, and as for the first time in their lives, colored people of Spanish, French, Dutch, Arabian, Danish, Portuguese, British and native African ancestry meet and move together, there comes into Negro life the stir and leavening that is uniquely American. Despite his inconsiderable numbers, the black foreigner is a considerable factor and figure. It is not merely his picturesqueness that he brings, his lean sun-burnt features, quaint manners and speech, his tropical incongruities: these as with all folkways rub off in less than a generation—it is his spirit that counts and has counted in the interplay of his life with the native population.[104]

Often quoted as Domingo's words, the changes in this paragraph almost certainly constituted Locke's editorial intervention: he was in sole editorial charge of *The New Negro*. Because the book went beyond the New York focus of the special issue, the title was changed as well as an early reference to Harlem being altered to "the Port of New York and America". The language of "gift" was very much part of the African-American lexicon, but not of the West Indian, so the new title was surely Locke's, as was the added sentence about "the gift of the black tropics to America". The first sentence is an addition, as, tellingly, are the adjectives "quaint" (twice) and "alien", as well as the reference to the West Indian's "tropical incongruities". The two boxed McKay poems disappear, although "The Tropics in New York" is printed in the poetry section, much earlier in the book. The phrase "alien heritage" belongs to a discourse very distinct from Domingo's, as does the new title: socialists like Domingo talked about rights, not gifts. However, always

104. From W. A. Domingo, "Gift of the Black Tropics", *The New Negro: An Interpretation*, ed. Alain Locke, New York: Albert and Charles Boni, 1927, pp. 341–352, at 341. Domingo's essay is rarely given much attention in discussions of *The New Negro*, perhaps because the framing of "the Harlem Renaissance" turns the anthology into a pre-eminently native African-American phenomenon: see, for example, Nathan Irvin Huggins, *Harlem Renaissance* [1971], Oxford, UK: Oxford University Press, 2007.

modest, Domingo kept quiet and gratefully accepted his royalty payment when it appeared in 1927: all of $5.[105]

Figure 5 "Hubert H. Harrison Teaching Class in 'World Problem of Race'" in Harlem, 9 September 1926. Domingo is in the middle of the front row holding a book. (Courtesy of the Hubert H. Harrison Papers, Series VI: Photographs, Box 15, folder 3, Rare Book and Manuscript Library, Columbia University, New York)

Towards the end of 1925, Charles S. Johnson asked for Eric Walrond's help in putting together a special Caribbean number of *Opportunity*. Domingo was asked to produce a general overview. His article, just called "The West Indies", starts by giving a succinct history of the region without mentioning Marcus Garvey, as if he were trying to explain to *Opportunity*'s readership that there was more to the West Indies than the one name with which they had all become so familiar in the previous five years.[106]

* * *

Throughout the 1920s Domingo's contact with Jamaica and Jamaicans continued, even though he didn't return to his homeland. Back in July 1917 he had been a founder member of the British Jamaicans Benevolent Association in New York,

105. W. A. Domingo, Letter to Alain Locke, 29 April 1927, ALP.
106. W. A. Domingo, "The West Indies", *Opportunity*, 4 (November 1926), pp. 339–341.

one of a string of such island organisations which, though more social than political, would eventually provide fertile soil for the movement for self-government; and there were plenty of other Jamaicans in Domingo's business and political circles.[107] Throughout the 1920s he kept a close eye on events in Jamaica, as a series of letters to *The Gleaner* shows, dealing with subjects as varied as the likelihood of US annexation, the work of the Jamaica Reform Club, the export of vegetables, and the local elections of 1925, as well as the nature of his connection to the UNIA [#15].[108]

Members of the Jamaican community in New York had kept political issues in the foreground during the 1920s and early 1930s, as witnessed, for example, by A. M. Wendell Malliet's pamphlet *The Destiny of the West Indies*, whose Introduction thanks various "dear friends", including Domingo for his "kind and helpful suggestions and criticisms".[109] Malliet was a fundamentally cautious figure, but he was at least raising the question of self-government and dominion status for the West Indies within the Empire, as well as drawing on the writing of Franz Boas to question claims of white racial superiority. He also underlined the importance of developing national consciousness—a sentiment to be distinguished from "rabid movements" such as Pan-Germanism, Anglo-Saxonism, and fascism. Where he fundamentally differed from Domingo was in his conviction that a self-governing British West Indies should remain as "one united group", in effect a federation.[110] This difference would shadow Domingo for most of the rest of his life, straining many of his friendships. He was probably never that close to Wendell Malliet, but over the years their disagreements would intensify. Indeed Malliet would become, after Garvey, Domingo's second great antagonist.

Arnold Mayhew Wendell Malliet (1897–1976), son of a French father, had come to the USA from Jamaica in 1918 and originally worked as a porter in a Park Lane drug store before making a career as an independent writer and publisher, eventually taking a staff position on the *New York Amsterdam News* from 1937 to 1950. He had founded and edited the *British West Indian Review* (the first and perhaps only issue appearing in April 1923), with the support of the British Consul General in New York, apparently as an attempted—though hardly successful—counterweight to Garveyite propaganda.[111] Among the journal's aims

107. See *Constitution, By-Laws and Member's Financial Book of the British-Jamaicans Benevolent Association, Inc.*, EEBP [EEBP = Egbert Ethelred Brown Papers, 1914–1956, Sc MS87, SCRBC], Box 1, folder 1.

108. W. A. Domingo, "Talks of US Annexation", Letter to *The Gleaner*, 21 May 1924, p. 10; "Work of Reform Club Appreciated", Letter to *The Gleaner*, 5 June 1924, p. 8; "Jamaica Can Export Vegetables", Letter to *The Gleaner*, 15 September 1924, p. 10; "The Recent General Election", Letter to *The Gleaner*, 10 March 1925, p. 8.

109. A. M. Wendell Malliet, *The Destiny of the West Indies*, New York: Russwurm Press, 1928, pp. 2–3.

110. Ibid., p. 20.

111. That opening issue carried a letter of welcome from Robert Wilberforce, the director of

Malliet emphasised promoting loyalty to the British Empire alongside supporting "to the fullest extent the idea of the confederation of the British West Indies".[112] He also floated the idea an "All West Indian Society", versions of which he would be involved in over the next 30 years.[113] *The Destiny of the West Indies* was published by the Russwurm Press, very much a one-man band. The back cover of the pamphlet listed five forthcoming titles "and others to be announced later", although none of the five—nor any others—actually appeared.[114]

Around the time he was writing his pamphlet, Malliet was appointed secretary to the new West India Committee of America, an umbrella organisation based at the New York office of the Victory Life Insurance Company, in which P. M. H. Savory had a stake.[115] C. A. Petioni was chairman, and other officers included Savory, James S. Watson, E. Elliott Rawlins, and C. Hendricks Powell.[116] Domingo was one of the speakers (on "Business Development") at the inaugural meeting at the Imperial Elks Hall.[117] Petioni had been a journalist in Port of Spain before medical training at Howard University: he was now a doctor and community activist; Savory became co-owner of the *New York Amsterdam News*, among other entrepreneurial successes; Rawlins was the health columnist for the *New York Amsterdam News*, infamous for describing jazz as a drug as intoxicating as cocaine; Watson was a lawyer who in 1922 had become Special Assistant Corporation Counsel to New York City in the Special Franchise Tax Division; Powell was a schoolteacher who'd moved to Harlem in 1920 and trained as a dentist.[118]

---

the British Library of Information (BLI) in New York. On Colonial Office support, see the documents in FO 371/8513, TNA. A covering note suggests that the journal might be "a means of cementing the interests of natives of the various islands … and offset to some extent the vicious propaganda being carried by the Universal Negro Improvement Association". On the BLI, see David A. Lincore, "The British Library of Information in New York: A Tool of British Foreign Policy, 1919–1942", *Libraries & the Cultural Record*, 46, no. 2 (2011), pp. 156–184.

112. A. M. Wendell Malliet, "Foreword", *British West Indian Review*, 1, no. 1 (15 April 1923), pp. 1–2, at 2.

113. A. M. Wendell Malliet, "West Indian Unity", *British West Indian Review*, 1, no. 1 (15 April 1923), pp. 12–13, at 13.

114. One of them, by Malliet himself, was to be called *The Confederation of the West Indies*; another, by Malliet and Domingo, *The West Indies and Some Prominent West Indians*. After the experience he gained from working for Oxford University Press in New York from 1929 to 1934, a later venture, Wendell Malliet Co., did publish several significant titles. In the 1980s, the Wendell Malliet Book Mart, established by his son Henry, was one of Kingston's leading bookshops: "Give Gifts of Books for Christmas from Wendell Malliet Book Mart", *The Gleaner*, 19 December 1986, p. 37. See the obituary: "The Late Wendell Malliet", *The Gleaner*, 28 April 1976, pp. 3 and 17.

115. See the advertisement in the *New York Amsterdam News*, 15 February 1928, p. 5.

116. See "Constitution and By-Laws of the West India Committee of America" [no date], James Watson Papers, Sc MG 464, Box 9, folder 6, SCRBC; "West Indians Elect", *Baltimore Afro-American*, 28 January 1928, p. 5; and "The West India Committee of the United States", *The Gleaner*, 21 February 1928, p. 11.

117. "Plank Tells West Indian Leaders' Aim", *Chicago Defender*, 4 February 1928, p. 4.

118. Charles Augustin Petioni (Trinidad, 1883–1951); Philip Maxwell Hugh Savory (British Guiana, 1889–1965); E. Elliott Rawlins (St Kitts, 1882–1928); James S. Watson (Jamaica, 1882–

So this was the professional West Indian class in New York, a group of self-made men, all still in their 40s, eager to be active in West Indian social and political matters. Malliet, ten years younger and not a professional, was apparently willing to do the organisational and secretarial work.

These men formed the nucleus of a new *West Indian* nationalism, which briefly found an outlet in yet another new journal, the *West Indian American*. As Mary Chamberlain summarises:

> The "new nationality" was to be like no other: an organically federated region whose borders were emotional rather than geographic, whose political identities and belongings had been shaped by the networks of transnational kin, and where an idea of Africa provided an authenticity and an awareness of race which made sense of dispersed networks of family and linked the black Atlantic experience.[119]

She rightly calls this a bold and imaginative step, outlined in Clyde Jemmott's essay in the opening number, but Domingo saw the "West Indian" range as a dilution that weakened the argument for self-government, and the idea of an African racial authenticity as too much of a concession to the ethnic nationalisms beginning to disfigure the European body politic.[120] Although he would work with Petioni and Savory, and even on occasion with Malliet, Domingo's nationalism was always specifically Jamaican while Jemmott's was explicitly racial—in clear continuity with Garvey's. The first page of the first issue proclaimed "Remember Marcus Garvey!", calling for Garvey's release from prison.

Despite this, Domingo wrote to welcome the establishment of the journal:

> The appearance of the *West Indian American* fills a long felt need in Harlem with its thousands of people of Antillean birth, descent and connections. It has always been a source of regret and dissatisfaction to me that despite their more than proportionate representation in other worthy fields of community endeavor, West Indians have failed to establish a journalistic organ which could be depended upon to give adequate expression to their point of view, besides

1952); Cecil Hendricks Powell (Jamaica, 1886–1971). Eric Duke recognises the importance of Petioni (*Building a Nation: Caribbean Federation in the Black Diaspora*, Gainesville, FL: University Press of Florida, 2016, pp. 89–92): see the obituary "Civic Leader Sparked Many Local Drives", *New York Amsterdam News*, 20 October 1951, pp. 1 and 4. Petioni added his paean to the West Indian contribution to African-American life: "Gifts from Abroad", *New York Amsterdam News*, 22 December 1934, pp. A6, 27, and 31.

119. Mary Chamberlain, "The 'Romance' of Foreign: Distance, Perspective and an 'Inclusive Nationhood'", in her *Empire and Nation-Building in the Caribbean: Barbados, 1937–66*, Manchester, UK: Manchester University Press, 2010, pp. 26–50, at 26. See Clyde Jemmott, "Nationalism and the Negro", *West Indian American*, 1, no. 1 (October 1927), p. 4.

120. Clyde Cardinald Jemmott (Barbados, 1893–?).

> furnishing authentic current news about the islands. I, therefore, hope that the new journal will occupy a permanent place in our midst and serve as a medium for educating West Indians about islands other than their own, and Americans about all the islands, thus educating both groups at one and the same time and helping to dispel the ignorance and prejudice which is the greatest obstacle to inter-insular and inter-racial rapprochement.[121]

Ironically, Domingo's letter appeared on the page opposite a short editorial announcing the paper's support for federation.[122] Frank Crosswaith and Wendell Malliet both contributed, but the journal seems to have lasted only four issues.[123]

* * *

Domingo was clearly by now a highly respected figure in West Indian Harlem circles, but there is a sense in which he stood slightly apart from many of his peers. Stuart Hall makes a distinction for early twentieth-century Jamaica between "the struggling, respectable country middle class" and "the well educated, well endowed, fast lane, city middle class".[124] He does so to point out that, despite later appearances, the eminent politician Norman Manley came from the former, as did Hall himself. Both, however, were exceptions inasmuch as their considerable talent and hard work led to Rhodes scholarships which took them to the heart of the Empire at Oxford, endowing them with an appreciation for at least some British institutions. Most of Domingo's West Indian peers in New York came from similar backgrounds to Manley and Hall but, without an Oxford scholarship, they had had to support themselves while getting the education and experience that would lead to careers in medicine, the law, teaching, journalism, or commerce. Very few, if any, of the New York West Indians of Domingo's generation came from the well-endowed city middle class: the fast lane tended to lead to England. In these terms, Domingo came from, at best, a middling fragment of the city working class. What he shared with his social "betters" was a New York education, in his case at what he called the "university of Harlem".[125]

That New York West Indian educated elite was by no means homogeneous. There certainly was a professional class of lawyers, doctors, and teachers, who at least had professional training and, in some cases, higher education: some of them would become successful business people too. Then there were the edu-

121. W. A. Domingo, Letter in *West Indian American*, 1, no. 2 (November 1927), p. 11.

122. "A Federated West Indies", *West Indian American*, 1, no. 2 (November 1927), p. 10.

123. A journal with the same name appeared in 1959 as a cheerleader for the West Indies Federation; it lasted until August 1961.

124. Stuart Hall, "Through the Passage of Time", in *The Norman Manley Memorial Lectures, 1984 and 1986*, London: Norman Manley Memorial Lecture Committee, 1986, pp. 7–20, at 8.

125. W. A. Domingo, "More Light on Harlem", *Public Opinion*, 30 August 1944, pp. 3 and 8, at 3.

Figure 6 W. A. Domingo in his 30s. (Lionel M. Yard, [W. A. Domingo], Association for the Advancement of Caribbean Education—Report on the Symposium Honoring Wilfred Domingo, 20 June 1976, cover)

cated (often self-educated to a high level) but not exactly *socially* elite: journalists and writers, for example, who might have to take menial jobs to support themselves. Those in commerce, like Domingo, would tend not to have the same social cachet as the professionals, unless they became very rich. As a small businessman with political views considerably to the left of most of his peers, Domingo doesn't seem to have moved at all in the purely social world of West Indian New York: his name only ever appears in newspapers in attendance at *political* events. Indeed, he separated himself from, and didn't have a high opinion of, most West Indian professionals in New York, at least judging from this frank assessment in a letter to Adolphe Roberts: "The local professionals of West Indian origin, with a few honorable exceptions, are either the biggest jackasses politically or they are so ignorant and self-centered that I despair at ever penetrating the thick wall of indifference with which they surround themselves."[126]

Another factor was family connections back home. Having attained success in New York, the West Indian professionals would visit family and friends in the home country, where their achievements would often be lauded in the local press. For Domingo there were no visits back home. Until he returned in late 1937, Domingo never visited Jamaica after leaving in 1910. With the disadvantage of illegitimacy and virtual orphanhood from an early age, there was no acknowledged family to be visited, no home to which the prodigal son could return. The contrast with his wife is stark. *The Gleaner* would refer to the arrival on the island of Mrs Domingo, better known as Eulalie Manhertz of Clarendon, acknowledging her rootedness on the island. Domingo's roots were less obvious and never acknowledged, indeed unacknowledgeable; which makes it intriguing that, although happy to operate within the larger West Indian orbit of New York, his nationalism was always decisively *Jamaican*. The New York West Indian professionals inclined towards federation—the political equivalent of their successful social and professional integration into a West Indian group in the city. For the most part Domingo kept a respectful distance; but with Malliet there seems to have been growing disrespect. There could have been several elements to this. Although Malliet had an impeccable family background in Jamaica, the two figures had similar New York trajectories, moving through menial jobs into journalism: eight years his junior, Malliet may well have regarded Domingo as something of a mentor. When Malliet started writing in favour of federation and acting as secretary to organisations committed to the establishment of a West Indian, rather than Jamaican, nation, Domingo could have felt a sense of betrayal. As we shall see, Malliet later represented the Jamaica Labour Party in New York, indicative of further political differences.

* * *

After the hectic political activity of the years following the end of the war, Domingo's life seems to have settled into a smoother rhythm. With a wife and young children to support, he developed his import business while writing occasional essays and making occasional appearances on public platforms.[127] His letter-writ-

126. W. A. Domingo, Letter to W. Adolphe Roberts, 6 August 1940, WARA [WARA = W. Adolphe Roberts Archive, National Library of Jamaica], Manuscript and Archive Collection, MS353], 2.3.5.

127. According to Ras Makonnen, Domingo imported the ingredients for pepper sauce, "and in his own little factory in Harlem he would chop them and produce the various chutneys and sauces. You can see something of his ability by the fact that Woolworths took his products—and they don't play ball with anyone who doesn't deliver goods on time" (Ras Makonnen, *Pan-Africanism from Within*, recorded and edited by Kenneth King, Nairobi, Kenya: Oxford University Press, 1973, p. 89).

ing was less frequent than usual in the early 1930s, but he did offer a series of practical suggestions as to how blacks in the USA might help Ethiopia in its struggle against Italian fascism.[128]

Domingo's most high-profile role in this period was in 1932 as head of the sponsoring committee for the trip to the Soviet Union of 22 black actors to take part in a film about race in the USA to be called *Black and White*. Louise Thompson was the driving force behind the project, but since she was a prominent Communist Party of America (CPUSA) member, Domingo provided a less obviously partisan chairman for the wide-ranging committee. There is a photograph of him alongside the departing actors.[129] A letter to Louise Thompson provides Domingo's only surviving comment about the film fiasco [#16].

* * *

For a memorial biographical sketch in 1971, Domingo's friends provided a picture of him in his prime. This is Domingo in, one might imagine, 1934, aged 45:

> Wilfred Adolphus Domingo was a rather attractive man with curly hair, a calm face and a disarming personality. He was over medium height, with a slim, erect figure. His movements reflected discipline and a concealed sensitivity. His eyes were peaceful, lips slightly sensuous, face oval and expression varied from deep contemplation to one of calm reflection. His voice, a little on the high side, rose in pitch as excitement or enthusiasm increased. His movements varied with his mood; they ranged from a gradual sweep of the arm to vigorous motions in the heat of driving home a telling point. His delivery could be slow and deliberate or rapid with quickly rising and falling inflection. He was not an orator but a speaker of genuine charm and sincerity. He was frank and this sometimes made him misunderstood. Being a fearless defender of people and institutions, he was not afraid to take any step he thought would substantiate his conviction.[130]

---

128. W. A. Domingo, "How to Help Ethiopia", Letter in *New York Amsterdam News*, 20 July 1935, p. 12.
129. "Goes to U.S.S.R. to Work on Soviet Film", *Afro-American* (Baltimore), 2 July 1932, p. 19; "22 Negros Sail to Russia to Work on Film", *The Washington Tribune*, 24 June 1932, p. 13; and "Announce Players for Soviet Picture", *New York Amsterdam News*, 8 June 1932, p. 7. Since he was photographed with the group on the docks as they were leaving, Domingo is sometimes mistakenly reported as having visited the Soviet Union.
130. Lionel M. Yard, [W. A. Domingo], p. 5.

1

The Press and the Negro

September 1917

In the spring and summer of 1917 three short-lived newspapers were founded to support the Liberty League of American Negroes, the brainchild of Hubert Harrison: *The Voice*, *The New Negro*, and *The Clarion*. Domingo seems to have been involved in at least the last two of these, possibly in an editorial capacity. Full runs of the journals don't survive, so he may have published more than this one article. It's perhaps appropriate that it should be his first, or at least the first to survive, given his long engagement with newspapers as editor, writer of articles, and correspondent. Domingo understood that the press is where ideas and images are presented and propagated, and therefore where they are best challenged.

The Clarion, 1, no. 1 (1 September 1917), p. 7

There is no phase in the so-called Negro problem that is more worthy of study than the attitude of the press to the Negro. Prior to the war and the consequent boom in American industries, we were not appreciated as of great industrial value; at best we were mere consumers and a "problem" that afforded the capitalists no considerable material for exploitation except in the agricultural South. This attitude was duly reflected in the metropolitan press, which is more or less under the control of the banks, trusts, and corporations that are the unseen powers that direct the industries of the country. With few exceptions the Southern press insisted that we were undeveloped human beings and an industrial liability who needed the sobering direction of the "superior" white Southerner, who from years of contact, knew us best. This specious plea found ready acceptance over the country especially when some of our prominent men re-hashed the doctrine by saying that "work" and "efficiency" were what we needed most of all. The Northern press, or rather, the controllers of it, not needing our labor, deliberately encouraged this view and, with notable exceptions, joined in the chorus of those who advised to "leave it to the South".

The interest of the South, needing cheap, docile labor to cultivate its fields, dictated that it should do everything possible to conceal the gross injustices imposed on the inarticulate members of the race, while at the same time misrepresenting the North in order to discourage our people from migrating. To this end the

Southern press dilated on the lack of industrial opportunity in the North, the coldness of the climate, the aloofness of the Northerners, and when a lynching took place above Mason and Dixie exaggerated it so as to be an effective deterrent to intending migrants. On the other hand Southern journalists would write articles for Northern newspapers and periodicals that portrayed the Negro as being insanely lustful for white women, lazy, improvident, criminal, and ignorant. With skill they avoided to explain that he merely responded to environments, and was the victim of conditions imposed upon him. Thus with unusual craftiness the Southern apologists poured vials of vitriol on the heads of our defenseless people, while covering themselves with the halo of saintliness and magnanimity. The only parallel of this campaign of slander is that launched against the German Kaiser and nation. With us it has resulted in poisoning the mind of the average, otherwise humane white individual to the extent that he is indifferent to the wrongs of an entire race of 10 millions of Americans.

With the advent of the war (and no quickening of conscience) the press bids fair to reverse itself and paint us in a fairer light. New industries have sprung up over night, immigration has stopped, labor is scarce, and our Southern brother is the only available material, hence he must be cajoled. Today, with conscious effort on his part, and because of his strategic position in the labor market, has forced fairer treatment from the Southern press. Competition for his labor with the odds in favor of the North has compelled the Southern press to confess Southern guilt in mistreating its most precious industrial asset—the Negro.

Today the Southern press balks with pleas for justice to us. Its attitude is briefly to exaggerate the unfavorable aspects of Northern conditions, while admitting with a newly stricken conscience the injustices of Southern life. Behind this is the desire to check the exodus and counteract the attractions and blandishments of the North—in other words induce our people to remain in the South. Today the Southern press pleads eloquently for better schools, higher wages, and justice in the courts.

In the North the talk of the press is more difficult especially with a portion (Hearst's) still unregenerate and its Southern corps of writers.[1] The Northern press will, from economic necessity and national self-interest, plead for the colored man, for his right to work and so as to influence the white worker with whom our unorganized element must compete, will paint the race more favorably than heretofore.

Reading the economic signs of the times it is safe to predict a more favorable attitude towards the Negro on the part of both the Northern and Southern press. Old and cultivated prejudices die hard, especially when they bolster up one's anthropological concerns, but die they must, when squarely confronted with

1. William Randolph Hearst (1863–1951) owned two of the most popular newspapers in the North, the *New York American* and the *New York Evening Journal.*

crass materialistic conditions. The inexorable law of supply and demand cannot be suspended by prejudice or any of its concomitants. While in the past we were misrepresented and maligned with impunity, today with the indispensability of our labor becoming cumulatively apparent in proportion to the intensifying of industry and the withdrawal of white labor to the battlefield.[2]

2. The piece ends here with the sentence seemingly incomplete.

2

Reconstruction in the West Indies

March 1919

When Marcus Garvey gave Domingo a free editorial hand in *Negro World*, he probably didn't realise quite how serious a socialist Domingo had become and quite how further radicalised he had been by accounts of the Soviet Revolution. The editorials for *Negro World* are where Domingo cut his journalist teeth, but no copy of the any of the issues of the paper edited by Domingo has survived. Fortunately, the Grenadian paper the *West Indian* reprinted one piece about the West Indies under the assumption that it had been written by Garvey, although its style and content are evidently Domingo's.

West Indian, 23 March 1919, rpt. in *MGP*, 11, pp. 187–189

There is hardly a section of the world that has remained untouched by the great war. If it has not actually participated by sending some of its sons to the battlefield, it has all the same felt the effects of the great conflict. In most countries the effects of the war have been dually experienced. Varying contributions of manpower have been made and many firesides and hearths are today mourning the loss of male relatives who died on some far off battlefield. But the principal way in which all countries have been affected by the war is economically; they have either gone backward or forward, but none of them has remained stationary. This is true of the British West Indies as of the other political divisions of the world. Being colonies controlled by a not altogether unaggressive capitalistic nation, these islands, by reason of that control, find themselves exposed to all the dangers that assail the mother country. Of themselves the islands are too small and too weak to cherish any notions of aggression, and having no voice in the formulation of British international policy, they are, without their consent or disapproval, compelled to share the fortunes of England, whether such fortunes are for weal or for woe or a result of aggressive or democratic motives on the part of the mother country. These islands went the limit and showed their attachment for England by taking on financial burdens of a character that is calculated [to] impoverish them for generations and also oversubscribed their self-allotted quota of men. So great is the former that taxes have been imposed in some of the islands which are at once a disgrace and a challenge to civilization, while the latter was such a drain upon their manhood that the Imperial government, with superior concepts of what should constitute a just contribution of manpower, ordered the disbandment of the West Indian contingent.

Out of the great European struggle a new world is in the making, and while due consideration is given to the desires and needs of Europeans, nothing is being said as to what form this reconstruction shall take in the British West Indies. If Englishmen, Canadians, and Australians fought, as they said, for ideals of democracy, it was for the same ideals that the sons of the Caribbean fought, even with their understanding of the ideals unclear and their perceptions dim. Beneath the surface of their self-sacrificing patriotism was an ineradicable belief that their sufferings and their participation in the war would result in the extension of some of the blessings of democracy and prosperity to their own homes. Unfortunately, there is no central authority in those islands which can be regarded as their mouthpiece; consequently the people, for the time being, are forced to look to Great Britain for application of the principles of democracy which she so loudly announced to the world. The British Empire cannot be half despotic and half democratic. If oligarchical rule is not to be tolerated by Englishmen in England, it should not be tolerated by them in sections of their own empire. In the reconstruction period Great Britain will have opportunity to prove to the world that her statesmen are not hypocrites; that they did not fight, as some allege, for mercenary reasons, but for freedom and democracy. If political freedom is good enough to be forced upon Germans, then it is certainly good enough for Jamaica, Trinidad, Barbados, St Kitts, and the other islands of the Antilles. If Prussian methods are to be eliminated from the world, they must also cease to exist in the possession of that nation which assures the world that it was its high mission to establish universal democracy. In the West Indies after the war there should remain not a single vestige of economic serfdom or political slavery. No longer should the people be denied a real voice in their government, nor should they be governed by a minority of the population. It is the duty of West Indians of light and leading who are domiciled in foreign countries to lead in the demand for a West Indian renaissance. They should not be satisfied with mere assertions of loyalty to any particular country, for they owe a higher loyalty to the islands where they were born. Therefore we suggest that these men and women get together now, even as the Irish, Czecho-Slovaks, Alsatians, Poles, and Hindoos have done, and begin to formulate plans for the betterment of the respective islands. This is not the time to be laggards; it is the time to be up and doing. WEST INDIANS, WAKE UP!

3

Socialism Imperilled, or the Negro—Potential Menace to American Radicalism

c. April 1919[1]

Drafted as a Socialist Party position paper, "Socialism Imperilled" was seized by the Lusk Committee and flourished as an example of the dangerous doctrines advanced by the Rand School. However, although it suited the Committee to treat Domingo's piece as Rand School policy, it turns out that it wasn't. The *New York Times* had reported on the Lusk Committee's public hearing.[2] The following day, the Rand School's secretary, Bertha Mailly, wrote to the *Times* to point out how misleading the presentation had been, since it neglected to say that Domingo's essay had been taken from the desk of the editor of the Rand School publication committee, David Berenberg, along with a self-addressed stamped envelope and a letter of rejection.[3] Far from being indicative of the American Socialist Society's views, Mailly pointed out, Domingo's essay had been rejected. It turns out that this wasn't quite true either. In fact, Berenberg had written to Domingo suggesting that he come into the Rand School to talk about how to proceed, but at the time of the raid hadn't got round to sending the letter, which the Lusk Committee seized, but didn't publish.[4] So Domingo's pamphlet hadn't been accepted, but it hadn't been rejected. In these precise months the SPA was in the process of tearing itself apart, and Berenberg—along with most of the other key players at the Rand School—belonged to its right wing: those who would remain after John Reed led the left-wing exodus into competing Communist organisations later that year. This internecine struggle was undoubtedly absorbing most of Berenberg's attention.[5] He probably didn't read Domingo's essay very carefully: questions of race would have seemed irrelevant to him in May and June 1919.

1. The piece itself is undated.
2. "Moves to Close the Rand School", *New York Times*, 28 June 1919, p. 1.
3. "Rand School Heads Plan Court Action", *New York Times*, 29 June 1919, p. 9.
4. Letter from David P. Berenberg to W. A. Domingo, 12 June 1919, Lusk Committee Papers, L0028, Box 1, folder 14, New York State Archives, Albany, NY.
5. See James Weinstein, "The Split of the Socialist Party, 1918–1919", in his *The Decline of Socialism in America, 1912–1925*, New Brunswick, NJ: Rutgers University Press, 1984, pp. 177–233; Theodore Draper, *The Roots of American Communism*, New York: Viking Press, 1957, pp. 139–167; and David A. Shannon, *The Socialist Party in America: A History*, New York: Macmillan, 1955, pp. 130–149.

Note that in this transcription "negro" appears with a lower-case initial, although Domingo would have written it with an upper-case initial.

Revolutionary Radicalism: Its History, Purpose and Tactics, with an Exposition and Discussion of the Steps Being Taken and Required to Curb It, Being the Report of the Joint Legislative Committee Investigating Seditious Activities, Filed April 24, 1920, in the Senate of the State of New York, 4 vols, Albany, NY: J. B. Lyon, 1920, pp. 1,489–1,510

At this time when a considerable portion of Europe is reorganizing itself; when for the first time in history millions of working people have begun to think in terms of their class; when the old form of political state is in danger of dissolution, and when sparks of proletarian unrest have passed from Russia to Germany, Argentina, Italy, and the Pacific coast of the United States, it is well for those who are agitating along radical lines in this country to comprehend all the dangers which beset them. Failure on the part of those who are immediately interested to recognize danger is sure to result in disaster—disaster which may set back economic radicalism in America for an indefinite period. On the other hand, the old adage, "Forewarned is forearmed" takes on significant importance to those who by failure to properly gauge a situation may precipitate their own destruction. Avoidance of such an eventuality should be the controlling influence in framing the tactics and strategy of American radicals. No element of the population should be despised nor should any reliance be placed upon a purely theoretical and dogmatic assumption that groups of the population can be depended upon, because of their sufferings and oppression, to arrive at an instinctive understanding of where their support should be cast when the crucial moment arrives. Tactics based upon such a fallacious premise must, and will, result in a catastrophe to those who so calculate, for at the bottom it rests upon no firmer basis than that the wish is the father of the thought.

Since the Russian revolution of 1917, when the revolutionists, Lenin and Trotsky, came into power, radical propagandists of all shades of belief have been encouraged to extend and intensify their propaganda in the United States. Every social theorist, every genuine social revolutionist is today fired with the determination to institute industrial freedom in America. "The home of the brave and the land of the free." All of these movements are maliciously labeled Bolshevism by the press, and ignorantly regarded as something dangerous by the majority of American newspaper readers and churchgoers. No section of the American people can claim to be immune from being influenced by this wicked characterization which is being made of Socialism and other species of economic radicalism by the press, the pulpit and the platform.

While during the war everything un-American (which means not profitable to Wall Street) was stigmatized as German propaganda, today it is Bolshevik. As a consequence, Socialist propaganda, although more intense and efficient than in the past, is being met by an equally efficient, less scrupulous and more intensive and extensive capitalistic counter-propaganda. That this counter-propaganda is at present very powerful will not be denied by anyone who is familiar with the political ignorance and national egotism of the average, so-called free American citizen. Abundant evidence of this is extant, notwithstanding the Seattle trouble, the Lawrence strike and the existence of the National Non-Partisan League.[6]

For proof we have only to note the stolid acquiescence of the masses to the fate of the Industrial Workers of the World (IWW), the persecution of conscientious objectors and Socialists, and the complacent willingness with which "Best Citizens" lead, presumably, the worst citizens to lynch or tar and feather a fellow citizen in the name of patriotism.[7] This attitude is national, permeating the country from the Atlantic to the Pacific coast, and from Maine to Texas, but, perhaps, its zenith is reached in the Southern states where Americanism is most rampant and least contaminated by contact with tolerant foreigners.

Revolutionary Socialists in the Socialist Party are agitating for a restatement of the party platform and tactics in terms of Bolshevik tactics which, with the class struggle as its basis, maneuver to establish a proletarian dictatorship in order to accomplish the transition from a capitalist to a Socialist state. Already Massachusetts, Michigan, and several other states have gone "Left" and New York is in the throes of an internal struggle for party control, waged between the Right and Left wings. This is, in itself, nothing strange as nearly every Socialist movement in Europe has had similar disputes, all of which centre on the question of tactics. The objective sought is the same, but how to attain it is the bone of contention. In France there are all kinds of factional splits in the movement; in Germany there are Majority Socialists, Independent Socialists, and Spartacides; in Norway, Denmark, and Sweden there are Left and Right wings; in Great Britain there are British Socialists, Independent Laborites, Industrial Workers of the World, and members of the Socialist Labor Party, and in the United States there are the Socialist Party and the Socialist Labor Party. There are some who bitterly denounce those who agitate for a restatement of Socialist tactics in terms of the present-day revolutionary Socialism; but, perhaps, this party shake-up is not altogether undesirable if it results in a clarifying of tactics and a readjustment of

6. In February 1919 a general strike had effectively shut down the city of Seattle. In 1912 the Industrial Workers of the World had led a strike of immigrant workers in the textile town of Lawrence, Massachusetts. The National Non-Partisan League, founded by Arthur C. Townley (1880–1959), had some success in the late 1910s in North Dakota and Minnesota, representing the interests of small farmers.

7. A famous 1918 poster, designed by Gordon Grant, proclaimed "The Best Soldiers Make the Best Citizens".

propaganda so as to reach every working-class element that is a potential danger to the establishment of the Socialist state whether achieved through a proletarian dictatorship or a majority vote. So long as there is a numerically considerable group that is a danger to the establishment of the co-operative commonwealth, every ounce of propaganda should be directed at that group. A potential danger should be recognized and steps taken to render it harmless or if possible transform it into a source of strength.

In the past the officials of the Socialist Party have been doctrinaires so far as their propaganda was concerned. Acting purely upon theory, and in some cases displaying an opportunism that played fast and loose with principles, they have confined most of their efforts to the industrial centers of the West, North, and Middle West. Little, if any, attention was paid to the farmers as a class (unless the maudlin and unscientific agrarian arguments that the *Appeal to Reason* used to send out can be regarded as such), and still less was paid to that unexplored continent of labor reaction—the South. On a few occasions speakers were sent to tour the South but with little success, for some, like Eugene V. Debs, refused to sacrifice their Socialistic principles upon the altar of race-prejudice.[8] In general, the Socialist Party might be said to have consciously or unconsciously adopted the tactics of the American Federation of Labor and neglected the white Southerner while leaving the negro severely alone.

The Industrial Workers of the World, avowedly non-political, on the other hand, did not confine their activities to any particular section of the country, nor did they excuse their failure to face facts and consider the circumstances surrounding any particular national element by making general statements that their appeals were made to all, and not to particular groups of the working class. Instead, these intrepid evangels of industrial unionism made special appeals to the migratory farm workers of the West, the ignorant white man of Louisiana, and the despised negro, with the result that they brought all these workers to realize the truth of the Marxian injunction: "Workers of the World, unite; you have nothing to lose but your chains. You have a world to gain!" So powerful is the unity achieved by the IWW that at their trial in Chicago there were men of all races as defendants, among them being Ben Fletcher, a negro, and among the witnesses for the defense were four negroes who gave their testimony despite military and secret service intimidation.

In recognizing the importance of reaching negroes with their gospel, the IWW are showing statesmanlike farsightedness. They are facing facts squarely and by so doing are removing potential dangers from their path. If the Socialist Party comes under the control of the "Left" or the "Right", let those who will be respon-

8. Eugene V. Debs (1855–1926), leading US Socialist in the first quarter of the twentieth century. In 1918 he'd been imprisoned for ten years under the Sedition Act for his opposition to US participation in the First World War.

sible for its success profit from the mistakes of the AFL [American Federation of Labor], which has shown such deplorable inaptitude as has resulted in making the negro an enemy of that organization and the scab of America. If they follow the methods of the IWW they will secure to themselves the adherence of over 12,000,000 people, and active support, without whose help no radical movement in America can hope to succeed.

There are over (?) negroes in the United States.[9] The majority live in the South and form the bulk of its laboring population. All the hard work which the white man with the traditions of slavery as a millstone around his neck refuses to do is performed by negroes. As a portion of the working class, negroes are industrially unorganized and in most cases bitterly antagonistic to organized labor. This is due to racial discrimination against them, the wages they receive, and the kind of work usually reserved for them. They are given low wages and are told to be grateful to those who gave them a chance to earn a living, hence, although hating their employers, still they regard them as friends, in that they are given work to the exclusion of members of their employer's own race. In addition to this is the subtle control exercised over negro opinion through negro schools, colleges, churches, and newspapers by Northern capitalists.

The South, that is, the dominant Bourbon South that needs ignorant, docile labor to exploit, is frankly hostile to negro education on the theory, founded in economic grounds, that "education spoils a negro for work". What is really meant is that education protects negroes from being mercilessly exploited. Due to Southern opposition to education, negro leaders naturally turn to the North for financial assistance in founding schools and colleges. By endowing Southern negro institutions of learning, Northern capitalists like Julius Rosenwald of Chicago and Andrew Carnegie of Pittsburgh control the various boards of trustees of these schools, and shape their policies.[10] Thus the curricula are usually framed in such a manner as to train potential industrial scabs, and the students very naturally regard those who endowed the schools as their real friends and benefactors.

The same thing is true of negro newspapers. For the most part they exist upon the bounty of the Republican Party, and, it is alleged, receive subsidies from big corporations for advising their readers to be hostile to organized labor and radicalism in general. Their policy is usually to denounce the white working class, while extolling the virtues of Mr Rosenwald, Mr Carnegie, and their ilk. They usually condemn every form of political and economic radicalism and laud patriotism.

---

9. The question mark is in the original. Presumably Domingo intended to check the number and insert it before publication. In 1920 there were around 10,500,000 African-Americans in the USA.

10. White industrialists and philanthropists: Julius Rosenwald (1862–1932) and Andrew Carnegie (1835–1919). Rosenwald was a major supporter of Booker T. Washington.

Negro churches are the real source of negro opinion. These churches are usually presided over by the graduates of schools endowed by Northern philanthropists, and true to their training they praise the rich while inveighing against the laboring class. Then there is the question of material interests. Many negro churches have had mortgages lifted, organs presented, or stained glass windows installed by philanthropically inclined millionaires. Thus every medium of negro thought functions in the interest of capital.

The individual negro is also subjected to influences that tend to make him defy those who profit from his oppression. For the most part negroes are a distinct caste in American life. They are mostly cooks, waiters, porters, and body servants who, because of their inferior social and economic status, place an exaggerated value upon opportunities common to others, but denied them. On the trains, in hotels, and other places where they work as menials they come in contact with people who can indulge in luxuries, and whose opinions are necessarily of a kind to extol conservatism and condemn radicalism. With the exception of the few who work in the garment industry in New York and come in contact with [the] wholesome radicalism of Russian Jews, the majority of negro men and women are deprived of the stimulating influence of advanced political thought.

Servants unconsciously imbibe their masters' psychology, and so do negroes. Nobody is more intolerant against foreigners than negroes, despite the fact that their lives are safer in the North where so many foreigners reside than in the South where there are so few. Occupational traits are also developed to a marked degree. Being of slave origin and depending on tips to a large degree, the tipper or those in a position to dole out tips take on magnified importance in the eyes of the tip receiver.

All of the foregoing influences exerted upon negroes have tended to make the race docile and full of respect for wealth and authority, while creating an immense gulf between the white and black workers, which is widened by the fact that white workers on their part exhibit racial prejudice in refusing to give negroes an opportunity to work under the more favorable conditions achieved by union labor. Smarting under the injustice of industrial discrimination and seeing the economic results upon himself and family, the average negro worker develops a not unnatural bitterness and hostility towards the white worker who, reacting to the cunning of the capitalist press that is intent on dividing the workers, reciprocates the hostility in terms of race hatred of the vilest and most unreasoning kind.

This results in a warping of the ordinary human instincts of both whites and negroes. They both become indifferent to the sufferings of each other and fail to recognize that most of what they suffer is both preventable and of common origin. So marked is this attitude that it is next to impossible to rouse a white audience of working men to the enormity of the crimes committed against society and the black race when the latter is denied elementary justice and fair play. Equally difficult is it to awaken in the breast of negroes any resentment against a vicious system that thrives on the labor of children, the sweating of adults, and the robbery of one class by another. Any attempt in that direction among negroes is usually met by them in the same questioning spirit as they meet the tale of any great disaster. If a railroad wreck occurs, or a ship is sunk, the attitude of the average negro is to scan the death list diligently and if none of his race is among the victims, ejaculate "Thank God, they are all white people. There are no colored folks among them." In short, negroes react to prejudice and discrimination by becoming distinctly race-conscious, but so far as their class-consciousness is concerned, it is not even as much as scratched. It is therefore the function of whichever wing, Right or Left, that controls the Socialist Party to transmute the race consciousness of negroes into class-consciousness. This will be necessary when cognizance is taken of some of the ingredients of negro ideology. Some of their ideas are contradictory and illogical, but that does not rob them of their vitality and power for good or evil. While it is true that, reacting to oppression, negroes become racially conscious and think that they hate all white people, still, because of the various influences exerted upon them, they nevertheless make a distinction and feel that the better class among the whites are their friends and should be protected from being encroached upon by the working class who, because of capitalistic tutelage and unfortunate experience, they regard as their enemy. They speak contemptuously of poor white trash and wreak vengeance upon them whenever possible. In their hearts, too, while they may have individual state governments, yet they look to the Constitution as their Gibraltar and the Federal government as their all-powerful protector. States may forfeit negro loyalty, but the Federal government has a firm grip upon it.

Jack London in his *Iron Heel* forecasts how mercenaries can be used to destroy Socialism if voted into power in the United States.[11] Sixty thousand armed White Guards in Finland are holding down a population of over 3,000,000 people who voted a Socialist government into power. Then there is the classic example of a few thousands of well-armed Czecho-Slovaks being deceived and being used by counter-revolutionary elements and foreign capital to render nugatory the Russian proletarian revolution. In Finland, through the martyrdom of 30,000 Socialists, it has been clearly demonstrated that one armed person in a population is able to cow and subdue 500 unarmed ones. The Czecho-Slovaks in Russia have shown how the just national aspirations of the oppressed people can be so successfully manipulated that they become instruments of their own ultimate enslavement. The tragic part that the Czecho-Slovaks played in the Russian revolution is too well known to radicals to render a recital necessary. Suffice to say

11. Jack London's *The Iron Heel* (1908) is a dystopian fiction based on the premise of the rise of a Socialist mass movement in the United States strong enough to have a real chance of winning national elections, getting to power, and implementing a radical Socialist regime. Jack London (1876–1916), journalist and novelist.

that, although oppressed Slavs longing for national freedom, they are being used by reaction as tools to restore a despotic Czaristic regime. Having these examples, and comprehending how much more dangerous the situation in the United States is for radicals, it will be the quintessence of revolutionary good sense and self-interest for those who contemplate the transference of industrial and economic power from the hands of the few to the hands of the many to consider the ominous possibility of three or four million black working men being used by the plutocracy as black White Guards, or Czecho-Slovaks in America.

Let it be supposed that the Right wing predominates in the Socialist Party; that it continues in the past policy of the party, concentrates its efforts upon vote getting in the North, flirts with the white South and ignores negroes except in Northern urban centers where their votes are needed to elect a municipal official. Let it be further supposed that a majority of senators and congressmen are elected along with a Socialist president. The moment such a result had been flashed over the wires, the bourgeoisie would realize that their days were numbered and would immediately begin to formulate plans for the prevention of their own social and economic extinction. This would be done as a measure of supreme self-preservation. Secret meetings would be held and the situation carefully gone over. Orders would be issued to the prostitute press, time-serving ministers of religion, lecturers, and the myriads of parasitical instruments that exist for the corruption of public opinion, to begin a campaign for the purpose of proving that the election was irregular, illegal, and consequently void; that the Socialists be not permitted to take control of the government as their program was un-American, atheistic, and anarchistic; that it would be the duty of all loyal citizens to save the country from a new form of slavery. In the meantime (and there would be five months between the election in November and induction of the Socialist administration into office in April of the following year) a careful survey would be made of the various sections of the country and groups of the population that were least affected by the virus of Socialism, and having the facts at their finger tips they would quickly turn to the white South and the negroes of the nation as the most likely defenders of the old order. They would play upon the ignorance of both and seek to use them against the class-conscious Northern proletariat. Soon all kinds of propaganda would flood negro sections. Negro ministers, past masters in the art of hypnotic emotional appeal and crude declamatory oratory, would preach diatribes against Socialism and warn their congregations, Cato-like, that the Bolsheviks, Socialists and Anarchists who seek to re-enslave the race and rob them of Jesus must be destroyed. In this the ministers would be actuated by their own material interest, as colored ministers are, perhaps, the most parasitic of celestial navigators. Evidence of their venality is easily supplied by the fact that most of them are quasi-politicians, and that after the Hylan-Hillquit-Mitchel mayorality campaign of 1917, the majority of colored preachers in New York City were proven to have participated in the notorious Mitchel slush fund.[12]

Leaflets and pamphlets condemning Socialism supposedly written by prominent negroes, but really written by skilled agents of capitalism, would be distributed broadcast among negroes. This form of propaganda was resorted to by a colored newspaper in New York in 1918 with the result that nearly all the negro votes which in a previous election had gone 20 per cent Socialist as a protest against Mitchel, went to the Republican candidates. Speakers who were secretly paid by the master class would appear on the street corners of negro sections, where from ladders and soap-boxes they would exhort their race-conscious, but politically ignorant and gullible fellow-negroes to die rather than submit to re-enslavement. From ministers, teachers, upstart military officers, newspapers, and the diversified tribe of race "leaders" would come arguments whose gravamen would be to recount the friendship of the capitalists and the enmity of the workers in the past. Eloquent and grateful references would be made to those whose generosity had furnished the beginnings of negro education; those who had out of their magnificent altruism endowed Fisk, Meharry, Talladega, Hampton, Atlanta, Lincoln, Livingston, Tuskegee, and other institutions of learning for the negro race; those who had from the fullness of their hearts done acts of charity and philanthropy to uplift the downtrodden race. References would be made to the fact that the race was just getting a grip upon the material things of life and that the white masses, jealous of negro improvement, were determined to confiscate what they had acquired after much personal privations and labor. By tongue, pen, and picture negroes would be reminded of the terrible things they had suffered at the hands of the white masses. The horrors of East St Louis would be painted and retold in harrowing language in order to excite the bitterest feelings of revenge in the breast of those who were of the same race as the victims of that terrible massacre that put the United States to shame when compared with Turkey.[13] The old hostility of the average American working man to permitting negroes to earn an honest livelihood in the industrial field among the class of best paid workers would be trotted out with telling effect. Then, to cap the climax, the pathetic and morbid desire on the part of negroes to gain prominence which was denied them in almost every walk of life except where it was criminal or it was military would be catered to by making a few spectacular military promotions

12. In the 1917 New York mayoral election, the incumbent, John P. Mitchel (1879–1918), a reform Democrat, was defeated by John F. Hylan (1868–1936), the regular Democrat supported by Tammany Hall and William Randolph Hearst. The Socialist Party candidate, Morris Hillquit (1869–1933), ran on a platform of opposition to US entry into the war: he got nearly 22 per cent of the vote.

13. Dozens, possibly hundreds, of blacks had been killed in the East St Louis pogrom in early July 1917. In protest, the NAACP organised the Silent Parade in New York City on 28 July, 10,000 black people marching down Fifth Avenue, women and children dressed in white, men in black.

and by giving negroes a little more meritorious publicity in the various organs of public information. These negro officers for the most part sharing the common status of their race in industries are not as far removed from the majority of their people as white officers are from theirs. On the contrary, when mustered out it is the dire fate of the black lieutenant or captain to find himself a competitor with his erstwhile private for the same menial job in a hotel or on the train as waiter or porter. This, apart from racial consciousness, more firmly cements the solidarity of the race, which on the whole takes place when any of its members can make even a temporary rise out of the common contempt to which they are all more or less condemned. All of this is already known to the plutocracy, but, unfortunately, it is not known to those for whom it constitutes a portentous peril. Already it has been suggested in the press that a sure preventive against Bolshevism (Socialism) in America would be to enfranchise the negro, which would mean a permanent increase of the Republican vote of the country.

Analysis of the recent municipal elections in Chicago proves that the election of Mayor Thompson was due to the solidly Republican negro votes which had been increased in number by large accretions of enfranchised negro emigrants from the South![14] Charles Schwab, the ironmaster of Bethlehem fame, is reported to have made a speech in New York in which he said that negroes can be relied upon to slay radicalism in this country.[15] Col. Watterson of Kentucky said some years ago that the South and the negro will be the firmest bulwarks of conservatism against which the waves of American radicalism will dash in vain.[16] After such testimony can anyone doubt that driven to desperation by a Socialist victory at the polls, the plutocracy would not hesitate to use force or fraud to prevent the establishment of a Socialist regime in the United States?

Let the hypothetical election of Socialism into office be further indulged in, and the fact that capitalism, beaten at the polls, has four months of grace before surrendering the scepter of power be kept in mind; let it be remembered that until the April when it is supposed to abdicate, that reaction still controls the army, navy, railroads, press, steamships, and all the various things that make for power in the modern world. Confident that there are 12,000,000 of racially conscious people friendly to it, that it can mobilize the petit-bourgeoisie and the various classes of the priest-ridden South, what is there to deter capitalism from boldly declaring the election null and void and its intention to retain power? To accomplish this, pretexts will have been found to declare martial law several weeks before April arrived; also specially trained armed mercenaries whose loyalty was unquestioned would be secretly mobilized and placed in charge of arsenals, railroad terminals, and all places of strategic or economic value. At

14. The notoriously corrupt William Hale Thompson (1869–1944) served as mayor of Chicago from 1915 to 1923 and again from 1927 to 1931.

15. Charles W. Schwab (1862–1939), steel magnate.

16. Henry Watterson (1840–1921), soldier and journalist.

the same time negro White Guards would be organized and held in readiness for any emergency. Perhaps Northern workers goaded to desperation by seeing their hard-earned political victory stolen from them might rise in revolt, but what measure of success could they hope to achieve without arms and without control of the means of communication? Finland gives the answer. And if one armed person can hold down 50 unarmed ones, how much easier will it not be for one armed negro to hold down less than ten unarmed white proletarians? Thus can the negro be the black White Guards of America: thus can they be as effectively useful to American Junkers as the Czecho-Slovaks are to the Kolchaks and Denekins of Siberia![17]

Let it be supposed that the other alternative happens, that the Left wing succeeds in gaining control of the party, that it adheres to a strictly theoretical position and shapes party propaganda on the purely theoretical syllogism, viz., the negro is a worker, he is part of the lowest stratum of the American proletariat, hence when mass action is galvanized into mass movement, he will be swept along with the rest of his class. Such reasoning has the appearance of logic but fails to recognize the existence of such a thing as group psychology and is out of harmony with the practical experiences of the Russian Bolshevik Party from which the extreme groups of American Socialists profess to have copied their tactics. Be it remembered that the program of that party is fundamentally sound although it had a suggestion of opportunism when it adjusted itself to the immediate needs of the Russian proletariat composed of peasants and workers. Land to the peasants and bread and peace to the people are the ultimate aims of Socialism, but in order to gain power Lenin had to give it an immediate application regardless of all else and thus secure the adhesion of the masses to his policies. In order to accomplish world revolution the Bolsheviki have not hesitated to encouch in their platform statements that are calculated to attract and gain for them the support of all the oppressed peoples of the world. They have made the declaration that they are willing to extend the principle of self-determination to even the toiling "masses of Africa, Asia and all the colonies"; they have gone further and encouraged the nationalistic ambitions of Ireland, India, and Egypt. Afghan emissaries are reported to have secured aid from Lenin for the purpose of recovering from England territory stolen in former years. Lenin, himself, has justified his employment of highly paid capitalistic experts, the signing of the Brest-Litovsk treaty with imperial Germany, and his treating with French monarchist officers on the ground that the international social revolution is a species of warfare and temporary alliance must be made in order to secure ultimate victory for the proletariat. All of this proves the willingness of Lenin to adjust his tactics to existing conditions provided there is no sacrifice of principle involved.

17. The Junkers were originally Prussian landed nobility. Anton Ivanovich Denikin (1872–1947) and Alexander Vasilyevich Kolchak (1874–1920) were anti-Bolshevik military leaders.

He is perfectly willing to use one enemy for the weakening of another with the deliberate intention of subsequently destroying this present ally, if capitalistic. In this respect Lenin reveals himself as a master strategist who is willing to adopt the tactics of the capitalists who do not scruple to use one race against another for the purpose of breaking a strike or suppressing incipient revolts. He uses realities, not theories to cope with the facts of a given situation. He, however, does not make the mistake of alienating from or failing to secure to his cause the friendship of those who by virtue of class affiliations are his logical adherents. To this end he stresses the needs of the poorest peasants and the industrial workers, and cements their loyalty by placing them in the first class in the scheme of rationing. Since it is the avowed object of the Left wing to establish Socialism through the medium of a dictatorship of the proletariat, how can they expect to accomplish it with a large portion of the American proletariat untouched by revolutionary propaganda?

Let the hypothesis of the Left-wing domination of the Socialist Party be further pursued. Having captured the party machinery the Left wing discards all old literature and prepares new and more revolutionary material. It is spread over the country broadcast. Negroes and white people receive it alike. The former, because of radical discrimination against them, attend no revolutionary mass meetings, do not come in contact with class-conscious workers, and are emotionally religious and intensely race-conscious. They attend lyceums and forums connected with their churches, read their weekly racial newspapers, and listen to lectures, besides reading the usual capitalistic daily, weekly, and monthly trash. From all of these sources directly and indirectly controlled by the plutocracy, they are poisoned against radicalism and abjured to fight it as the enemy of their most valuable possessions—the Constitution which secures to them the modicum of freedom they enjoy; their churches which are their social centers and the source of their spiritual exaltation and the other things that are to them sacred. Every subtle device would be exhausted to counteract radical propaganda, and with success.

On the other hand, let it be supposed that the propaganda among the whites makes headway and the workers of the great Northern, Eastern, and Western industrial centers reinforced by a few converts in the South, including agricultural workers, prepare for the day when the expropriators are to be expropriated. All radical groups submerge their differences and unite. A working arrangement is effected between the American Federation of Labor and the Industrial Workers of the World, and with the Left wing in control, a general strike is planned. Of course, it must not be forgotten that among the whites considerable numbers of the working class would be unaffected and would join the ranks of the bourgeoisie out of a perverted sense of patriotism. This would be particularly true of the South where the doctrine of state rights is a fetish even among the most ignorant and where new ideas on social and economic questions are resisted with intolerant fanaticism. It must also be remembered that the masters, unlike the working class, are very practical and ignore no factor that can be converted into a source of strength by making minor concessions. Being in control, the plutocracy would be in a position to make concessions to distinct radical or other groups so as to seduce them from working-class ranks. Informed by their spies in the ranks of militant labor of what is brewing, the capitalists would begin beforehand to mobilize their strength. And this is now being done with the negro. Witness the calling of a National Conference on Lynching immediately after the Union League Club discovered that Bolshevist propaganda was making headway among New York negroes, and Charles Evans Hughes, ex-Republican candidate for the presidency, a member of this club, making a radical speech against a practice which by silence he condoned for years before![18] Witness the plea of certain big capitalists to the dominant interests in New York to be a little more considerate to the negro in matters of employment and their rights. Witness the attitude of Samuel Gompers, member of the Civic Federation and president of the American Federation of Labor, the little brother of Big Business and in close touch with President Wilson and other political leaders, at the last convention of his organization held at Buffalo, for the first time openly inviting negroes into the ranks of organized labor, although, no doubt, fully cognizant of the racially discriminatory constitutions of many labor bodies.[19] These concessions and many others are straws that show the direction of the wind.

The scene for the general strike is set. Enthusiastic leaders fondly believe that this mass action will be transformed into mass movement and lay their plans accordingly. The strike is declared, but the plutocracy, already anticipating every move on the part of the proletariat, declares martial law, quickly mobilizes thousands of negroes and uses them as slave drivers to compel unwilling white working men to return to the shops, mines, and farms.

In Germany Noske pays his soldiers $2.50 a day.[20] What is to prevent any other government from doing likewise? Chaos reigns for a while but the plutocracy soon lets loose its unknown trump cards. Negro aspirations are played upon and their just human grievances are diverted so as to make them play the part that the Czecho-Slovaks played in Russia. Working men armed with nothing more formidable than propaganda, promises, and revolutionary zeal are beaten to their knees and their leaders seized and quickly executed. With their leaders dead or in jail the workers become panic-stricken as the White Terror employs black workers who are not class-conscious to render the mass movement one of

18. Charles Evans Hughes (1862–1948) was narrowly defeated by Woodrow Wilson in the 1916 presidential election.

19. Samuel Gompers (1850–1924) was a powerful labour leader, founder of the AFL.

20. Gustav Noske (1868–1946), Minister of Defence of the Weimar Republic during 1919–1920.

mass murder. Thus would perish some of earth's noblest in an abortive attempt to institute a dictatorship of the proletariat. Thus because of tactical error one set of workers will have brought defeat to their fellow-workers.

The point stressed in the foregoing imaginative pictures is that failure to make negroes class-conscious is the greatest potential menace to the establishment of Socialism in America whether by means of the ballot or through a dictatorship of the proletariat, and in this must all Socialists and radicals, whether Right- or Left-wingers, see their danger. For the sake of their cause, if not for the sake of negro workers, must they confront this problem squarely and firmly. How can the disaster portrayed be escaped, is the task of this booklet to point out. In the first place danger must not be ignored by a gesture or met by a theory. It must be removed. To do this it is necessary for American radicals to do the following:

First.—They must unequivocally condemn all forms of injustice practiced against negroes and encouch same in their declarations of principles and platforms, and Socialist officials and legislators must embrace every opportunity to make public denouncements of lynchings, etc.

Second.—They must give the negro more prominence in their discussions whether by speech or in their publications relative to injustices done in America.

Third.—They must seek to attract negroes to their meetings and to induce them to become members of their organizations.

Fourth.—Those who are members of labor unions must work for the repeal of all racially discriminatory practices in their organizations and endeavor to gain the admission of negroes into them on terms of equality.

Fifth.—They must have specially prepared propaganda showing negroes how they as a group are likely to benefit and improve their social and economic status by any radical change in the present economic system.

Sixth.—Radical negro publications must be supported financially even if subventions are to be made to them.

Seventh.—Radical white speakers must be instructed to try and reach negro audiences while competent paid negro speakers must be kept touring the country spreading radical propaganda. So far, the Socialist Party has taken a definite position on the 14th and 15th Amendments, but this fact is not known to the majority of negroes. It is only known to a few Northern negroes in districts where their votes were catered for. This, and even stronger pronouncements on the negro, should be distributed among the race in the South, because it is the Southern negroes who are most likely to be used as mercenary White Guards. Giving the negro more publicity would induce them to read more radical literature. Already many negroes read the *Call*, the *Liberator*, and

Pearson's for that reason. The same will, no doubt, be true of radical lectures. Induce intelligent negroes to attend radical meetings and to become members of radical organizations and radical propaganda will spread among them. Most negroes avoid these meetings at present because they fear social discrimination. More social contact carries great potential propaganda value. It has healing in its wings. If it becomes known among negroes that Socialists are fighting discrimination in labor unions they will soon learn that Socialists are their friends. At present, as a result of persistent capitalistic misrepresentation negroes identify Socialists with the discriminatory practices of the American Federation of Labor.

Specially prepared propaganda is absolutely essential. This propaganda should frankly discuss the economics of so-called race prejudice. It should avoid stressing the question of race and should be designed to wean negroes from their belief that all white people hate them. It should paint the advantages of the co-operative commonwealth and point out its inevitable destruction, if any of its component groups is exploited and discriminated against. It should expose the sham democracy today existing in America, with special reference to negroes. It should explain why metropolitan newspapers abuse negroes, labor, Socialism, and similar other exploited groups. It should explain how capitalists who control the Church, press, platform, and stage use these agencies for the purpose of dividing white and black workers, playing one against the other in order to make their exploitation all the more easy. It should point out that Christ, William Lloyd Garrison, Horace Greeley, John Brown, and Abraham Lincoln were abused as radicals in their day and that today they are esteemed as among the world's great benefactors.[21] In short, it should aim to change the race-conscious negro into a class-conscious worker. In supporting radical negro publications financially, white radicals will be making their best investments. Already a few such journals exist but they are woefully handicapped by lack of funds. The easiest avenues to approach negroes through are those used by the master class. Let negro ministers and newspapers preach Socialism and the negro race will be converted to it. At present many white speakers address negro audiences, but they are usually social patriots like Walling and Russell, anti-Socialists like John Wesley Hill, and patriots of the Roosevelt kind.[22] All make time-worn rhetorical allusions to negro loyalty, military records, etc. Socialist speakers should try to avoid this patronizing style and speak Socialism and its relation to the negro as a portion of the working class. As it

21. William Lloyd Garrison (1805–1879), abolitionist and social reformer; Horace Greeley (1811–1872), founder of the *New-York Tribune*; John Brown (1800–1859), abolitionist.

22. William English Walling (1877–1936), wealthy labour reformer and Socialist; Charles Edward Russell (1860–1941), journalist and one of the co-founders of the NAACP; John Wesley Hill (1863–1936), Methodist minister, political activist, and the chancellor of Lincoln Memorial University in Tennessee.

would be difficult for radical white speakers to get immediate access into negro churches as at present controlled, it will be necessary to maintain a few subsidized negro speakers to prepare the minds of their people and to hold mass meetings at which prominent radicals be invited to speak and deliver the message of class unity.

On their part radical negroes are doing a little, but it is indeed a little. The 21st A. D. branch of the Socialist Party, Local New York, is almost entirely composed of negroes. They are doing their best to enlighten their brothers and sisters to the doctrine of Socialism, but they are terribly handicapped by lack of funds. A Peoples' Forum is maintained and prominent radical speakers address it every Sunday afternoon, but the result, while encouraging, is entirely out of proportion to the enormity of the task. It may be argued that since negroes have so much at stake they must help to encompass their own salvation. Granted, but upon white radicals devolves the duty, out of consideration for their own self-preservation and the success of their cause, to aid to the limit of their greater ability to enlighten this most benighted section of the American proletariat.

It may also be argued that negroes are no more race-conscious than Jews and since the latter have become intensely class-conscious by reason of economic pressure and oppression negroes must of themselves realize that their racial salvation is ultimately wrapped up with the struggles and victories of labor. This argument is plausible but not true. In the first place, the founder of scientific Socialism, Marx, and its most active early propagandist, Lassalle, were Jews, hence it would have been absurd to think of carrying to Jews a doctrine formulated by members of their own race.[23] Next, there is no analogy between negroes and Jews, so far as propaganda is concerned. Jews have a distinctive language press which acts as a kind of screen against strictly "national" ideas; they are inter-racially arrayed against each other as capitalists and workers; they are essentially industrial proletarians—factory workers; and they have an almost unbroken tradition of resistance to oppression without scrupulous regard to the methods employed. On the other hand, these things are not true of negroes, who are most pathetically "Americans". They speak the same language, have the same ideals and have traditions which teach them to place reliance upon prayer to God, gratitude, and "constitutional" means for their liberation. Added to this is the constant pressure exerted upon them to convince them that they are inherently inferior to their fellow Americans. Then their circumscription tends to narrow their outlook, which rarely reaches beyond their own racial concern. The few negroes who have become radicals have been in many cases foreigners and, if natives, have been led to their way of thinking through mental curiosity stimulated by contact with white radicals. In New York, Jews, as ever great propagandists, have been instru-

23. Ferdinand Lassalle (1825–1864), a Prussian-German philosopher and political activist who initiated the social democratic movement in Germany.

mental in making more radicals among negroes than perhaps all the non-Jewish radicals put together. And this small success should be the most convincing sign to Socialists and other radicals that negroes constitute at present the most fertile field for their propaganda. Do not the enemies of radicalism poison and control the wells of public information from which negroes like other Americans freely imbibe? Are they not reached by the subtle propaganda of reaction? If so, are not white radicals justified by self-interest in making every possible effort and sacrifice to win over to themselves the support of over one-tenth of the population that is overwhelmingly of the working class? Was it not necessary to convert the majority of class-conscious workers to their present frame of mind by means of a Socialist tract, book or pamphlet? Look at the Christians! Do they not dispatch missionaries all over the world to convert the most benighted "heathens", and are not American negroes heathens so far as Socialism and economic radicalism are concerned? It is true that the "heathens" need salvation, but in order to keep the "saved" saved and avoid their destruction it is for them to see that the heathens are converted. Just as Christians follow the biblical injunction, "Go ye into all the world and preach the gospel to every creature", so must radicals preach their gospel to every member of the working class who is not a "convert".

Experience has taught the workers that Socialism will not be permitted to flourish in isolated spots. Russia, like the Paris Commune, realizes that international capitalism will ruthlessly destroy any government not built upon the pillars of rent, profit, and interest, hence no effort should be spared to hasten world revolution. Russian emissaries are sent everywhere and communist propaganda reaches from South Africa to England, Argentina to India, Cuba to Canada. Propaganda is not localized, but goes everywhere. In like manner must propaganda inside a nation reach every element. If America with her boundless resources remains non-Socialist, she will be a menace to world Socialism and America can remain non-Socialist if 12,000,000 negroes so will it. That some Socialists are getting to realize how serious a menace negroes are likely to be to the movement is proved by the willingness of the Rand School to institute lectures giving out the necessary facts relating to the race in America; but it is clear that the national leaders and the rank and file of the party do not comprehend their peril. Instead, they sentimentally flirt with the far-distance problems of India and China in blissful disregard of the material fact that they will never be in a position to render tangible aid to these oppressed peoples until they succeed in making allies out of American negroes. But perhaps this attitude on the part of American radicals is because of the fact that they are Americans and share the typical white American psychology towards negroes. If this is so, then their radicalism is not genuine and is deservedly doomed to failure. For anyone to think the negro unworthy of consideration is for that one to fly in the face of history. Mere acquiescence in a conventional national belittling of negroes will not make them race-conscious or remove their potentiality for being black White Guards or Czecho-Slovaks. Perhaps a few ominous and startling facts from history may disabuse the minds of those in doubt and sober the blind enthusiasm of the fanatical theorists. These facts contain lessons that even white radicals who are still under the influence of the American psychology which thinks in terms of races, not class, may well heed.

During the Civil War in which the freedom of negroes from the bonds of chattel slavery was incidentally involved, thousands of negroes were employed by the confederates as soldiers and in other capacities for the express purpose of perpetuating human slavery. Negroes, although an oppressed race, volunteered for service and were employed as soldiers to crush the uprising of the Filipinos under Aguinaldo for national freedom. In the present war, although denied a voice in the national government, lynched and prescribed against, negroes volunteered for military service in such numbers as to call for limits being placed upon their further acceptance.

When the interests of capital are endangered, governments do not hesitate to employ soldiers of any race to destroy those who menace it. This is proved by England and France scouring the universe for black, brown, and yellow soldiers to protect their interests against the enemy. At first the German capitalist government was the "enemy", now it is the Hungarian and Russian Soviet government, and negroes are being used against them. At Archangel, West Indian negro soldiers were attached to Canadian regiments, while American negro soldiers are alleged to have been rushed from the Philippines to participate in the taking of Vladivostok from the Bolsheviks. Official dispatches tell of 60,000 French colonials under General Mangin marching to capture Budapest and an official Bolshevik document states that negroes were being employed against them at Odessa.[24]

Colored West Indian troops, until recently demobilized, were stationed in England and Ireland, and some of them have said that they were told by their officers that in case of "trouble" (it was during the strikes in England and the intense Sinn Fein agitation in Ireland early in 1919) they would be called upon to do their "duty". In England some of them were given 50 rounds of ammunition while those in Ireland marched to church with fixed bayonets.

These are but a few examples showing that capitalists, or rather governments, do not discriminate as to the weapons they employ to achieve their ends; they also show that unless instructed, negroes, in their present state of ignorance of the real aims of Socialism, are liable to be willing tools of the plutocracy. History has a curious way of repeating itself, and it is quite possible that interested capitalists may help it to repeat itself on the American continent.

Having regard to the facts already outlined, to the future of mankind, amicable relations between races, the destruction of capitalism and the successful opera-

24. Charles Mangin (1866–1925), French general remembered for his advocacy of the mass recruitment of African troops into the French Army.

tion of Socialist principles, it devolves upon white radicals to concentrate their efforts and propaganda upon the negro race. Let white radicals remember and be guided by the fate of the Czecho-Slovaks in Russia. White Socialists, radicals, and liberals, remember that self-preservation is the first law of nature, and safeguard yourselves.

4

Race First!

July 1919

This was the last of Domingo's editorials for *Negro World*. With its title motto and striking line about the need to go armed in a world of wolves, the piece's words are often taken as Garvey's, even by a Garvey scholar such as Tony Martin.[1] The following spring, with Domingo critiquing Garvey in the pages of *The Emancipator*, Hubert Harrison, who had taken over the editorship of *Negro World* and who—temporarily—was closer to Garvey than to Domingo, reprinted the editorial with this comment attached: "This week we are reproducing an editorial written on July 26th last year by Mr W. A. Domingo, at present editor of *The Emancipator*, under the caption, 'Race First!' It makes quite interesting reading. Comment of our own is unnecessary. Each reader may furnish his own. H. H." Harrison republished the editorial probably in order to embarrass Domingo, who by 1920 was attacking Garvey; but Domingo always claimed that in many respects he agreed with Garvey's *ideas*, and certainly his constant quotation of Claude McKay's poem "If We Must Die" suggested a similar sentiment. In the 1919 Department of Justice report "Radicalism and Sedition among the Negroes as Reflected in Their Publications", this editorial was the first quoted.[2]

[anon.] "Race First!", *Negro World*, 26 July 1919, rpt. *Negro World*, 10 April 1920 (rpt. in *MGP* 1, pp. 469–470)

Perhaps no phrase has done more to consolidate the sentiment of Negroes of the world than that summed up in the two words: "Negro First". If we remember correctly, the slogan was coined by the well-known lecturer and scholar Hubert Harrison. It is a succinct paraphrase, for purposes of Negro propaganda and advancement, of the practices of all other races, particularly the white race.

Reasonably interpreted it means that in the situation of racial strife, existing Negroes should give their own racial concern precedence over all other matters

1. Martin, *Race First*, p. 22.
2. "Radicalism and Sedition among the Negroes as Reflected in Their Publications", Exhibit 10 in [US Senate], *Investigation Activities of the Department of Justice, 66th Cong., 1st sess. Doc. 153*, Washington, DC: GPO, 1919, pp. 161–192, at 163. The editors of *Negro World* are listed as Marcus Garvey and William H. Domingo. On this document, see Maxwell, *F.B. Eyes*, p. 53.

when such preference does not make for perpetuating racial efficiency or causing individual loss while enriching exploiters who operate under the camouflage of race loyalty. In other words, all things being equal, Negroes should give preference to members of their own race so as to conserve their resources to enable them more effectively to combat those forces that oppose them on racial grounds alone.

The present condition of Negroes forces them to assume an essentially defensive role; hence, practicing the principles of "Negro first" does not mean an abandonment of common sense or a disregard of individual interest; instead, the best defensive is sometimes achieved through employing tactics of offense, and individuals can better gain what they want by pooling their interests. The essence of "race first" is, therefore, co-operation among Negroes to protect themselves against the attacks of truculent and race-prejudiced white men. *This may be a new doctrine for Negroes, but it has been consciously practiced by Caucasians and others from time immemorial.*

It is the principle of race first aggressively misapplied that white men the world over practice when they discriminate against Negroes. But it is the same principle defensively and intelligently applied that makes the Chinese a self-sufficient people, although forming but a very small percentage of the population of New York, the West Indies, and other territories outside of China where they reside. The same principle partially accounts for the power and influence of the Jewish race, which power and principle seem to be in inverse proportion to the number of Jews in the world.

It may be argued that race first is racial selfishness, and as such will not remove the reasons that called it into being; but this argument loses its validity when recognition is taken of the fact that certain problems seem to suggest their own remedies. Fire is regarded or reputed to be an effective agent in fighting [fire], while steel is principally relied upon to cut steel. *To say that because Negroes are the victims of organized race first sentiment on the part of white people they should not organize along lines of race first to defend themselves is to inferentially condone their present oppression and counsel meek submission to its perpetuation.* Failure on the part of the oppressed to organize in terms of self as opposed to similar kinds of organizations on the part of their oppressors must naturally make their oppression more thorough. "Race First", "Negro First", or whatever the shibboleth adopted by Negroes may be, finds its highest justification in the practices and methods of their oppressors.

It is true that all races look forward to the time when spears shall be beaten into agricultural implements, but until that time arrives it devolves upon all oppressed peoples to avail themselves of every weapon that may be effective in defeating the fell motives of their oppressors.

In a world of wolves one should go armed, and one of the most powerful defensive weapons within the reach of Negroes is the practice of Race First *in all parts of the world.*[3]

3. See W. E. B. Du Bois: "we too must gather armed"; "Let Us Reason Together", *The Crisis*, 18, no. 5 (September 1919), p. 231.

5

Capitalism the Basis of Colonialism

August 1919

Freed from his commitment to *Negro World*, Domingo embarked on a series of essays for *The Messenger*. By the second half of 1919 he had acquired the Marxist analysis of colonialism that he would maintain for the rest of his life, pithily expressed in the first sentence of this piece.

The Messenger, 2, no. 8 (August 1919), pp. 26–27

The various colonial empires of the world are maintained by force and trickery and are devoid of altruism in any shape or form. The motivating influence that brought them into existence was the intention of a better armed race or nation to reduce weaker races and nations to the point where they would be compelled to directly or indirectly produce wealth for the benefit of the dominant class of the mother country. The true basis of all empires is economic in spite of the fact that apologists for colonial expansion exhaust all their ingenuity to assign moral intent to countries whose imperial rule is based upon openly exercised or slightly veiled force. This is as much true of the frank and brutal imperialism of Rome, Germany, France, Spain, Japan, and Great Britain as it is of the less visible imperialism of the United States. The former countries, more ingenuous than the latter, in acquiring new territory rarely, if ever, attempted to cover up their intentions with hypocritical cant or resort to the outward forms of a "purchase"; they usually took whatever they had the power to seize and explained the conquest afterwards.

A very natural question to ask is: "Why do countries have colonies?" This is easily explained. In the first place, because of the capitalistic development of most "civilised" countries the vast majority of the population have been expropriated from the land and live in cities in ever increasing numbers. In the cities, because of the wonderful productivity of modern machines more goods are produced than can be bought up by the population of the producing country, hence the need for outlets in foreign countries. This condition makes foreign markets necessary. The only markets than can absorb any appreciable portion of manufactured goods are located in such countries as cannot or ARE NOT PERMITTED to develop industrially. To safeguard and insure a market against other industrially developed and exploiting countries, political control of the market is essential.

Hence the imposing of the rule of the industrially developed exporting country upon the industrially undeveloped and importing country. However, sometimes the prospective colony may have infant industries of its own—enough to supply its own needs—or it may have ambitions to become self-sufficient. In such cases the "mother" or exploiting country ordinarily effectuates the death of the existing industries or renders the ambition to create new industries stillborn. This is illustrated by the manner in which the weaving and other industries of India were killed in the interest of English manufacturers and by the way in which the Jamaican government (which is dominated by English officials appointed by Downing Street, London) strangled the soap factory in Kingston some years ago. *The first reason for colonies is to provide safe markets for the surplus commodities of the mother country.*

Secondly, because of the needs of modern industry and the inability of manufacturing countries located in temperate regions to produce them, tropical products such as copra, rubber, coffee, cocoa, balatá, piasava, and hides have to be imported. In order that the supply will be steady and uninterrupted, political control of the source is necessary. This control manifests itself in the form of preferential tariffs between the colony and the mother country. It explains the insistent demands of the Unionists of Great Britain for a preferential tariff with the colonies and the reason why Cuban imports into America are given a substantial rebate of customs duties. *The second reason for the colonies is, therefore, to insure the mother country a safe and regular source of supply and raw materials.*

Thirdly, because of the contradiction of modern capitalist civilisation, instead of machines being a boon to the workers they have proven to be a curse. In all industrialised countries vast armies of unemployed exist who have been created by the man being displaced by his creature—the machine. These unemployed men and women serve two purposes. One, by their pressure on the factory gate to reduce wages to the lowest point of subsistence; two, by their ever-increasing numbers enlarge the proletarian population, thereby making of it a portentous menace to the system that created it. So as to avoid the latter phase from becoming too dangerous, the mother country, that is the class that controls it, needs some place to which the "surplus" population can be conveniently exported. Hence, the various efforts to send unemployed Europeans to Australia, Canada, South Africa, New Zealand, and other temperate countries. Germany, who came on the colonial field late, had to yield to this imperative economic law even though political control of her exported subjects was lost when they went to colonies of other exporting countries or to sparsely populated sovereign counties like Brazil. This in a measure explains the dual citizenship laws of Germany. *The third reason for colonies is to find congenial territory to which to export the "surplus" population of the mother country.*

The fourth and last important reason for colonies is the intention to create sinecures for impecunious sons of the mother country, who by virtue of lineage and tradition belong to the class from which bureaucracies are largely recruited. This last reason, which is the visible manifestation of actual political control of colonies, serves a dual purpose. First, it serves as a guarantee that the colonial government, dominated by sons of the mother country, will not be diverted into economic and political activities and alliances inimical to the interests of the land of their birth; and next by paying huge salaries and enormous pensions to these officials, substantial amounts are yearly extracted from the colonies and exported to enrich the mother country. To sum up: all empires, no matter how seemingly benevolent, are based upon force and maintain the structural form of a central manufacturing, exporting and exploiting mother country, whose influence radiates to the colonies through her possession of a merchant marine, political control, and expropriation of the natives. These bases of influence in their turn have behind them power in the form of an army and navy.

Colonialism, therefore, is a product of capitalism which may be defined as that system of wealth production and distribution that is based upon a favoured few living off and at the expense of the oppressed many. With the death of capitalism in the mother or central country, will come the collapse of imperialism and its train [of] murder, high taxes, poverty, oppression, and exploitation in the colonies.

6
"If We Must Die"
September 1919

The BI report "Radicalism and Sedition among the Negroes as Reflected in Their Publications" called the number of *The Messenger* containing this essay of Domingo's "more insolently offensive than any other of its issues".[1] The piece appeared as the issue's editorial, setting that "offensive" tone.

The Messenger, 2, no. 9 (September 1919), p. 4

America won the war that was alleged to be fought for the purpose of making the world safe for democracy, but in the light of recent happenings in Washington, the capital city, and Chicago, it would seem as though the United States is not a part of the world.[2] In order to win the war President Wilson employed "force, unstinted force," and those who expect to bring any desirable termination to a just cause can do no less than follow the splendid example set them by the reputed spokesman of humanity.[3] That the lesson did not take long to penetrate the minds of Negroes is demonstrated by the change that has taken place in their demeanor and tactics. No longer are Negroes willing to be shot down or hunted from place to place like wild beasts; no longer will they flee from their homes and leave their property to the tender mercies of the howling and cowardly mob. They have changed, and now they intend to give men's accounts of themselves. If death is to be their portion, New Negroes are determined to make their dying a costly investment for all concerned. If they must die they are determined that they shall not travel through the valley of the shadow of death alone, but that some of their oppressors shall be their companions.

This new spirit is but a reflex of the great war, and it is largely due to the insistent and vigorous agitation carried on by younger men of the race. The demand is uncompromisingly made for either liberty or death, and since death is likely to

1. "Radicalism and Sedition", p. 179.
2. See above, p. 22, n. 29.
3. At a speech in Baltimore on 6 April 1918, Wilson spoke of US war policy as: "Force, force to the utmost, force without stint or limit, the righteous and triumphant force which shall make right the law of the world and cast every selfish dominion down in the dust"; www.presidency.ucsb.edu/documents/speech-the-opening-the-third-liberty-loan-campaign-delivered-the-fifth-regiment-armory> (accessed 3 September 2024).

be a two-edged sword it will be to the advantage of those in a position to do so to give the race its long-denied liberty.

The new spirit animating Negroes is not confined to the United States, where it is most acutely manifested, but is simmering beneath the surface in every country where the race is oppressed. The Washington and Chicago outbreaks should be regarded as symptoms of a great pandemic, and the Negroes as courageous surgeons who performed the necessary though painful operation. That the remedy is efficacious is beyond question. It has brought results, for as a consequence the eyes of the entire world are focused upon the racial situation in the United States. The world knows now that the New Negroes are determined to observe the primal law of self-preservation whenever civil laws break down; to assist the authorities to preserve order and prevent themselves and families from being murdered in cold blood. Surely, no one can sincerely object to this new and laudable determination. Justification for this course is not lacking, for it is the white man's own Bible that says "Those who live by the sword shall perish by the sword", and since white men believe in force, Negroes who have mimicked them for nearly three centuries must copy them in that respect. Since fire must be fought with hell fire, and diamond alone can cut diamond, Negroes realize that force alone is an effective medium to counteract force. Counter-irritants are useful in curing diseases, and Negroes are being driven by their white fellow citizens to investigate the curative values inherent in mass action, revolvers, and other lethal devices when applied to social diseases.

The New Negro has arrived with stiffened back bone, dauntless manhood, defiant eye, steady hand and a will of iron. His creed is admirably summed up in the poem of Claude McKay, the black Jamaican poet, who is carving out for himself a niche in the Hall of Fame:

If we must die, let it not be like hogs
Hunted and penned in an inglorious spot,
While round us bark the mad and hungry dogs,
Making their mock at our accursèd lot.[4]

4. Domingo here quotes the whole poem. "If We Must Die" had appeared in *The Liberator*, 2, no. 7 (July 1919), p. 21. It was also reproduced in *The Crusader* (September 1919) and *Negro World* (October 1919).

7

Bolshevism and the Darker Races

March 1920

Bolshevism clearly galvanised Domingo and his colleagues. Lenin's thesis of self-determination for oppressed nations was particularly important in the long term for Domingo's campaign for Jamaican self-government, but the reputation of the Bolsheviks for defending minorities was also attractive to African-American activists. "Did Bolshevism Stop Race Riots in Russia?", Domingo had asked the previous September; "Will Bolshevism Free America?", he would ask in the September to come.[1] Claude McKay took note: "Bolshevism (as Mr Domingo ably points out in the current *Messenger*)", he wrote in the September 1920 *Negro World*, "has made Russia safe for the Jew .... It might make these United States safe for the Negro."[2]

[anon.] *The Emancipator*, 1, no. 1 (13 March 1920), p. 4

The *New York World* in the second of its series of articles on Soviet Russia quotes Leon Trotsky, War Minister, as expressing fear that the Allies, finding it impossible to maintain armed opposition to Bolshevism with literate white troops, may resort to the use of illiterate Senegalese, Anmanites, Malagasy, and other dark-skinned subjects of France and Great Britain. So far, the Allies have been completely beaten diplomatically and militarily by the superior methods of the Bolsheviks; armies have melted like snow; populations have been converted by seductive propaganda; and the Allies are forced to dicker with their foes for peace.

The economic situation of the world is forcing hypocrites like Lloyd George, fools like Churchill, and ignoramuses like a certain gentleman not living outside the United States to see the reasonableness of making peace with Lenin and his able co-adjutors. Clemenceau, that shriveled old gargoyle of Paris, has retired and is now traveling in Egypt, which he helped to enslave. The cordon sanitaire, the ring of bayonets around Soviet Russia, proved to be a cordon of paper. It is no more. England, with the blood of numberless Indians, Negroes, Egyptians, and

1. "Did Bolshevism Stop Race Riots in Russia?", *The Messenger*, 2, no. 9 (September 1919), pp. 26-27 [CB 31–34]; "Will Bolshevism Free America?", *The Messenger*, 2, no. 8 (September 1920), pp. 85-86. (Volume 2 ran over two years with inconsistent and repetitive numbering.)
2. Quoted in "Radicalism and Sedition", p. 164.

Irishmen upon her grasping, greedy hands, looks with nervous apprehension at the approach of Bolshevism to her Eastern colonies.

Everywhere Bolshevism brings terror to the heart of imperialism, secret diplomacy, hypocrisy, and oppression, and, yet, the chieftains of this liberating doctrine are afraid of some of the very races whom they would free. This is the great paradox, the great tragedy. Some of the very Indians and Negroes are the potential hangmen of their only disinterested friend—Soviet Russia. It is not idle fear that Trotsky voices. It is easy for propaganda to reach a literate people; but it is a tremendously more difficult task for it to reach an illiterate people. Poland and Rumania illustrate this.

However, there are signs of Negro awakening. All over the West Indies there are strikes and unrest; in South Africa, benighted and oppressed land, 40,000 natives are on strike, and two colored delegates to a labor conference in Johannesburg have been hailed as comrades and brothers. One of them even seconded a motion to support Soviet Russia to the limit. Social equality was also recognized as a prerequisite to industrial unity and racial harmony. The dawn is breaking in Negrodom! Black soldiers from the West Indies, South Africa, and a certain self-righteous republic, imbued with the spirit of the New Negro, will not be willing tools of those who now rule Egypt, India, the West Indies, Africa, and Arkansas with machine guns in the destruction of the people's non-imperialist government of Russia.

We appreciate Trotsky's fear, but feel that it is a little overdrawn. The war has opened the eyes of the darker races a little. They will no longer be their own enslavers. On the comrades of Trotsky in other lands devolved the duty of paying attention to the "needs" of the black masses whom the Russian war minister sees as the only possible material in the hands of the imperialism of the world.

8

Africa's Redemption

March 1920

Domingo's interest in and knowledge about Africa would grow throughout his lifetime, built on his extensive reading and meetings with young Africans who had come to New York to study. In this early sketch one senses him writing against the oversimplifications about Africa that Marcus Garvey had been foisting upon the African-American public. Garvey was about to have himself elected Provisional President of Africa, and generous subscribers to his fund-raising were being awarded Crosses of African Redemption.[1] Against such vacuous grandstanding, Domingo was concerned to spell out in more sober terms just what it would take to redeem Africa.

The Emancipator, 1, no. 3 (27 March 1920), p. 4

It is the natural instinct of any people who are bound together by ties of race to desire to control their destiny. Every right, natural or otherwise, justifies this feeling. It is based upon sound and logical principles. Control of a majority by a minority is odious; it is as objectionable as the domination of a man by a child. Deep down in the soul of every race there is the yearning after equality with other races, the longing to see one's own type achieve the highest, the best, the noblest. The Irishman, bound to Erin by many tendrils of cultural and historical affection, continues, and shows no sign of giving up the age-long fight of his fathers for freedom. It is impossible forever to enslave a people with the will to be free.

As education becomes more wide-spread and a people becomes conscious of themselves, there develops a constant struggle for the liberation of their racial souls. First comes liberation of the racial mind, next liberation of the group. Understanding this, empires have always striven to kill the racial and national individuality of a conquered people. In the case of Ireland, England sought to blot out the Irish language and put a blight upon peculiarly Irish industries. In India, little by little the English language is being forced upon the people, and definite attempts are made to destroy racial individuality by destroying Indian religions, industries, and culture. The Indian population is large and it is difficult to destroy

1. Grant, *Negro with a Hat*, p. 277.

the history of a people who have a written language. Study of their history, as well as economic and political oppression, has stiffened the national backbone of India and created unity where there was disunity, nationality where there were nationalities. In India nationality and race are becoming identical. When an Indian dies for India, he dies for his race, his nation.

Africa presents a different picture. It is a vast continent with no common culture of indigenous origin. The culture of North Africa is as different to the culture of South Africa as the culture of West Africa is different to that of Central Africa. There is no common African language which cements the various tribes together. In religion there are three major differences—Fetish, Mohammedan, and Christian, and, as is natural, a Mohammedan feels himself defiled if the shadow of a Christian swine falls upon him. All these tribes have their individual cultures which reach back to their earliest communal life and are compounded of traditional tribal animosities.

With one exception the African tribes have no indigenous written language in which to perpetuate their history or through which propaganda can function. Politically the native Africans are under the domination of Europe. The natural wealth of the vast continent is largely exported to enrich capitalists of the various European capitals. Prior to the advent of Europeans the aborigines had developed a very satisfactory communal system, a system for the inviolability of which the natives have fought most of their wars with England, France, Portugal, and Belgium. The natives, as Blyden and Dudley Kidd point out, are essential Socialists.[2] They think in terms of the "we" rather than the "I". On the coast European artillery has broken up the communal system, but it remains intact in the interior. To redeem Africa, then, means not the introduction of European political methods and social systems that are incomprehensible to the native, but recognition of the truism that to break up the African communal system is to injure, not aid, the natives. In West Africa and the coast towns of all Africa where the communal system has been destroyed, the natives are poor and have to resort to strike for relief. In the interior strikes are unknown and so is poverty—lack of the elementary needs of African existence! Freetown, Sierra Leone, is no better off economically and politically than Kingston, Jamaica, or Charleston, SC.

How then can Africa be redeemed? Not by a change of religion, for at the present rate of progress it would take a millennium to convert Africa to Christianity. By the sword? God help the fools who would try that method now. The serious problem of the African, his real problem, is how to overcome his present poverty and how to achieve ultimate self-government—self-determination. It cannot be forced upon the Africans from the outside; it must develop in Africa.

2. The Pan-African scholar and journalist Edward Wilmot Blyden (1832–1912) was born on St Thomas in the Danish West Indies but spent much of his life in Liberia: *African Life and Customs* (1908); the British ethnologist Dudley Kidd (1863–1921) wrote extensively about southern Africa: *Kafir Socialism and the Dawn of Individualism* (1908).

It must be African in character. But Africans abroad can help. They can help to destroy the system that dooms the majority of "civilized" Africans to poverty and denies a race the divine right to order their life as they deem best.

In America the heart of imperialism is Wall Street; in England, the counting houses; in France, the Bourse. And it is imperialism that enslaves Negroes everywhere. How can that power be broken? By aiding those who are today fighting the system in those countries. By trying to reach the heart of the hideous monster with a death stroke, by clipping the claws of the lion and the talons of the eagle Negroes can free Africa.

Does the redemption of Africa mean the foisting of Christianity upon the people? Or breaking up their communal system and introducing private ownership in land? Does it mean that descendants of Africans from the West Indies and the United States who have lost their true racial individuality must introduce their acquired culture into a land with a culture that reaches back into the dim past? Shall Africans of the dispersion try to supplant the communal organization of tribes like Fanti in which the dominant aim is the "many" as opposed to the "I" of the West Indies? Is the primitive socialism to give way to capitalist individualism with its brutal motto, "Every man for himself and the devil take the hindmost"? What is the experience of the Americo-Liberians with the Kroo tribe of that country?

To redeem Africa one must work with the materials in Africa; one must be practical. The best of European civilization in industry, art, literature, and science—particularly science—must be given to Africa, not to Europeanize the African, but to develop his racial culture to the zenith of its possibilities. To free Africans from the galling yoke of European domination one must first understand the nature of that yoke. Africa was partitioned at a time when capitalism had reached a point where it needed to stretch out in order to keep its industrial system intact. Africa was robbed of her sons, when a new world was discovered and labor to exploit that world was needed. Africa is dominated today because white capitalists—De Beers, Jameson, Thomas F. Ryan, King Leopold, Cecil Rhodes, Sir Alfred Jones—coveted its diamonds, rubber, gold, and other great mineral and agricultural wealth.[3] The oppression of Africa is, therefore, mainly economic and a fruit of the capitalist system.

---

3. De Beers was not actually a capitalist: it was the name given to a firm whose origins lay in a diamond mine found on their South African property by two Dutch settlers, brothers Diederik Arnoldus de Beer (1825–1878) and Johannes Nicolaas de Beer (1830–1883). Leander Starr Jameson (1853–1917) was a British doctor and colonial administrator in southern Africa who was closely associated with Cecil Rhodes. Thomas Fortune Ryan (1851–1928) was a US tobacco, insurance, and transportation magnate who invested in King Leopold II's Congo Free State and co-founded the American Congo Company with Daniel Guggenheim. King Leopold II of Belgium (1835–1909) was the founder and sole owner of the Congo Free State. Cecil John Rhodes (1853–1902) was a British mining magnate and politician in southern Africa. Sir Alfred Lewis Jones (1845–1909) was a Welsh shipowner with many financial interests in West Africa.

Negroes who live in countries where the strength of the system is located can best redeem Africa by helping to break up the system. Who are the real enemies of Haiti and Africa? The ignorant white soldier or the more ignorant black soldier who is thrilled at the sight of a certain chromatic arrangement; or is it the small group of men who get concessions for exploiting those places of their great agricultural and mineral wealth? Finally, to redeem Africa, Africans in Africa and Africans abroad must try to communalize science, art, and industry; they must recognize the true African soul which has its roots in the economic system of the native and try to develop that soul.

Africans abroad can aid Africa by striving to the limit to break a system that is responsible for the present political degradation of Africa and their own oppression in the West Indies, Central and South America, and the United States. To do this calls for clear thinking and recognition of the fact that Africans are not the only ones who are the victims of capitalist exploitation. Not by wild threats or sensational methods can these things be accomplished, but through organizations that function with a view to establishing co-operatives (like the Jamaica League in Jamaica), industrial organizations (like the National Brotherhood in the South and Labor Unions in Demerara and Trinidad), and by alliances with extreme radicals everywhere (like that of the natives of South Africa). As a fitting corollary of these three methods—consumers' co-operatives, industrial unions, and alliances with radicals—the race can have an educational system that will bring Negroes to a true conception and pride in their racial type which will expand their souls and give them the necessary weapons for achieving a great and glorious future.

9

The Maintenance of the Spirit of Radicalism among White Radicals

?May 1920

In *The Negroes in America*, which Claude McKay wrote in Russia in the spring of 1923, he includes a lengthy quotation from an article by Domingo, introduced like this: "About two and a half years ago W. A. Domingo, the Negro editor of the now defunct *Emancipator*, wrote the following article, which I quote in extracts and which ought to be distributed among the members of the Workers' Party." McKay's book was translated into Russian, and no sign has ever been found of his original text, nor of Domingo's article. McKay thought highly enough of the article to carry it to Russia with him when he went in November 1922 to attend the Fourth Congress of the Comintern. The article itself provides further evidence of Domingo's strategic thinking: black conservatives must be attracted, white radicals must be taught to see the importance of black workers .... Its existence also implies some closeness between McKay and Domingo, at least in these years, when both were attracted to the promise of the Russian Revolution. In the 20 September 1919 issue of *Negro World* McKay had advocated Bolshevism with reference to this article ("as Mr Domingo ably points out").[1] It appears here as back-translated into English from the Russian translation.

Claude McKay, *The Negroes in America*, ed. Alan L. McLeod, trans. from the Russian by Robert J. Winter, Port Washington, NY: Kennikat Press, 1979, pp. 38–40. Originally published as *Negry v Amerike*, trans. P. Okhrimenko, Moscow, Russia: State Publishing House, 1923

A great task lies upon Negro radicals who consider *their* radicalism to be something deeper than a simple innate protest against lynching and injustice; they must attract to their side Negro conservatives to struggle with other conservatives and to support the spirit of radicalism among white radicals .... Many whites call themselves radicals. They assure themselves and their friends that they are irreconcilable enemies of the existing order, with all its frightful injustices. They are ready to faint when they hear about the fact that white children are compelled to

1. "Radicalism and Sedition", p. 164.

work long hours in factories and on farms, and write lengthy articles, editorials, and letters of protest against repression in Ireland and against the introduction of African "savages" into "civilized" Germany. But their radicalism in many cases doesn't extend to colored peoples. This to a large extent applies to opportunistic elements inside various radical movements. Every time they have to defend American Negroes, they usually do it with far from the same ardor as when they are up in arms against injustice with respect to members of their own race. They must understand more profoundly what they themselves preach so eloquently: that capitalism is as deeply rooted in Africa as in Europe and that this system cannot be eliminated in England and continue to exist on the island of Haiti.

This the Russian Bolsheviks understand very well and use to good effect by supporting and encouraging the oppressed of all races, creeds, and nationalities. They have no scorn for Tartars, Mongols, Koreans, Hindus, Persians, or Negroes. In their first manifesto to the whole world, which was imbued with class-consciousness, the workers of Soviet Russia appealed to "the oppressed masses of Asia and Africa". The manifesto of the Third International contains the following significant declaration: "Colonial slaves! Know that the day of the victory of the proletariat in Europe will be the day of your emancipation."

For the victory of socialism in America, it is necessary that 15,000,000 Negroes be at least favorably disposed to it—and this they have not been, up to now, since they are not acquainted with the aims and aspirations of socialists. These aims and aspirations must reach their consciousness in the same way that the aims and ideals of the Bolsheviks have reached the Persians and the Koreans. And for this, radicals in their radicalism must abolish racial boundaries; they must throw off the American psychology which either completely ignores Negroes or gives them very little significance.

In America there are many active radical organizations. There are also active radical members in semi-radical organizations. Among the former the IWW stands in front. The workers who join this militant and revolutionary workers' organization profess the convictions set forth in their program. The persecution which they are subjected to is very similar to that which Negroes are subjected to, with the aim of restraining their feelings of protest against existing injustices.

The sincerity of the radicalism of a white man in America can be measured by his attitude towards Negroes. If he treats them patronizingly and opportunistically, or wants to compromise, then it is better to completely reject his "radicalism". If he agrees to recognize for Negroes the full right to all the privileges which he is striving to obtain for his own people, then one can trust him.

One can boldly say that in America the Negro question is the touchstone, the measure by which the sincerity of American radicalism can be measured. Negroes are sufficiently powerful to maintain or destroy American radicalism. Their strategic position in the industrial area gives them a power beyond their numbers. The Negro workers' power, correctly understood and intelligently and disinterestingly applied, could be used to obtain freedom for both black and white workers. And it is just this power which sooner or later will force white radicals to speak out.

Even the reactionary leaders of the American workers are beginning to see the power of black workers. Georgia and Florida are beginning to pay attention to black workers. The president of the AFL, Samuel Gompers, who for many years has treated black labor hostilely, recently has turned to the railroad brotherhoods with the request to eliminate their existing statutes which discriminate on the basis of skin color. All this indicates that the Negroes' day is close. They have the power to support conservatism in America or to create radicalism. Negro interests demand the support of radicalism, since there is the hope that by the victory of radicalism Negroes can expect a richer and fuller life; but in order to achieve this, the white radical has to make his radicalism manifest. And he will manifest it if he does not want Negroes to thwart all his efforts and to turn back the hour hand of human freedom.

The position of the Negro revolutionary in America is the position of national watchdog. At the same time that revolutionaries have an ear cocked and attentively watch each practical step of revolutionaries on the Negro question, the Negro revolutionary must occupy such a position that he has the opportunity to watch both reactionaries and revolutionaries. He absolutely must indicate to white comrades the root problems of the Negro working class and turn their attention to the snares which capitalist tricksters set while playing on racial inequality.

10

"Figures Never Lie, but Liars Do Figure"

October 1921

The Emancipator had published a long four-piece analysis of Garvey and the UNIA under Anselmo Jackson's name, although Domingo may well have been largely responsible. Now, bringing his business acumen into play, he offers an unsparing audit of UNIA finances, demonstrating Garvey's inattention to prevailing financial regulations.

The Crusader, 5, no. 2 (October 1921), pp. 13–14

It is a much frayed and time-worn aphorism that "figures never lie, but liars do figure". Sometimes a balance-sheet is a more valuable revealer of truth than is suspected by those responsible for its publication. Voluntary publication of a report or a balance sheet carries the clear implication that its publishers recognize that its contents are of public interest and as such subject to public scrutiny and criticism. Especially is this true when the publishers exhaust every trick of propaganda in trying to convince the public that the statement is true and, in that particular, different to those issued by other or similar organizations or institutions.

Ever since Marcus Garvey, president-general of the Universal Negro Improvement Association, president of the African Communities League, managing editor of the *Negro World*, president of the Negro Factories Corporation, provisional president of Africa, etc., etc., rose into prominence as a race leader, he has sought to give the impression that all the enterprises of which he is virtual dictator are typical and representative of the best efforts of Negroes. He has not advertised them as being merely so many Negro enterprises, but as being the only genuine undertakings of the race. Other enterprises are counterfeit: his are genuine. His 31-day convention is not a convention of his organization, but is tautologically described as an "International Convention of the Negroes of the World". With an ungenerousness that is despicable, and an unscrupulousness of methods that is beyond the pale of decency, he sends a cablegram broadcast to the world denouncing the Du Bois Congress in Europe as a fraud while glorifying the one presided over by him in New York as a Simon-pure, honest-to-goodness convention of the entire race.

Apart from the petty meanness of a rival resorting to "knocking", one cannot but be amazed at Mr Garvey's interpretation of social equality; and above all interpreting the phrase in such a manner as to endorse the prejudiced white man's oft-repeated lie that miscegenation and social equality are one and the same thing. Let Mr Garvey, Dr McGuire, Rev. Eason and the swarm of paid officials of the UNIA repudiate the right of Negroes to be treated as equals in a world no longer individually, but socially organized, and by so doing endorse segregation and its children: jim-crowism, lynching, disenfranchisement, etc., if they will, but can dishonesty sink lower than for the Garveyites to pass a resolution at the 12th Regiment Armory on 1 August, and send it broadcast to the world, giving the impression that it represents the sentiment of intelligent Negroes? No one will deny the right of the UNIA to oppose miscegenation or endorse social inferiority, for they should be the best spokesmen of their own concepts of anthropology and of what rights they are willing to forfeit while living in America! But it is unscrupulous, to say the least, for them to ascribe their own myopic views to all Negroes.

Not the least reprehensible of the many "fantastic tricks which make the angels weep" is the recent report of the parent body of the UNIA contained in the *Negro World* for 13 August.[1] Let us examine it a little. According to the Chancellor's report, the total receipts of the parent body from the alleged total of 4,500,000 members from 1 September 1920 to 30 July 1921 is $90,048. Of this amount $45,624.74 or over 50 per cent went for salaries; cables and telegrams alone reached $1,258, while travelling expenses were over $5,000.

The receipts disclose the true membership of the organization, despite the President-General's exaggerated claim of 4,500,000. Each member pays into the organization a death tax of 10 cents per month, which is remitted to the parent body. The report shows that $19,562.80 of death taxes were paid in during the ten months covered by the report, which proves that the actual membership, far from being the millions of Mr Garvey's fertile fancy, is less than 20,000! But according to the Auditor General, Elie Garcia, the amount that should have been collected is $88,227.60, which subjected to examination reveals a membership of a little less than 90,000! Speaking then for less than 1/4,000 of his alleged 4,000,000 Negroes, how can Mr Garvey honestly claim that his convention is any more genuine than Du Bois's? At least Du Bois has never been caught lying that the membership of the NAACP is 45 times larger than it really is!

Another illuminating disclosure is that the bank balance of the parent body is only $2,383, or £17,179 less than the amount of money collected as death tax, which amount is usually held intact by fraternal organizations for the specific purpose of paying out death benefits. The Universal Negro Improvement Associ-

1. "Man, proud man, / Drest in a little brief authority, / Most ignorant of what he's most assured, / His glassy essence, like an angry ape, / Plays such fantastic tricks before high heaven / As makes the angels weep" (*Measure for Measure*, act 2, scene 2).

ation is incorporated in the State of New York as a membership corporation and as such is subject to the law governing the limitation of the use of death tax to the purpose for which it is collected.

An item in the same report shows that $3,993.37 was received as "convention funds", yet nowhere is there an item of expenditure to show how much was spent on the convention, although the bank balance is less than the above-mentioned sum! Also, although local New York borrowed $643.89 and sundry loans amounting to $227.00 were made, yet neither sum is shown as being paid back to the parent body nor as being an account receivable! Nor is Liberty Hall entered anywhere as an asset of the organization!

So much for a swift glance at the Chancellor's report. Let us look at the Liberian Construction Loan. When this project was launched, in a signed front page letter addressed to "fellow men of Negro race", Mr Garvey stated that it was for the purpose of erecting administrative buildings and constructing railroads in Liberia. The uninitiated believed that it was to be loaned to the government of Liberia, and this view was amply justified by the utterances of prominent speakers at Liberty Hall. The loan netted $144,450.58. Of this large amount only $4,000, or less than 3 per cent of the money raised, reached Africa! A sawmill costing $4,463 was, according to Mr Garcia's report, still in Hoboken, NJ on 13 August.

But let us look at how the rest of the money was spent. Salaried officers and employers received nearly $27,000, or more than three times the amount spent on Liberia, and nearly seven times the amount that has actually reached the country for which the money was supposed to be raised! Traveling expenses were $10,872, which amount could have bought at least five of the wooden vessels now being sold by the US Shipping Board! But the most surprising feature of the affair is the fact that $80,994.20, approximately 9/16 or 56⅞ per cent of the money collected for Liberia, which did not go for salaries, etc., instead of being used to construct railroads or erecting administrative buildings, was invested in the Black Star Line [BSL] and the *Negro World*! In other words, 20 times as much of the Liberian loan as actually reached Africa was invested in Garvey's enterprises in America! How good an investment is the $34,440 of the amount placed in the Black Star Line can only be judged when the present market value of the stock of that concern is ascertained. Apparently the $46,555.20 invested in the *Negro World* have magical qualities for yielding profit, for the *Negro World* is estimated by the signer of the report, G. E. Stewart, minister of religion, dispenser of truth and chancellor of the UNIA, as being worth $60,000! A Baron Munchausen-like profit of $13,000 in a period of declined circulation among Negro newspapers!

The balance sheet, too, is an eye-opener. It might be remarked in passing that despite the great growth of the association claimed by its officers, the bank balance this year is less than that of last year for the organization's parent body. Last year it was $3,324.31. This year it is $2,383. In order that assets may offset the liabilities of the association and that a condition of solvency should appear, the association is credited with Black Star Line and Negro Factories stock at par despite the fact that the former corporation has not shown a cent's profit since its founding, and the latter had a severe set-back in the closing down of its only "factory"—a millinery store—months ago! Indeed, according to rumor the *Shady Side*, on which several thousand dollars were spent, is a wreck (certainly there have been no excursions advertised on that boat this summer) and, according to an uncontradicted report in the *Brooklyn Standard-Union* of Sunday 17 July 1921 the *Yarmouth* has been seized from the Black Star Line by its former owners, The North American Steamship Company. The *Kanawha* being a yacht (now reported held up in Cuba because of boiler troubles, although several thousand dollars were recently spent to put in new boilers) cannot be expected to do much in the way of earning money in carrying freight and immigrants to Africa.

Also of interest is the fact that, instead of marking off a reasonable portion of uncollected death tax, arrearage from branches, and uncollected checks as being dead and uncollectible, indeed, these items are credited as assets at their full face value. No depreciation is allowed upon either the building in Liberia or the furniture and fixtures in New York. Last but not least is the disclosure that contrary to the often printed statements of responsible officers of the UNIA, the organization as such never owned a single share of stock in the Black Star Line until the funds of the Construction Loan became available!

Possibly the newly conceived and launched African Redemption Fund might yield enough to redeem Africa by purchasing a huge block of BSL and BF stocks.[2] Certainly the above casual analysis of the various reports furnish proof or refutation of the aphorism referred to above: "Figures never lie, but liars do figure." Certainly some explanation should be forthcoming.

2. BF (Black Factories) may be a reference to Garvey's Negro Factories Corporation, another business venture that quickly became insolvent.

11
An Opponent of Garveyism
October 1921

Domingo's final publication in 1921 was a short but skilful letter to *The World Tomorrow*, which had published two thoughtful articles about Marcus Garvey by a young white teacher and aspiring writer, Worth Tuttle, who, after studying journalism at Columbia, had spent the academic year 1919–20 teaching at the all-black Dillard College in New Orleans.

In the first of these articles, Tuttle had reported on the powerful impact that Garveyism was having on the student body at Dillard (although she didn't use the college's name) and on the varying reactions of different sections of the staff, many confounded by the implication that Christian missions were now being seen as irrelevant to the future of Africa. Then, in August 1921 Tuttle had attended the public events of the UNIA convention in New York and had interviewed Garvey himself. Her cool and nuanced report was by no means hostile. She found Garvey "surprisingly unassuming, even modest … a forceful speaker, with a sincerity in his voice that is convincing". She reports his views clearly and without comment, before noting the skill with which he addresses the UNIA members, particularly when it comes to eliciting financial contributions by means of optimistic claims of probable returns on investment. Without going into detailed calculations, she notes the likely difficulty of the Black Star Line producing a profit any time soon and predicts that "the promise of cash return on Black Star stock may be the undoing of the entire movement". Unnecessarily so, she suggests in conclusion, since UNIA members see its business ventures as agents of racial regeneration rather than of monetary return, and would be prepared to support it on that basis. Promises of fabulous returns just risk causing disillusion.

Sensing an opportunity to reach a wider readership, Domingo wrote a letter complimenting Miss Tuttle for her insights (while making her article sound much more critical of Garvey than it actually was) and underlining his own key arguments that, despite Garvey's claim, he does not speak for the whole race, and that the white press are happy to accept his claim for their own nefarious purposes because they know that his enterprises will collapse, reflecting badly on the abilities of Negroes. He ends with his own barbed compliment that when it comes to understanding the art of advertisement and race capitalisation Garvey's only equal is Colonel Simmons, founder of the new manifestation of the Ku Klux Klan.

This remark proved prophetic when seven months later Marcus Garvey of the UNIA met with Edward Young Clarke, Imperial Wizard *pro tempore* of the Ku Klux Klan, and announced that the two organisations had much in common. *The World Tomorrow* was a radical Christian pacifist magazine edited by the prominent Socialist Norman Thomas (though he was just about to move to *The Nation*).

The World Tomorrow, 4, no. 10 (October 1921), p. 347

As a Negro and a West Indian who is familiar with most of the external and many of the internal manifestations of Garveyism, and especially as I was the first Negro journalist to subject the movement to critical examination from every angle, I must compliment Miss Tuttle upon having established in her article in your September issue a clear distinction between the UNIA and the Negro race.[1] By no means can the recent 31-day convention at Liberty Hall be regarded as having been a convention of the Negro race; it was only a convention of the UNIA, a Negro organization. In all of his outpourings to the press, in all of his bombastic, exaggerated, and misinformed statements, Mr Garvey has sought to convey the impression that he speaks for the race, that his satellites (who are mostly handpicked and recipients of handsome salaries from his bounty) are democratically elected, that he represents, in short, a point of view that finds endorsement among large numbers of his race. This position has been accepted by the white press, and no matter how strenuous a protest is offered, no effort is made to correct this erroneous view. This has led to the suspicion on the part of Negroes that the white press, or those who control it, realizing the inherent fallacies of Garveyism which have been so ably pointed out by Miss Tuttle, are consciously aiding in the growth of the movement by giving it undue publicity so as to make the ruin and consequent reflection upon the ability of Negroes all the more widespread when disaster comes, as it surely will, sooner or later.

Mr Garvey claims a membership of 4,500,000. According to a signed report covering ten months ending 31 July, the death tax of 10 cents per month collected from each member amounted to less than $20,000. By a process of simple arithmetic one [can] see that the membership of the movement is less than 20,000.

Miss Tuttle's criticism of the business projects is admirable. Mr Garvey's fundamental error rests in the fact that he does not understand the world in which he lives, although he does understand the unlettered of his race. If he understood the world of politics, intrigue, finance, and might, he would never have made the mistake of inextricably joining his propaganda and his business. When the material foundation is destroyed—as the ordinary laws of economics and the

1. Worth Tuttle, "A New Nation in Harlem", *The World Tomorrow*, 4, no. 9 (September 1921), pp. 279–281. Born Ella Worth Tuttle in North Carolina, the daughter of a Methodist minister, Worth Tuttle Hedden (1896–1985) later published several novels and collections of short stories.

machinations of those whom he thinks he is fighting surely will destroy it—the spiritual superstructure will cease to be. And as reaction is equal to action, the race will be plunged into despair and will lose faith in its own capacity for industrial leadership even within the narrow limits left to it by monopolistic capitalism and world-enslaving imperialism.

Speaking, as I believe, for the intelligent, dispassionate members of my race, it is my sober judgment that Mr Garvey is unfitted by intellect to formulate a program for the race. Unquestionably he is a man of great energy, a man who understands the art of advertisement and race capitalization to a degree comparable only to Col. Simmons of the Ku Klux Klan; but as to his being a leader of the intelligent among us, I must enter an emphatic protest.[2]

2. William Joseph Simmons (1880–1945). Inspired by D. W. Griffith's film *The Birth of a Nation*, he established the second Ku Klux Klan in 1915.

12
A Man's Best Friend
March 1923

This letter appeared in *The Messenger*'s Open Forum under the general heading "The Policy of The Messenger on West Indian and American Negroes: W. A. Domingo vs. Chandler Owen". We've supplied the new title. Owen's response fails to address any of Domingo's points. Domingo never wrote for *The Messenger* again. The final paragraph offers a particularly good example of Domingo's mode.

Letter to *The Messenger*, 5, no. 3 (March 1923), pp. 639–640

It is upon the principle that "a man's best friend is one who tells him his faults" that I am moved to write you this open letter. I have debated with myself the expediency of so doing since last October, and hesitated upon the supposition that reason would conquer pique and sound public policy outweigh personal prejudices. But as there might be misunderstandings as to my attitude towards some of the newer policies of the magazine on which I am listed as a contributing editor, I am compelled to state my position as clearly and as uncompromisingly as possible. I refer to the fight that *The Messenger* is waging against Garvey and the doctrines that have flowed from his oblique intellect. No one who knows me privately or publicly can accuse me of being in the remotest sense a subscriber to the illogical, race-injuring, and dangerous ideas of Mr Garvey. It is public knowledge and a matter of record that in New York City, as early as the fall of 1919, I raised my voice in protest against the abominable asinities of our black Barnum, culminating in Thomas Potter and myself being assaulted, kicked, and placed under arrest by Garveyites in the spring of 1920. Not a bit daunted by my experiences which brought me no fame as a leader, scholar, martyr, or orator, I persisted, published, and edited *The Emancipator* (for which you both write), and have not let up a single instant in my unequivocal opposition.

My position is, I think, clear. Garvey's doctrines are dangerous to Negroes everywhere, but more so to those in the United States and Africa; his doctrines and many disgraceful failures have resulted in giving partial confirmation to the Negrophobists' claims as to our essential inferiority and have been the means of weakening us politically, financially, and racially by driving away white friends and importing schisms into our ranks. But I am not discussing Garvey's doctrines, for we are agreed as to their intrinsic worthlessness. I am concerned about the doctrines of *The Messenger*.

I am a West Indian. I am so through no act of mine, and am neither proud nor ashamed of what is purely an accident. It is not the fault of Mr Randolph that he was born in Jacksonville and no[t] Rosewood, Florida. Mr Garvey was born in Jamaica, but according to him, he had rather been born in Africa. Despite his Jamaican birth, I, a Jamaican, find myself differing from him even as most native Negroes no doubt differ from Perry Howard, whom you have bracketed with Garvey as being of the same sinister sort.[1] Difference of opinion is purely a mental quality, and may exist between twin brothers and the closest relatives. Opinions are personal, not national.

Since *The Messenger* began its belated fight to rid the race of the disgrace of Garveyism, I have noticed that many of the articles dealing with that subject have stressed Mr Garvey's nationality. I have ascribed this to the early reactions of human beings who are engaged in a controversy with an unscrupulous antagonist, but the persistent and regular recurrence of this particular emphasis forces me to ignore past relationships and register my emphatic protest. Behind the unnecessary emphasis, the Cato-like repetition, there seems to lurk a national animus that finds a convenient vent in this particular subject. Believing that the editors of *The Messenger*, who wrote an editorial as recently as last summer protesting against the *Chicago Defender*'s irrational assaults upon Garvey's nationality, are amenable to unemotional, dispassionate argumentation, I desire to draw their attention to phases of the question that they may have overlooked.

In your righteous denunciation of Garvey you excoriate his demagogy, but with a strange inconsistency resort to the very methods you condemn. If Garvey is guilty of imitating white people with his black this and black that, aren't you emulating him when you adopt his own reprehensible methods of popular appeal without regard to principle? Isn't this a case of the oppressed becoming oppressors and the lynched becoming lynchers?

In the January *Messenger* there is an editorial entitled "A Supreme Negro Jamaican Jackass", which reads in part: "Of course, no American Negro would have stooped to such depths .... It was left for Marcus Garvey from Jamaica, etc." Yet in another editorial, "The Dyer-Johnson-Howard Triangle", speaking of Perry Howard, of Mississippi, U.S.A., you say, "Negroes of this country ... should hereafter class him along with Marcus Garvey." Elementary logic records an inconsistency here. If Howard is equal to Garvey in infamy, then Jamaica is not the only place to produce jackasses of Garvey's type! And to give Jamaica a monopoly in the production of jackasses after placing Percy Howard in parity

1. Perry Wilbon Howard II (1877–1961) was a black attorney twice tried on corruption-related charges stemming from his effective control over Republican patronage in Mississippi.

with Garvey is to involve yourselves in a contradiction! No; traitors and fools may be found anywhere and everywhere.

Youth can ever learn from age, and I refer you to your last issue and advise you to ponder over the reply of Kelly Miller to your own questionnaire, which, by the way, elicited a majority of answers that were a complete repudiation of your own policy of deportation of Garvey.[2] You argue for equality with white people, yet by giving their nationality unfavorable emphasis you deny equality to West Indians, and insinuate that only a West Indian would be guilty of the things you charge against Garvey! Consistency thou art indeed a jewel!

In the past you have called the 90 percent white people of this country cowards for their oppression of the 10 percent Negroes, and yet you advocate a policy, and practice a method that, carried out logically, will mean the oppression of 90,000 foreign-born Negroes (many of them citizens and fighters for your rights) by their 12,000,000 native-born brothers! Which is the greater oppression, nine oppressing one, or 400 oppressing three?) Suppose Garvey were an American, would you emphasize that fact? If not (and you could not), why emphasize his foreign birth?

I will not point out that it is incompatible with your professed Socialist faith for you to initiate an agitation for deportation or to emphasize the nationality of anyone as a subtle means of generating opposition against him, but I certainly maintain that to oppose Garvey on the score of his birthplace is to confess inability to oppose him formidably upon any other ground. By the penalties you advocate and the arguments you stress against Garvey one can determine what you regard as his greatest offense, namely his nationality. Certainly there is enough error and weakness in Garveyism for you to find a more intellectually dignified method of assault; and certainly the people you hope to rouse against this monstrous thing are sufficiently intelligent as to be entitled to a higher form of propaganda!

What is the object of emphasizing the nationality of an offender; to build up a feeling against the offender or against his nationality? The National Association for the Advancement of Colored People is interested in creating an unfavorable public opinion against Perry Howard, but do the leaders Johnson, Du Bois, and Pickens, always refer to their quarry as Mississippian?[3] Emphasizing nationality unfavorably can have only one result, whether it is desired or not, namely, extend public hostility from an individual to his group. Need I amplify this further when it is remembered that one of the greatest grievances of American Negroes is against white newspapers forever stressing the race of colored criminals. Need I point out that the policy you are now pursuing will logically culminate in dissension within the race and, if sufficiently disseminated, make the life of West Indians among American Negroes as unsafe or unpleasant as is the life of American Negroes among their white countrymen?

2. Kelly Miller (1863–1939), prominent African-American mathematician and sociologist.
3. William Pickens (1881–1954), writer, educator, and prominent figure within the NAACP.

The Messenger for which I wrote and which I loved prided itself upon its internationalism and valued this quality as its hall-mark of superiority: but today it seems to have fallen from its former high estate. So international was it that it formulated plans for the guidance of Negroes everywhere and catered to foreign subscribers; today its policy is one that is more intolerant and aggressively anti-West Indian than even those papers that it formerly condemned. Comparisons are odious but they can serve to drive home a point. *The Crisis* is no less opposed to Garvey, but neither Mr Johnson, Mr White, nor Mr Du Bois has forgotten the instincts of fair play, chivalry, and *noblesse oblige*, and appealed to popular protest against wholesale denunciation of West Indians for the sins (!) of one of their group.[4]

How can *The Messenger* reconcile its demand for the deportation of West Indians then un-convicted of crime, made in the November and December issues, with its fight against the deportation of Alexander Berkman, the Russian anarchist, in 1919, a man who had served nearly 20 years in prison for attempting to murder Henry C. Frick, the Pennsylvania steel magnate?[5] How can it reconcile its opposition to a group of Negro aliens while soliciting and accepting financial support from white aliens? And what of the financial, moral, and intellectual support these black aliens gave *The Messenger* and it[s] editors from 1916 to the present time?

And aren't these the same West Indians whom you praised during that period for their independence, radical tendencies, and lack of enervating traditions? Must I conclude that you only admire these traits when they coincide with your interests or promote any cause you espouse? Suppose those who now support the Universal Negro Improvement Association joined the Friends of Negro Freedom, would you sanctify them and render them acceptable to your new-born chauvinism?[6] *Et tu brute?*

It is surprising to learn at the Friends of Negro Freedom that the West Indians are a menace to the progress of American Negroes. Perhaps such careful, modest, and reliable scholars as W. E. B. Du Bois and Carter Woodson, Ph.D., are in error when they stress the part "played by West Indians" in the up-building of the race in this country.[7] Have you ever read the famous passage in *The Souls of Black Folk* in which the author refers to the contributions by West Indians

4. James Weldon Johnson (1871–1938) and Walter White (1893–1955) were both leading members of the NAACP, whose periodical, *The Crisis*, was edited by W. E. B. Du Bois.

5. Alexander Berkman (1870–1936) was a Russian-American anarchist who served 14 years in prison after his unsuccessful attempt to assassinate businessman Henry Clay Frick in 1892 during the Homestead strike. After campaigning against the draft, he was deported in 1919.

6. Friends of Negro Freedom was created by A. Philip Randolph and Chandler Owen to support black-owned businesses and help African-Americans train in the techniques of union organisation.

7. Carter Woodson (1875–1950), African-American historian and journalist; founder of the Association for the Study of African American Life and History.

in the early portion of the last century in formulating the manhood policies of native Negroes? Would the progress of American Negroes be greater without the achievements of foreign-born Negroes like Nathaniel Dett, Bert Williams, Prince Hall, Peter Ogden, Claude McKay, Straker, Crogman, Matzeliger, Russwurm, Marcus Wheatland, M.D., Bishop Derrick, Denmark Vesey, Dr M. A. K. Shaw, Margetson, F. Burton Ceruti, Giles of Ocala, Fla., and hundreds of teachers, doctors, ministers, lawyers, dentists, businessmen, and progressive folk in other walks of life?[8] Since when has meritorious achievement become a detriment to progress? And what of those like James Weldon and Rosamund Johnson, William Stanley Brait[h]waite, and Robert Brown Elliot with foreign-born parents?[9] And Du Bois with his Haitian-Bahamian ancestors?[10] If *The Messenger* is ignorant of these elementary facts, its knowledge of the race it affects to speak for is comparable only with the more complete unacquaintance with facts revealed by its *bête noire*, Marcus Garvey. The sober sense of *The Messenger* must deprecate anything that tends to destroy racial unity upon essential questions like lynching; and viewed by their consequences, would anyone seriously argue that Garvey's ravings are as dangerous to American Negroes [as] the unspeakable and despicable treachery of Perry Howard? Are his words more truckling than Moton's "Be modest and unassuming"?[11] If not, why emphasize the former's birthplace

8. R. Nathaniel Dett (1882–1943), born Canada, composer and musician; Bert Williams (1874–1922), born Bahamas, comedian and entertainer; Prince Hall (1748–1807), birthplace unknown but possibly Barbados, abolitionist and freemason; Peter Ogden (1820?–1870?), born Jamaica, founded the Grand United Order of Odd Fellows; Claude McKay (1890–1948), born Jamaica, poet; D. Augustus Straker (1842–1908), born Barbados, teacher, lawyer, and jurist; William H. Crogman (1841–1931), born Sint Maarten, educator and classicist; Jan Ernst Matzeliger (1852–1887), born Dutch Guiana (now Suriname), inventor; John Brown Russwurm (1799–1851), born Jamaica, abolitionist; Marcus Wheatland (1868–1934), born Barbados, doctor; William B. Derrick (1843–1913), born Antigua, African Methodist Episcopal bishop; Denmark Vesey (1767–1822), born St Thomas, executed for planning a slave revolt in Charleston; Dr Matthew A. N. Shaw (1887–1923), born Jamaica, president of the National Equal Rights League; Edward Henry Margetson (1891–1962), born St Kitts, composer and conductor; Edward Burton Ceruti (1875–1927), born Bahamas, attorney and founder of Los Angeles branch of the NAACP; George Giles (1863–1947), born Bermuda, one of the founders of Marti City and owner of the Ocala Knitting Factory.

9. James Weldon Johnson and his brother, the singer and composer Rosamund Johnson (1873–1954), were born in Jacksonville, Florida, their mother having been born in the Bahamas; William Stanley Braithwaite (1878–1962), literary critic and anthologist, was born in Boston: his father having been born in British Guiana; Robert Brown Elliott (1842–1884), a member of the United States House of Representatives for South Carolina, was probably born in Liverpool; his parents were possibly Jamaican.

10. Du Bois was born in Massachusetts: one of his paternal great-grandfathers was born in the Bahamas, his paternal grandfather in Haiti.

11. Robert Russa Moton (1867–1940) was named principal of Tuskegee Institute after the death of its founder Booker T. Washington. "Be modest and unassuming" were the words attributed to Moton in a famous *Messenger* cartoon, part of a pair that contrasted the "old crowd" Negroes (Moton, Du Bois, Kelly Miller) with "The 'New Crowd Negro' Making America Safe for Himself"; *The Messenger*, 3, no. 9 (September 1919), p. 17.

and ignore that of the latter? Or is discrimination inside the race another newly acquired policy of *The Messenger*?

Let us face certain fundamental facts regarding Garvey. Only so can we arrive at the truth and thus evolve a sound policy. Who are the bitterest and most persistent opponents of Garvey? Aren't they West Indians like Cyril V. Briggs, R. B. Moore, Frank R. Crosswaith, Thomas Potter, and myself? Who caused his arrests and indictments? West Indians: Grey, Warner, Briggs, and Orr![12] Who conducts the *Crusader Service*, Garvey's veritable nemesis? Briggs, assisted by the writer. The January *Crisis*, in justice to truth and elevated journalistic principle, concedes part of the work I did in unmasking Garvey.

Let us view the question from another angle: Who are the journalistic janissaries of Garvey, his intellectual bodyguard who play the role of his *diabolus advocatus advocates*? "Sir" John E. Bruce (Grit), "Sir" R. L. Poston, and "Sir" W. H. Ferris![13] Of what nationality are a majority of those be(k)nighted by Garvey. His Dukes, Ladies, and Clowns? Who subscribed the larger portions of his many funds? (Read the lists in the *Negro World*.) Are West Indians numerous in strongholds like Pittsburgh, Cincinnati, and Cleveland? But these facts do not constitute an indictment of American Negroes. Not a bit. One can understand how a people burdened with the naked and bitter realities of race prejudices and with traditions of despair and suffering will embrace something as chimerical and unsubstantial as the Black Star Line and an empire in Africa. It explains why they respond to Garvey's appeals even as they responded to those of Chief Sam, Bishop Holly, Bishop Turner, and the others related by Woodson in his book on Negro migration.[14] It explains, too, to a degree, the gullibility revealed by William Pickens in his article in *The Nation* a year ago. Mr Pickens, migrating from South Carolina to Arkansas, where he had to be acclimatized, had, buried somewhere in his sub-

12. Edgar M. Grey (1890–1963), born in Sierra Leone of Kittisian parents, joined the UNIA after the demise of his own Foreign-Born Citizens Alliance before becoming one of Garvey's fiercest critics. It was Grey who alerted the New York district attorney to Garvey's sale of Black Star Line stock without a licence, and he testified against Garvey in his 1923 trial. However, in 1921 he'd joined the ABB in order to provide information to the Bureau of Investigation and wrote to the Department of State to warn them of Domingo's radical tendencies. Theodore Kornweibel, Jr described him as possessing "a talent for walking both sides of an ideological street" (*Seeing Red*, p. 141); and see also Ernest Allen, Jr, "The New Negro: Explorations in Identity and Social Consciousness, 1910–1922", in *1915: The Cultural Moment*, ed. Adele Heller and Lois Rudnick, New Brunswick, NJ: Rutgers University Press, 1991), pp. 48–68, at 66–67, n. 44. Richard Warner (1883–1952), born St Kitts, was a reporter for the *New York Amsterdam News* and later an insurance broker; Edward Arnold Orr (1885–?), born Antigua. Both had also been officials in the UNIA before turning against Garvey.

13. Robert L. Poston (1890–1924) was general secretary of the UNIA. William Henry Ferris (1874–1941) was one of the editors of *Negro World*.

14. Carter G. Woodson, *A Century of Negro Migration* (1918). Alfred Charles Sam (1880–1930s?) was a Gold Coast-born merchant and Pan-Africanist who encouraged African-Americans to migrate to Africa, as did African Methodist Episcopalian Bishop Henry McNeal Turner (1834–1915). Bishop James T. Holly (1829–1911) was a proponent of migration to Haiti.

conscious self, some of the pioneer's optimism and became ever so enthusiastic over Garvey as to describe him as being "as brave as a Numidian lion". Mr Pickens has seen the light since.[15]

In the light of the foregone facts, historical and otherwise, is it hoping too much for me to expect that *The Messenger* will change its new policy of shifting personal responsibility to a group and penalizing a people who, despite their many faults and their misfortune in not choosing to be born in Mississippi or Alabama, so well described by Mrs Ratcliff and Clement Wood in *The Nation*, or Arkansas, whose eloquent description by Pickens in the January *Messenger* I richly enjoyed, are, when all is said and done, just as human as their brothers in the United States?[16]

---

15. See above, p. 100, n. 3. Originally an enthusiast for Garvey, as in his article "Africa for the Africans: The Garvey Movement", *The Nation* (28 December 1921), pp. 750–751, Pickens was one of the eight people who sent the 1923 "Garvey Must Go" letter to the US attorney general.

16. Ernest Gruening, editor of *The Nation*, commissioned a series of 56 articles to be published under the general heading "These United States": they included Beulah Amidon Ratliff on Mississippi (17 May 1922, pp. 587–590) and Clement Wood on Alabama (10 January 1923, pp. 33–35). Only one of the published essays was written by an African American—W. E. B. Du Bois's on Georgia: see *These United States: A Symposium*, ed. Ernest Gruening, 2 vols, New York: Boni and Liveright, 1923–24. In response, *The Messenger* commissioned its own series, called "These 'Colored' United States", with 31 essays, including Pickens's on Arkansas, which appeared between January 1923 and September 1926: see *These "Colored" United States: African American Essays of the 1920s*, ed. Thomas Lutz and Susanna Ashton, New Brunswick, NJ: Rutgers University Press, 1996.

13

The American Immigration Law

July 1924

Domingo sometimes wrote letters to *The Gleaner* under the pseudonym "Proletariat" to avoid seeming like even more a serial correspondent than he actually was. Such letters date back at least as far as 1924, as this one shows. Despite his falling out with the editors of *The Messenger*, Domingo is concerned to exempt such African-American periodicals from influencing the terms of the Johnson-Reed Act, signed into law by President Calvin Coolidge on 24 May 1924, which severely restricted immigration into the USA. In their diatribe against Garvey, Randolph and Owen had in fact called for such restriction, but Domingo is undoubtedly correct that the Act's framers needed no such nudges to incorporate the tweak by which the flow of black immigration could be reduced to a trickle.

At this point Domingo seems to think that the USA was applying a 2 per cent rule with respect to the 1890 census, which was the base line on which Johnson-Reed operated. In fact, it was the British authorities who—once they realised they had the power to do so—determined the quotas from each island. Lara Putnam recognises the importance of this letter, although she doesn't identify "Proletariat" as Domingo.[1] Putnam attends to the implications for the immigration of black West Indians into the USA, noting that total black immigration into the USA, made up almost entirely of black West Indians, dropped from over 12,000 in the first six months of 1924 to under 800 in 1925. As so often with immigration laws, the point was to restrict black immigration without seeming to do so, which Johnson-Reed achieved by the simple expediency of charging the colonies and dependencies of European powers to the respective mother countries. This initially caused confusion as it was unclear what proportion of the 34,007 allocated to the United Kingdom might be sub-allocated to the West Indies or

1. Lara Putnam, "Alien Everywhere: Immigrant Exclusion and Populist Bargains, 1920s–1930s", in her *Radical Moves: Caribbean Migrants and the Politics of Race in the Jazz Age*, Chapel Hill, NC: University of North Carolina Press, 2013, pp. 82–122, at 90–92. Other analysis of the 1924 Johnson-Reed Act has focused on the ways in which it attempted to exclude immigrants from southern European and Asians, such as, for example, Mae M. Ngai, "The Johnson-Reed Act of 1924 and the Reconstruction of Race in Immigration Law", in her *Impossible Subjects: Illegal Aliens and the Making of Modern America*, Princeton, NJ: Princeton University Press, 2004, pp. 21–55.

particular islands thereof. When the answer eventually came, the numbers were usually under 100 per island per year.

[Proletariat], "The American Immigration Law", *The Gleaner*, 6 August 1924, p. 8

THE EDITOR

Sir,—From a few belated copies of your paper I have learned of the consternation and hardships caused by the new Immigration Law which places natives of European colonies in the Western world on a quota basis chargeable to the yearly quota allotted to the "mother country" of each colony. That this limitation of immigration to 2 per cent of the number of Jamaicans in the United States in 1890 is tantamount to a complete stoppage of immigrants from the island is obvious when it is remembered that because of their fewness the census of that year made no special enumeration of West Indians.

There is considerable speculation here among West Indians as to the real reason for placing them on a quota basis, especially as they, like Canada and Newfoundland, were exempt under the 1921 quota law. Your correspondent, "Spirochette", in your issue of 30th June, essays the opinion that the inclusion of West Indians is traceable to agitation initiated by American Negro publications. I cannot agree with this, for while it is true that there is considerable friction between the two groups, it is unthinkable (and there is no evidence supporting an affirmative contention) that any considerable number of influential American Negroes who realise their numerical inferiority in this country would do anything that would result in cutting off a desired increase in their own number.

A certain proportion of intelligent (mostly naturalised) West Indians, noting the introduction and passage of a law to restrict emigration from the Leeward Islands and the introduction of a similar law in the Jamaica Legislature at the instance of the Imperial government, and the placing of West Indians on a quota basis if they desire to emigrate to the United States, believe that the latter was done at the request of the British government. From this view I dissent, not because I believe the British government incapable of making such a request, but for the simple reason that I am unable to see what Great Britain could possibly gain from such a step. Besides, the history of the agitation for a restriction of immigration clearly shows the true motives behind the matter.

Agitation against flooding America with immigrants started immediately after the Armistice and was a carry-over of the intense feeling against people who were dubbed as pro-Germans because they were human enough as to remember that they were blood relations of the Central Powers. It was also strongly stimulated by native-born labour because certain aliens, legally exempt from military service because of the neutrality of their country or because they were not obligated to serve as conscripts, reaped a veritable harvest from the high wages obtained in the various war industries. This anti-alien feeling was fanned to a blaze during the latter part of the Wilson administration by the pretended fear that unless restriction was resorted to the country would be overrun by hordes of Bolshevists from Russia. As a consequence Russians were treated by the agents of the Department of Justice, acting under orders of ex-Attorney General Palmer, with a ferocity and brutality that later came in for caustic condemnation from liberal-minded people throughout the country. It was enough for a malicious enemy to denounce a man as a Bolshevist and that man ran the risk of summary arrest, torture by inquisitorial methods, and final deportation. Hundreds of foreigners were so treated, a few dying in custody, while one was known to commit suicide rather than longer endure the infamous "Third Degree" tortures. That these illegal and brutal practices and frequent "Red" scares were but a smoke screen behind which the patrioteers and profiteers carried on their nefarious plundering of the public while posing as 100 per cent Americans is abundantly proved by the numerous suits to recover the millions of dollars stolen by the sale of German property and patents during the administration of A. Mitchell Palmer. Indeed, the revelations of graft made by Senator Burton K. Wheeler, now a candidate for the Vice-Presidency as a running mate with Senator La Follette, came very near having Mr Palmer indicted.[2]

Before the present Immigration Law was passed it was freely asse[r]ted by its leading proponents that they were desirous of admitting only immigrants of North European or, as they were pleased to call them, Nordic stock. Basing quotas on the 2 per cent of the census of 1890, they check the influx of Polish and Italian Roman Catholics, Russian and other Jews, and people of Slavic blood. It is argued that these people are inherently inferior to Anglo-Saxons, and what is most amusing, to Germans, who are a favoured group, and who but six years ago were regarded as "blond brutes", "baby-killers", etc.

It is my opinion that the West Indies are included primarily because believers in the theory of keeping out what is insolently and unscientifically regarded as inferior stock object to the influx of nearly 10,000 coloured persons yearly. Until 1st July these people were free to enter, like all people of the Western world; today they are barred, yet an exception is made in favour of Canada and Newfoundland. Certainly this difference cannot be explained on the basis of status, for although Australia and Ireland are self-governing they are on a quota.

Added to the racial reason I believe that Marcus Garvey and his noisy activities have attracted attention to what many white and coloured Americans regard as the dangerous and disruptive characteristics of West Indians. It is to be noted that in 1914 when an attempt was made to exclude people of African extraction along with Asiatics, American Negroes like Du Bois and the late Booker Washington protested vigorously and successfully against the measure. Up to now

2. Burton Kendall Wheeler (1882–1975), US Senator for Montana from 1923 to 1947.

not a single American Negro has uttered an audible word of protest against the present measure. While American Negroes may have taken no active step to have West Indians barred, it is nevertheless my belief that they are not sorry.

Personally I regret the ban on our immigrants, for despite their many shortcomings and the faults of this country, an opportunity is given the industrious and the ambitious to improve themselves financially and intellectually. With our people prevented from coming here and being forced to shift for themselves at home, it is to be hoped that they will exert themselves a little in an effort to make better conditions for themselves and their progeny.

I am, etc.
PROLETARIAT.
New York City,
25 July 1924

14
The Tropics in New York
March 1925

On Friday 21 March 1924 a number of black writers and intellectuals associated with the journal *Opportunity*—led by its editor, Charles S. Johnson—organised a dinner at the Civic Club in Greenwich Village to provide an opportunity for young black writers to meet white publishers and editors. At least three significant publications followed directly from this dinner: Paul Kellogg asked Alain Locke to co-edit the special issue of *Survey Graphic* that was published as *Harlem: Mecca of the New Negro* on 1 March 1925. Before the special issue even appeared, Albert Boni asked Locke to expand it into a book, published in December 1925 as *The New Negro: An Interpretation*; and that book was so successful that a second edition followed in March 1927. Domingo was not at the Civic Club dinner but was asked by Locke to contribute to the special issue. Claude McKay's poems "The Tropics in New York" and "Subway Wind" appeared in boxes at the foot of the first and fourth columns, both reproduced from his collection, *Harlem Shadows*, New York: Harcourt, Brace, 1922, pp. 8 and 54. Domingo's essay appeared, with small changes, in Locke's *The New Negro* (see above, p. 41).

Survey Graphic, 53, no. 11 (1 March 1925), pp. 648–650

Within Harlem's 70 or 80 blocks, for the first time in their lives, colored people of Spanish, French, Dutch, Arabian, Danish, Portuguese, British, and native African ancestry or nationality meet and move together. A dusky tribe of destiny seekers, these brown and black and yellow folk, eyes filled with visions of their heritage—palm-fringed sea shores, murmuring streams, luxuriant hills and vales—have made their epical march from the far corners of the earth to Harlem. They bring with them vestiges of their folk life—their lean, sunburnt faces, their quiet, halting speech, fortified by a graceful insouciance, their light, loose-fitting clothes of ancient cut telling the story of a dogged, romantic pilgrimage to the El Dorado of their dreams.

Here they have their first contact with each other, with large numbers of American Negroes, and with the American brand of race prejudice. Divided by tradition, culture, historical background, and group perspective, these diverse peoples are gradually hammered into a loose unit by the impersonal force of congested residential segregation. Unlike others of the foreign-born, black immigrants find it impossible to segregate themselves into colonies; too dark of complexion to pose as Cubans or some other Negroid but alien-tongued foreigners, they are inevitably swallowed up in black Harlem. Their situation requires an adjustment unlike that of any other class of the immigrant population; and but for the assistance of their kinsfolk they would be capsized almost on the very shores of their haven.

According to the census for 1920 there were in the United States 73,803 foreign-born Negroes; of that number 36,613, or approximately 50 percent lived in New York City, 28,184 of them in the Borough of Manhattan. They formed slightly less than 20 percent of the total Negro population of New York. From 1920 to 1923 the foreign-born Negro population of the United States was increased nearly 40 percent through the entry of 30,849 Africans (black). In 1921 the high-water mark of 9,873 was registered. This increase was not permanent, for in 1923 there was an exit of 1,525 against an entry of 7,554. If the 20 percent that left that year is an index of the proportion leaving annually, it is safe to estimate a net increase of about 24,000 between 1920 and 1923. If the newcomers are distributed throughout the country in the same proportion as their predecessors, the present foreign-born Negro population of Harlem is about 35,000. These people are, therefore, a formidable minority whose presence cannot be ignored or discounted. It is this large body of foreign-born who contribute those qualities that make New York so unlike Pittsburgh, Washington, Chicago, and other cities with large aggregations of American Negroes.

The largest number came from the British West Indies and were attracted to New York by purely economic reasons. The next largest group consists of Spanish-speaking Negroes from Latin America. Distinct because of their language, and sufficiently numerous to maintain themselves as a cultural unit, the Spanish element has but little contact with the English-speaking majority. For the most part they keep to themselves and follow in the main certain definite occupational lines. A smaller group, French-speaking, have emigrated from Haiti and the French West Indies. There are also a few Africans, a batch of voluntary pilgrims over the old track of the slave-traders.

Among the English-speaking West Indian population of Harlem are some 8,000 natives of the American Virgin Islands. A considerable part of these people were forced to migrate to the mainland as a consequence of the operation of the Volstead Act which destroyed the lucrative rum industry and helped to reduce the number of foreign vessels that used to call at the former free port of Charlotte Amelia for various stores. Despite their long Danish connection these people are culturally and linguistically English, rather than Danish. Unlike the British Negroes in New York, the Virgin Islanders take an intelligent and aggressive interest in the affairs of their former home and are organized to cooperate with their brothers there who are valiantly struggling to substitute civil government for the present naval administration of the islands.

To the average American Negro all English-speaking black foreigners are West Indians, and by that is usually meant British subjects. There is a general assumption that there is everything in common among West Indians, though nothing can be further from the truth. West Indians regard themselves as Antiguans or Jamaicans as the case may be, and a glance at the map will quickly reveal the physical obstacles that militate against homogeneity of population; separations of many sorts, geographical, political, and cultural tend everywhere to make and crystallize local characteristics.

This undiscriminating attitude on the part of native Negroes, as well as the friction generated from contact between the two groups, has created an artificial and defensive unity among the islanders which reveals itself in an instinctive closing of their ranks when attacked by outsiders; but among themselves organization among insular lines is the general rule. Their social grouping, however, does not follow insular precedents. Social gradation is determined in the islands by family connections, education, wealth, and position. As each island is a complete society in itself, Negroes occupy from the lowliest to the most exalted positions. The barrier separating the colored aristocrat from the laboring class of the same color is as difficult to surmount as a similar barrier between Englishmen. Most of the islanders in New York are from the middle, artisan, and laboring classes. Arriving in a country whose every influence is calculated to democratize their race and destroy the distinctions they had been accustomed to, even those West Indians whose stations in life have been of the lowest soon lose whatever servility they brought with them. In its place they substitute all of the self-assertiveness of the classes they formerly paid deference to.

West Indians have been coming to the United States for over a century. The part they have played in Negro progress is conceded to be important. As early as 1827 a Jamaican, John Brown Russwurm, one of the founders of Liberia, was the first colored man to be graduated from an American college and to publish a newspaper in this country; 16 years later his fellow countryman, Peter Ogden, organized in New York City the first Odd Fellows Lodge for Negroes. Prior to the Civil War, West Indian contribution to American Negro life was so great that Dr W. E. B. Du Bois, in his *Souls of Black Folk*, credits them with main responsibility for the manhood program presented by the race in the early decades of the last century. Indicative of their tendency to blaze new paths is the achievement of John W. A. Shaw of Antigua who, in the early 90s of the last century, passed the civil service tests and became deputy commissioner of taxes for the County of Queens.[1]

1. John W. A. Shaw (1859–1909), born in Antigua, also became the head of the United Colored Democracy, the first black Democratic club in New York.

It is probably not realized, indeed, to what extent West Indian Negroes have contributed to the wealth, power, and prestige of the United States. Major-General Goethals, chief engineer and builder of the Panama Canal, has testified in glowing language to the fact that when all other labor was tried and failed it was the black men of the Caribbean whose intelligence, skill, muscle, and endurance made the union of the Pacific and the Atlantic a reality.

Coming to the United States from countries in which they had experienced no legalized social or occupational disabilities, West Indians very naturally have found it difficult to adapt themselves to the tasks that are, by custom, reserved for Negroes in the North. Skilled at various trades and having a contempt for body service and menial work, many of the immigrants apply for positions that the average American Negro has been schooled to regard as restricted to white men only, with the result that through their persistence and doggedness in fighting white labor, West Indians have in many cases been pioneers and shock troops to open a way for Negroes into new fields of employment. This freedom from spiritual inertia characterizes the women no less than the men, for it is largely through them that the occupational field has been broadened for colored women in New York. By their determination, sometimes reinforced by a dexterous use of their hatpins, these women have made it possible for members of their race to enter the needle trades freely.

It is safe to say that West Indian representation in the skilled trades is relatively large; this is also true of the professions, especially medicine and dentistry. Like the Jew, they are forever launching out in business, and such retail businesses as are in the hands of Negroes in Harlem are largely in the control of the foreign-born. While American Negroes predominate in forms of business like barber shops and pool rooms in which there is no competition from white men, West Indians turn their efforts almost invariably to fields like grocery stores, tailor shops, jewelry stores, and fruit vending in which they meet the fiercest kind of competition. In some of these fields they are the pioneers or the only surviving competitors of white business concerns. In more ambitious business enterprises like real estate and insurance they are relatively numerous. The only casino and moving picture theatre operated by Negroes in Harlem is in the hands of a native of one of the small islands.[2] On Seventh Avenue a West Indian woman conducts a millinery store that would be a credit to Fifth Avenue.[3]

2. The Renaissance Theater and Casino, Seventh Avenue was located on the east side of Seventh Avenue between 137th and 138th Streets. The complex, built in 1921, included a casino, ballroom, 900-seat theatre, six retail stores, and a basketball arena. President and general manager was William H. Roach (1881–1963) from Antigua; vice-president and treasurer was Cleo Charity (1889–1964) from Montserrat; and secretary was Joseph Henry Sweeney (1889–1932), also from Montserrat. All three were one-time UNIA members.

3. Probably referring to the Odessa Millinery, 2221 Seventh Avenue, owned by Odessa Warren Grey (1883–1960), whose other claim to fame is as an actress who appeared alongside Bert Williams in the film *Lime Kiln Field Day* (1913). However, Odessa Warren was originally from Ohio.

The analogy between the West Indian and the Jew may be carried farther; they are both ambitious, eager for education, willing to engage in business, argumentative, aggressive, and possessed of great proselytizing zeal for any cause they espouse. West Indians are great contenders for their rights and because of their respect for law are inclined to be litigious. In addition, they are, as a whole, home-loving, hard-working, and frugal. Like their English exemplars they are fond of sport, lack a sense of humor (yet the greatest black comedian of America, Bert Williams, was from the Bahamas), and are very serious and intense in their attitude towards life. Always mindful of their folk in the homeland, they save their earnings and are an important factor in the establishment of the record that the money order and postal savings Departments of College Station Post Office have for being among the busiest in the country.

Ten years ago it was possible to distinguish the West Indian in Harlem especially during the summer months. Accustomed to wearing cool, light-colored garments in the tropics, he would stroll along Lenox Avenue on a hot day resplendent in white shoes and flannel pants, the butt of many a jest from his American brothers who, today, have adopted the styles that they formerly derided. This trait of non-conformity manifested by the foreign-born has irritated American Negroes, who resent the implied self-sufficiency, and as a result there is a considerable amount of prejudice against West Indians. It is claimed that they are proud and arrogant; that they think themselves superior to the natives. And although educated Negroes of New York are loudest in publicly decrying the hostility between the two groups, it is nevertheless true that feeling against West Indians is strongest against members of that class. This is explainable on the ground of professional jealousy and competition for leadership. As the islanders press forward and upward they meet the same kind of opposition from the native Negro that the Jew and other ambitious white aliens receive from white Americans. Naturalized West Indians have found from experience that American Negroes are reluctant to concede them the right to political leadership even when qualified intellectually. Unlike their American brothers the islanders are free from those traditions that bind them to any party and, as a consequence, are independent to the point of being radical. Indeed, it is they who largely compose the few political and economic radicals in Harlem; without them the genuinely radical movement among New York Negroes would be unworthy of attention.

There is a diametrical difference between American and West Indian Negroes in their worship. While large sections of the former are inclined to indulge in displays of emotionalism that border on hysteria, the latter, in their Wesleyan, Methodist, and Baptist churches maintain in the face of the assumption that people from the tropics are necessarily emotional, all the punctilious emotional restraint characteristic of their English background. In religious radicalism the foreign-born are again pioneers and propagandists. The only modernist church among the thousands of Negroes in New York (and perhaps the country) is led by a West Indian, Rev. E. Ethelred Brown, an ordained Unitarian minister, and is largely sponsored by his fellow-islanders.

In facing the problem of race prejudice, foreign-born Negroes, and West Indians in particular, are forced to undergo considerable resentment. Forming a racial majority in their own countries and not being accustomed to discrimination expressly felt as racial, they rebel against the "color line" as they find it in America. For while color and caste lines tend to converge in the islands, it is nevertheless true that because of the ratio of population, historical background, and traditions of rebellions before and since their emancipation, West Indians of color do not have their activities, social, occupational and otherwise, determined by their race. Color plays a part but it is not the prime determinant of advancement; hence, the deep feeling of resentment when the "color line", legal or customary, is met and found to be a barrier to individual progress. For this reason the West Indian has thrown himself whole-heartedly into the fight against lynching, discrimination, and the other disabilities from which Negroes in America suffer.

It must be remembered that the foreign-born black men and women, more so even than other groups of immigrants, are the hardiest and most venturesome of their folk. They were dissatisfied at home, and it is to be expected that they would not be altogether satisfied with limitation of opportunity here when they have staked so much to gain enlargement of opportunity. They do not suffer from the local anesthesia of custom and pride which makes otherwise intolerable situations bearable for the home-staying majorities.

Just as the West Indian has been a sort of leaven in the American loaf, so the American Negro is beginning to play a reciprocal role in the life of the foreign Negro communities, as for instance the recent championing of the rights of Haiti and Liberia and the Virgin Islands, as well as the growing resentment at the treatment of natives in the African colonial dependencies. This world-wide reaction of the darker races to their common as well as local grievances is one of the most significant facts of recent development. Exchange of views and extension of race organization beyond American boundaries is likely to develop on a considerable scale in the near future, in terms principally of educational and economical projects. Former ties have been almost solely the medium of church missionary enterprise.

It has been asserted that the movement headed by the most-advertised of all West Indians, Marcus Garvey, absentee "president" of the continent of Africa, represents the attempt of West Indian peasants to solve the American race problem. This is no more true than it would be to say that the editorial attitude of *The Crisis* during the war reflected the spirit of American Negroes respecting their grievances or that the late Booker T. Washington successfully delimited the educational aspirations of his people. The support given Garvey by a certain type of his countrymen is partly explained by their group reaction to attacks made upon him because of his nationality. On the other hand the earliest and most persistent exposures of Garvey's multitudinous schemes were initiated by West Indians in New York like Cyril Briggs and the writer.

Prejudice against West Indians is in direct ratio to their number; hence its strength in New York where they are heavily concentrated. It is not unlike the hostility between Englishmen and Americans of the same racial stock. It is to be expected that the feeling will always be more or less present between the immigrant and the native born. However it does not extend to the children of the two groups, as they are subject to the same environment and develop identity of speech and psychology. Then, too, there has been an appreciable amount of intermarriage, especially between foreign-born men and native women. Not to be ignored is the fact that congestion in Harlem has forced both groups to be less discriminating in accepting lodgers, thus making for reconciling contacts.

The outstanding contribution of West Indians to American Negro life is the insistent assertion of their manhood in an environment that demands too much servility and unprotesting acquiescence from men of African blood. The unwillingness to conform and be standardized, to accept tamely an inferior status and abdicate their humanity, finds an open expression in the activities of the foreign-born Negro in America. Their dominant characteristic is that of blazing new paths, breaking the bonds that would fetter the feet of a virile people—a spirit eloquently expressed in the defiant lines of the Jamaican poet, Claude McKay:

> Like men we'll face the murderous, cowardly pack,
> Pressed to the wall, dying, but fighting back.

15

Mr W. A. Domingo's Connection with the UNIA

June 1925

In the spring and summer of 1925 Domingo engaged in one of the long epistolary duels in which he clearly took such pleasure. Disturbed by signs of unrest during the local Jamaican elections, the journalist N. A. Parker had written to the governor asking him to rein in the mob. In a letter to *The Gleaner* Domingo objected to what he saw as these hysterical lucubrations, Parker clearly viewing any challenge to the rule of the established Jamaican oligarchy as indicative of imminent descent into anarchy and mob rule.[1] Parker responded, and they went at it hammer and tongs between March and July. Personal insults were exchanged. In his letter of 29 April, Parker accused Domingo of hypocrisy in his attitude to Marcus Garvey, which occasioned this helpful explanation by Domingo of his relationship with Garvey.

Letter to *The Gleaner*, 15 June 1925, p. 10

THE EDITOR:

Sir,—But for the fact that there are several misleading statements in his letter which appeared in your issue of 29th April, I would give N. A. Parker's latest effusion the contempt it so richly deserves by ignoring it. There is an old saying that one can never tell where a fire will end, and the same thing can be said of—well, an inaccurate statement, hence my imposing on your generosity for space to reply to Mr Parker's "comments" on my letter in your issue of 20th ult. "dissecting some of his arguments".

In the first place, be it observed that the doughty patriot has again failed to expose to public opprobrium the demagogue and malignant individuals to whom he had often made reference. He has also failed to explain why he cut the quotation praising Jamaicans at a comma. He has failed to meet a single point I made, but contented himself by claiming that I am a past-master at twisting arguments. It seems to me that I cited the deliberate misquotations and distortions made by honest Mr Parker and challenged him to substantiate his charges of a

1. Nathaniel Alexander Parker (1875–1952), editor of the *Jamaica Mail.*

similar nature made against me. If I am to believe the opinions of a few friends in Jamaica as typical, it would appear that I am, to judge from my controversy with Mr Parker, not altogether incapable of pulverising his arguments.

Mr Parker is clearly an incorrigible individual. He seems to have a notion, presumably an original one, that social progress is predicated upon "singleness of thought" in a community. May I not direct the gentleman's attention to the fact attested to by history that singleness of thought—tribalism—is a sure indication of social stagnation? Need I point to the indubitable fact of sociology that progress is greatest where opinions are diversified? The veriest tyro in that science knows what Mr Parker seems blissfully ignorant of, namely, that society in its development moves from the simple to the complex, or, as Herbert Spencer has it, from the homogeneous to the heterogeneous. In other words, from the single thought to many thoughts. "Singleness of thought" leads to "political quiescence" of the kind in Barbados, and ultimately to isolation from world opinion. The countries that are most progressive are those with warring philosophies and creeds.

Beyond question Mr Parker entertains a dislike for a majority of his countrymen for if he did not he would not be so persistent in making a vicarious transference of my individual act from me to them. I am solely responsible for my acts, and what I do should not be charged to a majority of my compatriots as "one of their deplorable characteristics". Surely, because Mr Parker is oblivious to certain elementary sociological facts and to the unaccustomed necessity for observing the rules usually adhered to by honest controversialists is no reason why I should ascribe his shortcomings to all Jamaicans!

Mr Parker places great importance on the telegram I sent to Mr Mattuck regarding the imprisonment of Marcus Garvey.[2] He thinks that by emphasising this point he can curry favour with the masses of the island. As he is obviously misinformed as to the relationship that existed between Mr Garvey and me, and as his letter contained several statements that are at wide variance from the truth, I am compelled to expose either the ignorance or the mendacity (or both) of Mr Parker.

In the summer of 1918 on the first appearance of the *Negro World*, Mr Garvey engaged me to write two editorials for the paper every week. I consented on the distinct understanding that I should be free to express my personal opinions and not be a propagandist for the UNIA. This Mr Garvey agreed to, as I was not, and never was, a member of his organisation. This does not mean that I disagreed with the programme advanced by Mr Garvey at that time. I agreed with most of it for I believed then as I believe now, that every group of the human family has the right to desire a "place in the sun". However, I did disagree with the wildness

2. Maxwell S. Mattuck prosecuted the mail fraud case against Marcus Garvey. It was reported in the *New York Times* (4 February 1925) that after the guilty verdict Domingo had sent Mattuck a telegram which read "Right-thinking negroes will congratulate you for having caged the tiger at last" (reprinted in *MGP*, 6, p. 87).

of many of Mr Garvey's statements, and insisted that I should have a free hand. Besides, I had known Garvey and had business dealings with him in Jamaica.

I edited the paper for about eleven months. During that time Mr Garvey became very dissatisfied because I did not boost his ideas, so he used the front page of the paper for a signed article setting forth his personal propaganda. So much at variance were our views on the character of his propaganda that he had me "tried" before the executive committee of the UNIA for writing editorials not in keeping with the program he had outlined. I convinced the nine persons who composed the committee that I had not violated the terms of my engagement and they gave me a sustaining verdict. This happened a little after Mr Garvey had launched his idea of the Black Star Line. Prior to this he had asked me to write editorials and speak on street corners in support of the project, and I refused because I believed the undertaking unsound economically. A few weeks after my "trial", I sent him my resignation and stated, among other reasons, that I differed wildly from his methods, which were mediaeval, obscure, and dishonest, even characterising the Black Star Line as "bordering on a huge swindle". That was in the summer of 1919, and I severed my connection with him and the organisation. Be it understood that during that time I had my private business when I was not engaged in the US Postal Service.

Knowing something of the inside of the movement and of Garvey's methods, training, competency, and honesty, I took the stump and openly attacked his ideas in Harlem. In the spring of 1920 I published a weekly newspaper, *The Emancipator*, and devoted ten issues to exhaustive exposure of the philosophical and industrial foundation of the Garvey movement. So vigorous were my attacks that Garvey brought action against me for libel to the tune of $400,000! He did not dare go to trial and the case was thrown out of court last year. Among other things I published the official statement of the Canadian government that the SS *Yarmouth*, first ship of the Black Star Line, was not owned by that company at the time Mr Garvey was advertising all over the world that the boat was the property of his company.

Believing that Garvey by his flamboyant method would influence a few unthinking people in Jamaica, I sent *The Gleaner* several letters exposing him, most of which were published. Whether it is something to be proud of or not, I think that the records will show that I have consistently and vigorously opposed Garvey since he floated the Black Star Line. I have in my possession everything I wrote in the *Negro World*, also copies of *The Emancipator*, *The Messenger*, *The Crusader*, and *The Crisis*, which will bear out my statement that I never wrote a line exhorting the public to invest in a single project of the many that emanated from the fertile, if twisted, mind of Garvey.

When Mr Parker states that I painted roseate pictures about "back to Africa", as well as the launching of a shipping enterprise, and generally, to achieve their aspirations even if they had to wade knee-deep in blood, he proves himself a greater inventor than Baron Munchausen. I can only assign that statement to pure, undiluted imagination prompted by pique at the inability of the writer to meet my arguments, or, if I must be severe, there is only one word—a short and ugly one—that is an apt description.

I challenge Mr Parker, if he is not a peddler of falsehoods, to produce a single piece of writing by me that can justly be regarded as bearing out the statements quoted from his recent letter. It may not be immoral to admonish me, but I am sure that Mr Parker will agree with the respectable opinion of the world that it is decidedly immoral to peddle inaccurate statements.

As for my causing anything to be published in any journal, Mr Parker, a journalist, knows full well that was impossible. If a private telegram to an acquaintance is given publicity without the consent or approval of the sender, it seems to me that the latter should not be blameable for more than the sentiment of the message.

In conclusion, let me express a few more hopes: that Mr Parker will learn a little about social progress, about history, about journalistic ethics, about substantiating statements of a slanderous nature before giving them currency; to refrain from indicting all his countrymen for the failings of a few, from deliberately misquoting, from giving uninvited advice, and, finally, that he will make it a practice in the future to verify every statement before rushing into print.

I am, etc.
W. A. DOMINGO
110 West 143 St,
New York City,
8 May 1925

P.S.—This is my last communication on the subject and I apologise for the personal references which were made necessary by the highly "ethical" methods of my opponent.

16

Letter to Louise Thompson

October 1932

This is the only surviving document written by Domingo about the failure of the Soviet plan to make a film about US racism, and also the only surviving letter which shows any trace of his personal life, to wit the break-up of his marriage with his wife and daughter returning to Jamaica. "Had me all upset" is almost the only truly personal note in the whole of this collection of his writing.[1]

Letter to Louise Thompson (6 October 1932), Louise Thompson Patterson papers, MSS 869, Box 1, file 82, Stuart A. Rose Manuscript, Archives, and Rare Book Library, Emory University, Atlanta

110 West 143rd Street
New York City
6 October 1932

My dear Miss Thompson,

At the outset I must apologize for not answering your letters dated 15th and 25th August before now. Much as I dislike making excuses, I am forced to do so in this case. First, Mrs Domingo and Yolanda sailed for Jamaica early in August, and that fact had me all upset, especially as she took most of the furniture with her in anticipation of permanently settling there. The proposed voyage entailed a considerable amount of shopping which tended to take up a good deal of my time and energy. Following that, the famous dispatch from Moscow to the *Herald-Tribune* alleging that the picture had been abandoned and the members of the group stranded had me all confused and worried for a time.[2]

---

1. On the ill-starred film plan, see Joy Gleason Carew, "Langston Hughes and the *Black and White* Film Group", in her *Blacks, Reds, and Russians: Sojourners in Search of the Soviet Promise*, New Brunswick, NJ: Rutgers University Press, 2008, pp. 115–139; Steven S. Lee, "From Avant-Garde to Authentic: Revisiting Langston Hughes's 'Moscow Movie', in his *The Ethnic Avant-Garde: Minority Cultures and World Revolution*, New York: Columbia University Press, 2015, pp. 119–148; and Meredith L. Roman, "Forging Freedom, Speaking Soviet Anti-Racism: African Americans and Alternate Strategies of Fighting American Racial Apartheid", *Critique*, 39, no. 3 (2011), pp. 365–383. On Louise Alone Thompson Patterson (1901–1999), pioneering black social activist, see Keith Gilyard, *Louise Thompson Patterson: A Life of Struggle for Justice*, Durham, NC: Duke University Press, 2017; on her and Domingo, see ibid., pp. 76–80.
2. "Negroes Adrift in 'Uncle Tom's' Russian Cabin", *Paris Herald Tribune*, 12 August 1932, p. 5.

When I saw the article I went to downtown headquarters and urged the powers that be to send a cablegram demanding a denial or explanation. Three cables were sent before the answer came, which was signed with your name. I turned it over to Briggs and a very good story was made stating the facts as you had advanced them in the cablegram. I also saw Haywood and he told me about Lewis's conduct and his unsavory escapades.[3] The information contained in the cable from you and what I gleaned from Haywood reassured me despite the more damaging second dispatch which contained portions of the minority's appeal to the Comintern. Nevertheless, I was greatly disturbed because I was being bombarded right and left by various people for definite information.

The skeptical ones were quite sure that Russian Communists were no different from white Americans who were not committed to doctrines espousing human brotherhood. Your mother got in touch with me and I did everything possible to set her mind at rest. With the situation as it was, I waited for a letter from you with details and was very glad to get yours of the 25th giving a lucid and chronological review of events in the Soviet Union with respect to the film *Black and White*.

I'm glad that you were very frank in the matter. I cannot truthfully say that I am surprised at the conduct of Poston.[4] What I saw of him at the meetings left me with the impression that he was not a very serious person and that he was given to frivolity and wise-cracking. Lewis I could not appraise. Truthfully, I thought that you knew him well and I trusted to your judgment in the matter. However, I must admit that I thought Moon could hardly be influenced in the way you said he was.[5] Having some contact with the radical movement, I thought he would not allow the internal intrigues of a struggle over authorship to get the better of him.

Of course I am writing from the point of view advanced in your letter. In fairness I will say that Alberga sent me a very long and detailed letter dated the 25th August in which he made as strong a case as possible.[6] The main points were that Col. Cooper, who has easy access to Stalin, tried to dissuade McKenzie from having any part in the picture as it would be hurting America.[7] Alberga also said that the papers (presumably those in Russia) admitted that the picture had been abandoned. This latter point I doubted. I suspect that he assumed that postpone-

3. Harry Haywood (1898–1985) was born Haywood Hall, Jr in Nebraska. After serving in the army during the First World War, he was radicalised by the Red Summer, joining the ABB and then the CPUSA. He spent five years in Moscow and then, as head of the CPUSA Negro Department, led the campaign to free the Scottsboro Boys. Thurston McNairy Lewis (1901–1998) was born in Mississippi and lived in Nashville and Indianapolis before moving to New York in 1932.

4. Theodore Roosevelt Augustus Major (known as Ted) Poston (1906–1974) was at this time a reporter for the *New York Amsterdam News*, later moving to the *New York Post*.

5. Henry Lee Moon (1901–1985) was a colleague of Poston's on the *New York Amsterdam News*. He later worked for the NAACP.

6. Laurence Osmond Alberga (1901–1944), Jamaican agricultural worker.

7. Alan McKenzie (1895–1973), born in British Guiana, was a CPUSA member. Col. Hugh Lincoln Cooper (1865–1937) was a US consultant engineer invited to the USSR to build a hydro-electrical station. He tried to get the film stopped.

ment, as Ralph W. Barnes, who sent the news from Moscow, did, is, in Russia, tantamount to abandonment.[8] In any case I decided that the evidence advanced by the Moon faction was purely circumstantial. On the other hand, your letter contained the positive state that the picture will be made in the spring when a suitable scenario is ready and the Meschrabpom outfit is technically prepared for the work.[9]

Taking everything into consideration and remembering the history of the Soviet Union and the Comintern and the philosophy motivating the entire Communist movement, I find it difficult to believe that there has been any surrender on their part to American or any other kind of race prejudice. Stalin and his followers are fully aware that nothing is to be gained by courting the distrust of the millions of black people in the world; they know instead that for the Communist movement in Russia to be free from the constant fear of intervention it is necessary to make the colonial and other oppressed peoples at least sympathetic to the USSR. It is a great pity that the group could not stick together and always act as a unit. I know you are anxious to know of the effect of the alleged abandonment on work among our people. I think it has hurt. The Negro editors pounced upon the story and broadcasted it all over.

Myra Page's interviews with you and Langston Hughes were fine, but so far as I know confined to the pages of the *Daily Worker*, which paper is unfortunately not very much read by whites, not to speak of Negroes.[10] I think that Meschrabpom should have made a denial and handed it to Barnes with a gentle hint that he encouch it in a dispatch or be in danger of being expelled from the country. I mean that steps should have taken to force the denial being published in the *Herald-Tribune*.

This week's *Amsterdam News* contained the Moon-Poston philippic mailed from Berlin. The *Times* mentioned it. The editor of the *Amsterdam News* wrote an editorial and reinforced it with a vicious cartoon.[11] I think the cumulative consequences will be disastrous. The only way that all this can be overcome, I think, is for the Meschrabpom to make the film in the spring as promised. Failure to do so will be fatal. Remember, the charge is made that the word "postponement" is really a diplomatic way of saying that the picture has been killed. If the picture is made on schedule the lie will have been given to Moon et al., and the Soviet

8. Ralph W. Barnes (1899–1940), foreign correspondent for the *New York Herald-Tribune*.

9. Meschrabpomfilm was the German-Soviet film studio behind the *Black and White* project. It operated from 1922 to 1936.

10. Myra Page was the pen-name of Dorothy Markey (born Dorothy Page Gary, 1897–1993), a Communist writer, activist, and intellectual who had studied with Franz Boas and Melville Herskovits at Columbia University. The poet James Mercer Langston Hughes (1901–1967) was the most eminent of the African-American contingent who travelled to Moscow.

11. T. R. Poston and Henry Lee Moon, "Amsterdam News Reporters Tell Why Soviet Union Dropped Film", *New York Amsterdam News*, 5 October 1932, p. 1.

Union will stand vindicated in the eyes of Negroes while those who believed otherwise will occupy an unenviable position.

Whatever happens now THE PICTURE MUST BE MADE.

I am very pleased to learn from you and Alberga of how well received you have been; and I am delighted to know that you have had an opportunity to travel in the country as honored guests. It is to be hoped that those who obtain jobs will make good and reflect great credit on our race. The terms arranged with the company for your reimbursement, etc., are fair and I believe will be lived up to. Like you I believe keenly that the behavior of a few should have been reprehensible, but in every group there is bound to be "bad eggs". Remember me to the others and accept from me best wishes for continued enjoyment in the vast territories now ruled by workers, for workers.

Sincerely,
W. A. Domingo

PART II

Seeking Freedom: Jamaica, 1936–1947

Firmly believing that any people that has seen its generations come and go on the same soil for centuries is in fact a nation, we pledge ourselves to work for the attainment of self-government for Jamaica, so that the country may take its rightful place as a member of the British Commonwealth of Nations.

Jamaica had never fallen off Domingo's radar. He had business contacts there and clearly kept a close eye on *The Gleaner*. However, his full re-engagement with Jamaica began in the summer of 1936 when he was involved in the foundation of the Jamaica Progressive League (JPL) in New York. Over the next eleven years he visited the island of his birth on three occasions: a short visit in early 1937 and a longer one stretching from late 1938 into the spring of 1939, returning in 1941 for what became a very extended visit indeed after he was first interned without charge for 20 months by the colonial authorities and was then unable to get a visa to return to the USA. The increase in political activity on the island was fuelled by a new newspaper published in Kingston called *Public Opinion*: Domingo wrote for it from the start. After his release from internment, he continued writing for the newspaper, and for others, building a valuable running analysis of the political and labour struggles on the island. Meanwhile, his marriage broke down very publicly in 1943 when, with Domingo still locked up, Eulalie wrote to *The Gleaner* to announce that "Mr Domingo has consistently refused to fulfil his obligations to his family for several years prior to his detention."[1]

* * *

In March 1933 Wendell Malliet founded a new organisation, the West Indian Federation of America (WIFA), with himself as secretary, Joseph C. Morris as president, and Hodge Kirnon and C. H. Powell as vice-presidents.[2] A friendly

1. Eulalie Domingo, "Detainees Defendants' Fund", Letter to *The Gleaner*, 12 January 1943, p. 4. Eulalie sued for divorce, and on 6 October 1943 was granted a decree nisi on the grounds of cruelty. Her house at 5 Osborne Street, Kencot in Kingston, Jamaica and its contents, were put up for auction in December ("Divorce Courts", *The Gleaner*, 7 October 1943, p. 6; "For Sale By Auction", *The Gleaner*, 4 December 1943, p. 18). The decree absolute came on 14 June 1944 ("Divorce Courts", *The Gleaner*, 16 June 1944, p. 12). She continued her career as a pianist and music teacher, re-opening her school as late as 1968. She died in 1988.
2. Joseph C. Morris (British Guiana, 1898–1966) was a lawyer, and Hodge Kirnon (Montserrat, 1891–1962) was a writer and journalist.

interviewer allowed him to outline his views: "the big problem is one of political unity. For, without this union in federation, Dominion status can never be obtained." The islanders are too insular, Malliet claimed, but he thought that the federation movement would gather momentum. He envisaged a large federation: the British West Indies, but also Guiana, Honduras, the Bahamas, and the Bermudas.[3]

Federation had been on the West Indian agenda for many years, but as late as the Wood Report in 1922 on constitutional problems in the West Indies, the official British government view was that federation would simply be "inopportune and impractical" unless there was substantial growth in local support for the idea.[4] In fact, within the Eastern Caribbean local voices had begun speaking in favour of some form of federation from as early as 1912, when the colonial administrator C. Gideon Murray advocated the establishment of a federation of the eastern units on the grounds of administrative efficiency.[5] Domingo would have taken Louis S. Meikle's 1912 book more seriously, both because of his Jamaican origin and on account of his ideal federation consisting of all the British possessions in the Caribbean under "a government by the people for the people".[6]

The next British move came with the recommendation of the West Indian Sugar Commission in 1929 that an administrative union of the Windward and Leeward Islands would make sense. Moving with characteristic speed, the government announced a Closer Union Commission (CUC) in March 1932.[7] Commissioners were appointed in September 1932; their report appeared in 1933—and its recommendations were ignored. Meanwhile, the local Caribbean voices had been getting louder. From 1915 the Grenadan newspaper *The West Indian*, edited by T. A. Marryshow, had been prominent in its support for the idea of federation, soon drawing into its orbit figures such as Alfred Cipriani (Trinidad), Ebenezer Duncan (St Vincent), and C. E. A. Rawle (Dominica)—all from the eastern Caribbean.[8] In October 1932, with the CUC in the offing, the West

3. "Nationalistic Spirit Seen as Basic Need of the West Indies by American Federation", *New York Amsterdam News*, 8 November 1933, pp. 1 and 9. On the long history of the idea of West Indian federation as viewed from outside the area, see Jesse H. Proctor, Jr, "The Development of the Idea of Federation of the British Caribbean Territories", *Caribbean Quarterly*, 5, no. 1 (June 1957), pp. 5–33, and Eric D. Duke, *Building a Nation: Caribbean Federation in the Black Diaspora*, Gainesville, FL: University Press of Florida, 2016.

4. *Report by the Hon. E. F. L. Wood on His Visit to the West Indies and British Guiana*, Cmd. 1679, London: HMSO, 1922, p. 32. Edward Frederick Lindley Wood (1881–1959), 1st Earl of Halifax.

5. C. Gideon Murray, *A United West Indies*, London: West Strand Publishing, 1912.

6. Louis S. Meikle, *Confederation of the British West Indies vs. Annexation to the United States of America: A Political Discourse on the West Indies*, London: S. Low, Marston & Co., 1912. See #35 for Domingo recalling the book.

7. From this point, "Closer Union" was the term preferred by the Colonial Office until the plans for a West Indian federation took final shape.

8. Theophilus Albert Marryshow (1887–1958) was one of the leading West Indian journalists and political figures of the first half of the twentieth century, often referred to as "the father of

Indian Conference, commonly referred to as the Roseau Conference, and hosted by the Dominica Taxpayers' Reform Association, brought many of these figures together and arguably marked the true beginning of the movement that eventually led to The West Indies Federation in 1958.[9] Plausibly, too, though, it led to the failure of that Federation. The argument that the islands' case for self-government would be stronger if they made it together, after discussion, was impeccably logical. However, the participants' assumption that they couldn't hope to become self-governing unless they federated was true, if at all, only for the islands of the eastern Caribbean. The eventual inclusion of Jamaica in the federative framework would alter the picture, as would Britain's eventual decision to dismantle its empire, but the participants would never alter their initial assumption. In any event, that 1932 Roseau conference called for a self-governing federation, and the train was set in motion.[10]

One reason for this federative tide not easily being gainsaid was that it had broad, if uneven, support across the political spectrum. Although Marcus Garvey's focus was more on Africa than the Caribbean, one of the resolutions carried at the Fifth Annual UNIA convention in August 1926 said that "The Confederation of the British West Indies and the responsible home rule should be diligently sought." That resolution was carried by Richard B. Moore to the International Congress Against Colonial Oppression and Imperialism in Brussels in February 1927, where it was underlined by a similarly worded common resolution drafted by Moore to the effect that "The Confederation of the British West Indies should be achieved and the Union of all these peoples accomplished."[11] Also on the radical left, in 1930 Otto Huiswoud described the pursuit of a "Federated West Indies" as a fight for "native rule" of the colonies.[12] And George Padmore was

Federation". Alfred Cipriani (1875–1945) fought with the West Indies Regiment in the First World War before becoming president of the Trinidad Workingmen's Association and oft-times mayor of Port of Spain. Ebenezer Duncan (1876–1968) was a historian and local politician, and Cecil Edgar Allan Rawle (1891–1938) was a lawyer, activist, and newspaper owner.

9. *Proceedings of the West Indian Conference Held at Roseau, Dominica, B. W. I., October-November 1932*, Castries, St Lucia: Voice Printery, 1932.

10. See Duke, *Building a Nation*, p. 85; John Mordecai, *The West Indies: The Federal Negotiations*, London: George Allen and Unwin, 1968, pp. 22–24.

11. The UNIA resolution appeared in the Congress report as "Resolution adopted by the Fifth Annual Convention of the Negro Peoples of the World, New York, August 1–31, 1926", entitled "The Social and Political Status of the Negro Peoples of the World; Means for Its Improvement", League Against Imperialism Archives, https://hdl.handle.net/10622/ARCH00804.54 (accessed 20 April 2019), and the other resolution as "Résolutions communes sur la question nègre", League Against Imperialism Archives, https://hdl.handle.net/10622/ARCH00804.55 (accessed 20 April 2019). The English version appeared as "The Colonial Congress on the Negro", *The Crisis*, 34, no. 5 (July 1927), pp. 165–66.

12. Otto Huiswoud, "World Aspects of the Negro Question", *Communist* (February 1930), pp. 132–147, reprinted (abridged) in Louis J. Parascandola, *"Look for Me All around You": Anglophone Caribbean Immigrants in the Harlem Renaissance*, Detroit, MI: Wayne State University Press, 2005, pp. 246–255.

furthermore on record as proclaiming that *The Negro Champion*, the newspaper of the American Negro Labor Congress, "stands ready to give its full support to a militant movement among the islanders for the federation and the freedom of the West Indies".[13]

Increasingly, too, the colonial government was by no means opposed to a greater degree of federation, although its interest was always more in decreasing the costs of administration than in fostering any nationalistic spirit. Sir Charles Ferguson, the ex-Governor-General of New Zealand, chaired the CUC in 1933, but Jamaica wasn't even on the agenda, and Trinidad was smartly removed after a swift taking of the temperature on the island.[14] Nonetheless, in New York Wendell Malliet seized on the CUC report as an opportunity to foreground "closer union", and WIFA discussed the matter on 17 June 1934 at the Imperial Elks Auditorium on West 129th Street, with Domingo presiding.[15]

A few weeks later, on 1 August 1934, the centenary of the start of emancipation in the West Indies, WIFA hosted an event at St James Presbyterian Church on West 141st Street. Malliet was the chair of the programme committee, and Lucien Brown chaired the day's events, attended by 2,500 people.[16] Joseph C. Morris suggested the federation of the nine crown colonies in the Caribbean "into one self-governing dominion ... in which native sons of the island may hold the highest posts".[17] Calling for "national solidarity", Malliet proposed a national organisation with branches in each of those nine colonies. Here, clearly, the *nation* was intended as the British West Indies as a whole. Eulalie Domingo provided piano entertainment, but this time there was no sign of her husband. Morris followed up with a letter to Ebenezer Ray, the Barbadian-born columnist for the *New York Age*, in which he offered the slogan "The West Indies for West Indians, and all West Indians for a United West Indies".[18] So, broadly speaking, in the Caribbean itself federation was seen primarily as an eastern idea: Jamaica very rarely entered into the picture. But in New York federation meant *all* West

13. *The Negro Champion*, 8 August 1928, p. 12, quoted in Joyce Moore Turner, "Richard B. Moore and His Works", in Richard B. Moore, *Caribbean Militant in Harlem: Collected Writings 1920–1972*, ed. W. Burghardt Turner and Joyce Moore Turner, Bloomington, IN: Indiana University Press, 1988, pp. 19–108, at 82.

14. Her Britannic Majesty's Government, *West Indies: Report of the Closer Union Commission*, C.P. 171 (33), Printed for the Cabinet, July 1933. CAB/24/242, TNA.

15. "Indies Report Will Be Discussed Here", *New York Amsterdam News*, 16 June 1934, p. 6.

16. "Centenary of Emancipation of West Indians to Be Observed at St James' Church Program", *New York Age*, 28 July 1934, p. 3. Dr Lucien M. Brown (1895–1960) was a Jamaican immigrant who had graduated from Long Island College Hospital in 1923. He was a vice-president of the National Urban League and a life member of the NAACP.

17. "New Deal in B.W.I. Sought", *New York Amsterdam News*, 4 August 1934, p. 16. See also "W. Indians in New York Honour Centenary of Emancipation", *The Gleaner*, 17 August 1934, p. 5.

18. Joseph C. Morris, Letter to Ebenezer Ray, in "Dottings of a Paragrapher", *New York Age*, 11 August 1934, p. 6.

Indians, underlined by the prominence in various organisations of the Jamaican Wendell Malliet.

* * *

The spark that lit Domingo's close engagement with Jamaican politics came in early July 1936 at 117 West 120th St in the southern reaches of Harlem, the rather grand home of Jamaican-born Judge James S. Watson, recently elected as the first black judge in New York State. In this instance Malliet was the important link since he was the person approached by the white Jamaican W. Adolphe Roberts, who was seeking an introduction to the black Jamaican community in Harlem. A party was arranged at the house of Judge Watson—Malliet's good friend—and other eminent Jamaicans were invited, including Claude McKay and Wilfred Domingo.[19]

Three years older than Domingo, Walter Adolphe Roberts (1886–1962) had grown up in rural Manchester parish, the son of a downwardly mobile white family. If the National Club was Domingo's formative Jamaican experience, then the early nationalist flourish associated with the Jamaican press at the turn of the century was Roberts's: the short story competitions in which he himself competed and, above all, the example of Tom Redcam at the *Jamaica Times* who was committed to the attempt to develop a native Jamaican literature.[20] By the time Roberts was 17 he had a job on *The Gleaner*. He later recalled that his first assignment was to cover the Legislative Council: "The farcical nature of the proceedings converted me to self-government for the island."[21] Those feelings remained dormant for nearly three decades as Roberts forged a career as a writer and editor in New York, based in Greenwich Village. In the early 1930s he published a biography of the pirate (and governor of Jamaica) Henry Morgan, the book containing an appendix outlining the case for self-government, a case Roberts would often make, in similar form, over the next few years.[22]

19. McKay and Domingo clearly kept in touch during the 1930s: at the beginning of his book on Harlem, McKay thanks Domingo for informal conversation (*Harlem: Negro Metropolis*, New York: E. P. Dutton, 1940, p. vii), and Domingo recalls that McKay sent him a copy of *A Long Way from Home*, published in 1937 ("A Noble Englishwoman", *Public Opinion*, 23 August 1944, pp. 3–4, at 3).

20. Tom Redcam was the pen-name of Thomas MacDermot (1870–1933), poet, novelist, and forthright proponent of the need for a Jamaican literature.

21. W. Adolphe Roberts, "Sir Henry Morgan", *Times Literary Supplement*, no. 1,660 (23 November 1933), p. 840. This would have him converted just before Gilbert Cox started the National Club in Kingston in March 1909.

22. W. Adolphe Roberts, *Sir Henry Morgan: Buccaneer and Governor*, New York: Covici Friede, 1933. W. Adolphe Roberts, *These Many Years: An Autobiography*, ed. Peter Hulme, Kingston, Jamaica: University of the West Indies Press, 2015 is the main source for the early years of the Jamaica Progressive League, supplemented by his scrapbooks and journal (WARA 10.1; 3.3) and by two rather unsatisfactory memoirs: Walter G. McFarlane, *The Birth of Self Government*

After the Watson party, things moved swiftly. Probably through Domingo, Roberts was invited to speak to the British Jamaicans Benevolent Association on 15 July 1936, where he seems to have impressed the membership.[23] Roberts and Domingo arranged to meet again, which they did on 3 August 1936 at the Harlem office of Dr Lucien Brown. The JPL was then formally established on 1 September 1936 with Roberts as president, Domingo as vice-president, and E. Ethelred Brown as secretary. Lucien Brown, the Harlem dentist T. E. Hanson, and the counsellor Stanley McPherson formed an advisory council which quickly faded from the scene.[24] Other early members of the JPL were Ben and Theophilus Burrell (who had worked with Domingo on *The Crusader*), Jaime O'Meally, Ivy Bailey-Essien, Thomas R. Bowen, and F. Theo Reid.[25] Roberts recalled that at this point Malliet refused nomination as secretary and "dropped out of the picture". "Unfriendly critics"—who perhaps included Domingo—" said that he was an agent of the British Consulate General, paid to observe Jamaican activities in Harlem. If so, he had already learned enough to file his report on us."[26]

Roberts wrote the JPL's founding declaration, adopted on 1 September 1936, the words by which he and Domingo lived for the rest of their lives: "Firmly believing that any people that has seen its generations come and go on the same soil for centuries is in fact a nation, we pledge ourselves to work for the attainment of self-government for Jamaica, so that the country may take its rightful place as a member of the British Commonwealth of Nations."[27] This was the first statement of Jamaican nationhood, with no mention of race and with that clever formulation "its generations come and go", which allows into the national picture the migrants who have arrived and those who have left, but might return—such as Domingo and Roberts themselves. The principles articulated in the declaration also included universal adult suffrage, economic and social reform, and an

for Jamaica and the Jamaica Progressive League 1937–1944 [1957], revised edn, Kingston, Jamaica: self-published, [1974], and John S. Young, *Lest We Forget: Based on the Jamaica Progressive League, 1936–1979*, New York: Isidor Books, 1981. The best study is Birte Timm, *Nationalists Abroad: The Jamaica Progressive League and the Foundations of Jamaican Independence*, Kingston, Jamaica: Ian Randle, 2016.

23. Young, *Lest We Forget*, p. 31.

24. Ibid., p. 32. Dr Brown involved himself—as genteelly as possible—in Jamaican nationalism, without ever formally joining the JPL. Theodore E. Hanson (1884–?), a leading Harlem dentist, had previously been chairman of the Caribbean Union. Stanley Gilbert McPherson (Jamaica, 1901–?).

25. Benjamin Ebenezer Burrell (1892–1959) and Theophilus Burrell (1894–1938). Jaime O'Meally (1891–1942), originally James Augustus O'Meally, worked for the UNIA before suing it for unpaid salary. He had married Alejandrina Retamozo, presumably Cuban, in Kingston in July 1915. They may have lived for some time in Cuba since O'Meally was fluent in Spanish. Anna Ivy Bailey Essien (Jamaica, 1892–1989) worked as a stenographer at the children's court. Thomas R. Bowen (Jamaica, 1886–1955?), was a real estate and insurance dealer. Ferdinand Theodore Reid (1891–1973) was a well-known Jamaica-born Harlem physician.

26. Roberts, *These Many Years*, p. 271.

27. Jamaica Progressive League, *Constitution and By-Laws*, 1 September 1936, in EEBP 4/7.

encouragement of the study of the history, geography, and literature of Jamaica. Based on two of his early talks to these meetings, Roberts produced a 16-page pamphlet, *Self-government in Jamaica*, published in New York, which served as the movement's touchstone.[28] The pamphlet starts by simply describing Jamaica's system of government, then reviews the island's political history before looking briefly at other colonies and quoting some expert opinion. It says that the moment has come for Jamaicans to realise that if they are to develop politically, "they must set about the shaping of their own future …. They must begin to act as a people." They *are* in fact a people, Roberts argues, repeating the founding definition: "for national entity is a gift of God to every society that has seen its generations come and go on the same soil for centuries. The awakening of a consciousness of nationality is what is needed today." He then offered some final recommendations: the immediate founding of a political party in Jamaica pledged to work for self-government; and the waging by Jamaicans in Jamaica of a campaign of cultural development. The stated ideal is a *national* one: national sentiment and national consciousness, created through political action and artistic fruitfulness.[29]

As Roberts later recalled:

> We now campaigned in the manner common to all agitators. We rented halls and staged mass gatherings. We lectured on such subjects as libertarian struggles everywhere, the history of government in Jamaica, the abuses of the crown-colony system, and the right of the people to conduct their own affairs. We adopted resolutions, which were sent to the proper authorities in London and Jamaica. We published pamphlets. The meetings were held in Harlem, because we wanted the support of the masses, and most of the Jamaicans we could reach had gravitated, being colored, to Harlem. Nevertheless, a handful of white islanders came.[30]

The anti-colonial contingent among the large West Indian community of Harlem was relatively small: after all, in May 1937 5,000 West Indians turned out for a ball in Harlem to celebrate the coronation of King George VI.[31] And even within this anti-colonial contingent, the JPL was an anomaly. Already by 1936 there had

28. W. Adolphe Roberts, *Self-Government for Jamaica*, New York: Jamaica Progressive League of New York, 1936. Other pamphlets followed: E. Ethelred Brown, *Injustice in the Civil Service of Jamaica*, New York: Jamaica Progressive League, 1937; the collectively authored *Onward Jamaica!*, New York: Jamaica Progressive League, 1937; and Jaime O'Meally, *Why We Demand Self-Government*, New York: Jamaica Progressive League, 1938.

29. Roberts, *Self-Government for Jamaica*, pp. 14–15.

30. Roberts, *These Many Years*, p. 171. In addition, the JPL published a short-lived typewritten journal, *Jamaica Tomorrow*, which seems to have run for three issues. Numbers 2 and 3 (October 1937 and January 1938) can be found in CO 137/827/1, TNA. They were sold at George Young's People's Book Shop at 135 West 135th Street, New York, the address of Domingo's first import firm in 1914.

31. Jervis Anderson, *This Was Harlem: A Cultural Portrait, 1900–1950*, New York: Farrar, Straus and Giroux, 1982, p. 300.

been enough straws in the wind for Domingo and Roberts to understand that they were running against the federation tide by insisting on island self-government for Jamaica as the central policy of the JPL.

Until the early 1950s the JPL's line on federation caused no serious divisions within the ranks of the Caribbean "awaymen". As a white Jamaican, Adolphe Roberts was less involved in the issues that had brought black West Indians and African Americans together; and as a self-identifying liberal, he was no longer involved in left-wing politics. Even he, though, would on occasion have to share platforms with proponents of federation.[32] Domingo had a more difficult line to steer, which during the 1930s he did largely by avoiding organisations and meetings that endorsed the federal idea while himself constantly hewing to the prime importance of self-determination. Nonetheless, the two of them were pretty much on their own in their insistence that self-government and federation were separate ideas, and that the first should take absolute primacy.

However, as the JPL gathered momentum during 1937, the cause of West Indian self-government was undoubtedly helped by the outbreak of labour disputes on several islands, Barbados foremost among them, which prompted the formation in September of the West Indian Defense Committee by the Barbadian-born journalist Reginald Pierrepointe.[33] Other prominent members included Moore, Petioni, Morris, Osborne, Malliet, and Watson. A mass meeting was called for 31 October to protest "against the wanton slaughter of West Indians in Trinidad-Barbados-Jamaica-St Kitts and the Bahamas".[34] Further meetings took place before the end of the year, ensuring that the attention of New York West Indians was firmly focused on the islands.[35]

32. So, for example, at a meeting to celebrate the 103rd anniversary of Emancipation, Roberts derided the absurdity of Crown Colony government while Vernal J. Williams spoke in favour of federation ("West Indians Celebrate", *New York Times*, 2 August 1937, p. 4). Vernal J. Williams (1896–1952) was a Jamaican-born lawyer, once prominent in the UNIA, and a founder of the Consolidated Tenants League.

33. See O. Nigel Bolland, *On the March: Labour Rebellions in the British Caribbean, 1934–39*, Kingston, Jamaica: Ian Randle/London: James Currey, 1995; "Troubled West Indies Are Aided", *New York Age*, 18 September 1937, p. 12. Reginald St Aubyn Pierrepointe (1898–1984) emigrated to New York in 1920 after serving with the British Expeditionary Forces in Egypt and Palestine. He studied journalism and engineering, then worked for the *New York Amsterdam News* and established the West Indies News Service, ending his career at the American Broadcasting Corporation.

34. "West Indian Defense Committee (U.S.A.). Protest Mass Meeting", *New York Amsterdam News*, 30 October 1937, p. 2.

35. See "Sunday Afternoon, 500 People Met at Dunbar Place", *New York Amsterdam News*, 4 December 1937, p. 23; Ebenezer Ray, "Dottings of a Paragrapher", *New York Age*, 25 December 1937, p. 6. A different organisation, though involving some of the same individuals, was the American-West Indian Defense Committee: see "Correction", *New York Amsterdam News*, 2 July 1938, p. 5. The American-West Indian Defense Committee was actually a committee of the National Negro Congress, founded by Max Yergan: see Ken Post, *Arise Ye Starvelings: The Jamaica Labour Rebellion of 1938 and Its Aftermath*, The Hague, the Netherlands: Nijhoff, 1978, quoting US State Department Memorandum 18, 1 July 1938, 844G.00/26, NARA.

* * *

After the successful launch of the JPL in New York, Roberts, Domingo, and Brown all realised that the next stage in the process was to take their message to Jamaica: they knew perfectly well that any political party pushing for self-government needed Jamaican roots.[36] In February 1937 Ethelred Brown announced that the JPL would be seeking to establish itself on the island.[37] Domingo arrived in Jamaica on 6 February and stayed until 26 March. There's no record of his activity during these six weeks but this was precisely when the new weekly newspaper *Public Opinion* was launched, with its first issue on 20 February, so it seems likely that he had contact with at least some of the group involved: O. T. Fairclough, Frank Hill, Ken Hill, Richard Hart, and H. P. Jacobs.[38] On 20 March the newspaper published a piece quoting extensively from Roberts's pamphlet, which Domingo had almost certainly brought with him to the island.[39] Then, while Domingo was in Jamaica, the *Gleaner* journalist Ken Hill wrote an impassioned column about the need to emulate the JPL by forming a Jamaica National Movement to press for economic and political reform, which he duly created on 31 March.[40] By the

36. While Domingo and Roberts had been away, various political reform movements had flourished and faded in Jamaica: the Jamaica League (founded 1913), the Jamaica Representative Government Association (1921), and the Jamaica Reform Club (1923). Domingo wrote in support of this last short-lived venture ("Work of the Reform Club Appreciated", Letter to *The Gleaner*, 5 June 1924, p. 8). Then, more equivocally, there was Marcus Garvey's People's Political Party (1929). On all of these, see Timm, *Nationalists Abroad*, pp. 9–21.

37. E. Ethelred Brown, "Jamaica Progressive League", *The Gleaner*, 15 February 1937, p. 12. Although Brown here gave an early indication of his tendency to stray from the official JPL line when he announced that when the JPL asks for self-government "it is really asking for a restitution of the Constitution that was surrendered in 1865": that was not what Roberts and Domingo had in mind.

38. On the early years of *Public Opinion*, see Raphael Dalleo, "The Public Sphere and Jamaican Anticolonial Politics: *Public Opinion, Focus*, and the Place of the Literary", *Small Axe*, 14, no. 2 (June 2010), pp. 56–82. Domingo's first piece for the newspaper appeared in June 1937. Osmond Theodore Fairclough (1904–1970) was a black banker who was one of the key figures behind the formation of the People's National Party. He had previously worked in Haiti's National Bank for eight years. Ken Hill (1909–1989) was an outspoken and eloquent journalist, trade unionist, and politician with connections at various points in his career with Bustamante Industrial Trade Union, the People's National Party, and the Jamaica Labour Party. His brother, Frank Hill (1902–1980), was a nationalist, intellectual, and maverick who later became chairman of the board of governors of the Institute of Jamaica under a Jamaica Labour Party government. Born in Yorkshire, Hedley Powell Jacobs (1904–1985) was a Fabian socialist who taught history at Jamaica College and was president of the Jamaican Historical Society. For the political background to Domingo's time in Jamaica in the late 1920s and 1940s, see Richard Hart, *Towards Decolonisation: Political, Labour and Economic Development in Jamaica, 1938–1945*, Kingston, Jamaica: Canoe Press University of the West Indies, 1999.

39. "The Jamaica Progressive League", *Public Opinion*, 20 March 1937, p. 12.

40. Ken Hill, "Things We Need", *The Gleaner*, 9 March 1937, p. 6; "National Movement Launched", *The Gleaner*, 3 April 1937, p. 10. Present at the launch were Fairclough, N. N. Nethersole, Hugh C. Buchanan, Una Marson, and Eulalie Domingo. Noel Newton Nethersole (1903–1959), known affectionately as Crab, had been a Rhodes scholar and was a keen cricketer

end of the year Domingo had published four pieces in *Public Opinion*, including "The Case for Self-Government" [#17]. *Public Opinion* remained Domingo's main outlet over the next ten years. His contributions fall into two periods separated by his internment. There were 31 between June 1937 and March 1941, and an astonishing 686 between February 1943 and August 1947. The 13 that we reprint here are therefore just a small selection from a large body of journalistic work just for this single newspaper.

After seeing a notice in *The Gleaner* of a JPL meeting in New York, Walter McFarlane—who himself had recently returned to the island after 13 years in the USA and had been involved with the local Federation of Citizens' Associations (FCA)—wrote to New York to ask whether he could start a Jamaican branch of the JPL.[41] Co-ordinating their plans, McFarlane set up a launch meeting in Kingston for 27 November, with Roberts due to arrive on the island a week later. On his arrival on 2 December Roberts was interviewed by Ken Hill and allowed to present his views, not least on the need for a nationalist party to press for self-government.[42] Roberts first addressed the local JPL group on 15 December at the Metropolitan Hall, reading the JPL's Declaration and its objectives and stressing its commitment to self-government as a dominion.[43] The first monthly meeting of the Kingston wing of the Jamaica Progressive League (JPL(K)) took place on 30 December 1937.[44] Roberts left Jamaica early in the new year. Meanwhile, the Jamaican authorities had kept a close eye on the JPL. The local Criminal Investigation Department (CID) obtained a copy of *Jamaica Tomorrow* and asked the New York Police for a report on the activities of the JPL, which the governor, Edward Denham, forwarded to the Colonial Office.[45] From New York Domingo closely followed events in Jamaica, contributing to a discussion in *Public Opinion*

and solicitor who became a leading light in the PNP. Hugh Clifford Buchanan (1908–1964), a mason by profession and a Marxist by belief, who had been a member of the UNIA in Cuba in the 1920s, co-founded with A. G. S. Coombs the Jamaica Workers and Transport Union in 1936 and was general secretary of the BITU. A founder member of the PNP, he later formed the Progressive Independent Party to fight federation. Una Marson (1905–1965) was a black feminist with a career full of achievements despite a difficult life marred by depression. She turned her hand to many forms of writing: journalism, editing, poetry, playwriting, as well as working for the BBC during the Second World War. She would later found the Pioneer Press before handing over to W. Adolphe Roberts when she left Jamaica to live in Washington, DC. Others involved were Richard Hart and H. P. Jacobs. The movement soon changed its name to the less ringing National Reform Association and in September 1938 folded itself into the new People's National Party.

41. "Jamaica Progressive League Celebrates Its First Anniversary", *The Gleaner*, 23 September 1937, p. 19. Confusingly, a local community organisation already existed, called the Jamaica United and Progressive League.

42. Ken Hill, "W. Adolphe Roberts Says: Seek Self-Government", *The Gleaner*, 7 December 1937, p. 12.

43. "Self-Govt. for Jamaica", *The Gleaner*, 22 December 1937, p. 23.

44. "League to Work for Self Govt.", *The Gleaner*, 5 January 1938, p. 8.

45. Edward Denham, Letter to W. C. A. Ormsby-Gore, Secretary of State for the Colonies, 22 March 1938, CO 137/821/16, TNA.

between Richard Hart and Jaime O'Meally over the relevance of the JPL's programme to the problems facing Jamaica [#18].

The period between Domingo's first two returns to Jamaica was momentous. Labour riots at the beginning of May 1938 on Frome Estate, owned by the West Indies Sugar Co., were met with extreme police brutality, leading to further strikes and solidarity protests across the island. Kingston was soon paralysed, with most shops closed and public transport severely disrupted.[46] The labour disputes across the island created widespread unrest and a new generation of political activists began to flex their muscles. As the situation in Jamaica erupted into violence, it was Wendell Malliet who reported the news and gathered together the outrage of prominent Jamaicans in New York.[47] Domingo had to rely on newspaper reports, supplemented by correspondence with Richard Hart. Meanwhile, he pushed ahead with growing the JPL in New York, addressing a series of meetings during the summer.

Discussions over the formation of a political party in Jamaica, soon given the name People's National Party (PNP), under the leadership of Norman Manley, took place in the spring and summer of 1938. Manley was trying to draw various interest groups together and didn't want to commit to immediate self-government even if he privately made it clear that he thought the new party should work *towards* such a target.[48] With Roberts and Domingo in New York, the JPL's position was represented in the discussions leading up to the founding of the PNP by McFarlane, who was elected to three of the early planning committees and the original steering committee, where his was—according to his own account—the only voice strongly in favour of self-government.[49] The PNP was formally constituted on 18 September 1938, with its key opening conference scheduled for the following April. Domingo immediately welcomed this development in *Public*

46. See Hart, *Towards Decolonisation*, pp. 8–18.
47. For example, in A. M. Wendell Malliet, "Harlem's Jamaica Colony Shocked by Sugar Cane Field Shootings of Fifty", *New York Amsterdam News*, 14 May 1938, p. 5; and "Warns England of Possible Rebellion in West Indies", *New York Amsterdam News*, 20 August 1938, p. 7. For analysis, see Richard Hart, *Rise and Organise: The Birth of the Workers and National Movements in Jamaica (1936–1939)*, London: Karia Press, 1989; O. W. Phelps, "Rise of the Labour Movement in Jamaica", *Social and Economic Studies*, 9, no. 4 (December 1960), 417–468; O. Nigel Bolland, "Jamaica", in his *On the March*, pp. 132–166; David Scott, "Memories of the Left: An Interview with Richard Hart", *Small Axe*, 3 (March, 1998), pp. 65–114.
48. Norman Manley, Letter to E. Ethelred Brown, 15 September 1938, NMP, 4/60/2B/2 [NMP = Norman Manley Papers, Jamaica Archives and Records Department, Spanish Town, Jamaica]. Norman Washington Manley (1893–1969) was one of Jamaica's leading lawyers. With his cousin and rival Alexander Bustamante, he would dominate Jamaican politics over the next 30 years, serving as the colony's chief minister from 1955 to 1959 and as premier from 1959 to 1962.
49. McFarlane, *Birth of Self-Government*, p. 23. On this period, with some attention to the JPL in Kingston, see Post, *Arise Ye Starvelings*, pp. 221–237. For Manley's perspective, see Rex Nettleford, "Manley and the Politics of Jamaica: Towards an Analysis of Political Change in Jamaica, 1938–1968", *Social and Economic Studies*, 20, no. 3 (September 1971), pp. 1–72. On the establishment of the PNP, see Hart, *Towards Decolonisation*, pp. 30-32.

Opinion [#19]. A further essay for *Opportunity* [#20] brought his US readers up to date with a summary of the labour disturbances, the resulting social ferment, the Moyne Commission (the West Indian Royal Commission, headed by Walter Guinness, 1st Baron Moyne, established after the recent unrest to investigate conditions in the region), and the history of Jamaica from 1865 to the recent founding of the PNP: "The Party is a coalition of the various progressive organizations in the island, including the Jamaica Progressive League. Self-government is the goal of the Party." That was what Domingo wanted the party's goal to be, but not as yet how Manley was describing it: "I do not say that I think Jamaica is to-day ripe for self-government."[50] Manley's February 1939 memorandum on constitutional change talked about "a real measure of" (that is, not complete) "self-government after four to eight years", a much more extended time scheme than Domingo and Roberts had in mind.[51]

The big JPL guns would all soon visit the island again. On 11 September in New York the JPL held what was advertised as a "History-Making Mass Meeting" under the title "Revolution in Jamaica" in which "All Patriotic Jamaicans" were invited to hear the programme that Brown was taking with him to Kingston to present to the Moyne Commission. Brown arrived on the island on 23 October, the commissioners on 1 November. Brown carried with him two pamphlets: the statement of their main aim, W. Adolphe Roberts's pamphlet *Self-government for Jamaica*, and another containing a new programme formulated by the JPL that August, which advocated, *inter alia*, civil liberties, a minimum wage, pensions for all, unemployment insurance, compulsory elementary education, establishment of a University of Jamaica, and forest protection, positioning the JPL as something much more than a one-issue pressure group.[52] However, with the local JPL members diffident, Brown found it impossible to successfully convey to Moyne the views he was there to represent; a hastily written supplementary memorandum didn't even mention self-government. Neither, for that matter, did the PNP's submission: it just stressed that it was in favour of gradual reform.[53] Brown left the island on 20 November, having achieved little.

50. "Jamaica Not Ripe To Manage Own Affairs", *The Gleaner*, 19 September 1938, p. 7. Manley repeated the sentiment at a speech in St Thomas on 5 November 1938.
51. Arthur Richards, Letter to Malcolm MacDonald, Secretary of State for the Colonies, 24 February 1939, CO 137/834/7, TNA, enclosing Norman Manley, "Memorandum for Constitutional Change for Jamaica" (9 February 1939).
52. McFarlane, *Birth of Self-Government*, pp. 57–62; "Dominion Status Sought in Memorandum to Royal Commission", *The Gleaner*, 2 November 1938, p. 6; *We Advocate a Social and Economic Programme for Jamaica*, New York: Jamaica Progressive League of New York, 1938.
53. See the detailed account in Timm, *Nationalists Abroad*, pp. 151–157. *Supplementary Memorandum of the Jamaica Deputation Committee under the Auspices of the Jamaica Progressive League Presented to the West Indies Royal Commission 1938*, signed by Ethelred Brown and W. G. McFarlane, EEBP 4/6.

Figure 7 "Revolution in Jamaica". Poster advertising a meeting of the Jamaica Progressive League to be chaired by W. A. Domingo on 11 September 1938. (Courtesy of the W. Adolphe Roberts Archive, MS353, National Library of Jamaica)

* * *

The JPL strategy at this point was to ensure that the PNP—yet to fix its political platform in any detail—would declare itself in favour of self-government. In a long letter to the *Gleaner*, Domingo prepared the way, recapping the brief history of the JPL and associating it with Manley and the PNP.[54] Domingo then arrived in Jamaica on 11 December 1938, and Roberts on 1 January 1939, bring-

54. W. A. Domingo, "Self-Government for Jamaica", Letter to *The Gleaner*, 8 December 1938, p. 5.

ing with them stacks of the four JPL pamphlets published in New York to be circulated across the island. The close relationship between the JPL and the PNP was also emphasised in Roberts's first interview after his arrival: the differences between them over self-government were a matter of timing, not substance, he suggested, and the JPL "feels itself affiliated with the PNP and will support it". And he himself would, he said, after a short return to New York later in 1939, settle permanently in Jamaica and eventually qualify for election as member for one of the parishes on the Legislative Council.[55]

The local JPL had a welcome meeting at which Norman Manley spoke alongside Roberts and Domingo, setting the tone for the months to come. In this speech Manley gave his fullest acknowledgement of what he (and therefore the PNP) owed to Roberts and Domingo. He noted that he didn't claim to have originated the idea of a national Jamaica nor that of self-government—"which was the logical and inevitable corollary of the progress they had made", only to have recognised, and that in a tardy fashion, the value of the ideas that Roberts had outlined to him in his chambers a year ago. The ultimate aims and ambitions of the JPL and the PNP were now identical, Manley concluded.[56] This was not, however, exactly what Manley would put into practice at the forthcoming PNP conference. In his own speech Domingo recalled his participation in the National Club, and mentioned recognising the faces of old schoolfriends in the audience: "He had never lost touch with his native land", he was reported as saying. Domingo threw himself into working for the PNP and was elected second vice-chairman of the party's Metropolitan Group.[57] Domingo and Roberts were now both prominent in PNP meetings, Domingo often chairing them.[58] Stuart Hall calls the movement of "the national progressive wing" in Jamaica between 1938 and 1944 "one of the most audacious political attempts ever tried in the history of decolonisation".[59] Domingo was at the heart of that movement; indeed, arguably he was one of its chief ideologists.

The other figure who had come to the fore during 1938 was Alexander Bustamante (1884–1977). Born William Alexander Clarke, a cousin of Norman Manley's, Bustamante said that he took his surname to honour a Spanish sea captain he claimed had adopted him during his youthful years of travelling. At the age of 48 he returned to Jamaica, setting himself up as a money lender and

55. "Progressive League Chief Here on Visit", *The Gleaner* 3 January 1939, p. 11.
56. "Self-Government for Jamaica Stressed at Welcome to Progressive League Leaders", *The Gleaner*, 9 January 1939, p. 21. For that meeting in chambers, see Roberts, *These Many Years*, p. 276.
57. "City Group of People's Party Elects Officers", *The Gleaner*, 28 December 1938, p. 9.
58. For example, on the evening of Monday 13 February 1939: see "Much Interest at City Party Group Meeting", *The Gleaner*, 15 February 1939, p. 21.
59. Stuart Hall, "Through the Passage of Time", in *The Norman Manley Memorial Lectures, 1984 and 1986*, London: Norman Manley Memorial Lecture Committee, 1986, pp. 7–20, at 11–12.

gaining a local reputation through his frequent letters to the press. In 1937 he was elected treasurer of the Jamaica Workers' Union, founded by labour activists Allan G. S. Coombs and Hugh C. Buchanan, but during the 1938 labour rebellion, thanks to his fiery oratory, he became identified as the spokesman for striking workers, soon re-organising the union as the Bustamante Industrial Trade Union (BITU).[60] On 14 February 1939 Bustamante responded to a minor clash in Montego Bay by calling a general strike, precipitating the declaration by the governor, Sir Arthur Richards, of a state of emergency. Manley used his influence with Richards, who allowed him some leeway to try to persuade Bustamante to call off the strike. Manley asked Domingo and Roberts, along with the black barrister E. E. A. Campbell, to talk to Bustamante.[61] On the night of 17 February they presented an agreed compromise to him: a mass meeting would enunciate a programme of unified action on behalf of the working classes; Bustamante would read a prepared address, accepting the authority in labour disputes of the new Trades Union Advisory Council (TUAC), of which he would be a member; and he would call off the strike.[62] Grudgingly, Bustamante assented: the strike was immediately ended. On Tuesday 21 February Domingo chaired the mass meeting at the Kingston race course: 10,000 people attended, the most ever to that date at a single event in Jamaica. Bustamante strayed from his script, but duly announced the members of the Advisory Council, which included Domingo and Roberts, supposedly "selected" by him, but in fact imposed upon him.[63] Bustamante was temperamentally incapable of working on equal footing with others, and he and Domingo soon clashed. At the end of April Bustamante withdrew from TUAC in order to plough his own union furrow, and TUAC morphed into the Trade Union Council, a PNP organisation for all unions not within BITU. This set the scene for the fearful symmetry of Jamaican politics: if the PNP was going to have an affiliated union organisation, then the rival union organisation must have an affiliated political party, although it would take four years before that came to pass. Roberts and Domingo both had a low opinion of Bustamante, Domingo calling him "an unmitigated charlatan".[64]

At the first annual meeting of the JPL(K) in Kingston at the end of February 1939, Roberts was elected president and affirmed the strategy of supporting the PNP while retaining the JPL's own identity. He also announced the educational and cultural campaign to "Jamaicanise Jamaica", perhaps suggesting that the JPL

60. Allan George St Claver Coombs (1901–1969), trade unionist.

61. Ethelred Erasmus Adolphus Campbell (1888–1969). After originally training as a biochemist, Campbell became a barrister and a leading figure in the FCA. For the cousinly rivalry between Manley and Bustamante, see Colin A. Palmer, *Freedom's Children: The 1938 Labor Rebellion and the Birth of Modern Jamaica*, Chapel Hill, NC: University of North Carolina Press, 2014.

62. Roberts, *These Many Years*, p. 293.

63. Ibid., p. 294.

64. W. A. Domingo, Letter to W. Adolphe Roberts (21 July 1939), WARA 2.3.5.

was beginning to see itself as the cultural wing of the PNP rather than as an electoral force in its own right.[65] A campaign was launched at the end of April 1939, and a Research Committee formed—though one senses in the newspaper reports some impatience on Roberts's part at the lack of progress: the project only really bore fruit after the war, when Roberts finally settled in Jamaica and made this cultural work his career.[66]

Although Roberts and Domingo never quarrelled and seemed instinctively to know the importance of a united front in the struggle to get self-government onto the political agenda, their characters, inclinations, and wider politics were not identical. Roberts was more single-minded, in that for him self-government was the be-all and end-all: he was chary of confusing the issue by embracing unionism and working-class struggle. They'd both been socialists—if of very different kinds—in their twenties in New York, but Domingo's Leninist sympathies remained, and found some echo in the left-wing circles of the PNP, while Roberts was now happy to style himself as a liberal in general political ideas. Roberts also realised that while Domingo was a fine stump speaker, his own style and temperament made any kind of electoral victory unlikely. He was also—perhaps most important—a writer with a book to finish, so he withdrew in March 1939 to a house outside Kingston to write; while Domingo had taken a divergent route in December 1938 by joining the editorial staff of the *Jamaica Labour Weekly* whose Marxist editors, H. C. Buchanan and Stennet Kerr Coombs had been imprisoned for seditious libel of the police.[67] He now had two outlets for his writings—with different readerships—and the *Jamaica Labour Weekly* began to enthusiastically embrace the idea that self-government was essential for the improvement of the lot of the working class. However, when released from prison in April 1939, Kerr Coombs, who owned the press, was not best pleased with the rest of the staff, and so Domingo's involvement proved short-lived.

At the PNP conference in April 1939, Domingo, Roberts, and McFarlane had to fight for the principle of immediate self-government to be party policy.[68] Initially reluctant, Manley was eventually persuaded, although his lawyerly skill seems to have found a form of words that, as Birte Timm explains, offered "a sophisticated

65. "League Re-Affirms Pledge to Back P.N.P.", *The Gleaner*, 28 February 1939, p. 13.

66. "Progressive League to Start New Drive", *The Gleaner*, 22 April 1939, p. 7; "Jamaica Progressive League Leader Presents Programme", *The Gleaner*, 1 May 1939, p. 20; "Research Work on Island's History Planned by League", *The Gleaner*, 31 July 1939, p. 4. However, there was a public function in honour of Edward Jordon in February 1940 with Manley giving the keynote speech ("City Folk Pause to Pay Tribute to Great Jamaican", *The Gleaner*, 9 February 1940, pp. 1 and 7). Edward Jordon (1800–1869) was a leading campaigner for the rights of free people of colour. With Robert Osborn he started a bookshop and then launched a newspaper, *The Watchman*, the first to represent the views of the Jamaican free coloured population, forging ties with the humanitarian movement and the Anti-Slavery Society in England.

67. Stennet Kerr Coombs (1911–1993), Garveyite and labour activist.

68. See the account in Timm, *Nationalists Abroad*, pp. 179–186.

representation of the agreement at the conference that left room for a more moderate interpretation".[69] In the years ahead, the New York branch of the Jamaica Progressive League (JPL(NY)) was rarely satisfied with PNP commitment to the cause of self-government. The JPL(K) affiliated with the PNP while keeping a separate identity, but there was considerable cross-membership, and McFarlane was elected a member of the PNP General Council, a post he held until 1947.

FAREWELL TO P.N.P. ORGANIZER

Scene at Esquire restaurant Friday night when a smoker was given in honour of Mr. W. A. Domingo (right) 2nd. Vice-President Metropolitan Group of the People's National Party. Mr. N. N. Nethersole (standing) was toast master; Mr. N. W. Manley, K.C., Party leader, (second from left) proposed the health of the guest of honour. Third from left is Mr. W. Adolphe Roberts, colleague of Mr. Domingo, in the Jamaica Progressive League.

Figure 8 "Farewell to P.N.P. Organizer". Photograph taken at Domingo's farewell dinner in Kingston on 21 April 1939. (*The Gleaner*, 24 April 1939, p. 21)

When Domingo was about to leave Jamaica in April 1939, he was given a warm send off by the PNP at a mass meeting in Metropolitan Hall and a dinner and reception at the Esquire restaurant. Norman Manley made the main speech. "He had often wondered", Manley was reported as saying, "why it was [that] the Jamaicans who had been abroad were far more appreciative and devoted to Jamaica than they who had spent their lives at home." Manley suggested two reasons. First, that going abroad allowed for a "true picture of what Jamaica was like". Second, "a Jamaican abroad got a truer picture of the relationship between Jamaica, its political life and its problems. They see similar problems on a bigger scale in other parts of the world" and despair that Jamaicans were not doing more to solve their own problems.

Replying to the warm tributes, Domingo said that "Ever since he had left the island he had always hoped to return to take part in bettering the conditions of his

69. Timm, *Nationalists Abroad*, p. 183.

countrymen."[70] He promised to act as a PNP ambassador in the USA and to return for the 1940 elections. Over the summer, the main political event on the island was a protest against the new law giving the governor the power to ban public meetings, a harbinger of the wartime powers that would shackle anti-colonial activity. Roberts—still in Jamaica—presided over a meeting where Manley gave a powerful speech against the law, and back in New York Domingo organised a meeting in sympathy, denouncing the law as unnecessary and repressive.[71]

The outbreak of war in Europe stymied everybody's plans. Roberts left Jamaica on 20 August for New Orleans to do work on the French and Spanish sections of his book on Caribbean history, intending to return at the end of the year. In the event, he sat out the war in New Orleans, writing a trilogy of historical novels. Domingo would return to Jamaica, but not until June 1941.

* * *

With Roberts in New Orleans, Domingo assumed effective control of the JPL in New York and was clearly the driving force behind the resolutions adopted at its meeting on 24 September 1939 in which it pledged support for the British government in its fight against Nazism while nevertheless declaring "that it does not abate its campaign or abdicate its right to struggle for self-government for Jamaica in order that the people of the island may enjoy some of the political blessings for which they are willing to make the supreme sacrifice on behalf of others".[72] Meanwhile, the PNP decided to refrain from agitation for constitutional reform for the duration of the war as a show of loyalty to Britain.[73] This was in all probability Manley's decision. He had, after all, fought in the British Army during the First World War and spent some formative years at Oxford: his commitment to Britain and British institutions was visceral. Even in the depths of 1940, when a British defeat looked distinctly possible, the PNP remained in a "sort of coma", as Domingo put it in a letter to Roberts.[74]

---

70. "Mr Domingo at Farewell Functions Promises to be P.N.P. Ambassador in U.S.", *The Gleaner*, 24 April 1939, p. 21.

71. "Protest Public Meetings Law", *The Gleaner*, 7 July 1939, pp. 1, 6; "Edict Wipes Out Islanders' Rights", *Chicago Defender*, 29 July 1939, p. 4.

72. "Jamaica League in New York Strong for Self-Government", *The Gleaner*, 12 October 1939, p. 6. One of Domingo's white radical friends in New York, Alfred Baker Lewis, recalls that, despite his earlier sympathies with Communism on account of the Soviet Union's anti-imperialism, Domingo denounced it on the signing of the Hitler-Stalin Pact. Lewis quotes Domingo's words to him: "I have been fighting the British imperialists in the West Indies all my life. But, when it comes to a war between the Nazis and the British imperialists, I will shoulder a gun for the British imperialists every time. For the British imperialists let you fight them; the Nazis kill their racial and political opponents" (Alfred Baker Lewis, *A Political Odyssey: Alone and Together*, Hicksville, NY: Exposition Press, 1979, p. 118). Lewis (1897–1980) was a lawyer, union organiser, socialist, and civil rights activist. He served on the board of the NAACP and as secretary of the Socialist Party of Massachusetts.

73. "Policy of the P.N.P. Party Is Outlined", *The Gleaner*, 23 December 1939, p. 1.

74. W. A. Domingo, Letter to W. Adolphe Roberts, 24 June 1940, WARA 2.3.5. Roberts

Figure 9 The Moore/Domingo debate in Harlem, 21 April 1940. *Left to right:* Domingo, J. A. Rogers, Richard B. Moore. (Courtesy of the Schomburg Center for Research in Black Culture, Manuscripts, Archives and Rare Books Division, New York)

Shortly after Domingo had returned to New York, and in response to British policy approaching and after the outbreak of war, the Caribbean Union (headed by Charles A. Petioni) organised a conference (14 May) and then a protest (2 June) against the British anti-alien bills. Together with the Harlem Legislative Conference, it then sponsored a Latin American-West Indian Conference (16–17 June) to discuss common problems. On 15 November it gave a dinner in honour of Jacques Roumain. On 17 December it staged a debate at the Renaissance Casino titled "Should British Colonial Negroes Support the British Empire in the War?", Domingo and Moore affirming and negating.[75]

The year 1940 proved a particularly difficult one for Domingo. He and Roberts wrote constantly to each other about possible strategies, particularly should

reported that Edna Manley had told him that the PNP leaders "are sunk in gloom and frantic with uncertainty" (W. Adolphe Roberts, Letter to W. A. Domingo [1 June 1940], WARA 2.3.5).

75. In April 1940 it began to publish the short-lived *Caribbean Review*. See "A Brief Review of the Activities of the Caribbean Union", *Caribbean Review*, 1, no. 1 (April 1940), pp. 2–3. Domingo and Moore reprised these debates over the next few months at various venues in New York (see Duke, *Building a Nation*, pp. 120–121). As Moore's daughter recalls of the relationship between Moore and Domingo: "they were giving the appearance of ardent opponents to some who did not fully understand their deep friendship and their ardor for forensic forays" (Turner, "Richard B. Moore and His Works", p. 76).

Britain lose the war, and neither of them had much faith in the local JPL(K). Roberts was keen on putting together a secret group that might be able to declare and maintain Jamaican independence if the need arose. Domingo was on board with the idea, but with communication with Jamaica censored, it was impossible to sound out people on the ground. Meanwhile, in Jamaica, Governor Richards was behaving increasingly like an autocrat, constantly overruling the decisions of the Legislative Council. The JPL(NY) cabled the Secretary of State for the Colonies demanding his recall: Richards was dismissive, suggesting to his superiors that the JPL had no support on the islands: "They stand essentially for self-government by the unfit."[76] Next on Richards's agenda was the Undesirable Publications Bill in May 1940, designed to keep out of the island anything in print the governor chose to find undesirable. Seeing itself as a target (which it probably was), the JPL(NY) swung into action with a resolution deploring the decision, which it had learned about "with astonishment and indignation".[77] Writing under his pseudonym "Proletariat", Domingo weighed in with sarcastic remarks at the governor's expense [#21].

Whereas Domingo had played only a peripheral role in the various West Indian umbrella groups that had sprung up in the 1930s, often with federation on their agenda, he was the driving force behind the foundation of the West Indies National Emergency Committee (WINEC) established in New York in June 1940 to confront the very real possibility either that Nazi Germany would defeat Britain, with the West Indian islands becoming German colonies, or that the USA, to avoid the potential threat to the security of the Panama Canal, would move to acquire the islands for itself.[78] Domingo wrote to Roberts about how he was trying to get as broad a representation as possible: "I even included Malliett," he wrote—misspelling his name, as he often did—"He has been splendid up to now."[79] Malliet was on board, and published a piece in the *New York Amsterdam News* about the new organisation, although he slipped in a reference to the West Indies as a "national unit", which was very much his idea rather than Domingo's.[80] In any case, the rapprochement would not last long. Domingo wrote to Roberts about his difficulties in getting the council up and running, but the members

76. "League in New York Protests Invoking of Paramount Importance", *The Gleaner*, 27 April 1940, p. 12; Arthur Richards, Letter to Malcolm MacDonald, Secretary of State for the Colonies, 29 April 1940, CO 137/846/10, TNA.

77. Ethelred Brown, "Protest Against 'Undesirable Publication Bill'", Letter to *The Gleaner*, 18 May 1940, p. 12.

78. "Suggest U. S. Acquire West Indies Islands", *Brooklyn Daily Eagle*, 20 May 1940, p. 2. Domingo was interviewed about the WINEC on 30 September 1940: Sydney H. French, "The West Indies National Emergency Committee", SCRBC, https://digitalcollections.nypl.org/items/aocb42co-74ff-0133-d021-00505686d14e (accessed 4 September 2024).

79. W. A. Domingo, Letter to W. Adolphe Roberts, 4 June 1940, WARA 2.3.5.

80. "West Indians Stirred over German Progress", *New York Amsterdam News*, 1 June 1940, p. 19.

finally met on 15 June and established a planning committee to be chaired by Domingo. The occasion had been successful, Domingo reported, although "Our friend Malliett did everything possible to sabotage the meeting" by not giving it publicity in his column.[81] Apart from Domingo, Moore was probably the most committed and dynamic of this group, but he was also a communist (though expelled from the CPUSA in 1939) and a federationist, and Domingo tried to make sure that the WINEC's public statements stuck to the issue of self-determination: he didn't want the waters muddied.[82] Indeed, with most of the other members of the WINEC in favour of federation, Domingo had to try to finesse the discussions, which wasn't always easy. For example, after he'd written to the *New York Amsterdam News* just as the WINEC was being formed, to underline the importance of West Indians in New York at least discussing how to react in the event of a German victory, a supportive letter from George Padmore in London suggested consideration of political independence of the West Indies—but based on a federation of the islands.[83]

When the Pan-American Foreign Ministers' Conference was summoned by President Roosevelt to meet in Havana in July 1940 to discuss the governance of the American colonies of European countries taken over by Axis powers, Roberts (in New Orleans) and Domingo (in New York) wrote to each other, their letters crossing.[84] As usual, they were on the same page, this time in thinking it vital that Jamaica's right to self-determination should be taken into account in the conference's deliberations, particularly since the PNP was showing no interest in the event. Roberts wrote a statement on behalf of the JPL while Domingo co-ordi-

81. W. A. Domingo, Letter to W. Adolphe Roberts, 16 July 1940, WARA 2.3.5. Domingo suggested that Malliet was two-faced, claiming to support the WINEC, but sabotaging it because of his dislike for three individuals, Domingo among them. He called Malliet "a very petty and spiteful individual" (W. A. Domingo, Letter to W. Adolphe Roberts, 5 August 1940, WARA 2.3.5).

82. By November the organisation had been renamed the West Indies National Council (WINC), with Domingo elected president, Richard B. Moore, Charles A. Petioni, Ivy Bailey-Essien, and Trystam Ebenezer Chalwill (Tortola, 1888–1951) as vice-presidents, Herman Percival Osborne (Trinidad, 1903–1982?) as secretary, and Arthur E. King as treasurer. Other members were Hope R. Stevens, F. Theo Reid, and Reginald Pierrepointe. So there was a core of JPL members plus others from various islands. For documentation on the WINEC/WINC, see the papers in RBMP [RBMP = Richard B. Moore Papers, Sc MG 397, SCRBC], box 8, and WINCC [WINCC = West Indies National Council Collection, SCRBC].

83. W. A. Domingo, "Status of West Indies", *New York Amsterdam News*, 8 June 1940, p. 8; George Padmore, "Self-Government", *New York Amsterdam News*, 10 August 1940, p. 8. According to the International African Service Bureau's pamphlet *The West Indies Today*, published anonymously but written by W. Arthur Lewis, looking ahead towards political change, "the constitution must be federal" (*The West Indies Today*, London: International African Service Bureau, 1939, p. 38). The International African Service Bureau was founded by several of Domingo's soulmates, including George Padmore. W. Arthur Lewis (1915–1991) was a St Lucian economist and later Nobel laureate. George Padmore, born in Trinidad as Malcolm Ivan Meredith Nurse (1903–1959), was a Pan-Africanist, journalist, and author.

84. Roberts, *These Many Years*, p. 301.

nated a response from the WINC [#22].[85] The West Indian attorney Hope Stevens went to Havana as the representative of both organisations.[86]

If occupation of European colonies were to prove necessary, the US government favoured trusteeship, with administration via commissions consisting of one member from each of three nearby republics until the full pan-American body could determine the best outcome, but with no time limit announced and no guarantee that a colony's inhabitants would be consulted. Stevens needed an ally among the delegates who would support the Caribbean case. He found one in Dr Leopoldo Melo, foreign minister of Argentina, who argued that an organic law should be adopted after consultation with the inhabitants and that trusteeship should be limited in the first instance to three years: he name-checked Jamaica as a unit for which tutelage would be an insult: "He insisted", the *New York Times* reported, "that the American republics take action only on a judicial basis and even then only after consulting the population to be affected and each other."[87] Melo's proposals weren't adopted, but the USA did shift its views, recognising the possibility that if any pan-American "administration" came to an end, the colonies might be "organized into autonomous territories".[88] Roberts speculates that Governor Richards was less than pleased that Jamaicans had gone over the head of the colonial regime to speak directly to a pan-American grouping from which Britain and France had been excluded—on the grounds, as Roberts puts it, that the discussion would involve "how their own autopsies might have to be conducted".[89] In a singular propaganda coup, the JPL and the WINC had been seen to speak for Jamaica.[90] That fact in itself was more important than the minor concessions gained by Melo's intervention.[91]

85. [W. Adolphe Roberts], *The Jamaica Progressive League: A Memorandum to the Havana Conference* [1940], in WARA Scrapbook no. 8, 10.1.17.

86. W. Adolphe Roberts, "The Act of Havana", *Jamaican Historical Review*, 3, no. 2 (1959), pp. 66–69. Hope Reynolph Stevens (1905–1982), born on Tortola, in the British Virgin Islands, and brought up on Nevis, had spent five years in the Dominican Republic before getting to New York, where he trained as a lawyer. His knowledge of Spanish made him a good choice for this Cuban trip. On the Havana conference, see Post, *Strike the Iron*, pp. 114–117; Timm, *Nationalists Abroad*, pp. 224–232.

87. Harold B. Hinton, "Argentina Blocks Trusteeship Plan", *New York Times*, 26 July 1940, pp. 1 and 6. Leopoldo Melo (1869–1951) was an Argentine politician, lawyer, and university professor. He served as minister of the interior (the political arm of the executive power in Argentina) under the conservative president Agustín P. Justo from 1932 to 1936, presiding over the Argentine delegations to the Inter-American conferences in Panama (1939) and Havana (1940).

88. "The Havana Agreement", *New York Times*, 29 July 1940, p. 5.

89. Roberts, *These Many Years*, pp. 302 and 301.

90. Post, *Strike the Iron*, p. 115.

91. Although Domingo and Roberts were aware that Melo's motivation had more to do with Argentine and pan-American politics than it did with his sympathy for Jamaica, Melo did keep up the contact, both in letters to the WINC and the JPL and then in a book he wrote (which Roberts obtained and read and made use of): Leopoldo Melo, *Panamericanismo y la Reunión de la Habana*, Buenos Aires, Argentina: Pesce y Cia, 1940.

Stevens was welcomed back to New York at a mass meeting for Emancipation Day on 5 August at the Renaissance Casino.[92] With the eventual defeat of Germany, the Act of Havana proved academic but its safeguards were valuable as a precedent, even though the conference had made it clear that the USA now regarded itself as the dominant power in the region, both an indication of post-war realities and a warning to the JPL that it might need to keep a weather eye open with respect to US plans. This apprehension was immediately underlined by the signing on 2 September of the bases-for-destroyers deal, negotiated, needless to say, without involvement from any actual West Indians.[93] In return for a 99-year lease to establish naval and military bases, 50 antiquated US naval destroyers were given to Britain, while US bases were established in seven British Caribbean territories, giving the USA a foothold in the region. Domingo's position was that the lease of island property without local consent could be construed as a violation of the Act of Havana.

Roberts and Domingo had both been writing constantly to Manley, updating him on the WINC and the preparations for the Havana conference, and sharing their fears of what might happen if Britain was defeated by Germany. Eventually, Manley saw the light and announced that he wanted to propose a shift in policy, back to advocating self-government.[94] Domingo immediately wrote an open letter to the September 1940 PNP annual conference to encourage the party to align its actions with those of the WINC.[95] The party fell in line, approving a statement which explained that there was no reason why a campaign for self-government should not be carried on without conflicting in any way with the larger interests of the British Empire. At the same time a strong national movement would ensure a popular voice should events conspire to see the USA take control of the islands.[96] During 1940 Domingo was, in effect, the PNP's unpaid advisor, and one for whose knowledge and commitment it was increasingly grateful. He also took the direct route with a letter to the US president, filling him in on what had happened in Havana and raising West Indian concerns about the operation of the new US bases on the islands [#23].

92. "West Indies National Emergency Committee to Present Attorney Hope E. Stevens at Mass Meeting", *New York Age*, 3 August 1940, p. 1.

93. Struck through an exchange of notes between the British and US governments. On the deal, see Jason C. Parker, *Brother's Keeper: The United States, Race, and Empire in the British Caribbean, 1937–1962*, New York: Oxford University Press, 2008, pp. 16–39.

94. Letter from Norman Manley to W. A. Domingo, 16 August 1940, NMP.

95. W. A. Domingo, Letter to the PNP Conference, Kingston, 25 August 1940, NMP.

96. "P.N.P. Now Socialist", *The Gleaner*, 30 August 1940, p. 6. And, as *The Gleaner* headline indicated, the PNP was also now—on Manley's recommendation—declaring itself as a Socialist party, somewhat to the surprise of its Marxist "inner circle", who regarded such an announcement as premature, but could hardly oppose it (Hart, *Towards Decolonisation*, p. 40). It was a declaration that did not improve the PNP's electoral prospects.

The victory at Havana was a small one, but it was a victory.[97] One of its consequences was that in the event of a British defeat, a pan-American commission would investigate whether colonies were ready for self-government. Roberts—whose strategic vision was exceptional—insisted that Jamaican leaders, and he would have Manley in mind above all, were prepared with a declaration of independence should the occasion arise. Meanwhile Domingo approached the NAACP to ensure broader African-American backing and the WINC directed itself to the Colonial Office to underline West Indian readiness to assume self-government.[98]

In Jamaica, however, things were going from bad to worse. In July 1940 it was reported that the JPL(K) had adopted a resolution about the desirability of Jamaica exploring the possibility of joining with sister colonies to become a West Indian province of Canada.[99] Domingo and Roberts were not pleased. Brown wrote to McFarlane to underline that demand for self-government was the appropriate strategy, and to ask the JPL(K) to abstain from any further action. By September the local branch was back in line.[100] At no point had Domingo and Roberts had real confidence in McFarlane and his Kingston allies, but by this time they were, in letters to each other, openly disdainful: "spineless asses", "numbskulls and weaklings" were typical descriptions. Roberts spoke of the need to "shove them outside and found a new organization".[101]

* * *

The Moyne Commission's report painted such a devastating picture of poverty, disease, and malnutrition that the British government decided that publishing it in full would provide fodder for German propaganda, so only a few of its recommendations were made public in February 1940, notably advocacy of a West Indian Welfare Fund to provide £1 million of extra expenditure on the colonies.

97. Domingo and Manley both discussed the outcome: "W. A. Domingo from New York", *Public Opinion*, 17 August 1940, p. 11; Norman Manley, "The Act of Havana", *Public Opinion*, 14 September 1940, pp. 3–14. Manley berated the West Indian legislatures for not sending observers to Havana.

98. Under the letterhead of the WINC, Domingo sent several letters to Walter White at the NAACP offices on Fifth Avenue in New York without receiving an answer (NAACPRDPS, pp. 3–4 [NAACPRDPS = NAACP Racial discrimination and political sovereignty in the British West Indies Folder 001432-002-0252 Found in Papers of the NAACP, Part 13 NAACP and Labor, Series A Subject Files on Labor Conditions and Employment Discrimination]). Herman P. Osborne, Secretary of the WINC, "A Letter to Lord Lloyd", reproduced in *Public Opinion*, 25 January 1941, pp. 2–3. George Ambrose Lloyd, 1st Lord Lloyd (1879–1941) died shortly after the letter was written.

99. "Hope to See Jamaica a Province of the Dominion", *The Gleaner*, 3 July 1940, p. 9.

100. "Progressive League Moves on Questions Affecting Jamaica", *The Gleaner*, 30 September 1940, p. 5.

101. Letter from W. Adolphe Roberts to W. A. Domingo, 15 September 1940, WARA 2.3.5.

On political matters, the 1940 recommendations merely noted the commission's rejection of the "extreme proposal" for immediate and complete self-government based on universal suffrage while suggesting, somewhat ambiguously, that while political federation "is not of itself an appropriate means for meeting the pressing needs of the West Indies", it is, nevertheless, "the end to which policy should be directed".[102]

A large meeting was organised by the PNP at the Ward Theatre on 15 January 1941 to discuss constitutional change. Other organisations were invited to send representatives to speak, including not only the FCA and the JPL(K), but the BITU. Something close to a united front emerged on the pressing need for reform of the constitution.[103] And Manley was now *so* on message that he attended the annual meeting of the JPL(K) to encourage it to push harder for self-government, spending most of his speech giving an account of WINC activities in New York, which he knew in detail through Domingo's letters.[104] He also publicly aligned himself with the JPL position, stating in an interview with *The Gleaner* on 9 January 1941 that the PNP now stood "uncompromisingly on our demand for the grant of immediate self-government".[105] Richards remained intransigent, speaking disparagingly about "every platform politician, and every fireside financier who confuses the aspirations of the people with a personal craving for power".[106]

Meanwhile, a committee of the Legislative Council in Jamaica under the leadership of J. A. G. Smith proposed a new constitution similar to the one that had operated in Jamaica between 1854 and 1866.[107] The JPL and the PNP were scornful, Governor Arthur Richards was not enthusiastic, and so the Colonial Office sketched a new version based on the Moyne proposals: the Legislative Council would be enlarged to at least 40 members, 28 of them elected; the governor could still pass a bill he considered of paramount importance whatever the view of the Legislative Council; and universal suffrage would be introduced after a new census. The PNP was prepared to accept this proposal, but asked for the creation of ministries to be headed by elected members of the Legislative Council. The Legislative Council eventually voted in August 1941 to turn down the proposal and ask for Smith's proposal to be reconsidered—though in March 1942

102. *West India Royal Commission, 1938–39—Recommendations*, Cmd 6174, London: HMSO, 1940, p. 25.

103. "Call Sounded at Ward Theatre Mass Meeting for Change in Island's Constitution", *The Gleaner*, 17 January 1941, pp. 6 and 9.

104. "P.N.P. President Urges Unity for Self Government", *The Gleaner*, 25 January 1941, pp. 5 and 9.

105. "Governor's Visit Linked to Change in Constitution", *The Gleaner*, 10 January 1941, p. 3.

106. "Governor Hits Out at 'Political Quacks and Fireside Financiers'", *The Gleaner*, 16 December 1940, p. 13.

107. This paragraph draws from Ronald V. Sires, "The Experience of Jamaica with Modified Crown Colony Government", *Social and Economic Studies*, 4, no. 2 (June 1955), pp. 150–167. James Alexander George Smith (1877–1942) was a barrister and politician, anti-colonial in his views, although he stayed aloof from political parties.

it changed its mind. The PNP then brokered an agreement with the FCA, the Jamaica Imperial Association, and the elected members of the Legislative Council to produce a compromise proposal based on a bi-cameral system, an executive committee made of elected members who would serve as departmental ministers, and the severe restriction of the governor's power of veto. The Colonial Office agreed, except—predictably—with respect to the governor's veto. A five-year trial period was suggested, with further instalments of self-government to follow if the first period proved a success. Morley Ayearst describes it as "responsible government on a leash".[108] A new constitution would eventually come into effect in 1944.

* * *

For some time Domingo and Roberts had discussed whether one of them should return to Jamaica, both to give some backbone to McFarlane and the others in the JPL(K) and to help keep the PNP on its new track.[109] Norman and Edna Manley constantly encouraged them to return.[110] Edna wrote to Roberts that the PNP needed Domingo "more than ever before".[111] Roberts felt that Domingo would be more effective than he would, and he lobbied the Manleys to persuade him.[112] Manley did his best. He wrote to Domingo:

> I need hardly tell you that we miss you not less but more every day. We have a very devoted band of propaganda workers who has stood up to severe tests but we do need men of experience and knowledge of organization. I still look forward to the day when you will return because I feel that the future is full of possibilities which will want all the best people to help to realize them.[113]

Meanwhile, Domingo contributed regularly to *Public Opinion*, usually on the topic of nationalism, on one occasion reminding his readers of its earlier history in Cox's National Club.[114]

Finally, early in 1941 Manley asked Domingo to come from New York and work as a paid organiser for the PNP for six months, which was as long as Domingo thought he could spare from his business, which had been suffering during the

108. Morley Ayearst, *The British West Indies*, London: Allen & Unwin, 1960, p. 73.
109. Shortly after Roberts finally returned to Jamaica in 1950, the Kingston branch of the JPL was quietly closed ("League Records Go to Archive", *The Gleaner*, 20 June 1950, p. 7).
110. Edna Swithenbank Manley (1900–1987) was a Jamaican sculptor. Daughter of an English cleric and his Jamaican wife, she married her cousin Norman Manley in 1921 and moved to Jamaica with him.
111. Edna Manley, Letter to W. Adolphe Roberts, undated, WARA 2.3.4.
112. W. Adolphe Roberts, Letter to W. A. Domingo, 9 February 1941, WARA 2.3.5.
113. Norman Manley, Letter to W. A. Domingo, 16 August 1940, NMP.
114. W. A. Domingo, "Rise of a National Consciousness in Jamaica", *Public Opinion*, 22 March 1941, pp. 12–13.

war.[115] One potential problem was that Domingo had been exchanging very frank letters with his old friend Martin Luther Campbell. Referring to this correspondence, Domingo wrote to Roberts just before he sailed:

> Letters from me to everybody else in Jamaica were opened [censored] while those to him [Campbell] were invariably unopened. It looked as if they had set a trap and were waiting to catch me. That is my real fear. I may have written something carelessly long ago (though I can't think of any) and it might be held against me. Still, regardless of everything, I am determined to go. Let them do their worst.[116]

As it turned out, they were perfectly prepared to do their worst.

A testimonial dinner was held for Domingo at the Harlem Young Men's Christian Association on the evening of Monday 26 May 1941. Ethelred Brown was MC, and spokespeople for various groups provided tributes. Domingo sailed for Jamaica on 29 May.[117] When his boat docked at Port Royal on 17 June 1941 he was immediately arrested and placed in an internment camp at the governor's pleasure, to the outrage of PNP leaders and of his friends in New York, both groups launching lengthy campaigns to try to secure his release.[118] The *New York Amsterdam News* wrote that Richards had acted "with the might and ruthlessness of a Hitler blitzkrieg", and with a touch of exaggeration, that under Jamaica's draconian Defence Regulations he had more power than Hitler, Stalin, and Mussolini combined.[119] West Indians and African-Americans in Harlem also protested Domingo's detention.[120] The WINC sent a strongly worded telegram to the governor demanding Domingo's unconditional release while issuing

115. In August 1940, Domingo told Roberts that he'd already lost more than $14,000 and was living off his capital, while now he had so little cash that he needed Manley to buy his passage to Jamaica (W. A. Domingo, Letters to W. Adolphe Roberts, 6 August 1940 and 24 March 1941, WARA 2.3.5). Nonetheless, despite four and a half years away (four years more than planned), he returned to New York in 1947 with considerable funds in various bank accounts.

116. Roberts, *These Many Years*, p. 305.

117. "W. A. Domingo Paid Homage", *New York Amsterdam News*, 31 May 1941, p. 4. There were 85 guests at his farewell dinner (W. A. Domingo, Letter to W. Adolphe Roberts, 3 June 1941, WARA 2.3.5).

118. "P.N.P. Declare Against Detention of Domingo", *The Gleaner*, 21 June 1941, pp. 1, 6. On Domingo's detention, see Jason Parker, "'Capital of the Caribbean': The African American-West Indian 'Harlem Nexus' and the Transnational Drive for Black Freedom, 1940–1948", *Journal of African American History*, 89, no. 2 (Spring 2004), pp. 98–117; Timm, *Nationalists Abroad*, pp. 271–298; Palmer, *Freedom's Children*, pp. 256–263.

119. "W. A. Domingo, Nationalist Leader, Lands in Concentration Camp in Jamaica", *New York Amsterdam News*, 28 June 1941, pp. 1 and 3.

120. "Plan Protest Meeting Here Against Arrest Of Domingo", *New York Amsterdam Star-News*, 12 July 1941, p. 13; "Harlemites Protest Arrest of Domingo in West Indies", *New York Amsterdam Star-News*, 19 July 1941, pp. 1–3.

a statement referring to his detention as a new Dreyfus case.[121] Adolphe Roberts had no doubts: "We now know to what length the British government intends to go, to silence voices that demand real self-government. Let us not be deceived. The arrest of Domingo is due not to the fact that he was entering Jamaica to work for the PNP, but to his connection with the Jamaica Progressive League and the West Indies National Council."[122] Manley said that he had "never been more shocked and amazed in my life at any act done by this government".[123] Two days later Manley's second statement was reported, focusing on the talks Domingo had given in New York defending the proposition "Why the coloured peoples of the world should support Britain against the menace of fascism", and the lawyer Ansell Hart (father of Richard Hart) published a letter in *The Gleaner* in which he wrote that "As a student of history I cannot fail to observe that submission to aggression from without is preceded by submission to aggression from within", a statement which—had he not been so respectable—might well have resulted in his own detention.[124]

The earlier legislation on "undesirable publications" and the banning of public meetings had given strong indications of Richards's autocratic tendencies, and Domingo's outspoken letters to *The Gleaner*, alongside—doubtless—police reports on his political activities in the early months of 1939, would have alerted the governor to the danger, as he would see it, of Domingo's presence on the island. Here was somebody who could not be trusted to show the deference that Manley and other members of the PNP had so far displayed.

After Domingo's detention, the WINC wrote to Walter White at the NAACP, who contacted the Department of State: it became a US matter of interest and an under-secretary of state, George Hall, was sent to investigate.[125] It soon, however, became apparent that because Domingo was not a US citizen, the USA could play no direct role in the matter, which did not stop it exercising pressure behind the scenes, as we shall see shortly. White tried to be helpful, offering the suggestion "that it might be well for you to ask the Colonial Secretary the specific question as to whether or not Mr Domingo's well known position favoring independence for the people of the various West Indian islands would be construed by the Governor as an act 'prejudicial to public safety and defense'".[126]

121. NAACP(RDPS), p. 98; "Freedom of West Indian Is Linked with Effort to Destroy Hitlerism", *New York Amsterdam Star-News*, 29 November 1941, p. 2.
122. W. Adolphe Roberts, Letter to E. Ethelred Brown, 21 June 1941, WARA 2.3.6.
123. "P.N.P. Declare Against Detention of Domingo", *The Gleaner*, 21 June 1941, p. 1.
124. [Norman Manley] "The Case of Mr Domingo", *The Gleaner*, 23 June 1941, p. 3; Ansell Hart, "What History Teaches", *The Gleaner*, 23 June 1941, p. 8.
125. "Colonial Secretary to Probe Arrest, Detention of Domingo", *New York Amsterdam Star-News*, 13 September 1941, p. 1.
126. Letter from Walter White to Ethelred Brown (NAACP[RDPS], p. 75). That phrase was taken from a reply to Brown from the Colonial Secretary in Kingston (dated 12 July 1941), a copy of which Brown had sent to White.

Domingo was not alone. On 8 September 1940 Alexander Bustamante had been detained by the governor under the Defense Regulations Act for giving a rabble-rousing speech in which—according to the police report, in all probability fallacious—he threatened bloodshed while demanding revolution and self-government.[127] Among the other people detained was a *Gleaner* journalist, the English-born G. St C. Scotter, ironically a supporter of Richards's draconian methods, but apparently a pessimist as regards the outcome of the war, which provoked the governor's ire.[128] His detention inevitably swung his newspaper behind a critique of the governor's sweeping powers—much more sweeping, an article in the *Gleaner* pointed out, than those in force in Britain itself, which was geographically rather closer to the German enemy than was Jamaica.[129] A Council for the Protection of Civil Liberties was formed, ensuring that the protests against Domingo's detention spread beyond the ranks of the PNP. A June 1941 meeting was addressed by Leslie Ashenheim and Manley, and attended by H. G. de Lisser, J. A. G. Smith, Ansell Hart, and E. E. A. Campbell as well as by O. T. Fairclough and Florizel Glasspole.[130] In his opening remarks Ashenheim declared the meeting to be the most representative group *ever* to meet on the island, "And we are determined that for this evening we are Jamaicans and Jamaicans only."[131]

This wide alliance was possible because, as a report from the US consul put it:

> None of the interned British subjects, so far as is known, is in any way pro-German; probably none of them is anti-British in the broad sense of the term; all of them are bitter critics of the present government of Jamaica. By many people, therefore, it is considered that the government is using a power given for a specific purpose under War Defense Regulations to accomplish ends for which it was never intended and which could not be accomplished under civil law.

The result was, he continued, that "people from all walks of life, of different colors, and creeds, among them a few prominent citizens, have joined with the avowed purpose of protecting their liberties against what they consider to be a form of despotism".[132] Such a grouping might have no permanence, but this was

127. Palmer, *Freedom's Children*, pp. 184–197.

128. G. St C. Scotter, "To-Day", *The Gleaner*, 15 May 1940, p. 3. Gordon St Clair Scotter (1890–1978).

129. L. E. Ashenheim, "The Pathway to Detention: English Safeguards Omitted in Jamaica", *The Gleaner*, 27 May 1941, pp. 3, 6. Ashenheim was a member of one of Jamaica's most prominent business families.

130. "Civil Mass Meeting Protests Local Defence Regulations", *The Gleaner*, 25 June 1941, pp. 1, 18. Florizel Augustus Glasspole (1909–2000) was the general secretary of the TUAC and a prominent member of the PNP. After Jamaican independence, he spent 18 years as governor-general.

131. Ibid., p. 18.

132. Hugh H. Watson, "Political Developments in Jamaica (Semi-Annual Report)", 16 July 1941, pp. 4–5, 811.34544/675, NARA, quoted in Post, *Strike the Iron*, p. 179.

very much the kind of national sentiment that the JPL wished to foster—even if Domingo would have preferred a trigger that didn't involve his being locked up.

On the back foot, Richards acknowledged Domingo's arrest for the first time and on 12 July stated the government's position that it was necessary to hold Domingo in order to prevent any activities on his part likely to:

> (a) promote and foster anti-British and defeatist sentiments, (b) embarrass and impede the policy of the Imperial and local government in relation to the war effort, (c) promote and foster anti-American sentiments, (d) excite opposition to and embarrass and delay the rapid and successful execution of the plans for the completion of the United States Defense Bases in Jamaica, (e) cause disaffection, unrest and disorder in the coloured population of Jamaica by exciting feelings of colour prejudice and racial animosity.[133]

With questions also being raised in the British House of Commons, the British government moved in August to bring the Jamaican Defence Regulations Act into line with its home counterpart.[134] As a result, only in those instances where persons had actually been engaged in activities likely to endanger the defence of the island or public safety could a governor exercise the powers vested in him to hold persons for security reasons. Moreover, he was obliged to provide detainees with an explanation of the reasons for their detention, and they were allowed a right to appeal.

* * *

133. *The Case of Domingo*, Kingston, Jamaica: The People's National Party, 1941, p. 3.

134. The question of Domingo's detention was consistently raised in the House of Commons by a series of Labour MPs, notably Arthur Creech Jones (1891–1964), who vouched for Domingo's "integrity". Domingo's case was raised nine times in the Commons, but the government simply stonewalled. Creech Jones's remark about Domingo's integrity came in the first series of questions on 9 July 1941 (*Hansard*, Fifth Series, vol. 373, cols 153–154). The final raising of the issue came on 8 July 1942 (*Hansard*, Fifth Series, vol. 381, col. 759). In a discussion of the colonial issue on the House of Commons, Creech Jones made the point fairly bluntly: "I feel strongly that, time and time again, civil liberty has been outraged in Jamaica .... The long imprisonment of Domingo seems to me to be completely indefensible from the point of view of any standards of civil liberty" (*Hansard*, Fifth Series, vol. 387, 16 March 1943, cols 1,094-1,095). Another MP who continued to press the case was the Grenada-born Dr Hyacinth Bernard Morgan (1885–1956), the most consistent parliamentary advocate for the West Indies in the middle of the twentieth century. In a letter to Harold Macmillan, the Colonial Under-Secretary, dated 5 November 1942, Morgan noted of Domingo that "The whole history of his original high-handed (if not illegal) arrest and his persistent imprisonment is worthy of a Hitlerian regime" (CO 968/689, TNA). On Morgan, see Edward L. Cox, "A West Indian Lobbyist in England", *Journal of Caribbean History*, 47, no. 1 (2013), pp. 49–72. Even after his release, Domingo was named at the 1945 London Subject Peoples Conference in a protest against political imprisonment (Hakim Adi, "Pan-Africanism in Britain: Background to the 1945 Manchester Congress," in *The 1945 Manchester Pan-African Congress Revisited*, ed. Hakim Adi and Marika Sherwood, London: New Beacon Books, 1995, pp. 11–32, at 20).

Sir Arthur Richards had been hurriedly installed as governor in a "crisis transfer" after the sudden death of Edward Denham. He had no experience of the Caribbean, but arrived with a reputation for hard-nosed efficiency.[135] He quickly developed a low opinion of Jamaicans in general and of the elected members of the legislature in particular. In opposition to universal local demands for constitutional reform, he opined in a letter to the Colonial Office that the existing constitution was "quite workable", representing as it did "as great an advance on the road of democratic control as is warranted by the state of development, political and educational, of the people". The group clamouring for self-government consisted, he pronounced, of "the half-educated middle classes" alongside "professional agitators with a foreign training", and "a sprinkling of educated idealists, fanatics, and men with a colour complex".[136] He would probably have regarded Domingo as fitting into the latter two categories. Richards's use of the "paramount importance" clause in the constitution, which allowed the governor to override the votes of elected members to get his way on small local issues, prompted a letter of outrage from the JPL in New York demanding his recall. Richards's response to the colonial secretary was to comment that the JPL "largely represents Jamaicans who have left their country for their country's good".[137]

The only partial exception in Richards's dyspeptic panorama was Norman Manley, the one person on the island whom Richards seems to have regarded as his intellectual peer. In this February 1939 letter Richards enclosed a memorandum he had asked Manley to write about constitutional change, and he was even prepared to accept much of Manley's analysis, recognising that some change would be necessary in order to meet the strength of local opinion.

Richards and Manley continued to co-operate inasmuch as the governor forwarded Manley's second memorandum on constitutional reform to London in December 1940, although his covering letter doubled down on his low opinion of Jamaicans in general ("The Jamaican is so intractable and so unlovable, with very few exceptions, white or black") and of Manley's colleagues ("a group of dis-

135. Sir Arthur Richards (1885–1978) had held appointments in North Borneo, Gambia, and Fiji before becoming Governor of Jamaica, holding the office for five years, from August 1938 to July 1943. He ended his colonial career as governor of Nigeria, where he became known as "Old Sinister". The Nigerians were not impressed by what J. S. Coleman calls his "special knack for antagonising the educated elements" (J. S. Coleman, *Nigeria: Background to Nationalism*, Berkeley, CA: University of California Press, 1958, p. 275). For a sympathetic view, see Richard Peel, *Old Sinister: A Memoir of Sir Arthur Richards, GCMG, First Baron Milverton of Lagos and Clifton in the City of Bristol, 1885–1978*, Cambridge: [R. Peel], 1986. For a less sympathetic view, with a focus on Domingo's detention, see Palmer, *Freedom's Children*, pp. 244–296.

136. Arthur Richards, Letter to Malcolm MacDonald, Secretary of State for the Colonies, 24 February 1939, CO 137/834/7, TNA, enclosing Norman Manley, "Memorandum for Constitutional Change for Jamaica" (9 February 1939).

137. Ethelred Brown, Letter to Malcolm MacDonald, Secretary of State for the Colonies, 10 April 1940, and Arthur Richards, Letter to Malcolm MacDonald, Secretary of State for the Colonies, 29 April 1940, CO 137/846/10, TNA.

gruntled failures in life whom laziness or incompetence have denied the position they crave to occupy, or of rabid Communists, largely inspired by hatred of the white man, or pure theorists with no practical knowledge at all").[138] The outbreak of war with Germany hardened Richards's attitude, and his detention of Domingo broke his relationship with Manley, who refused to speak to him for twelve months.

* * *

After the change in the defence regulations, Richards now had to either release Domingo or charge him with some specific act. He chose the second course, and on 2 September 1941 Domingo was given a copy of an amended order which declared that the governor "has reasonable cause to believe that Domingo has recently been concerned in acts prejudicial to the public safety or the defence of the realm or in the preparation or instigation of such acts".[139] Domingo appealed. The appeals committee—appointed by Richards—consisted of Justice D. T. J. Sherlock, an Anglo-Irish judge on the Jamaican High Court, Sir Charlton Scott Chomeley Harrison, a white Jamaican-born plantation owner who had served as a colonial official in India, and Mr J. G. Kieffer, the English-born retired head of the United Fruit Company in Jamaica, who had settled on the island. All were friends of Richards.

The particulars that Richards now had to provide were produced on 3 September. "They proved astonishing," as a quickly produced PNP pamphlet remarked. These "prejudicial acts" turned out not to refer to any public activity or publications, but rather to correspondence between September 1939 and June 1941 with four people in Jamaica "taking an active part in politics": M. L. Campbell, N. W. Manley, V. L. Arnett, and E. E. A. Campbell. At the very least the charges seemed to involve considerable sleight of hand, as the PNP pamphlet was quick to point out. Can private letters really be said to promote, foster, or excite anything at all? Perhaps—stretching a point—if they are directed at persons in public life who might see fit to broadcast the content of the letters. Hence, presumably, the reference to Domingo's four correspondents as "taking an active part in politics". But then, when it came to the actual content of the letters, the only ones the government took objection to were those written to Domingo's old friend Martin Luther Campbell, who played no part at all in the island's political life. The four letters to E. E. A. Campbell were inconsequential; there were 35 in that period written to Manley and Arnett, for the most part dealing with the Havana conference and the proposed establishment of US bases on Jamaica and other West Indian islands.

138. Arthur Richards, Letter to Lord Lloyd, Secretary of State for the Colonies, 23 December 1940, CO 967/132, TNA.
139. *The Case of Domingo*, p. 5.

The Case of Domingo announced on its cover: "Domingo is a Victim of Fear and Prejudice. Is it too much to hope that right will be done?" The epigraph immediately laid waste to the claim that Domingo was any kind of traitor with a quotation from one of his letters: "we must fear and fight fascism. If England loses, all hope of Freedom in Jamaica is dead." The four sections of the pamphlet then answered four questions: "Who is Domingo? What is he charged with? How was he tried? What did he write Campbell?"[140] After explaining the background to Domingo's arrival in Jamaica—invited by the PNP—the pamphlet explained that no reasons had been given for Domingo's detention until his solicitor (N. N. Nethersole) received a communication from the governor.[141]

Before contesting these claims, the pamphlet gave a short "personal sketch", one of the very few we have of the man:

> Domingo is a Jamaican somewhere over 50 years of age, dark complexioned (Sambo to use a colloquialism), with strong, blunt features and an independent, incisive mind. Thoroughly democratic, both in outlook and personal conduct, he has acquired a vast storehouse of knowledge by his wide reading and personal contacts during his more than 20 years in the United States. He is a good mixer, a clever conversationalist, friendly yet outspoken.[142]

Outlining Domingo's involvement in the JPL, the pamphlet made a point of the organisation's insistence on excluding questions of colour and race from the campaign for self-government, quoting a resolution Domingo had moved on 18 October 1938, seconded by Jaime O'Meally: "That the Board of Directors hereby condemn the raising of the Race issue as an argument for Self-government, it being the settled conviction of this body that this is a nationalist and democratic movement including all races which go to form the Jamaican people".[143] The clear conclusion is "that to suggest that Domingo would stir up racial hatred is deliberately to ignore the whole of the public life and activity of the man".[144]

During the hearing itself none of the three political correspondents was called, despite Domingo's urging. None of the other witnesses he asked for was called. His solicitor was not allowed to be present, and none of the material he requested be put into evidence proving his views on the matters at issue was taken into con-

140. Ibid., p. 2.

141. Ibid., p. 3. Manley, who clearly felt guilty for his pressing invitation to Domingo, hired Nethersole to represent Domingo and, with his wife Edna frequently visited Domingo in the Up Camp detention centre. Domingo was only allowed to send two letters a week. His prison number was #994.

142. Ibid., p. 4.

143. Ibid., p. 4.

144. Ibid., p. 5. W. Adolphe Roberts underlined these points, particularly emphasising Domingo's hope for a Nazi defeat, expressed in private letters: "Postscript to the Case of Domingo", *Public Opinion*, 14 February 1942, p. 5.

sideration. The first day's hearing was taken up with questions put to Domingo about whether he was a Communist—irrelevant since he wasn't charged with being one. On the third day M. L. Campbell was called, but Domingo wasn't allowed to be present. Whatever evidence Campbell gave was never published or even referred to. Later in September Domingo was informed that his appeal had failed and that he would be held in detention at the governor's pleasure. On 8 October the government issued a statement that was published in *The Gleaner*:

> Mr W. A. Domingo has been detained by His Excellency the Governor in exercise of the powers conferred on His Excellency by Defence Regulations which enable him to order the detention of persons who, *inter alia*, have recently been concerned in acts prejudicial to the public safety or defence, or in the preparation or instigation of such acts.
>
> Evidence is available which indicates that Mr Domingo has been engaged in defeatist and anti-war propaganda including propaganda designed to stimulate opposition on racial grounds to the establishment of United States Bases in the West Indies.
>
> Mr Domingo has exercised his right to make an objection to his detention before the Advisory Committee under the Jamaica Defence Regulations, and the Advisory Committee has stated that the grounds on which the Detention Order was issued support the Order.[145]

No evidence was offered in support of this judgement. All Domingo's public statements were pro-British and in favour of the US bases, as the PNP pamphlet pointed out in some detail.[146] Even if the statements in his letters to M. L. Campbell could be construed as more equivocal, they were written to a private individual and could therefore not, by definition, be read as "propaganda". Perhaps the most "anti-British" was his argument about British censorship: "That is why the British are so disliked everywhere. They pretend that they believe in democracy while as a matter of fact they are the worse tyrants on earth save the Fascists whom they so closely resemble and whom they long antedated."[147] But even this was in the midst of constant reiterations of the hope that Britain would win the war.

So why would Domingo's "communist" activities be up for debate, and why would British authorities consider Domingo a person who would "stimulate opposition on racial grounds" despite the irrelevance of both to the legal proceedings and given Domingo's clear support for the British war effort? The answer tells us about the operation of British colonialism in the West Indies as well as the importance of Domingo's ideas, with his statement about censorship providing several clues. First, Domingo's comparison between British policy and fascism was not a

145. "Domingo Detained for Duration", *The Gleaner*, 8 October 1941, p. 1.
146. *The Case of Domingo*, pp. 7–8.
147. W. A. Domingo, Letter to Martin Luther Campbell, 23 August 1940, 11 September 1940, NMP.

new argument for him, nor was he alone in marking the close proximity between certain colonial policies and fascist behaviour. There was an extensive debate on such issues in the pages of the black press in the United States, France, the United Kingdom, West Africa, and the Caribbean.[148] But the internal and external threat of fascism was a particular focus for Domingo and his writings proved a major intellectual contribution to the debate [#19, 20, and 28]. In 1938, while still in Harlem, Domingo declared in the pages of *Public Opinion* that the history of fascism could be traced back to "British Imperialists decades ago" and the dictums "sung by Kipling."[149] These were uncomfortable comparisons for British officials, and Domingo's rooting of fascist thinking in the racialist jingoism of Kipling and the high tide of British imperialism provided a lasting intellectual genealogy.[150]

Secondly, in the 1930s colonial authorities throughout the British Empire applied Seditious Ordinances—and passed new ones based upon older legislation—that enabled charges of sedition and the seizure of "undesirable" literature. This was one prong of British anti-communist activity in the 1920s and early 1930s, when anxiety about international communism increased, particularly in response to the activities of the League Against Imperialism and the training of several anti-colonial activists in Moscow.[151] International communist movements at this time espoused anti-imperialist ideas. British colonial authorities perceived the threat to their authority posed by colonised subjects who could draw on communist resources. In the British West Indies and British African territories, the two major targets for censorship were communist and Garveyite literature.[152] In

148. Leslie James, "Blood Brothers: Colonialism and Fascism as Relations in the Interwar West Africa and the Caribbean", *American Historical Review*, 127, no. 2 (June 2022), pp. 634–663; Imaobong Umoren, "Anti-Fascism and the Development of Global Race Women, 1928–1945", *Callaloo*, 39, no. 1 (2016), pp. 151–165; Neelam Srivastava, *Italian Colonialism and Resistance to Empire, 1930–1970*, Basingstoke, UK: Palgrave, 2018, pp. 21–32.

149. W. A. Domingo, "Jamaica in a Fascist World," *Public Opinion*, 16 April 1938, p. 5.

150. Hannah Arendt, *The Origins of Totalitarianism* [1951], San Diego, CA: Harvest Books, 1968, pp. 185–221.

151. Michelle Louru, "The Johnstone Affair and Anti-Communism in Interwar India", *Journal of Contemporary History*, 53, no. 1 (2018), pp. 38–60. There is a wide literature on international communism and anti-imperialism, but for its relevance to the Caribbean and individuals in Domingo's circle, see Margaret Stevens, *Red International and Black Caribbean: Communists in New York City, Mexico and the West Indies, 1919–1939*, London: Pluto Press, 2017; Hakim Adi, *Pan-Africanism or Communism: The Communist International, Africa and the Diaspora, 1919–1939*, Trenton, NJ: Africa World Press, 2013; S. Ani Mukherji, "'Like Another Planet to the Darker Americans': Black Cultural Work in 1930s Moscow", in *Africa in Europe*, ed. Eve Rosenhaft and Robbie Aitken, Liverpool, UK: Liverpool University Press, 2013, pp. 120–241; Holger Weiss, *Framing a Radical African Atlantic: African American Agency, West African Intellectuals, and the International Trade Union Committee of Negro Workers*, Leiden, the Netherlands: Brill Academic Publishers, 2014; and Jonathan Derrick, *Africa's "Agitators": Militant Anticolonialism in Africa and the West, 1918–1939*, New York: Columbia University Press, 2008.

152. Yaw Twumasi, "Press Freedom and Nationalism under Colonial Rule in the Gold Coast (Ghana)", *Journal of the Historical Society of Nigeria*, 7, no. 3 (1974), pp. 499–520; Stephanie Newell, "Paradoxes of Press Freedom in Colonial West Africa", *Media History*, 22, no. 1 (2016), pp. 101–122.

1937 Domingo contributed a letter to the International Trade Union Committee of Negro Workers' *Negro Worker*, a copy of which is held in Colonial Office files, arguing that Jamaicans must "weaken the capitalist forces ... by organizing labour unions, by forming cooperative societies, and by demanding self-government everywhere".[153]

As for Garveyite literature, this very letter in the *Negro Worker* roundly criticised Garveyite plans regarding the Back to Africa movement. But Domingo's ideas in this regard proved nuanced once again. As Myles Osborne has shown, Domingo argued, in an article entitled "Back to Africa" no less, that Jamaicans should emulate African leaders who embraced their African heritage by rejecting European food and dress. He praised the ingenuity of those who frequented Kingston's Coronation Market, a space that would "soon become one of the first spaces in which Rastafari were welcomed and mixed with those who were not members of the faith".[154] Domingo was unapologetically committed to strengthening black pride, utilising his journalism to broadcast black achievement in science, medicine, the arts, and business. In 1945, when asked by a reader to explain the significance of his column "Do You Know", Domingo explained that "I cite our racial achievements because I am convinced that most of my readers are ignorant of them and because I am hopeful that the information will be relayed to relatives, acquaintances and friends, thus helping to lift the racial self-respect of our people in Jamaica." Domingo was committed to spreading knowledge as "the antidote to ignorance", an ignorance he roundly placed at the feet of "European propaganda which engenders a sense of inferiority in us". His own learning had been inspirational to him, and he wanted to inspire the same confidence in others:

> It was a revelation to me when I discovered that there were hundreds of black inventors. Before that I believed that people of my own colour had never invented anything. Also not knowing of the existence of Negro poets, authors, scholars, explorers, generals, scientists, etc. ... It is to give my readers knowledge of themselves why I publish acts about our racial achievements.[155]

The promotion of "racial feeling" was a consistent paranoia of colonial officials in British Africa and the Caribbean.[156] When wartime censorship came into effect, it was delimited in terms of "prevent[ing] the circulation of material which would

153. W. A. Domingo, "Our Letter Box," *Negro Worker* (January 1937), p. 15, in CO 323/1518/9, TNA.

154. Myles Osborne, "Africa in Jamaica: W.A. Domingo, George Padmore and *Public Opinion*", in *The Edinburgh Companion to British Colonial Periodicals*, ed. David Finkelstein, David Johnson, and Caroline Davis, Edinburgh, UK: Edinburgh University Press, 2024, pp. 519–530, at 524.

155. W. A. Domingo, "Knowledge Will Destroy Our Inferiority Complex", *New Negro Voice*, 10 March , 1945, pp. 1 and 3.

156. Stanley Shaloff, "Press Controls and Sedition Proceedings the Gold Coast, 1933–1939", *African Affairs*, 71 (1972), pp. 241–263, at 248.

provoke ill-feeling between the various races in the Colony".[157] These are precisely the terms on which Domingo was interned. Colonial officials missed the nuances of Domingo's thinking that could be confined neither to a Garveyite or communist line. But they rightly perceived his work as threatening the social and political fabric of the colonial order.

* * *

Domingo's incarceration united the New York West Indians, but there were some variations in their responses, which did eventually cause faultlines to form. The WINC kept up the pressure with meetings in Harlem.[158] Malliet returned to the subject in September 1942, reporting a reply that Ethelred Brown had received from the private secretary of Lord Cranborne (Secretary of State for the Colonies) to an earlier letter Brown had written to Richards.[159] The reply noted that Domingo's detention would shortly be reviewed by the Advisory Committee, with Brown's representations slated to receive "due consideration". Malliet took this as offering some "slight hope" for expecting Domingo's release, doubtless unaware of the meaning of "due consideration" within the British bureaucratic lexicon.

Although Malliet was clear enough in his call for Domingo to be freed and to be allowed to re-enter the United States, there was a note of equivocation in his remark "whatever the charges against Domingo may have been and regardless of how well-founded they were"—which ignored the full refutation contained in the PNP's pamphlet *The Case of Domingo*. This was sufficient for Herman P. Osborne, Domingo's old colleague at the WINC, to weigh in with a letter criticising Malliet. Osborne's particular gripe was that Malliet had not recognised the fact that the reason for Domingo's detention had been his championing of West Indian nationalism: "Merely to say what you have said and leave matters to stand as they are is not enough, and, to say the least, is unconvincing."[160]

Malliet and Osborne aired their disputes in the columns of the *New York Amsterdam Star-News*, establishing (in reality very slight) differences between the WINC (represented here by Osborne) and an organisation calling itself the American West Indian Association on Caribbean Affairs (AWIACA). The AWIACA was founded by several of the more conservative members of the JPL(NY), such as Ethelred Brown and T. E. Hanson, along with Joseph C. Morris (as president), Lucien Brown, H. S. Boulin, Hodge Kirnon, Wendell Malliet, and Isaac Braith-

157. Mr Macdonald's Private Secretary to E. Cook, 15 February 1940, CO 323/1749/1, TNA.
158. "Free Domingo Party", *New York Amsterdam Star-News*, 28 March 1942, p. 9.
159. A. M. Wendell Malliet, "World Fronts", *New York Amsterdam Star-News*, 5 September 1942, p. 7.
160. Letter by Herman P. Osborne, in A. M. Wendell Malliet, "World Fronts", *New York Amsterdam Star-News*, 10 October 1942, p. 7.

waite, all of whom feared that the WINC was leaning too far to the left.[161] The AWIACA produced a short book, *Caribbean Charter: A Program for the West Indies* (1942), but doesn't seem to have lasted long.

For the next round Osborne got his own column as part of the newspaper's "The People Speak" feature. He immediately upped the rhetoric, claiming that it was "unfortunate that our mutual friend should seek to hide his malice, his motives and his political ineptitude behind meaningless attacks against me and against the leading political organization of the West Indian people in the United States—the West Indies National Council".[162] The escalation of insults tended to hide the fact—and perhaps resulted from the fact—that the differences between the two positions were relatively small. Osborne defended the WINC's record, with particular reference to the Act of Havana, and called the fear of US annexation of the West Indies "so much eye-wash". He also praised US action in sending a substantial number of black soldiers to Trinidad, and ended with an unequivocal demand for the unconditional freedom of colonial peoples. But among the "central questions" which Osborne offered as the aims to which all New York West Indians should be working—self-government, freedom for Domingo, development of economic resources—was "support for the People's National Party of Jamaica and its program". This, it would turn out, was the nub of the matter.

* * *

Under the terms of the Atlantic Charter (14 August 1941), the USA and the UK announced "certain common principles in the national policies of their respective countries on which they base their hopes for a better future for the world". The third of these principles was that "they respect the right of all peoples to choose the form of government under which they will live; and they wish to see sovereign rights and self government restored to those who have been forcibly deprived of them".[163] As with Woodrow Wilson's equivalent statement in 1918,

161. Herbert Simeon Boulin (1883–1952?) was a Jamaican-born businessman who had served in the British Army in Africa before coming to the USA and working for the Pinkerton Detective Agency. After a brief spell as president of the Berry and Ross Toy Company, which manufactured brown and black dolls, he was employed by the BI to spy on Garvey and others. According to Kornweibel, he reported that Domingo was a paid party propagandist who would blindly follow any dictate of Lenin or Trotsky (*Seeing Red*, pp. 26–27) and urged the deportation of Domingo, Briggs, and Moore (p. 31). Terminated in August 1921, he established the Boulin National Detective Agency, in which capacity he was described as a "sensational divorce raider" (*Inter-State Tattler*, 3 December 1931, p. 2). He later organised the Foreign-Born Citizens League, which competed with the WINC. By 1941 he was again working for the FBI. Isaac Newton Braithwaite (Barbados, 1887–1964).

162. "H. P. Osborne Answers A. M. Wendell Malliet", *New York Amsterdam Star-News*, 14 November 1942, p. 8.

163. "Atlantic Charter", https://avalon.law.yale.edu/wwii/atlantic.asp (accessed 4 September 2023).

these ringing words turned out, when glossed, to have considerably narrower parameters than had seemed apparent: in particular, "all" never actually meant "all".[164] In the House of Commons in September 1941 Winston Churchill clarified what he had *really* meant when he said "all":

> At the Atlantic meeting, we had in mind, primarily, the restoration of the sovereignty, self-government and national life of the States and nations of Europe now under the Nazi yoke, and the principles governing any alterations in the territorial boundaries which may have to be made. So that is quite a separate problem from the progressive evolution of self-governing institutions in the regions and peoples which owe allegiance to the British Crown. We have made declarations on these matters which are complete in themselves, free from ambiguity and related to the conditions and circumstances of the territories and peoples affected. They will be found to be entirely in harmony with the high conception of freedom and justice which inspired the Joint Declaration.[165]

Arthur Creech Jones pressed Churchill to publish those declarations "free from ambiguity", probably suspecting—correctly—that Churchill had never made such declarations.[166]

The Anglo American Caribbean Commission (AACC) was established in March 1942 as a further co-operative effort of the USA and the UK to deal with the Second World War emergency. The Moyne Commission report had indicated that rampant poverty in the islands could lead to social and political volatility. German submarine activity in the region made colonial defence a priority. Charged with advising their respective governments, the commission surveyed ways to cope with the basic social and economic problems of the region and formulated emergency war measures.

President Roosevelt appointed Charles W. Taussig to head the US side of the AACC, turning the commission into an instrument of US policy.[167] Taussig believed in the necessity of political reform through universal suffrage, and the democratisation of local government in order to tackle social and economic issues. With a British defeat on the cards, the USA was clearly preparing for the possibility that it would inherit a set of dysfunctional colonies. When Taussig undertook an extensive tour of the British possessions in the Caribbean, the British gritted their teeth and co-operated. His tour ended on 5 January 1941, before Domingo

164. See above, p. 28.

165. Winston Churchill, Statement in the House of Commons on 9 September 1941, *Hansard*, Fifth Series, 1940–41, vol. 374, col. 69.

166. See Hart, *Towards Decolonisation*, pp. 136–137.

167. See Charlie Whitham, *Bitter Rehearsal: British and American Planning for a Post-War West Indies*, Westport, CT: Praeger, 2002. Charles William Taussig (1896–1948) was president of the American Molasses Company and a confidant of FDR.

reached Jamaica.[168] Taussig was not one to pussyfoot. He understood the seriousness of the 1935–37 riots ("a revolt against intolerable conditions"[169]) and the inadequacy of the Moyne Report recommendation of an annual grant of £1 million for 20 years. He was generally impressed by the black labour leaders and political radicals whom he met, less so by members of the plantocracy and the colonial administration.

In the wartime context the question of subversion was on Taussig's agenda, but he reported that the police commissioners on the British West Indian islands were, generally speaking, "not troubled either with actual subversive activities nor with potential activities of this nature".[170] Domingo's name appears in this section of the report in a somewhat garbled account of the WINC, but none of these references suggest that Taussig saw anything untoward in Domingo's activities, so he was probably as surprised as anyone when Richards ordered Domingo's detention.[171]

After his tour Taussig wrote an overview of the area for the US social work magazine, *Survey Graphic*. In tone it was fairly emollient, praising Roosevelt's New Deal and Moyne's Royal Commission as offering ways forward for the area; but it must have made for uneasy reading in London (and Kingston) on the occasions when it didn't mince words about "reactionary planters and merchants" and "unspeakably bad" sanitary conditions.[172] After Domingo's detention, Walter White wrote to Taussig to keep him informed, offering the opinion that "the arrest is exceedingly unwise if not stupid as it is, in the first place, useless, and in the second place, will increase suspicion of the integrity of the British war aims far more than would any speeches or other acts by a dozen Domingos".[173]

On Taussig's staff at the AACC was the redoubtable figure of Paul Blanshard (1892–1980), a socialist lawyer and secular humanist who'd been appointed as, in his own words, "a sort of research quasi-diplomat".[174] Based in Jamaica, Blanshard was tasked by Taussig with touring the Caribbean colonies in order to compile a

168. "State Dept: Taussig Report, 1941", FDRP [FDRP = Franklin D. Roosevelt, Papers as President: The President's Secretary's File (PSF), 1933–1945, Franklin D. Roosevelt Presidential Library & Museum, Hyde Park, NY], Box 76.

169. Ibid., p. 28.

170. Ibid., p. 61.

171. Ibid., p. 63. In March 1942 R. L. M. Kirkwood, managing director of the West Indies Sugar Company (and another of Richards's *bêtes noires*), wrote a glowing pen portrait of Taussig ("Charles Taussig", *Public Opinion*, 14 March 1942, p. 5).

172. Charles W. Taussig, "The Caribbean", *Survey Graphic*, 30 (March 1941), pp. 146–148 and 198–200, at 199. For Taussig's continuing interest in the Caribbean after Roosevelt's death in 1945, see Jason Parker, "Remapping the Cold War in the Tropics: Race, Communism, and National Security in the West Indies", *International History Review*, 24, no. 2 (2002), pp. 318–347.

173. Letter from Walter White to Charles W. Taussig, 28 July 1941, NAACPRDPS, p. 72.

174. Paul Blanshard, *Personal And Controversial: An Autobiography*, Boston, MA: Beacon Press, 1973, p. 176. Domingo mentions Blanshard as if he knew him ("Sparks from My Anvil", *Public Opinion*, 5 January 1945, p. 3).

secret study of local leaders and social conditions designed to answer the question "Who would rule these territories if the predominantly black peoples were given the right of self-government?"[175] Much of what he learned ended up in his outspoken critique of British colonialism, *Democracy and Empire in the Caribbean*, published after the war—and after he had left his State Department employment.

Blanshard much preferred socialising with the radical black leaders than he did with the white plantocracy, whom he clearly despised. His book's main antagonist emerges as none other than Sir Arthur Richards—although Blanshard never actually mentions his name. Even more than his boss, Blanshard was not one for pulling his punches. The book compiled from his four years' experience in the Caribbean opens by noting that "The odor of black burning flesh still hangs over the Caribbean, and the white ruling class will never escape it."[176] He paints a scathing picture of British officialdom. Governors "deal with and rule over subject peoples all their lives, and their techniques are the techniques of servitude and patronage". They are "not primarily responsible to the people of the colonies" since their "roots and lines of promotion are all abroad".[177] So a governor will almost always arrive "without any first-hand knowledge of the colony": "He comes, let us say, from British Malaya and has never been in the Western Hemisphere", hardly an accidental example given that Richards had spent 25 years in Malaya and had never served in the western hemisphere before his appointment to Jamaica. Governors, Blanshard notes, "tend to maintain feudal standards of expenditure and display", for which his exemplar is, by no coincidence at all, the governor of Jamaica, who lives in a large private park and is properly referred to as "Knight Commander of the Most Distinguished Order of St Michael and St George, upon whom has been conferred the Decoration of the Military Cross, Captain-General and Governor-in-Chief in and over the Island of Jamaica and Its Dependencies".[178] His opinion of the US presence on the islands was equally clear-sighted. Pointing out that the army, navy, FBI, and State Departments all had agents on Jamaica, he noted that "There was no coordination in our quadruple 'intelligence' services, and not much intelligence."[179]

* * *

In June 1942 Richards wrote a long personal and secret letter to H. F. Downie, the Assistant Secretary to the Colonial Office, offering him a background analysis

175. Blanshard, *Personal and Confidential*, p. 177.
176. Paul Blanshard, *Democracy and Empire in the Caribbean: A Contemporary Review*, New York: Macmillan, 1947, p. 9.
177. Ibid., p. 15.
178. Ibid., p. 82.
179. Blanshard, *Personal and Confidential*, p. 179.

of the situation in Jamaica—but also revealing a man in the grip of paranoia.[180] "Unrest is in the air", he warned, singling out as particular dangers the conservative newspaper *The Gleaner*, run by "hard-bitten Jews and Syrians", and Norman Manley and the PNP, who are now seeing the consequences of "preach[ing] the gospel of hate with such unscrupulous passion for years to a very ignorant and emotional people". One of the "local aggravations" he listed was "the indiscretion of Taussig" and the AACC's "drift under him towards positive interference in the domestic affairs of Jamaica". Taussig, Richards asserted, had, on the basis of a superficial knowledge of the area, "an incurable itch to interfere in local politics while steadfastly denying any such intention". Taussig had also clearly raised the Domingo case with Richards—much to the governor's annoyance.

Another local irritation was the dispute between Bustamante and Manley, which had flared up after Bustamante's release from detention. Richards's analysis of Bustamante was astute: he is "a damned nuisance, admittedly", stirring up trouble all over the island, but "he is first and last out for Bustamante". As a result his activities are sporadic and incoherent, and "[h]e is not fundamentally anti-government". On the other hand, Richards announced, "the Manley group is fundamentally anti-government and subversive". It aims at "complete self-government and at an entirely Communist set-up". This was paranoid nonsense, but Richards wasn't finished. "Its methods and techniques", he continued, "are closely modelled … on the Nazi plan—to end in the dictatorship of Manley." This was deranged fantasy.

Richards had evidently seen the danger that, with Bustamante detained, Manley and the PNP could gain effective control of the labour movement. As his letter to Downie suggests, he recognised Bustamante as the lesser of two evils: the BITU leader's egomania prevented him from having an effective political programme that might threaten the government, so the governor was prepared to release him in order to stymie what he regarded as the more dangerous PNP plans. With Domingo still detained, the PNP didn't have a charismatic speaker who might go toe-to-toe with Bustamante among his own constituency. Bustamante was smart enough on his release in February 1942 to stress that he had no complaints with Richards himself ("I do not blame the Governor"), only with the person who had made the false accusation against him ("the wretch who framed me").[181]

As soon as Bustamante was released he went on the offensive against Manley, accusing him of bringing Domingo into Jamaica to run the BITU in Bustamante's absence and wrest control away from its rightful owner.[182] In addition, he came

180. Arthur Richards, Letter to H. F. Downie, 1 June 1942, CO 137/854/14, TNA.

181. "Bustamante Tells All", p. 12. For evidence that the interests of Richards and Bustamante coincided, see the speech Richards gave to honour Bustamante in London in 1971 (Peel, *Old Sinister*, pp. 181–183).

182. "Labour Leader Hurls Accusations at Head of People's National Party", *The Gleaner*, 27 February 1942, p. 11. During Bustamante's imprisonment, the BITU had survived thanks to the

out against self-government. There were suggestions that taking such a stance was a prerequisite for his release from internment, but it's also the case that Bustamante's political instincts told him that this was the one issue on which he could create a clear dividing line between the PNP and the new political party he soon created, the Jamaica Labour Party (JLP), which he did via the inaccurate but effective slogan by which he characterised self-government: "brown man rule".[183]

The question as to why Domingo had come to Jamaica was much debated. One of the elected representatives to the Legislative Council, C. A. Reid, a loyal supporter of the governor, used a local Mandeville meeting called to discuss the Moyne Commission recommendations to suggest that 5,000 people ought to have been detained and then to pose the question: "I should like to know if there is any truth in the rumour that Domingo was being brought out here to take Bustamante's job?"[184] Manley hit back, suggesting that he could guess the source of Reid's information, since prominent BITU members had received a pseudonymous letter, signed "Ethel", asking the same question. The letter was "written in a very characteristic hand", Manley reported, indicating that he knew very well the source of the question.[185] "Ethel" was probably Gladys Longbridge, Bustamante's lover and amanuensis. Bustamante was quick to stir the pot further. During a rambling speech in front of thousands of his supporters on the evening of 30 March, he told how he and Domingo had originally been in different compounds, but that when Domingo was transferred to an adjoining room, Bustamante began to wind him up by pointing out that Manley hadn't been to visit him for six weeks, prompting Domingo to bring out a letter in which Manley invited him to come to Jamaica to work for BITU: "I saw it with my own eyes," announced Bustamante.[186]

Although Bustamante certainly had his own axe to grind, and increasingly saw Manley and Domingo as threats to his plans, and although *The Gleaner* and those loyal to the colonial government were certainly eager to sow division within the nationalist forces, it is true that Manley gave different accounts as to exactly what Domingo had been asked to Jamaica to do. The official story was that Manley had requested Domingo to come to Jamaica "to assist in the organisational work of the Party having in mind particularly his thorough understanding of the organisation of study programmes for political purposes which forms the basis of the

---

efforts of the PNP, with Manley clearly doing his best to get his cousin released. Gratitude was not among Bustamante's qualities.

183. Richard Hart quotes Vernon Arnett's unpublished memoir recalling that Arnett had been told by Manley that Bustamante had told him that Richards's release of Bustamante from internment was dependent on him coming out against self-government (*Towards Decolonisation*, p. 151).

184. "Manchester Study Moyne Constitution", *The Gleaner*, 29 July 1941, pp, 6 and 7, at 6. Charles Archibald Reid (1887–1944) represented Manchester for many years on the Legislative Council.

185. "Mr Manley Replies To Hon. C. A. Reid", *The Gleaner*, 4 August 1941, p. 10.

186. "Bustamante Tells All", *The Gleaner*, 1 April 1942, p. 12.

educational programme of the Party which is today one of their main activities".[187] But Manley also wrote to Herman Osborne in New York shortly after Domingo was detained: "I wanted him to do work in connection with Union organisation. Domingo realized certain weaknesses in Union structure which he observed in Jamaica and which are unnecessary for me to discuss and I think that his gift for organisation would have been invaluable at a time when the movement is at a critical stage of development."[188] Indeed, in 1939 Domingo had written to Manley complaining about Bustamante's leadership and autocratic style: "You can depend upon me to fight with my last breath for the extensions of the rights of the masses."[189] Of course, despite his undoubted commitment to the PNP and to the labour movement, Domingo himself may have imagined that his major efforts in 1941 would be directed towards the fight for self-government.

In a further move, Bustamante began to associate himself with the recently deceased Marcus Garvey, no doubt realising that a large number of his followers had been Garveyites and that he had a chance to ascend the now vacant pedestal. "Garvey paid the price for leadership," Bustamante announced. "The price of leadership is suffering and persecution .... Thousands who once turned their backs upon Marcus Garvey regret to-night that he is not among us."[190] The invitation to identify the two leaders could hardly have been more blatant.

* * *

With Domingo's re-entry permit due to expire in mid-1942, his supporters began to demand his return to the USA, hoping that the British authorities would be content with seeing the back of him. Governor Richards was not convinced:

> I presume it is fully realized that if Domingo is released to go to the U.S.A., he will immediately start a virulent anti-British campaign in America and will no doubt be clever enough to keep under cover himself. I have the gravest doubt of the wisdom of letting him go, even if the U.S. authorities were unexpectedly to agree to receive him.[191]

On 11 March 1942 Ethelred Brown wrote to the interned Domingo. Manley had sent Brown copies of 39 letters that Domingo had written to Campbell. Brown announced that the letters proved that Domingo's arrest had been justi-

187. "P.N.P. Declares Against Detention of Domingo", *The Gleaner*, 21 June 1941, pp. 1 and 6, at 6.
188. Norman Manley, Letter to H. P. Osborne, 28 June 1941, NMP; quoted after Timm, *Nationalists Abroad*, p. 292.
189. W. A. Domingo, Letter to Norman Manley, 28 July 1939, NMP.
190. "Bustamante Tells All", *The Gleaner*, 1 April 1942, p. 12.
191. Sir Arthur Richards, "Memorandum", 30 September 1941, WINCC.

fied. It apparently never occurred to Brown that his letter would be opened by the British censors—who would obviously be delighted that even some of Domingo's friends and colleagues were not supporting him. When Roberts—in New Orleans—heard about Brown's letter, he was livid.[192] The JPL(NY) put out a statement that tried to repair the damage.[193] With Roberts in New Orleans and not on the JPL(NY) committee, Domingo interned, and O'Meally possibly ill (he would die later that year), Brown was the senior figure, less politically savvy than the other three and more fearful of implication with left-wing radicalism.[194] His craven response—openly in a letter to US Secretary of State Cordell Hull and internally in meetings reported to J. Edgar Hoover by FBI informants—did Domingo no favours at all.[195] Indeed, US authorities were not eager to welcome him back. While Domingo was still interned, J. Edgar Hoover received an anonymous letter from "A Native American War Veteran", suggesting that Domingo shouldn't be allowed back into the country "because he has been for the last 20 years a special agent of the Soviet government and is one of the chief trouble-makers among the Negroes".[196]

On 6 October 1942 Hoover sent a note to the Visa Division at the Department of State noting that the FBI files "reflect that Wilfred A. Domingo … has been exceedingly active in Communist activities, both in the United States and in Jamaica".[197] The FBI's grasp of Jamaican events is indicated by the remark that the PNP "had its inception at a mutiny of the National Reform Association in Kingston, Jamaica on August 10, 1938". Of Domingo, "it is said that he was sent to Moscow, Russia, for training in 1931". This misinformation was passed by Hoover (24 February 1943) to Adolf A. Berle, Assistant Secretary of State. By 22 April, in a further memorandum to the Visa Division, Hoover had omitted the reported speech in favour of the plain statement: "is known to have left the country in 1931 to undertake certain training at Moscow, Russia". In fact, Domingo never

192. Roberts told Brown that he had "blundered seriously"; Roberts, Letter to Ethelred Brown, 4 April 1942, WARA 2.3.6.

193. 24 April 1942, in ibid.

194. Jim O'Meally, as Domingo and Roberts called him, was clearly trusted by both, and his early death was a significant blow to the JPL(NY).

195. In his letter to Cordell Hull, Brown referred to Domingo's "indiscrete and improper remarks" (27 March 1942, DF 1940–1944, Box 3029, 800.2021, Domingo, W. A./3), RG59, NARA), while it was reported to Hoover that Brown had told a meeting that the JPL(NY) was going to drop all work pertaining to the Domingo case (FBI report by Special Agent Torrens, 10 April 1942, CDF 1940–1944, Box 3083, 800.00B. Jamaica Progressive League, RG59, NARA), and then that Brown had suggested that Domingo's letters showed support for the Axis powers (J. Edgar Hoover to Adolf A. Berle, 20 May 1943, CDF 1940–1944, Box 3083, 800.00B, Jamaican Progressive League/5, RG59, NARA): all quoted after Timm, *Nationalists Abroad*, pp. 287 and 289.

196. Letter to J. Edgar Hoover, 22 February 1942, FBIWAD.

197. J. Edgar Hoover to Visa Division, Department of State, 6 October 1942, FBIWAD.

travelled further east than Brooklyn. With these kinds of calumnies flowing, Domingo was very unlikely to get a sympathetic hearing.

* * *

Richards was not for backing down. The formation of new trade unions, some involving government workers, and evidence of the activities of an organised left-wing within the PNP disturbed what was left of his equanimity. The PNP, increasingly frustrated by Richards's hard line, made a further hard move by declaring again for self-government: "The cornerstone of our economic recovery and stability is the immediate transfer of responsibility and power to the people of Jamaica. … Full self-government for Jamaica becomes a necessity the delay of which increases the hardships and sufferings which our people are forced to bear day after day."[198] For Richards, Britain was at war, and he was inclined to view all such activities as implicitly treasonous, leading him to further and even more blatantly misuse his wartime emergency powers. On 3 November 1942 he ordered the detention of Ken Hill, Frank Hill, Richard Hart, and Arthur Henry, soon referred to in the local press as the 4Hs.[199] Unfortunately for Richards, his high-handedness was increasing the ranks of the opposition, both within Jamaica, where even moderate voices could see that his detentions were politically motivated rather than having anything to do with the war effort, and even more importantly outside, to the north, where the US government was taking a greater interest.

While the British had always thought that social and economic improvement could come within the framework of the Empire, the USA thought differently, pressing the British government both to improve the socio-economic situation and to make a constitutional move towards self-government. This and other factors meant that during Domingo's detention the tectonic plates of British colonialism began to shift. The replacement of Lord Moyne as colonial secretary by Viscount Cranborne indicated some movement on these fronts.[200] Cranborne's tenure was brief, but his successor, Oliver Stanley, was of the same disposition. "We are pledged to guide Colonial people along the road to self-government within the framework of the British Empire," he announced.[201] The new constitution would be reviewed after five years with the hope that "further advances" could be made. The language was still deeply paternalistic, but the phrase "self-government" was at least now in use.

198. "P.N.P. Plans Special Campaign on Self-Government", *Public Opinion*, 31 October 1942, p. 1.
199. For a participant's account, see Hart, *Towards Decolonisation*, pp. 194–210.
200. Robert Arthur James Gascoyne-Cecil, 5th Marquess of Salisbury 1893–1972), known as Viscount Cranborne from 1903 to 1947.
201. Col. Oliver Stanley, COLONIAL AFFAIRS HC Deb 13 July 1943, vol. 391 cc47–151.

In late 1942, by which time Domingo had already been locked up for 18 months, Roosevelt sent Taussig to London to consult with the British government.[202] The discussions—which involved meetings with Prime Minister Winston Churchill and King George VI—were wide-ranging, but the Domingo case was firmly on the agenda of the formal conference.[203] A sub-committee of six people, including Taussig and Sir George Gater, the Permanent Under-Secretary of State for the Colonies, "considered certain matters concerning internment of Domingo", and its conclusions were approved by the conference as a whole.[204] The group met on 14 December and produced a note that read in full:

> It was agreed that the Colonial Office should raise with Sir Arthur Richards the possibility of Domingo being released in Jamaica subject to good behaviour and on the understanding that, if his conduct over a period of twelve months was such as to satisfy this condition, the question of granting authority for his readmission to the United States would be sympathetically considered by the State Department. That Department would, of course, not be bound by the views of the Jamaica government but would exercise an independent judgment on the question whether Domingo had in fact shown good behaviour during the period of probation in the Colony.
>
> If the procedure suggested above proved acceptable to Sir Arthur Richards, the next step would be to sound the State Department, through Lord Halifax. Simultaneously through this approach, Mr Taussig would be informed and would use his good offices with the State Department to secure their promise of sympathetic consideration for Domingo's readmission if his behaviour in Jamaica during the twelve months following his release should prove to be satisfactory.[205]

Towards the end of the main conference, Taussig raised some political questions which Stanley asked to be discussed in camera, with just the two of them present. Stanley admitted that Jamaica provided the most dangerous situation in the West Indies, one he was resolved to address via major constitutional reform, "which would include greatly increased franchise and a limitation on the reserve powers of the Governor". In addition, "Colonel Stanley told Taussig of his intention to recall Governor Richards to London for a consultation and the possibility of Richards not returning to Jamaica. Taussig and Stanley discussed in some detail Governor Richards and his present difficulties in Jamaica."[206]

202. See the account in Whitham, *Bitter Rehearsal*, pp. 89–110.
203. "Report of the Visit of Chas. Taussig Chm. Anglo American Caribbean Comm. to London, Dec. 9–19, 1942", FDRP, Box 166. The report was secret.
204. Ibid., pp. 38–39.
205. Ibid., p. 58. The note is also in CO 318/455/11, TNA.
206. "Report of the Visit of Chas. Taussig", p. 78.

Post haste, Richards was summoned to London, leaving in the first week of January 1943. On his return to Jamaica, Domingo was released on 19 February and the 4Hs on 18 March. There are no records of the conversation Richards had with Stanley. Indeed, there is very little in the Colonial Office files about Domingo's detention, despite (or perhaps because of) the *cause célèbre* it became. Richards had previously announced that he would prefer to leave Jamaica at the end of his first term (due on 19 August 1943), but would be happy to stay if asked. The suspicion must be that Taussig, with FDR's weight behind him, suggested in his *tête-à-tête* with Stanley that it would be best for the Anglo-American relationship if Domingo were released and Richards transferred. Stanley may have needed little persuading since his plan for constitutional reform would get nowhere with Domingo still detained and Manley not playing ball. His constitutional proposals were published on 10 February, Domingo's release providing a boost for their discussion in Jamaica.[207]

The suggestion that Richards released Domingo under duress has two bases. Richards—a stubborn man at the best of times—refused to indicate any reason for the release. In August 1942 his Advisory Committee (very much in his pocket) had reviewed Domingo's case and reported that it was unable to modify its original recommendation. In 1943 its views were not sought. Richards even went so far as to announce, as late as 16 February, that he had no reason to believe that Domingo's sentiments had changed—and therefore there was no reason to release him other than pressure from London.[208] This put the Colonial Office into something of a funk as they tried to find a form of words for Stanley to use in the House of Commons. Since the decision had to be presented as Richards's—to save his face—it couldn't be announced that Richards had decided that he was satisfied that Domingo, if released, would not act in a manner prejudicial to public safety and defence: he clearly wasn't thus satisfied, and would not say so. Stanley was, a note on the Colonial Office file announced, "on a sticky wicket". His only stroke (backward defensive) would be to say that he had no knowledge of Sir Arthur's reasons for releasing Domingo.[209] Stanley followed the playbook. Three of the Labour MPs who had taken an interest in the Domingo case pressed Stanley in the House on 10 March.[210] David Adams asked whether there were conditions to Domingo's release (there were not), and Sam Silverman followed up with the

207. *Jamaica Constitution: Despatch from the Secretary of State for the Colonies to the Governor of Jamaica Dated 10th February 1943*, London: HMSO, 1943.

208. "The release is believed to have been inspired by very important moves to come in the British Caribbean, as it came almost simultaneously with announcements regarding large-scale expenditures for the development of social welfare and economic adjustment programs and the grant of a new constitution with other political reforms" ("Long Fight Wins Release of W. A. Domingo In Jamaica", *New York Amsterdam Star-News*, 6 March 1943, p. 1).

209. The relevant documents are in CO 967/132 and CO 968/68/6, TNA.

210. Benjamin Riley (1866–1946), Labour, Dewsbury; David Adams (1871–1943), Labour, Consett; Samuel Silverman (1895–1968), Labour, Nelson.

expected googly: "What information has the Governor had to induce him to change his mind? He was satisfied at one moment that the detention was necessary and satisfied much later that the detention was not necessary." "I cannot go into details," deadbatted Stanley: "The Governor was satisfied that the detention was no longer necessary."[211] After a suitable interval it was announced on 21 June that Richards had been appointed Governor of Nigeria, doubtless a reward for keeping his mouth shut, even though he would encounter some equally intractable anti-colonialists in his new posting, as Domingo would report in his *Public Opinion* column.[212]

* * *

Domingo's return was welcomed by a 3,000-strong rally at Edelweiss Park.[213] Manley very much wanted Domingo to stay in Jamaica, but Domingo decided against running for public office: he needed to sort out his business affairs in New York.[214] Getting back to the USA, however, proved challenging.[215] For a start, the FBI was ratcheting up its hunt for Communists, and Domingo was firmly in its sights. Seemingly unaware that his letters were still being opened and read in Kingston even after his release, Domingo wrote to various friends in New York, contrasting the British colonial system of internment with the free trials of the USA, but even this didn't count in his favour. Back in New York, in May 1944 the FBI started investigating the WINC for the possible association of some of its officers with "communist elements": the phones of Stevens and Petioni were tapped.[216] This didn't bode well for Domingo's chances of being allowed back, and in February 1945 the FBI advised the US Consulate in Kingston not to issue Domingo with a visa.[217] As he'd promised, Taussig tried to help via the State Department, which contacted the US Consulate in Kingston. Consul Kemp's priceless answer was "I know of no specific act on which to base a refusal for a visa, on the other hand I would consider a visa highly inadvisable."[218]

211. *Hansard*, Fifth Session, vol. 387, 10 March 1943, cols 651–652.
212. Domingo, "Sparks from My Anvil", *Public Opinion*, 6 June 1946, p. 6. Reporting from London, George Padmore quoted a PNP spokesman as saying that Richards's high-handedness had made him the most unpopular governor of the past century and that his departure would improve co-operation between Jamaicans and the British government ("London West Indians Hail Jamaica Change of Governor", *Chicago Defender*, 3 July 1943, p. 5).
213. "Welcome to Domingo", *The Gleaner*, 1 March 1943, p. 7.
214. "Mr Domingo Anxious to Return to America", *The Gleaner*, 23 February 1943, p. 6.
215. Roberts thought that Domingo "had suffered morally to the extent of a nervous breakdown while held in the internment camp" and reports that Manley spoke of a "psychic hypochondria", though it has to be said that there is little evidence of this in Domingo's writing (Roberts, *These Many Years*, p. 327).
216. J. Edgar Hoover, "Memorandum for the Attorney General", 30 May 1944, WINCC.
217. Timm, *Nationalists Abroad*, p. 313.
218. Ibid., pp. 313–314.

A summative FBI memorandum described Domingo as "a British West Indian negro agitator ... particularly interested and effective in fomenting disturbances among the colored population of the British West Indies and the United States". His internment is described as resulting from "his activities in Jamaica in connection with the native agitation"—a bit rich since he was arrested before he even set foot on Jamaican soil.[219] At the same time a War Department document described Domingo as "a Communist organizer of the West Indian National Council".[220] A further memorandum from the US Secret Intelligence Service liaison officer in Kingston was more openly hostile: "Domingo has been the subject of frequent communications to the Bureau," he began: "He is the foremost exponent of race prejudice .... He is one of the few individuals in Jamaica who seems to be engaged internationally in demanding that the negro in negro majority countries be given the right to rule themselves, and that the dominating white element be eliminated." Sullivan was clearly a very poor reader, but his opinion was unequivocal: "Domingo is a dangerous rabble raiser who is in a position, particularly at this time—that is with the advent of the new constitution—to do a great harm."[221]

The end of the war in 1945 marked a shift in power in the Caribbean, with the USA now in the ascendency and the UK beginning the long process of decolonisation. The global map was taking a new form too, with the San Francisco conference set up to establish the United Nations in April and the Pan-African Congress meeting in Manchester in October. Stranded in Jamaica, Domingo had no way of attending these events: instead, he publicised them.[222] Despite the disappointment at not being allowed back to the USA for a further four and a half years, Domingo threw himself into his political journalism and worked closely with the PNP, often chairing meetings, speaking alongside Manley, and acting as a delegate to the constitutional conference in which the PNP participated. In August 1943 he was granted an ex-officio seat on the party's general council. On 21 December 1944 he addressed a large meeting at PNP headquarters in Edelweiss Park.[223] Ironically, while Domingo was trying to get out of Jamaica, W. Adolphe Roberts was trying to get in. At first the Executive Council refused him entry, prompting Domingo's ire. When he finally returned, a dinner was given in his honour at the Myrtle Bank Hotel, with Domingo as one of the speakers.[224]

* * *

219. S. S. Alden, "Memorandum for Mr Ladd. Re: W. A. Domingo, Visa Applicant", 8 July 1943. CC-287, FBIWAD.

220. MID 201. Domingo, Wilfred Adolphus, 15 March 1943, FBIWAD.

221. John F. Sullivan, Memorandum to Director, FBI, 7 February 1944, FBIWAD.

222. He covered the Manchester Pan-African Congress in W. A. Domingo, "Speaking Out Loud," *Public Opinion*, 31 October 1945, p. 3.

223. "P.N.P. Will Work for Success of New Constitution", *The Gleaner*, 27 December 1944, p. 5.

224. "Mr W. Adolphe Roberts Honoured at Dinner: Work as Journalist, Patriot, and Idealist Praised", *The Gleaner*, 9 August 1946, p. 10.

Immediately after his release Domingo had written a short piece for *Public Opinion* to thank his local supporters, quickly followed by two cheers for the new constitution [#24].[225] After that he wrote for *Public Opinion* almost weekly. When the paper went daily on 4 April 1944, he began a daily column, becoming a mainstay of the main mouthpiece of the PNP, and producing several thousand words a week on a wide variety of topics. A series of shorter observations began to appear under the title "Sparks from My Anvil", sometimes with a sub-title, sometimes not. There was even a "Sparklets from My Anvil". Occasional longer pieces would run across two or more days. The 31 months between April 1944 and November 1946 were by far Domingo's most productive period as a writer. In November 1946 *Public Opinion* went back to being a weekly due to a lack of printing equipment. And while this reduced the number of pieces by Domingo it could publish, he responded by writing supplementary pieces under the transparent pseudonym "Ognimod".

Producing a weekly and then a daily column, Domingo's writing started to become more personal, inasmuch as he began to construct an image in his readers' minds of a plain-speaking man committed to factual accuracy, nationalist to his core, but with wide international interests, and by turns self-deprecating, sarcastic, and sometimes angry. He described himself on one occasion as "a bull in a china shop", willing to break the crockery: "I have a bad habit of thinking ruthlessly, allowing logic to lead me to the final conclusion."[226] On another he was "a journalistic gadfly, a disturber of consciences, an agitator of people's cerebrums".[227] He clearly wanted to come across as an independent voice, although his partisanship on behalf of the PNP became clearer and clearer as the 1944 election approached: he described election day (14 December) as "Our Rendezvous with History".[228] Part of this independent voice, however, involved assuming, simultaneous to his most prolific period of writing for *Public Opinion*, the editorship of *Negro Voice*. Initially under the editorship of Garveyite Z. Munroe Scarlett, *Negro Voice* regularly reprinted front-page extracts from Garvey's "Philosophy and Opinions" and news of the activities of the Kingston UNIA.[229] A column from J. A. G. Edwards, "As I See the Negro World", announced that he "subscribed one hundred percent" to the principles of the UNIA.[230] Around the time Domingo assumed editorship, a title change occurred, the *New Negro Voice* adding a reference to Harlem's "New

225. W. A. Domingo, "Domingo Says 'Thanks'", *Public Opinion*, 27 February 1943, p. 1.

226. W. A. Domingo, "Speak Up, Please", *Public Opinion*, 1 May 1944, pp. 3, 4; "A Personal Statement", *Public Opinion*, 26 May 1944, p. 3.

227. W. A. Domingo, "The World Is My Province", *Public Opinion*, 11 January 1945, p. 3.

228. W. A. Domingo, "Our Rendezvous with History", *Public Opinion*, 13 December 1944, p. 2.

229. Zephenia Munroe Scarlett (1902–1984). Scarlett was a long-time member of the UNIA and later of the Afro-West Indian League. In 1961 he travelled with the Jamaican government delegation to Ethiopia, where they held conversations about Rastafari repatriation.

230. J. A .G. Edwards, "As I See the Negro World," *Negro Voice*, 2 January 1943, p. 3.

Negro" movement with which Domingo had been associated. Taken in isolation, this editorship has led to the misapprehension that at this time Domingo could be "best described as a Garveyite".[231] Nothing could be further from the truth. After their rift, Domingo's views on Garvey himself never changed, as this volume amply demonstrates, but their ideological differences shouldn't be overstated: certainly their views on what was wrong with Jamaican society were not all that far apart. And with Garvey dead, the UNIA in Kingston was free to make its own political decisions, which included working with the PNP: J. A. G. Edwards also announced that after watching the PNP closely, he now claimed affiliation "under the banner of the UNIA and as a PNP member".[232] A final factor may have been Domingo's personal friendship with Garvey's widow, Amy Jacques Garvey. Jamaica's political landscape was certainly shifting.

Occasionally in his *Public Opinion* column Domingo would recall incidents from his internment: how, for example, he and Sam Marquis (both black) were forbidden from using the one shower in their compound, which was reserved for the four white Germans in custody.[233] The following month he recalled that of the nine British citizens detained at Up Camp, six were members of the PNP, but that the attack on the party backfired, strengthening the resolve of the PNP membership and eliciting sympathy even from the more liberal members of the elite.[234] On another occasion he remembered that when he was arrested, his luggage contained an abridged copy of Thomas Paine's works, about whose subversive qualities Domingo was quizzed by Judge Sherlock. Domingo pointed out that FDR had quoted extensively from Paine in a 1942 radio broadcast and that Paine's works were freely available at the Institute of Jamaica.[235] This is one of several references to Richards's three friends who constituted the kangaroo court that confirmed the governor's decision to detain Domingo: "When I was taken off a ship and imprisoned for 20 months, and my business in America ruined; when I was taken before three hand-picked men who were manifestly unfit psychologically and politically to give me a fair 'hearing', it was because Sir Arthur Richards and his advisers feared that I might spit out some unpleasant truths."[236] Sherlock is a frequent recipient of Domingo's barbs: "I confess that I never felt greater

231. Myles Osborne, "Africa in Jamaica: George Padmore, W. A. Domingo and *Public Opinion*", in *The Edinburgh Companion to British Colonial Periodicals*, ed. David Finkelstein, David Johnson, and Caroline Davis, Edinburgh, UK: Edinburgh University Press, 2024, pp. 519–530, at 524.
232. J. A .G. Edwards, "As I See the Negro World", p. 3.
233. W. A. Domingo, "The Double Standard in the Empire", *Public Opinion*, 5 February 1944, pp. 3 and 6. Samuel Charles Marquis (1912–1945) was secretary of the Propaganda Committee of the PNP.
234. W. A. Domingo, "We Celebrate", *Public Opinion*, 25 March 1944, p. 4.
235. W. A. Domingo, "Jamaica—A Republic", *Public Opinion*, 20 April 1944, p. 3.
236. W. A. Domingo, "By Way of Explanation", *Public Opinion*, 20 June 1944, p. 3.

contempt for a human being than I did for him."[237] The experience of prison, he reports, "soured my disposition", although his remark about Sherlock is one of the few traces of real bitterness in his writing.

Perhaps understandably, Domingo couldn't resist a few parting shots at his nemesis, now removed from the Jamaican fray. Soon after his release Domingo waded into the issue of racial minorities in Jamaica, furiously debated in the pages of *Public Opinion* [#26], even finding a way of laying the blame for racial segregation at Richards's door.[238] On his next posting Richards managed to antagonise Nigerian activists, as Domingo was not slow to point out, quoting the *Eastern Nigerian Guardian*'s less than complimentary view of the colony's governor.[239] In 1948 Richards (now Baron Milverton) retired from the colonial service to dedicate himself to British politics as a member of the Labour Party in the House of Lords. Domingo would not have been surprised by Richards's rapid move across the political spectrum, first to the Liberal Party and then in 1951 to the Conservatives.

Payback also came for those who supported Richards, notably a son of the soil and ardent supporter of the British Empire, C. A. Reid, who had become an elected member of the Legislative Council and was appointed Privy Councillor by Richards. Domingo recalled a speech in which Reid deplored that five Jamaicans (including Domingo) were in detention: he thought the number should be 5,000. Domingo commended Reid for wanting to mitigate his loneliness by providing him with so much company. Though the tone is good-humoured, Domingo's words drip with sarcasm as he professes to await Reid's contributions with bated breath because every one can be guaranteed to contain one such gem of wisdom. The Legislative Council also featured when in 1943 Domingo commended its disruption by two Rastafarians who injected some real world issues into the arena of colonial pomposity [#26]. His sympathy for these tactics was also obvious in 1945 when he again praised the ingenuity of those who circumvented protocol to disturb the respectable veneer of official proceedings [#34].

Domingo's writing for *Public Opinion* ranged far and wide. Among the topics discussed, often across several articles, were the tourist trade, the discovery of bauxite, the progress and then aftermath of the war in Europe (including the Nuremburg trials), the abuse of Jamaican bus conductors, the development of nuclear weapons, standing (or not) for the national anthem, the racist treatment of Jamaican airmen in England, athletics, the discarding of hats and umbrellas, lynching in the USA, the freedom of the press, industrialisation, the need for a university in Jamaica, tourism [#31], and the appalling living conditions

237. Domingo, "Sparks from My Anvil", *Public Opinion*, 22 February 1945, p. 3. David Thomas Joseph Sherlock (1881–1964) had previously been chief justice of North Borneo.

238. W. A. Domingo, "Racial Segregation: Sir Arthur Richards' Legacy to Jamaica?", *Public Opinion*, 21 August 1943, p. 3 and 28 August 1943, p. 4.

239. Domingo, "Sparks from My Anvil", *Public Opinion*, 6 June 1946, p. 6.

in Kingston [#36]. Also touched upon more than once were the etymologies of Jamaican words, nutrition, science, and religion. He called out frequent examples of racial discrimination and prejudice in Jamaica. Always interested in visitors' views of Jamaica, he reported on the visits of his Trinidadian friend from New York Charles Petioni, and of his JPL colleague Adolphe Roberts. He pronounced himself both a nationalist and in favour of "internationalisation", on the grounds that an international perspective was necessary to understand the global currents affecting Jamaica [#29]. He wrote praise songs to several individuals, including the journalist Dorothy Thompson, the veteran Grenadan politician T. A. Marryshow (despite his support for federation), Sylvia Pankhurst on her unwavering support for Ethiopia, Norman Manley on his receipt of an honorary degree from Howard University, the PNP politician Ivan Lloyd, Adam Clayton Powell, Jr on his election to Congress, Nwafor Orizu, Eleanor Roosevelt, H. G. Wells, and Arnold Lescene ("the most obdurate and daring writer" on the subject of self-government).[240] We here include his paean to the Nigerian activist Nnamdi Azikiwe [#29]. Domingo often reported on what he'd read in the foreign press or in official documents: common sources included *The New Statesman*, *Time*, the *Miami Herald*, and the London *Daily Mail*, though he was also capable of quoting from journals such as *Scots Socialist*, the magazine of the Scottish Socialist Party, which was pushing for independence—to Domingo's surprise, and delight.[241] And he also quoted liberally from his favourite writers: Paul Laurence Dunbar, Alexander Pope, Shakespeare, Wendell Phillips, Anatole France, Thomas Paine, John Strachey, and Joseph McCabe.

In another sign of the turning tide, Domingo remarked with surprise and delight the foundation of the Jamaica National Republican Party by M. K. Kandekore.[242] Beyond Jamaica, he covered events in Trinidad and Barbados, as well as giving detailed attention to the situation in Cuba. The USA inevitably featured heavily. A three-part essay traced the history of Jamaicans in New York, and another assessed Father Divine, who had intrigued him in Harlem.[243] He compared US and British attitudes to race while monitoring the behaviour of US troops stationed in the West Indies: although prepared for the worst, Domingo reported that his own investigations had shown that US troops based in Jamaica had behaved well, and that any colour-related incidents had been dealt with swiftly by shipping the miscreants back to the USA. He offered a careful comparison of the situations of West Indian and US blacks, based, of course, on long

240. Domingo, "Sparks from My Anvil", *Public Opinion*, 6 July 1946, p. 6.

241. W. A. Domingo, "Nationalism in an Unexpected Quarter", *Public Opinion*, 7 July 1944, p. 3.

242. W. A. Domingo, "Jamaica—A Republic", *Public Opinion*, 20 April 1944, p. 3: see "Current Items", *The Gleaner*, 6 March 1944, p. 4. Menelik R. O. Kandekore (1909–1971) was also president of the Jamaica National Labour Union, and therefore a bitter opponent of Bustamante.

243. Possibly born in Georgia, USA as George Baker, the full assumed name of the controversial black spiritual leader, Father Divine, was the Reverend Major Jealous Divine (*c.* 1876–1965).

personal experience in both Jamaica and New York. There were also constant comparisons between Puerto Rico and Jamaica, to the former's advantage.

He often remarked on British neglect of its colonies—despite the debt it owed them [#25]. On persistent rumours that the USA was about to purchase or otherwise acquire the British Caribbean islands, Domingo was of the view that there was nothing to fear: the Southern political elite would always object to the acquisition of responsibility for further black majority countries.[244] One proponent of this fear was Wendell Malliet, with whom Domingo took issue, though referring to him only as "our Harlem friend", taken to task for claiming to know better what was happening in Jamaica than Jamaicans on the island, such as Domingo himself.[245]

He frequently turned to constitutional matters, often voicing support for the PNP and its policies, and commenting—usually unfavourably—on the doings of the Jamaican legislature, pointing out that because of the war the elected representatives had not faced an election in nine years. He often bemoaned the fact that some of the most conservative people in Jamaica were those who would most benefit from change: "Conditioned by their degraded lot, they dread any proposed improvement."[246] Others were equally decried for their reluctance to involve themselves in their country's political struggles. A constant theme was the need for Jamaica to take control of its own destiny and to Jamaicanise the culture of the island. Signs of progress were noted: "Jamaica is developing a healthy national consciousness. Its people are taking an active interest in their own affairs. They are thinking as Jamaicans."[247] One piece focused on forgotten Jamaican authors [#35].

This spotlight on Jamaica's cultural productivity aligned with many of the themes of his writing in *New Negro Voice*. His "Are Negroes Men?" [#28] bears the hallmark of many of the points he was simultaneously making in *Public Opinion*. In this *New Negro Voice* contribution Domingo reiterated his belief in opposing all forms of racial discrimination. He insisted that governments who quash the airing of grievances and public protest are "Fascist in their outlook", along with voicing his firm belief that democracy was the best path forward. But Domingo also departed from his *Public Opinion* prose, translating the same points more explicitly into language familiar to UNIA followers. He applied the familiar adage to "think clearly and stiffen our backbones", to convert "wishful thinking" into "purposeful doing". Remnants of this language are visible in *Public Opinion* [#31], but without the UNIA maxims. Domingo's modulations between his two main

244. W. A. Domingo, "The U.S.A. and the West Indies", *Public Opinion*, 15 January 1944, p. 3.

245. W. A. Domingo, ""Give the Devil His Due", *Public Opinion*, 18 April 1944, p. 3; "There Is No B. W. I. Unity, It Seems", *Public Opinion*, 2 June 1944, p. 3. The second piece sees an early shot against federation.

246. W. A. Domingo, "A Call for Service", *Public Opinion*, 29 January 1944, p. 3.

247. W. A. Domingo, "Nationalism and Unity", *Public Opinion*, 31 July 1944, p. 3.

publishing venues at this time show consistencies of theme alongside conscious decisions to write differently for two different audiences.

Of Domingo's various epistolary antagonists, the one that became a particular bugbear was the white expatriate editor and writer Esther Chapman. Born in London, the youngest of six children of a Russian-Jewish immigrant family, Esther Hyman (1894–1987) had trained as a journalist in London before getting a job in Jamaica as editor of the *Jamaica Times* and then the *Jamaica Review*. Chapman was nothing if not productive. Alongside publishing three novels, in 1934 she founded an ambitious literary and cultural journal with a pan-Caribbean remit, *West Indian Review* (*WIR*), which ran until 1974, usually appearing monthly. Her play *West Indian* was performed in Kingston in 1936, the same year in which she began writing "Woman's World: A Weekly Page for Women" for *The Gleaner*; and in 1939 she started a weekly penny paper called *Jamaica*. In the 1940s she was on the Board of Governors of the Institute of Jamaica as well as being editor of the Kingston *Daily Express*, as reliably pro-Empire as its London namesake, and of the *West Indian Review*. She also wrote features for the *Express* under the pen-name John Blunt, and then began writing an opinion piece for *The Gleaner* under the pen-name Peter Simple: Domingo immediately recognised her style and took great pleasure in outing her as the author.[248] So by the 1940s Esther Chapman was one of the most formidable and widely heard voices in Jamaican life, a worthy successor to a man of broadly similar views, Herbert G. de Lisser, who died in 1944, and one with a number of outlets for her opinions. She was clearly an efficient editor, business-oriented, and accomplished at promoting her various ventures. She operated comfortably within the British expatriate social circle, being on good terms with the various governors during her extended sojourn on the island.

Until 1938 Chapman had largely kept her political views to herself. An early correspondent to the *WIR* had asked: "Might not the review in breaking down the barriers of insular prejudice which in a way estrange the British Colonial communities break down as well those barriers which exist to British West Indian Federation?"[249] Chapman dampened his hopes by responding that the magazine "cannot adopt the principle for British West Indian Federation or any other political Platform".[250] She maintained her opposition to federation into the 1950s, but—unlike Domingo—clearly on the grounds that federation was associated with a degree of political autonomy for which she thought Jamaica was not prepared.

248. W. A. Domingo, "'Peter', the Simple", *Public Opinion*, 16 October 1944, p. 3.

249. "Sylvester", "Correspondence: The Birth of an Idea", *West Indian Review*, 1, no. 2 (October 1934), pp. 5–6.

250. "Forward: A Federation of Ideas", *West Indian Review*, 1, no. 2 (October 1934), p. 11. See also "Federation: A Cautionary Note", *West Indian Review*, n.s. 4, no. 3 (1946), pp. 13–15.

Her first public announcement of her political views came in response to the labour disturbances of 1938: she published three articles in the *WIR* under the title "The Truth About Jamaica", which were then collected into a pamphlet with the same name and distributed widely in Jamaica and in the UK.[251] In England during the summer of 1938 she had some contact with a Conservative MP, Ralph Assheton, and then with the British Council, discussing the possible use of the *WIR* to represent the views of the British government.[252] She also requested information about an organisation which she described to Lord Lloyd, chairman of the British Council, as "sending out some very good stuff": the Imperial Policy Group, a right-wing pro-Empire group of MPs who favoured appeasement of the Nazis and the regency of the Duke and Duchess of Windsor, and which a CIA report (no less) called "an extremely right-wing conservative organization formed in 1934".[253] And to round off her trip she gave an interview to the London *Daily Express* which appeared under the headline "Negro's 'Public Enemy No. 1' Editor is A Woman", which was reproduced in *The Gleaner*.[254] It quoted her as saying: "London officials come out to the West Indies feeling all romantic about the negroes. They have a sentimental prejudice in favour of what they think is the subject race. But the negroes are not a subject race in Jamaica. They have a great deal to do with running the internal affairs of their country." She showed the *Express* reporter a copy of her weekly paper *Jamaica*, in which she had written: "It seems incompatible to ask for self-government and Jamaica for the Jamaicans, and in the same breath demand that existing and all new industries be heavily subsidised. The man who pays the piper calls the tune." Then at the end of the year Chapman turned to the newly founded PNP, and by extension the influential JPL, voicing her reservations concerning the introduction of self-government on the grounds that "Jamaica is not ready for that day; her people are backward, she has few honest leaders, and the country is riddled with graft. To give her an advanced status before she is ready for it will be a retrograde step, not a constructive one."[255]

Her instincts were, Domingo unsurprisingly thought, inimical to the development of a national culture. Mrs Chapman was not, he asserted in September 1944, a Jamaican "by birth or in spirit".[256] "She has openly opposed the aspira-

251. Esther Chapman, *The Truth About Jamaica*, Kingston, Jamaica: n.p., 1938.
252. See Claire Catherine Irving, "The Wrong Side of History: Esther Chapman and The West Indian Review", in *Printing the West Indies: Literary Magazines and the Anglophone Caribbean, 1920s–1950s*, PhD thesis, Newcastle, UK: Newcastle University, 2015, pp. 144–152, at 151.
253. Irving, "The Wrong Side of History", p. 152; "Kenneth de Courcy and the Intelligence Digest", 2 January 1951, www.cia.gov/readingroom/docs/CIA-RDP80R01731R000400280006-6.pdf (accessed 4 September 2024).
254. "Negro's 'Public Enemy No. 1' Editor Is a Woman", *The Gleaner*, 2 August 1939, p. 6.
255. Esther Chapman, "Criticism and the People's Party", *West Indian Review*, 5, no. 3 (November 1938), p. 17.
256. W. A. Domingo, "National Culture", *Public Opinion*, 25 September 1944, p. 3.

tion of Jamaicans for political autonomy", he declared: "No opportunity is ever neglected by her to tell Jamaicans of their alleged financial indebtedness to the 'mother country' and to the English workingman." Her attitude to Jamaican writers is "patronising and belittling". The nub of Domingo's complaint is that Chapman's political attitudes mean that she can never be in favour of the development of a *national* culture. Imperialists like her will always oppose anything that is capable of strengthening the will of the people to achieve national autonomy.

Despite their antagonism, her analysis of Jamaica's problems in *The Truth About Jamaica* contained some elements in common with Domingo's: they certainly shared the view that the chief problem facing the island should not be regarded as racial in nature, and both expressed scorn for the lucubrations of the Legislative Council, and admiration for Norman Manley. The main difference between them lay in their very different perceptions of the country's political future. For Chapman, Jamaicans were "a simple people whose best interests can only be served by adherence to the Mother country, at all events for a long time to come".[257] Her racist assessment of the majority of Jamaicans ensured Domingo's pointed criticism.

One major engagement with Chapman came in late 1944 in the throes of a national debate about the new constitution. The gulf between Manley and Bustamante was growing ever wider, and Domingo never missed an opportunity to attack him.[258] In an editorial in her paper, *Jamaica*, Chapman had taken issue with one of Domingo's critiques of Bustamante in which he had asked him how he could reconcile his professed love for the black and brown working classes of Jamaica with his boast of having fought in the Spanish Army against the Moors of North Africa. Chapman found this question "dishonest". She continued: "There is nothing in common between the Moors of North Africa and the coloured people of Jamaica except the negative fact that they are not white. Nor is Bustamante."[259] Several cans of worms were thereby opened, and Domingo proceeded to pore over their contents. One of the cans concerned Bustamante's parentage. His father was a white Irish Catholic planter. He often claimed his mother was "Indian", meaning indigenous, which was clearly a ridiculous way of denying black ancestry. Oddly, given his leadership role in the black community, Bustamante was never keen to identify with blacks on a racial basis. Domingo points out that there are plenty of people in Jamaica who knew his mother as "a splendid lady of Negro extraction". Another can concerned Bustamante's mysterious past about which all anyone knew (and still knows) is what he chose to reveal or invent, including his

257. Chapman, *The Truth About Jamaica*, p. 16.

258. For example, W. A. Domingo, "Bustamante Under The Microscope", *Public Opinion*, 19 October 1944, p. 3; "Bustamante Under Examination", *Public Opinion*, 24 October 1944, p. 3 and 25 October 1944, p. 3; and "Bustamanteism Must Go", *Public Opinion*, 27 October 1944, p. 3.

259. Quoted by Domingo, in his "Mrs Chapman, Bustamante, Walter Lewis et al.", *Public Opinion*, 31 October 1944, p. 3.

joining the Spanish Army and fighting in North Africa—under Franco, Domingo speculates. Domingo's friend Adolphe Roberts spent a considerable time investigating Bustamante's claims about his past and found most of them either false or exaggerated.[260] For Domingo, the claim to have fought is as revealing as the possible fact. However, the can that most interested him was Chapman's statement about the non-relation between the North African Moors and the coloured population of Jamaica. Both, Domingo points out, suffer from imperialism and "are interested in procuring self-government for themselves". He notes that there had been international conferences of colonised people from the British, French, Dutch, Portuguese, Spanish, Belgian, and Italian empires "for the sole purpose of working out a formula for their freedom from imperialism", and that people with nothing in common are unlikely to meet in conferences.

Chapman was a frequent target for Domingo's criticism after she made herself a kind of unofficial spokesperson for Bustamante, and therefore to Domingo a symbol of how the Jamaican colonial elite were wooing Bustamante as a way of trying to head off the kind of political progress embodied by the PNP. This was a two-way process, with Bustamante taking his cues from what Chapman wrote in the *Express*. Domingo's language describing Busta also got more and more robust: "a pretentious, dishonest and aggressive ignoramus" is a representative assessment.[261]

* * *

As the December 1944 elections approached, Wendell Malliet reported from New York that other political parties had taken to the field: Bustamante had formed the JLP, the Syrian immigrant and businessman E. A. Issa the Jamaica Democratic Party (JDP), and J. A. G. Smith was organising a Garveyite party. The article was illustrated by pictures of Manley and Domingo, Manley described as "head" of the PNP, Domingo as "the most outstanding leader".[262] Domingo played a prominent role in the run-up to the elections.[263] The JDP and the smaller Jamaica Conservative Party had little chance of winning seats under universal suffrage, and so tried to paint the PNP as a Communist-influenced organisation. But the main threat to the PNP came from Bustamante, now he headed a political party. Like Arthur Richards before them, the Jamaican conservative and business elite saw Bustamante as the lesser of two evils—perhaps thinking that they would be

260. W. Adolphe Roberts, "The Bustamante Story" (1959), WARA 5.5.1. This was written as an obituary for *The Gleaner*, but turned down by the editor, T. E. Sealy. By then Bustamante's standing was too high for such a forensic analysis to be published.
261. Domingo, "Sparks from My Anvil", *Public Opinion*, 10 April 1946, p. 3.
262. A. M. Wendell Malliet, "Rival Parties and an Empty Treasury Mar Jamaica's Attempt at 'Self-Rule'", *New York Amsterdam News*, 5 February 1944, p. 4B.
263. "P.N.P. Meetings", *The Gleaner*, 26 February 1944, p. 12.

able to exert some control over him. Domingo spoke at the final PNP rally before the election as well the first one after the heavy defeat of the PNP left Bustamante as unofficial leader of the government.[264]

A wholly elected Lower House and universal suffrage were substantial steps towards self-government. This eroded one of the principal reasons why some leaders had wanted federation: they had thought self-government was impossible without it. But federation was not off the table. Indeed, this long-standing idea gained traction because it began to appeal to a diverse range of interests, from British policy planners to those arguing for self-government. Postwar conferences and meetings facilitated contact between leaders who increasingly felt a truly *West Indian* nationalism might be created. The Moyne Report, published in full in 1945, offered some support for federation, pronouncing that "the combination into one political entity of all the British possessions in the Caribbean area is the ideal to which, in our opinion, policy should be directed".[265] Out of its initial recommendations had come the Colonial Development and Welfare Organisation, established in 1940. Its purpose was to distribute the annual grant that Moyne had recommended, but its practice—treating the West Indies as a whole, travelling extensively across the constitutive territories—prepared everyone concerned to think about the West Indies as a single unit. So the Moyne Report could be seen as helping pave the road to federation. However, while noting the existence of sentiments in the region favouring federation, it tellingly reported that while every witness questioned "was in favour of closer union, ... few of them were able or prepared to define the degree or nature of federation which they considered desirable". The conclusion was prophetic: "There is room therefore for doubting the readiness of West Indian opinion to accept federation in principle. Even if that doubt could be removed, the practical difficulties still seem to be insuperable."[266]

Nevertheless, there was no doubt that the federation train was gathering speed. With the war over, the immediate goal of the WINC was Caribbean representation at the United Nations on International Organization conference scheduled to take place in San Francisco between 25 April and 26 June 1945. A preliminary WINC conference, chaired by Charles Petioni and involving, *inter alia*, Hope Stevens, H. P. Osborne, Richard B. Moore, and Reginald Pierrepointe, listed seven demands. One of them was indeed "Forthright recognition of the inalienable right of the Caribbean peoples to self-government and self-determination", but another

264. "St Andrews Big Three", *The Gleaner*, 13 December 1944, p. 2; "P.N.P. Meeting", 22 December 1944, p. 12. The JLP won 22 of the 32 seats.

265. *The Moyne Report. Report of the West Indian Royal Commission* [1945], with an Introduction by Denis Benn, Kingston, Jamaica: Ian Randle Publishers, 2011, p. 327. See John Gaffar La Guerre, "The Moyne Commission and the Jamaican Left", *Social and Economic Studies*, 31, no. 3 (September 1982), pp. 59–94, and Post, *Strike the Iron*, pp. 85–92.

266. *The Moyne Report*, pp. 326–327.

was "Practical recognition of the age-long objective of the West Indian peoples for voluntary federation".[267] Stuck in Kingston, there was nothing Domingo could do about the WINC's change of policy.[268] He admitted the "emotional appeal" of the idea of federation, but would consistently write against the project.[269]

Manley moved forward on several fronts. He began a series of visits to the USA, seeking finance for the PNP and attempting to bring various West Indian and African-American organisations together to further the movement for West Indian self-government. In a talk he gave to the Board of Directors of the NAACP on 8 October 1945 he announced that he had come north "seeking to meet all the West Indian organizations in America to ask them to help with what we are trying to do in the West Indies, getting them together on a common and useful platform of thought and action, as well as to get their practical assistance".[270]

By the end of the war, self-government without federation had no champions in New York. Ethelred Brown, now JPL president, was working closely with Manley, who was now leading the way on federation, while Malliet and Osborne—though politically at odds—were in agreement when it came to arguing that federation was the only way forward. In 1946 Osborne got the opportunity to put the West Indian case in *The Crisis*, stressing that "the West Indian people are indeed a nation, albeit an oppressed nation" and putting Norman Manley front, back, and centre—or in his words, heart, brain, and lifeblood—on the "rugged road to federation and self-government".[271] Following the example recently set by Eric Williams, Osborne made prominent reference to Winston Churchill's speech at a banquet of West Indian planters in London that "Britain got her start from her West Indian colonies from which she derived great wealth which was used to lay the basis of the British Empire."[272]

267. "Program Adopted by the Conference Committee", RBMP, Box 8. A report from the British Consulate in New York noted that Pierrepointe "is radical and can be a trouble maker, and like Petioni should be watched" ("Negro Opinion and the San Francisco Conference", CO 968/121/4, TNA).

268. As early as August 1940, Domingo had spoken of letting the WINC fade away, perhaps alert to the possibility that it would become an instrument for supporting federation (W. A. Domingo, Letter to W. Adolphe Roberts, 6 August 1940, WARA 2.3.5).

269. Domingo, "Sparks from My Anvil", *Public Opinion*, 25 January 1946, p. 3, and "Federation of the B.W.I", *Public Opinion*, 29 January 1945, p. 3.

270. "Remarks of Mr Norman Manley of Jamaica, British West Indies, before the Board of Directors of the National Association for the Advancement of Colored People—Monday, October 8, 1945", NAACPACWIF [NAACPACWIF = NAACP 1940-55. General office file. Leagues—American Committee for West Indian Federation, 1945–48], pp. 1–4, at 4.

271. Herman P. Osborne, "The Road to West Indian Federation", *The Crisis*, 53, no. 1 (January 1946), pp. 14–15 and 27–28, at 27, 14, and 28.

272. The words are Osborne's paraphrase. Churchill's words, spoken at a dinner on 20 July 1937 at the Dorchester Hotel in London given for the Duke of Kent by the West India Committee, were: "Our possession of the West Indies … gave us the strength, the support, but especially the capital, the wealth, at a time when no other European nation possessed such a reserve, which … enabled us not only to acquire this appendage of possessions which we have, but also to lay the foundations of that commercial and financial leadership which … enabled us to make

It did seem as if everyone was coming out in favour of federation. In many ways the influential black sociologist Ira de Augustine Reid swam against the tide when he quoted extensively from the writings of Roberts and Domingo and declared that "Politically the British West Indies is an anachronism." But he also looked forward to "a federation of states and protectorates forming the hemisphere's first English-speaking Negro republic".[273] Even Adolphe Roberts was prepared to contemplate—with apparent equanimity—the possibility of two federations, a western one consisting of Jamaica, the Bahamas, and British Honduras, and an eastern one with Trinidad, British Guiana, and the Windward and Leeward Islands.[274] However, Roberts was probably swayed by the sense that Jamaica and Trinidad would so clearly be the leading players that these would look more like enlarged states than actual federations. And in Jamaica, where Domingo could exercise some influence once he'd been released from detention, the federative idea still continued to gain ground. The 1944 PNP conference approved a resolution on federation pushed through by Manley with little discussion.[275] In November Domingo seized the opportunity to state, perhaps with a growing tinge of desperation, that there was no sentiment in Jamaica in favour of federation [#33].

* * *

In August 1947 Domingo finally got his US visa and left the island for New York, ironically just a month before two of the most important West Indian political meetings in many years took place in Jamaica. After considerable delay following the Labour election victory in 1945, the new Colonial Secretary, Arthur Creech Jones, called for a conference on closer association to be held in Montego Bay in September 1947. This would be immediately preceded by a conference of the Caribbean Labour Congress (CLC), founded in Barbados in 1945 with T. A. Marryshow as president and Grantley Adams as vice-president.[276] This was the first time a popular organisation in Jamaica had significant contact with similar organisations in the eastern and southern Caribbean, although the BITU didn't

our great position in the world"; quoted in Eric Williams, *The Negro in the Caribbean* (Washington, DC: Associates in Negro Folk Education, 1942), p. 14. Williams provides no source, but the only account of the speech is to be found in "Jamaica Figures Largely in Speeches Delivered at West India Club Dinner", *The Gleaner*, 11 August 1937, pp. 1 and 6.

273. Ira de A. Reid, "The Negro in the British West Indies", *Journal of Negro Education*, 10, no. 3 (July 1941), pp. 524–535, at 535.

274. W. Adolphe Roberts, "The Future of Colonialism in the Caribbean: The British West Indies", in *The Economic Future of the Caribbean*, ed. E. Franklin Frazier and Eric Williams, Washington, DC: Howard University Press, 1944, pp. 37–39.

275. Hart, *Towards Decolonisation*, p. 295. No documentation has survived.

276. Grantley Herbert Adams (1898–1971) was a Barbadian politician. After serving as the inaugural premier of Barbados from 1953 to 1958, he became the first and only prime minister of the West Indies Federation from 1958 to 1962.

respond to the invitation and the PNP hesitated before sending Richard Hart—who proceeded to make a strong speech about the need for "the development of the Caribbean area as one economic entity".[277] Keeping a wary eye on events, Domingo was not overly impressed.[278] In the event, Hart was appointed CLC assistant secretary, giving Jamaica a seat at the table, and indeed Hart would quickly become the organisation's driving force after taking over as secretary in January 1947. The secretariat was underfunded, so progress was slow, but minds were concentrated when the British government called that conference for September 1947 in Montego Bay to discuss closer association of the West Indian territories, clearly a code for federation. The CLC council—basically its officers plus Norman Manley and V. C. Bird from Antigua—met in Antigua in January 1947 and drew up a statement concerning federation to be discussed at the CLC meeting in Kingston in September, just a few days before the Montego Bay conference.[279] That was the situation when Domingo left Jamaica.

He had arrived in 1941 with the prospect of becoming an important spokesperson for the PNP and therefore of influencing its policy with respect to self-government. He left the island just in time to avoid the meeting of the CLC at which Manley waxed lyrical about "forging West Indian unity": "Are we satisfied", he asked, "to be obscure and small nonentities in a world in which larger groupings have the only chance of survival and success?"[280] Domingo had put his heart and soul into the establishment of the PNP. He had come to Jamaica on Manley's invitation and been incarcerated for 20 months. Denied a US visa, he'd spent a further 45 months on the island, writing thousands of words in *Public Opinion* to develop and explain the PNP's platform. Now, just as he was finally able to go home, Manley took the PNP away from the Jamaican nationalism that provided the bedrock of Domingo's political views. Domingo no doubt breathed a deep sigh, but he wasn't going to back down now.

---

277. *Official Report Caribbean Labour Congress*, 17–27 September 1945, Barbados: Advocate Co. Ltd, 1945, quoted in Mordecai, *The West Indies*, p. 34. Confusingly, the PNP was a more traditional "labour" party in the British sense than the Jamaica Labour Party. Hart recalls that the PNP originally had so little interest in the CLC that it nearly sent the avowed anti-federationist Domingo as its representative (Richard Hart, "Federation: An Ill-Fated Design", *Jamaica Journal*, 25, October 1993, pp. 10–16, at 11).

278. Domingo, "Sparks from My Anvil", *Public Opinion*, 12 October 1946, pp. 3 and 6.

279. Vere Cornwall Bird (1910–1999) was a labour activist and first prime minister of Antigua and Barbuda.

280. "West Indian Federation: A Cause Vital to Our Progress" [1947], in *Norman Washington Manley and the New Jamaica: Selected Speeches and Writings, 1938–68*, edited with notes and introduction by Rex Nettleford, Kingston, Jamaica: Longman Caribbean, 1971, pp. 162–170, at 163 and 165.

17

The Case for Self-Government

August 1937

This piece follows on from the JPL's founding document, W. Adolphe Roberts's pamphlet *Self-government for Jamaica* (see above, p. 131, n. 28). Also relevant is C. L. R. James's *The Case for West Indian Self-Government* (1933).[1]

Public Opinion, 7 August 1937, pp. 5 and 11[2]

Man is by nature conservative. He is reluctant to leave old moorings. He distrusts the future and clings to the familiar. Only a few bold and far-visioned spirits are willing to sail into uncharted seas. Yet all the progress of the world is a direct result of the daring of the few who blazed new trails over which the multitude later trod in comfort. Progress is the legitimate fruit of the efforts of inventors, explorers, composers, authors, experimenters, and thinkers in all fields of human endeavour and relationship. But for the activities of the Cromwells, George Washingtons, Wilberforces, Lincolns, De Valeras, L'Ouvertures, Frederick Douglasses, and the numberless host of lovers of their fellow-men and women who believed sincerely in democracy—the right of all human beings to a fuller life and to participate in the governing of themselves—mankind would still be in the feudal or slave era of history. Fortunately there were individuals who had a vision of human freedom and dedicated their life to its achievement.

In raising the question of self-government for Jamaica, the leaders of the Jamaica Progressive League are fully conscious that they will meet with powerful opposition at home and in England. They agree with the sage dictum of Lord Acton: "Voluntary abdication of power is unknown in history and absurd in psychology."[3] The League has no illusions regarding the nature of its task, but the enormity of an undertaking is no reason for evading it. There are political and economic forces in Great Britain, and for that matter, throughout the Empire,

---

1. See Christian Høgsbjerg, "'A Thorn in the Side of Great Britain': C. L. R. James and the Caribbean Labour Rebelliions of the 1930s", *Small Axe*, 15, no. 2 (July 2011), pp. 24–42.
2. Because the numbering of *Public Opinion* is so inconsistent, we've chosen to refer to issues just by date.
3. Domingo may have taken this quotation from D. N. Bannerjea, "India's Case for Independence", *Current History*, 38, no. 2 (May 1933), pp. 169–175, at 169. Bannerjea seems to have invented it.

that will leave no stone unturned to prevent any genuine democratic advance for mixed-racial or non-white communities. Those same interests resisted the Irish nation's right to govern itself and it is not to be thought for one moment that they will be in a hurry to accord Jamaica any real self-government unless they are forced to do so. Regardless of the beautiful fiction taught in British countries about the altruistic nature of British imperialism, the bald fact remains that all imperialisms are in essence the maintenance of the rule of outsiders over people who are governed by open or concealed force. The government may be semi-benevolent, but in the last analysis it functions to a large degree in the interests of the real rulers of the so-called mother country.

In the case of colonies like Jamaica the use of force is not as naked as in India or South Africa or as it was in Ireland, but no sensible Jamaican can fail to realise that behind the government stands the military power of Great Britain. Let there be a broad and emphatic demand for wage increases as there was in Trinidad recently, and immediately English ships of war begin to converge on the little island to impress the unarmed inhabitants with the most powerful argument that the British never hesitate to employ—FORCE. Let the people of India demand their right to self-government, and there is immediately a strong exercise of force to deter them. But in periods of comparative quiescence there are subtler means for reinforcing imperialistic chains in places like Jamaica. All the media of tradition and public opinion and all the subtleties of propaganda through schools, press, pulpit, literature, etc. are brought to bear in a continuous effort to condition the people into meek acceptance of the prevailing political status.

In effect they are made to believe that their status is the best they merit; that they would revert to barbarism but for the wisdom and God-given capacity of their rulers to preserve and advance civilisation in communities with Negroid or other non-white populations. In short, the people are subtly impressed with the idea that they are inferior and should not aspire to be the masters of their own land. Of course, it is not always stated in that crude fashion, but the implication is clear to anyone who is willing to understand. To placate those who believe in progress for all peoples and who deny the libel of the inherent incapacity of Jamaicans to rule themselves, the statement is often made in responsible quarters that whenever Jamaicans demonstrate a fitness for self-government it will be given to them. The hub of the question rests on the point that in the opinion of the permanent officials of the Colonial Office who get their ideas from governors, retired colonial officials, and army officers, coloured people seem never fit for self-government. It is hardly likely that officials drawn from the ruling classes of Great Britain, who themselves fought every democratic advance for the white English working class, will grant increments of democracy to coloured peoples unless they are compelled to do so. That this is the policy of the Colonial Office is easily proved when a study is made of the history of Canada, South Africa,

New Zealand, Tasmania, and Australia and contrasted with the history of the peoples of the West Indies. While the colonies with large white populations steadily progressed to the point where they are now equals with Great Britain in the Commonwealth of British nations, the non-white Caribbean colonies definitely retrogressed. The West Indies lost ground politically while the white colonies gained.

Behind the situation stands the clear fact that in the minds of powerful groups in England certain colonies exist for exploitation [by] British capitalists. They never say that openly, but deeds are often more eloquent than words. All major questions affecting the crown colonies are decided finally, not by the local legislators, whose function is purely consultative, but by an Under-Secretary of State for the Colonies who may know absolutely nothing about the people whose fate he is deciding. The economic connections may not be obvious, but let no one be so simple as not to realise that the banks, insurance companies, traders of one sort or another, pensioners, army officers, racial chauvinists, and others exert tremendous influence upon the British Colonial Office. Linked to them are their representatives in the Crown Colonies whose fortunes, prestige, and general interests motivate them to oppose, secretly or openly, any move that tends to broaden the democratic foundations of colonies where the majority of the people are non-Caucasians. Stated plainly, colonies exist as sources of raw materials, markets for capital and manufactured goods; they provide sinecures for sons of Englishmen who are later pensioned at the expense of the colony, and in these days of militarism, soldiers to be shock troops for their imperial masters.

Among the very people most likely to benefit from any increase in democracy will be found defenders of the *status quo*. Usually they are the timid souls who fear every progressive move and whose spiritual ancestors resisted freedom when slavery was abolished, feeling that they could not make a success of their new condition. Freedom had to be thrust upon that kind. There is another type that reflects the ideology of the master-class and mouths his opinions without reflection. Then there are a few who have been seduced by the propaganda of their detractors into believing that people of their racial type are really incapable of governing themselves. They refer to Haiti and Latin America in proof, but will never point to the chaos in the Balkans, Poland, Austria, and other parts of the white world. They will not refer to the history of England with its Luddites and Chartists and Cromwell, nor to France with its Commune and frequent changes of government.

Briefly stated, self-government, dominion status, for Jamaica is justified by the history of mankind. It will free the people from being slavishly dragged into wars and quarrels not of their making; and it will give them greater control over their economic lives. It will give Jamaicans the power to regulate immigration into their country; make it possible for them to legislate in defence of their people when they are discriminated against in Latin America and other places. It will give Jamaicans the power to negotiate commercial pacts that are primarily beneficial to the island and not subordinated to so-called imperial exigencies; it will make possible a greater industrialisation of the country, which will result in benefits to local capitalists and provide more work for the people. It will open up new types of political and government employment to natives, such as being trade representatives abroad, and remove the colour barriers now existing in the Police Force. It will make it possible for Jamaicans freely to legislate to penalise steamships which use their ports and discriminate against coloured passengers. In short, self-government will create national pride, release new energies and stimulate the literary and artistic expression of a people who will have cast off much of the sense of colonial inferiority that a crown colony engenders. Our goal must be—JAMAICA, A DOMINION!

18

Nationalism and the Masses

March 1938

Like Richard B. Moore in New York, Richard Hart was a close friend of Domingo's with whom he liked to argue. At this point Hart (A.R.H.)—a committed leftist—was sceptical of the movement for self-government and had clashed on the matter with Jaime O'Meally in the pages of *Public Opinion*. At the same time Arnold Lecesne was voicing the case for full independence—Jamaica as a republic. Domingo here hews to the JPL line against both positions. Hart would later commit to self-government, just as Domingo would commit to independence.

Public Opinion, 5 March 1938, pp. 3, 13, and 15

The controversy waged in your columns between A.R.H. and Mr Jaime O'Meally over the merits of the programme of the Jamaica Progressive League as an instrument for improving the condition of the masses has been reduced to its essentials by the former writer in your issue of 12 February.[1] A.R.H. condemns the aims of the League on the ground of their inadequacy, but adds that they "are better than no aims", implying that his only objection is that they do not go far enough for him. He concludes that "Self-government within the capitalist shell will be of no appreciable benefit to the masses."

In every progressive movement there are bound to be extremist points of view. These have found expressions in Jamaica during the current agitation for improvement in the political status of the country. They are represented by the demand of Mr Lecesne for independence from Great Britain, and in the opinions of A.R.H. quoted above.[2] There can be no question as to the sincerity of the proponents of both views. Mr Lecesne voices what [are] primarily the ideals and aspirations of those who believe in freedom for all people and of those who resent the self-assumed right of outsiders to impose their rule upon others; A.R.H. is anxious to effectuate social, as well as political changes in order to bring benefit to the masses.

1. A.R.H. (Ansell Richard Hart, 1917–2013) was a Marxist political activist and historian, and founding member of the PNP.
2. Arnold Lecesne (1877–1942) was a descendant of French refugees from the slave insurrection in Saint Domingue.

I personally welcome the existence of an independence movement, even though it consists of a microscopic minority, for it proves that the love of freedom is not dead. But I cannot endorse it as a practical political programme capable of rallying the masses of Jamaica to its defence. It is commendable idealistically, but romantic and inept politically. The pre-requisites for a healthy and unconquerable movement for national independence seem lacking in the Jamaica of today. Such a movement requires historical or traditional roots or both. There is neither a tradition nor an historical popular belief in the necessity of separation from England extant in Jamaica, hence the projection of any such demand into the political arena at this moment is unreal and bound to fail. It is not capable of inducing the masses to make the sacrifices which such a struggle will necessarily entail and can only result in confusing the people and playing into the hands of the reactionaries who are loath to concede even the most elementary national democratic rights to our country.

Before there can be a strong movement for independence there must be a flourishing nationalism. Jamaicans must feel that Jamaica is their country, not England; and that they have national interests which are in conflict with those of the British Empire. They must feel that they constitute a NATION and as such are hampered in their development because of being tied to England as a mere colony, without voice or effective part in determining the policies of the Empire, not to mention the subordination of Jamaican interests to those of England. A few intellectuals and idealists may cherish such feelings and may even be willing to die for them, but in the Jamaica I saw a year ago they would be to all intents and purposes leaders and martyrs without a mass base, and as such the demand for independence must, despite its lofty aims, fail.

The programme of the Jamaica Progressive League is designed to provide the basis for a strong national spirit. In common with the National Reform Association and *Public Opinion*, it seeks to orientate the minds of Jamaicans towards the needs and problems of their country. It seeks to create a truly national spirit to take the place of the anachronistic imperial spirit with which the people have been deliberately inoculated for decades. With the definite emergence of a genuine national consciousness, there is no telling what other political demands will find expression at the proper time.

All the forces of public education in Jamaica operate to make Jamaicans belittle and despise their country, its products, history, and people, whilst glorifying England and everything English. As a result, despite a deplorable social condition and a humiliating political relationship to the British Empire, there is practically no hostility on the part of the people to British imperialism. The inhabitants are convinced that the British Empire is a benevolent organisation and that they are important units in it. Regardless of class or colour, Jamaicans recognise no grievances against England as such, although they may grumble about this or that condition or this or that official from abroad. Not knowing the real functions of commercial banks in the modern world, they are utterly unconcerned that the credit of the country is completely in the hands of foreigners and they have no realisation of the part played by banks, insurance companies and various other alien institutions in exploiting the country and draining away its wealth to strengthen the treasuries of financial tycoons abroad.

Even such obvious insults and injustices as the exclusion of "natives" from higher forms of employment in private banks and the limitations placed upon promotion in the police force of the country, have not roused and sustained indignation or protest in any quarter, not excepting the liberals, nascent nationalists, and proponents of independence, which tends to confirm my view that there is as yet no widespread national spirit justifying the advancement of what can be called extremist programmes.

I disagree with A.R.H. in his dogmatic statement that there can be no appreciable benefit to the masses under capitalism. Like him, I hate capitalism with its hypocrisy, race prejudice even in religion, oppression of the weak, and, as expressed in Jamaica, its illiteracy, poverty, and mass stupidity. But I do not think it necessary to wait for the world revolution before attempting to improve existing conditions in my country. Giving a man a tuxedo suit will not appease hunger, but it will protect his body from the rigours of the elements. The attitude of A.R.H. represents a sort of philosophy of futility. Logically, he would counsel the people of Jamaica to remain politically inactive until they have a programme which calls for social revolution. But he himself has pointed out the overwhelming military forces at the disposal of the British, and it does not take a prophet to predict just what would happen if a serious movement should arise with the bursting of the capitalist shell as its objective.

There can be no question about the unwisdom of advancing at this time any slogan or precipitating any crisis that is likely to bring the unarmed people of Jamaica into conflict with the military and naval strength of England. Such a situation would result in the slaughter of the masses. Not only would the odds be hopelessly uneven, but of greater importance is the fact that the people lack a philosophy or ideal worthy of the sacrifice. Then, too, Jamaicans would be at a terrible disadvantage internally because of the unlikelihood of any considerable class co-operation even for national progress. The majority of the sufferers would be from the masses, and one can easily imagine the kind of lurid propaganda about African barbarism that would be broadcast to the world by the "defenders" of "law and order".

Implicit in A.R.H.'s position is the belief that it is useless to make purely political changes; that for the masses to benefit it is necessary to have aims that comprehend a bursting of the capitalist shell, in other words, social revolution. This view sounds very radical, but as a matter of fact it is reactionary. The history of labour abounds with instances of leaders who feel that there should be no immediate demands; that so-called immediate demands were reforms designed to patch up the tottering edifice of capitalism. Some have gone further and objected to any sort of political activity, insisting that only industrial action can be of any benefit to the workers.

A.R.H., in effect, repudiates the possibility of the masses (workers) of Jamaica benefiting under capitalism. This is in flat contradiction of the experience of the workers in England, America, France and even some fascist countries. Hours have been reduced, illiteracy decreased, living conditions bettered, child-labour lessened, wages increased, and the franchise democratically broadened under capitalism. And these gains are so precious to the workers that they are never willing to surrender them without a struggle.

It will doubtlessly be argued that those same benefits can be achieved for Jamaica without self-government. Quite true, but with self-government the size of the opposition to them will be decreased and the possibility of their achievement made easier. Without self-government the opposition is maximised, and it will take a longer time making gains that already are ancient in countries where the people theoretically govern themselves. The imperial government claims that it is the trustee for the growth of civilisation in the colonies. It arrogates to itself the role of sole judge of the fitness of a people for self-government.

There is no instance on record showing that the imperial government has ever voluntarily initiated a movement for increasing the political responsibilities of any part of the British Empire. On the contrary, every demand for self-government has met with fierce opposition from the Colonial Office, and concessions were usually made grudgingly.

Viewed realistically, the imperial government, operating through the Colonial Office, is the defender of capitalism and alien rights against those of the indigenes of a colony. Should the people of Jamaica through mass meetings and other democratic agencies, including our consultative Legislative Council, decide that a certain measure will benefit the masses, they will have not only the local reactionaries to oppose them, but they are likely to have the opposition of the Colonial Office as well. The forced resignation and rebuke of Sir Arthur M. Fletcher, Governor of Trinidad, during the labour riots is an eloquent case in point.[3] The exploitation of the labourers by foreign capitalists had become unbearable and there was an explosion. The officials on the spot, appointees of the Colonial Office, acting as humane persons, sought to avoid bloodshed and to improve the condition of the workers by making small concessions, but instead of receiving approval from the supposedly impartial trustee, they were condemned for being "weak" and "undignified". In other words, the masses of Trinidad were fought

3. Sir Arthur George Murchison Fletcher (1878–1954) became governor of Trinidad shortly before an oil workers' strike paralysed the colony.

not only by their local exploiters, but also by the defenders of foreign capital who operate along political lines from the office of the Secretary of State for the Colonies.

Will A.R.H. argue that it would not have been easier for the local officials to have initiated measures likely to have benefited the masses if they were not controlled, intimidated, and balked by the form of constitutional connection existing between Trinidad and England? Without the backing of the Colonial Office (which now, as ever, is under the powerful influence of financial forces hostile to labour improvement in the colonies), would not the oil companies of Trinidad have been forced by the Governor and Mr Nankivell to grant the workers a fairer part of the profits made out of their sweat and blood?[4] Would not the exploiters of labour in Jamaica be more inclined to listen to reason and be more humane in their treatment of their workers, if they did not realise that behind them stand not only the local police force and militia, but the mighty British Navy?

The Jamaica Progressive League asserts that self-government would reduce the strength of the forces opposed to measures that can appreciably benefit the masses, by leaving the workers confronted only by their local capitalists and not by the entire British Empire as is the case now. It would leave the workers on the sugar and banana plantations to face their masters even as the British and American workers face theirs without the interference of outsiders.

Even in our external relations, self-government can be used to benefit the masses. Take a concrete example. The masses of Jamaica need cheap food, clothes, shoes, building materials, etc., because many of those articles have to be imported and the income of the people is miserably low. Japan is capable and willing to supply the island with cheap cloth and shoes, but because Jamaica lacks self-government she has to accept the dictates of England and impose a prohibitive tax on the very articles which the low incomes of the masses drive them to secure from sources outside the British Empire. From the Jamaican point of view, self-government would benefit the masses in a definite way by making it possible for their low wages to secure for them more of those commodities which their physical being demands. Instead, without self-government, they are deprived of concrete advantages in order to benefit the British Empire! Accepting his implied advocacy of the need for social revolution if the masses are to benefit, may I ask A.R.H. this question: Will it be easier to achieve social revolution with the full power of England in opposition than it will be under self-government?

As A.R.H. employs Marxian phraseology, I am led to believe that he is a Marxian student. The outstanding example of Marxian theories is the Soviet Union, and it will be fruitful to pay some attention to the experience of the architect of that

4. Howard Nankivell (1894–1938), Trinidadian, assistant colonial secretary. Both Murchison Fletcher and Nankivell expressed sympathy for the oil workers, as a result of which the oil companies destroyed their careers. Fletcher tendered his resignation on grounds of ill-health in January 1938, and shortly afterwards Nankivell died in a mysterious fall from a train in France.

great edifice which is dedicated to the imperishable genius of Karl Marx. Lenin was a practical man. After the Bolsheviks had conquered political power, the dispossessed capitalists and their foreign allies sabotaged industry and the country was going to ruins because of economic malnutrition. Lenin saw the situation dialectically and instituted the New Economic Policy which permitted private trading. Immediately the capitalists were gleeful and confident that socialism could not work and it would not be long before Russia would be back in the ranks of capitalism. Dogmatic Marxists raged at Lenin and denounced him for abandoning the revolution and encouraging a return to capitalism. To all of this, the great leader replied in a pamphlet called *Left Infantile Sickness of Communism*, in which he demonstrated that his radical critics lacked an understanding of a need for compromises at certain stages of progress.[5] Answering the critics of his own party who accused him of retreating from the ultimate goal of the Bolshevik Revolution, Lenin said that as long as the workers held the commanding heights (in Russia, the banks, foreign trade, the land, the army, communications) he was not afraid to make progress at the rate of two steps forward and one step back. Stalin is still denounced by Trotsky and his followers for his belief that Socialism can be built up in one country. According to Trotsky, Russia should have concentrated upon the attainment of world revolution [before] attempting to initiate measures likely to be of appreciable benefit to the masses of his own country. History shows that Stalin was right.

A.R.H. confuses immediate with ultimate aims. The aim of the Jamaica Progressive League is political change, not social revolution. It believes that there is nothing prohibiting self-government from being of benefit to the masses politically and materially. It is convinced that with self-government and its democratic concomitants of universal suffrage and freely functioning labour unions, Jamaica can initiate moves likely to benefit the masses to a greater extent than is possible under the present archaic and out-grown system of Crown Colony government which is subject to the will of aristocratic bureaucrats and financial harpies outside the island.

5. Now usually known as *"Left-Wing" Communism: An Infantile Disorder*, first published in June 1920.

19
The People's National Party
October 1938

The launching of the PNP was a triumphant moment for Domingo and his allies. After some initial reluctance, the eminent barrister Norman Manley had agreed to lead the new party, although his commitment to self-government was as yet hesitant, at best. The party was given a boost by the presence at the launch of Stafford Cripps, whose fervent anti-imperialism made the Jamaican politicians seem moderate by contrast.

Public Opinion, 15 October 1938, pp. 6 and 10

The speeches delivered by Mr Norman W. Manley and Sir Stafford Cripps to an overflow audience when the People's National Party was formally launched on the Ward Theatre on Sunday 18 September marked another epoch in the recent political life of Jamaica.[1]

Only a year before, Mr Adolphe Roberts, founder and president of the Jamaica Progressive League, at considerable expense to himself, fired by the same political idealism animating Mr Manley and his band of supporters, toured the island and placed the cause of Jamaican self-government before the world. Prior to that pioneering trip, the League was regarded by local mossbacks as an exotic that existed only in the minds of a small group of Jamaican malcontents residing in New York. Even before Mr Roberts's memorable tour of the island, he, Mr Jaime O'Meally and the present writer, officers of the Jamaica Progressive League, had taken advantage of the courtesy of the columns of *Public Opinion* to agitate for self-government. Arguments were advanced laying the theoretical bases of the demand for a genuine Jamaican national policy free from the dictation of British imperialism. It was repeatedly emphasised that Jamaican national interests should not be subordinated to those of Great Britain.

In keeping with its ideals, the League published several pamphlets, the last being Mr O'Meally's *Why Self-Government?* The literature was sold at a reasonable price to Jamaicans at home and abroad, and in order to reach the widest circle of readers large portions of it were distributed free of cost. *Public Opinion* with its

1. Sir Richard Stafford Cripps (1889–1952) was a British Labour Party politician, barrister, and diplomat.

splendid corps of writers courageously analysed and exposed some of the worst features of the political, social, and economic life of our country. Considering the complete journalistic monopoly that it had to face, *Public Opinion* deserves the gratitude of every truth-loving Jamaican. Subjects that were formerly tabooed in the local press as conducive to stirring up strife or regarded as "bad taste" were freely, frankly, and fully discussed.

Political agitation is not new in Jamaica. Many persons still living will remember the activities of S. A. G. Cox and Dr J. Robert Love. Those men, and others, laboured to improve their country, but with the exception of Cox they failed to realise that the basic trouble with Jamaica was the system of imperialism of which it is still a victim. The people had long been lulled into the belief that British imperialism is a beneficent institution which should be endured and defended under all circumstances. The local oracles of the daily press, loaded down with meaningless titles and making comfortable incomes as the reward of their treachery, subservience, or ignorance, flooded the country with imperialistic propaganda, disregarding the true and vital interests of the masses. Outdated political concepts were paraded as the last word of wisdom, and for anyone to suggest that the island was being exploited for the benefit of a few capitalists was to expose that individual to the satire or abuse of boot-licking journalistic thugs. But a change had to come about. Jamaicans found themselves woefully behind the rest of the world politically. Little by little they had to realise that to depend on England for improvement of their lot was only to continue the prevailing evil conditions indefinitely. Immigration laws of other countries openly based upon race or language, and the natural increase of our population, created a serious labour problem.

Far-sighted individuals knew that some kind of revolt was inevitable. People, no matter how misguided or docile, will not tolerate bad conditions for ever, and last spring a large-scale labour revolt swept the island from end to end. The local seers were nonplussed. Their infallible knowledge of Jamaican workers went awry. But deplorable as the disturbances were, they revealed Jamaica to itself. It was discovered that the despised "lower orders" were dissatisfied; that they were willing to make the most serious sacrifices for self-improvement; that they knew the value of cohesive group action; and that they would follow a leader.

The people were in a state of ferment. They were in a rebellious state of mind needing informed, honest, devoted, and unselfish leadership. Industrial action is absolutely necessary if the workers are to get anywhere, but that alone is insufficient. It cannot bring approximately permanent relief. Political change is imperatively necessary. It needs to be fundamental and must affect the relation of forces in the regulation of affairs of the country. A mere palliative would be like putting a poultice over a cancerous sore. The cry was for a new deal in the political life of the country.

There can be no doubt that Mr Manley, like Mr Roberts, had long been dissatisfied with the conditions of the majority of his fellow Jamaicans. In every country there are men and women whose patriotism and humanity are deeper than their personal or class interests. Jamaica has had, and still has, its quota of such persons. They have been willing to risk misunderstanding, ostracism, misrepresentation, and libellous accusations for their humanitarian ideals. In Jamaica, with its peculiar social pattern of blended class, colour, and educational considerations, it takes unusual courage and idealism for members of the upper class voluntarily to champion the cause of the lowly and inarticulate black peasants and workers. Worse than that is the treason of even hinting that the British government is not the most altruistic and the purest political institution on earth. Of course, the recent unconcealed antics of Chamberlain, Hoare, and Runciman have been so raw that even the most obtuse person, if he is not morally dead, must realise that the beautiful fiction of lofty-minded and honourable gentlemen conducting the affairs of the Empire along lines of the Sermon on the Mount is not in accordance with the facts of reality.[2]

It was therefore natural that someone of ability and standing should yield to the compelling influence of humanity and local nationalism and come forward to supply the necessary guidance for the people. The Jamaica Progressive League welcomes the entrance of Mr Manley into the struggle for Jamaican self-government. It hopes that his patriotic and courageous action will be emulated by others of equal prominence. Soon a delegate of the League will be in Jamaica to present its considered programme to the Royal Commission which is soon to arrive in the island. It is the intention of the League to stress the political aspects of the needed reforms. The League stands uncompromisingly for SELF-GOVERNMENT and means to fight for it regardless of the difficulties ahead.

The League is a component part of the People's National Party, which is a coalition of the progressive organisations working for national improvement. Agitation is useless unless it has a definite goal, and the goal of the People's Party *must be unflinchingly that of self-government.* The speech of Sir Stafford Cripps and his letter to the people of Jamaica, through Mr Manley, were a much-needed political education. While the Parkers, Scotters, and de Lissers have been trying to prove that the agitation for self-government is unjustified, and the local daily newspapers do everything to discredit the movement and its leaders through vicious misrepresentations, along comes an Englishman, not a "spiritual" one, but an honest-to-goodness Englishman, and an aristocrat to boot, direct from the seat of the mighty, to tell the people of Jamaica that they have an inalienable right

2. Neville Chamberlain (1859–1940), Samuel Hoare (1880–1959), and Walter Runciman (1870–1949) were all associated with the British policy of appeasement towards Nazi Germany. On 30 September 1938 Chamberlain had signed the Munich Agreement, following Runciman's diplomatic mission to Czechoslovakia. Hoare was the author of the 1935 Hoare-Laval Pact, which had partially recognised the Italian conquest of Ethiopia.

to rule themselves and that they should place their national interests ahead of those of the Empire. The speech reads like some of the pages of *Public Opinion* on the same subject.[3] But treason of treason, Sir Stafford Cripps said, "The whole administration of a colony must always be determined primarily by the imperial needs of the Empire, that is why self-government is withheld in so many cases, especially where the numerically dominant race is not the white race." That is letting the cat out of the bag with a vengeance.

Many Jamaicans seem disturbed over the fate of Jamaica if self-government is achieved. Many of the timid souls confuse self-government within the Empire with independence. Independence is the logical goal of all nations whether they are large or small, rich or poor. As the Spaniards say, "It is better to be the head of a mouse than the tail of a lion." Better be the poorest freedman than the best-fed slave. Jamaica is a nation. It has all the characteristics of a nation. It is one territory. The people speak a common language. The overwhelming majority is of the same blood. They have a common economic destiny. They have a history. Class divisions are not peculiar to Jamaica. They exist everywhere and form the basis of the struggle between capital and labour that so often results in violence in England, the United States and practically every other "civilised" country. There is no better definition of the nation than the one written by Mr Roberts and accepted by the Jamaica Progressive League. *Any people who has seen its generations come and go on the same soil for centuries is, in fact, a nation.*

Many people do not understand the true working of the colonial system, which is another name for imperialism. They naively believe that colonies do not pay the "mother country" and that the latter holds them for the benefit of the "poor natives", acting like a sort of St George to protect them from attacks by rapacious neighbours. Sir Stafford laid that nonsense bare by pointing out that there are many small nations existing in cantankerous Europe itself and that small countries everywhere exist by virtue of treaties. In the special case of Jamaica, the Monroe Doctrine would operate to protect it from the European wolves. Some may fear America, but the history of that country in its relation to Cuba and Haiti shows that it is more liberal than England in giving small nations freedom to regulate their affairs. Were America as rapacious as England, not a single small nation could maintain a semblance of independence in the western world.

Despite her attitude towards people of colour, it cannot be denied that America gives to the people of Porto Rico and the Philippines greater control over their affairs than England accords to Jamaica. Porto Ricans and Filipinos enjoy a substantial amount of self-government and are given opportunities for advancement that coloured British subjects are systematically denied. Even in colour-preju-

3. See the extensive report: "Theatre Packed at Launching of Peoples Party", *The Gleaner*, 19 September 1938, pp. 1, 7, and 21. Domingo's quotation in the paragraph that follows has been slightly amended in order to correspond with the newspaper account.

diced America there are Negro army officers, police lieutenants (equivalent of inspectors), consular agents, etc. These men occupy positions and receive salaries that no Jamaican of colour can ever dream of.

It is generally conceded that the British Empire may be broken up as a result of the suicidal class policy of the Tories. If this should happen Jamaicans will face the possibility of their country being seized by, or ceded to, the United States. If we come under American influence in our present condition of political helplessness, our future will be difficult and we will not be in a position to demand from our new master a status which is superior to the one we now occupy; but if we struggle for improvement of our present status, then, come what may, we will be in an immeasurably better position to defend ourselves and our interests against those features of American domination that we have a right to fear.

But the question is not one of changing masters. If we achieve self-government under the British flag, we would have the right, if the Fascists succeed in dismembering the Empire, to demand independence from all external control, including that of America. Independence is not the pressing issue for Jamaicans. Their immediate task is to gain self-government. It is not an unreasonable ambition. There are enough precedents in the British Empire. Coloured people of the British Empire with the facts of history before them should not be willing to leave their destiny in the hands of imperialists of any school of thought. There can be no doubt of the essential kinship of imperialism with fascism. Fascism, it cannot be repeated too often, is a philosophy and practice of government that means slavery and death for non-white and all weak peoples. It is well that the middle classes of Jamaica realise this and stop dreaming.

A self-governed New Zealand is free to say whether or not it agrees with the pro-fascist policies of Chamberlain and can refuse to send its sons to die for ideals and causes that are opposed to their own best interests as human beings desiring a world of freedom and equality for all men. It can also initiate and put into effect, without outside interference, legislation of the greatest social benefit to the masses of that self-governing unit of the British Empire. Jamaicans, with so much at stake, must fight for similar rights for themselves.

Considering all the facts, no liberty-loving patriotic Jamaican can stand aloof from the newly organised People's National Party. The Party must be uncompromisingly national in outlook and democratic in character. It should operate on the principle of "the greatest good for the greatest number". In such a party there is room for all classes of Jamaicans. Colour and its follies must not be a barrier to membership or leadership. Lines of social demarcation must not invade its ranks.

The greatest desideratum of the moment is discipline and loyalty. Enthusiasm without knowledge and loyalty without discipline can lead us nowhere and will discredit the great movement of national regeneration that is now in motion. Hail to the PEOPLE'S NATIONAL PARTY and its goal of SELF-GOVERNMENT FOR JAMAICA!

20

Jamaica Seeks Its Freedom

December 1938

Opportunity, the house magazine of the Negro Urban League, was not quite the prestigious venue it had been under Charles Johnson's editorship when Domingo had contributed to a West Indian number in 1926. However, its readers were the movers and shakers of the African-American community and, with the JPL now in full flow, Domingo was offering them an update on the movement for Jamaican self-government.

Opportunity, 16, no. 12 (December 1938), pp. 370–371

What little the average American Negro knows about the British West Indies is derived from contact with a few West Indians, from books, and from an occasional dispatch in his newspaper reporting a natural disaster or a local riot. Practically no serious study of the social, economic, and political condition of the islands has been made by colored Americans. It is generally hazily believed that social and political conditions in the islands, while not perfect, are at least tolerable.

In the mind of Americans, colored West Indians are a homogeneous group. It is but vaguely realized that the islands are in some instances hundreds of miles apart and that among West Indians at home there is little knowledge of any island other than their own. It is in America that West Indians develop a geographical consciousness. In the islands they maintain, naturally enough, their distinct insular prejudices, interests, and loyalties—their major loyalty being, of course, to Great Britain. The newly acquired group consciousness results from the attitude of Americans who are unable or unwilling to recognize the insular differences which exist among the English-speaking immigrants from the Caribbean area.

For the last two years events have taken place in the West Indies, British Honduras, and British Guiana which may exert a great influence upon the destiny of the inhabitants. Serious labor disturbances have resulted in the loss of many lives and the destruction of considerable property. The fundamental grievance is dissatisfaction with the prevailing low wage scale. Other factors responsible for the upsurge are the return of large numbers of disgruntled workers from Cuba and Central America, strict enforcement of immigration laws in those countries and the United States, and the ignoble part played by Great Britain in the Italo-

Ethiopian war. All of this created a social ferment that was bound to end in an explosion.

Disturbed by the series of disorders in its "model" ancient colonies, the British government recently sent a Royal Commission, under the leadership of Lord Moyne, a wealthy aristocrat, to the West Indies to study the situation and make recommendations calculated to prevent a recurrence of the unrest. Unfortunately, the Commission is composed entirely of Englishmen. Its first stop is Jamaica. Because of its geographical location, historical background and singular economic dependence on bananas, Jamaica has little if any contact with the other colonies. In consequence, the point of view in Jamaica is not exactly the same as the point of view that may be found in Trinidad, Barbados, or British Guiana. Jamaica is the largest insular possession of Great Britain in the Caribbean area and has about one half of the total British West Indian population. Over 90 percent of the people are of African descent in varying degrees. They are active and progressive. Given a fair opportunity they are capable of giving a good account of themselves. Their achievements, at home and abroad, are impressive. Until the so-called rebellion of 1865, Jamaica had representative government. Political power was in the hands of a small clique of white planters and merchants, but there were very definite limits over which the Colonial Office did not dare step. The black population was practically disenfranchised. As an aftermath of the serious agrarian troubles which swept the eastern part of the island, the House of Assembly, composed of planters and their supporters, surrendered the constitution because, as they confessed, they feared that Jamaica would become a second Haiti.

Between 1865 and 1884 the affairs of the island were administered by officials directly responsible to the Colonial Office in London. Considerable dissatisfaction ensued, and a new constitution was granted to the people in which a feeble form of representative government was provided. The Colonial Office reserved to itself rights that it never had under the old constitution. However, specific constitutional guarantees were provided against legal discrimination based upon race. The Governor, who is appointed from England, may not give his assent to any bill "whereby persons not of European birth or descent may be subjected or made liable to disabilities or restrictions to which people of European birth or descent are not also subjected or made liable". Despite the clear and unequivocal language of the constitution there are many disabilities and restrictions imposed upon colored people by custom.

* * *

The deplorable situation in Jamaica had the effect of rousing the dormant nationalism of the people and induced several prominent, patriotic citizens to take an active interest in the political future of their country. A People's National Party was launched by N. W. Manley, KC, perhaps the leading barrister of the country, on 18 September 1938. The Party is a coalition of the various progressive organizations in the island, including the Jamaica Progressive League. Self-government is the goal of the Party. The movement is receiving considerable support from the hitherto indifferent middle class and from militant sections of the workers. As was expected, it is vigorously opposed by reactionary elements which benefit from the *status quo.*

Jamaicans in New York, long dissatisfied with the stagnant social, political, and economic conditions of their country, organized the Jamaica Progressive League two years ago under the leadership of W. Adolphe Roberts, poet, editor, biographer, and war correspondent. It is the avowed aim of the League to agitate and fight for self-government and achieve dominion status for the island. This is unquestionably a tall order, for it is in effect a bold challenge to the British system of colonial government that is based upon the theory of "the white man's burden". It is the contention of the League that the time is long past when West Indians should tamely continue to accept and endure the anomalies of anachronistic Crown Colony rule. The time has arrived when a breach must be made in the debasing and oppressive system of government which has fettered the political ambitions of a virile and civilized people for decades.

The Jamaica Progressive League makes the declaration that Jamaica is a nation by every acknowledged definition and as such fully capable of self-government. It demands a status for the island similar to that enjoyed by New Zealand, Canada, Ireland, or South Africa. It has held several mass meetings in Boston, Montclair, and New York and flooded the West Indian colony in New York, and the island of Jamaica, with written propaganda setting forth its program for the political regeneration of the country. The ideals of the League have found ready acceptance and response in the homeland. Following a propaganda tour of the island by Mr Roberts last winter, the League was established there, and in conjunction with its sister body in New York played an important part during the wave of strikes which swept the island last summer. The League recently sent its secretary to appear before the Royal Commission and present its social and economic program for needed reforms in the island. It charged him with the heavy responsibility of making the demand for complete self-government for Jamaica within the British Commonwealth of Nations.

The aspiration of Jamaicans for self-government is a legitimate one. It is the indefeasible right of every nation to govern itself. Responsible British spokesmen have frequently stated that self-government will be accorded to colonies which exhibit a fitness for it. Jamaicans contend that they are as capable to govern as Englishmen or any other people. They point with pride to scores of their countrymen who have risen high in the service of the government and in private life as proof of their capacity as administrators. They refuse any longer to accept an inferior status in the British Empire. They want to know quite definitely what their future position in the Empire is going to be. The struggle for self-government is not and cannot be waged along racial lines, although it is quite obvious that any political gain will necessarily transfer considerable power to an important section of the colored race. It will give a million and a quarter Jamaicans control over their future and endow them with powerful weapons to be used in self-defense against imperialism and fascism. Its repercussion will be felt in the other British colonies, and even as the Haitian Revolution affected America, the elevation of Jamaica to the coveted status of a dominion may react beneficially upon the Negroes of this country.

* * *

Leaders in the movement for Jamaican self-government need and invite the co-operation and encouragement of all liberty-loving peoples. Any gain made by Jamaica will be an object lesson for Trinidad, Barbados, and the other colonies of the Caribbean area. It will make similar demands by them easier. Better still, the inauguration of similar movements in those colonies will be irresistible and compel the British government to make substantial political concessions.

Believing that they have a clean-cut case for the right to self-determination, Jamaicans are unwilling to confuse the issue by the intrusion of any controversial questions. The British government must be maneuvered into a position where it recognizes the right of its 283-year-old colony, with its large colored population, to self-government, or openly expose its true policy. The fight is likely to be bitter and will entail many sacrifices, but Ireland fought for 700 years and never lost courage. Jamaica's fight should not be long drawn out, but come what may, *The Battle For Freedom Is On*.

Jamaica is a nation and its people are fit and able to govern themselves.

21

"Undesirable Publications": Protest from a Jamaican Residing in New York

May 1940

The accrual of arbitrary powers by Governor Richards under the shield of necessary measures in time of war was of constant concern to Domingo—who would soon enough become a victim of those powers. Here he uses his old pseudonym "Proletariat" (see #13) to unleash his most sarcastic tone in objecting to the proposed Undesirable Publications Law.

The Gleaner, 20 May 1940, p. 8.

THE EDITOR: Sir,—In a letter from a friend in Jamaica I first learnt of the intention of the government to introduce in the next session of the Legislative Council a bill entitled the "Undesirable Publications Law". The letter in question breathed alarm and contained the significant phrase that the Governor would be the sole arbiter of what kind of literature will be allowed entry into the island if the law is passed. Since then I have read the highpoints of the proposed law and want to add my word of protest and present some arguments why I think the elected members should not pass the bill and grant the Governor the extraordinary and arbitrary powers that the law would confer on him.

Most people in Jamaica believe, and the world has been told by leading British spokesmen, that the war now waged against Germany is for the purpose of eliminating Hitlerian practices from the world. I humbly submit that Jamaica is in the world and part of a democratic empire (if the two words can be reconciled). I further submit that one of the first acts of Hitler, whose principles and practices Jamaicans are urged to destroy, was to place a ban upon certain types of literature. He confiscated and destroyed every book or other kind of publication that did not conform with his ideas, and it stands to reason that the Governor, if vested with "absolute discretion", will exclude from entry into the island all literature that in his opinion is undesirable. For a book or pamphlet to be undesirable it only has to meet his personal disapproval. I feel sure that the innate modesty of Sir Arthur must quail at the idea of finding himself, an ordinary mortal, suddenly invested with the attribute of omniscience in literary matters.

The proposed law is retroactive, for possession of a banned publication (even obtained before passage of the law) will render the owner liable. A peculiar feature of the law is that it will make no exemption for books or pamphlets that originate in England and circulate there freely. In other words, it means that what is safe for Englishmen to read may be undesirable for Jamaicans. Underlying this is the clear assumption that there is an inequality between the two peoples. Englishmen can be trusted to read the ideas and philosophy of Stalin and Hitler, but not Jamaicans.

But there are many English writers whose books may very likely be placed under the ban. I suppose that the monumental works of Beatrice and Sidney Webb on Soviet Communism will be prescribed, also the works of Leonard Barnes and Edward Mo[r]rell, MP. Will the literature of the Fabian Society of England, of which a former Governor of Jamaica was an outstanding ornament, be declared undesirable?[1] Carried out logically it is conceivable that the propaganda literature of the Jamaica Progressive League with its uncompromising insistence on the right of Jamaica to self-government will be denied entry by a Governor who regards such an ambition as "dangerous".

In an editorial on the subject you feel confident that the Elected Members will vote for the measure. I grant that you probably know the members better than those of us who are living abroad, but it is difficult to believe that they will be so blind and reactionary as to approve a law that has as its object the shutting out of modern knowledge. Freedom of thought and of the press is one of the most priceless achievements of humanity. Jamaicans should not be barred from intellectual contact with the outside world. To establish an *index expurgatorius* in Jamaica will be a retrograde step.

I agree with Voltaire, who said, "I disagree with your opinions but will fight to the death that you have a right to express them." If our English rulers are sincerely out to destroy Hitlerism and all that the term connotes, they are doing their cause a grave disservice by introducing dictatorship practices in Jamaica. People should not be judged by their speech but by their actions, and the test of the sincerity of British protestations of democracy is to be found in the colonies. In England there is freedom of speech and the free circulation of ideas, but in Jamaica there is to be suppression of thought. In Japan they have a law against dangerous thoughts, and I suppose, following the precedent of the proposed Undesirable Publications Law, an act, similar to the one in Japan, will be introduced in the Council.

1. Martha Beatrice Webb (1858–1943) and Sidney Webb (1859–1947) were socialists and co-founders of the London School of Economics. Together they authored *Soviet Communism: A New Civilisation?* (1935) and were prominent members of the Fabian Society alongside George Bernard Shaw and Sydney Olivier, the former governor of Jamaica. Leonard Barnes (1895–1977) was an anti-colonialist writer and journalist. Domingo probably had in mind his *Empire or Democracy* (1939). Philip Edward Morrell (1870–1943) was a British Liberal politician.

It is unfortunate that Jamaicans are not alert in the defence of their liberties. Too often they allow their rights to be lost by default due to sheer laziness and indifference, only to realise it when it is too late. Everybody seems to fear the awakening of the average man to an interest in himself and the social and political life of his country. He was alright when he allowed everybody to walk on him without a word of protest, but today he is suddenly discovered to be dangerous and capable of upsetting the social and economic apple cart.

As one who has always taken an interest in the affairs of his native land, I regard the proposed law as the gravest and most dangerous invasion of the rights of the people. It will lead to an unhealthy regimentation of the intellectual life of the country; it will develop stagnation. No country is truly progressive that prohibits the intellectual pollen of other countries from entering. Were such a law in existence a hundred years ago, pamphlets issued by the English abolitionists would have been banned on the ground that they contained "dangerous propaganda" when they denounced the institution of slavery and urged the manumission of slaves.

The Elected Members, for the most part descended from men and women who were freed because some people dared to preach "dangerous doctrines", if they vote for the proposed law will be guilty of inferentially disapproving the very propaganda that liberated their ancestors. They will be admitting that certain literature is good enough for Englishmen, but bad for Jamaicans and confess that they accept the doctrine of their own racial inferiority. They will show that people who benefited from the advance of progressive ideas have themselves become the defenders and champions of reaction. Civilisation as we know it is the result of the free circulation of ideas. Civilisation developed in proportion as thought was liberated. Not all the specious arguments in the world can show that mankind has not stagnated whenever it has been subjected to the kind of intellectual blockade and mental blackout implied in the proposed bill.

Finally, it is my opinion that every progressive person should lift his voice NOW in opposition to the bill. The People's National Party and its affiliates should hold monster mass meetings in order to make the Elected Members responsive to democratic and modern principles.

I am, etc.,
PROLETARIAT
New York City, 7 May 1940

22

Declaration of Rights of the Caribbean Peoples to Self-Determination and Self-Government

July 1940

This declaration is unsigned, although the fact that the easiest available copy is in the Richard B. Moore Papers has sometimes led to it being attributed to Moore: his daughter refers to it as "largely the work of Moore".[1] However, in a letter to W. Adolphe Roberts, Domingo explained: "I did the original work and was aided by a committee in having the language refined, but the essential ideas are mine and I did everything possible (and I think I succeeded) to exclude anything of a red aspect from the document."[2] Accordingly, Domingo was careful to emphasise self-government at every turn but never mentions the word "federation", instead always using the plural forms such as its title phrase, "Caribbean peoples", then "West Indian peoples", "peoples of these areas", etc. Richard Drayton is therefore mistaken in saying in this connection "that the future of the entire Caribbean was to be sovereign *and united*".[3] Adom Getachew stresses the importance of the WINEC Declaration: "this document precedes the Atlantic Charter but already contains the anticolonial refashioning of self-determination as a human right".[4] Copies were circulated widely by Domingo, including to Rayford Logan and to George Padmore. As Domingo explains in his letter to Padmore:

> The Declaration was printed on fine paper, translated into Spanish and Portuguese, and copies were sent by registered air-mail to every American Foreign

1. Joyce Moore Turner, "Richard B. Moore and His Works", in Richard B. Moore, *Caribbean Militant in Harlem: Collected Writings 1920–1972*, ed. W. Burghardt Turner and Joyce Moore Turner, Bloomington, IN: Indiana University Press, 1988, pp. 19–108, at 75. The Declaration is reproduced on pp. 262–270, but without its appendices. A slightly abbreviated version also appeared as "Self-Determination Declaration Text", *New York Amsterdam News*, 3 August 1940, p. 11, with Domingo's name heading the list of signatories.
2. W. A. Domingo, Letter to W. Adolphe Roberts, 24 June 1940, WARA 2.3.5.
3. Richard Drayton, "Commonwealth History from Below? Caribbean National, Federal and Pan-African Renegotiations of the Empire Project, c. 1880–1950", in *Commonwealth History in the Twenty-First Century*, ed. Saul Dubow and Richard Drayton, London: Palgrave Macmillan, 2020, pp. 41–60, at 43; italics in original.
4. Adom Getachew, *Worldmaking after Empire: The Rise and Fall of Self-Determination*, Princeton, NJ: Princeton University Press, 2019, p. 87.

Office, every legation at Washington, to every delegation at Havana, to President Roosevelt, to Secretary Hull, and to the press of the entire world through the various news agencies. We sent copies to the Foreign Policy Association, the liberal magazines and the daily press and to the most important South American Newspapers.[5]

West Indies National Emergency Committee, submitted to the Pan-American Foreign Ministers' Conference, Havana, Cuba, July 1940. Included in a letter from Domingo to Rayford Logan, 9 November 1940, Rayford Logan Papers, Coll. 166, Box 23, folder 1, Moorland-Spingarn Research Center, Howard University, Washington, DC.[6]

There comes a time in the affairs of every people when it becomes imperative for them to examine their conditions of existence and to take such steps as they deem necessary for the protection of their vital interests and for the enjoyment of their unalienable rights to "life, liberty, and the pursuit of happiness". Such a time has arrived in the history of the peoples who have for centuries inhabited the Caribbean colonies of Britain, France, and the Netherlands. These peoples, whose total aggregate is over three and a half million and who occupy territories approximating 231,314 square miles, are specifically designated in an appendix to this declaration.[7]

The war now raging in Europe has brought to the fore the question of basic political and economic adjustments for the peoples of the West Indies and of both American continents. This grave situation has compelled the democratic and peace-loving nations of the western hemisphere seriously to consider the best possible collective measures for their mutual defense, security, and welfare. The existence of strategically situated and economically important European colonies in the New World constitutes, and will always constitute, a basis for aggression and a threat to the security of the nations of Pan-America. For many years responsible statesmen of the Americas have enunciated the doctrine that this hemisphere should be kept immune from the rivalries and wars of the Old World. The vital interests of the inhabitants of the Caribbean regions, as part of the Americas, are indissolubly bound up in the practical establishment and actual maintenance of this basic principle.

The political control of the peoples of these territories by non-American powers is now recognized to be a menace to the safety and security of all American

5. W. A. Domingo, Letter to George Padmore, 2 August 1940, CO 137/846/10, TNA. Presumably the letter is in the Colonial Office files because it was opened by MI5, which was spying on both of them.

6. Rayford Whittingham Logan (1897–1982) was an African-American historian and Pan-African activist.

7. Not included here.

nations. Opinion is being developed in the United States of America appealing to this sentiment and advocating the sale, transfer, forcible seizure of, or establishment of trusteeship or mandate over these Caribbean areas. But any such menace can best be removed only by the integration of the West Indian peoples into the Pan-American family of nations strictly on the basis of the right of self-determination. Only thus will it be possible to create an enduring foundation for genuine "Good Neighbor" relations. Taking full cognizance of the grave nature and the serious implications of these proposals for change of sovereignty, the West Indies National Emergency Committee regards it as its solemn duty to present the case and the cause of the peoples most directly involved to the Pan-American nations and to the entire world.

The Committee identifies itself with and whole-heartedly supports every effort honestly directed towards keeping the continents of America out of war. It realizes and submits that conflicts over colonies constitute the major source of war in the modern world. Therefore, the assurance of the right of self-determination and self-government to the West Indian peoples is unquestionably necessary to remove this major danger of war from the western hemisphere. Reflecting and expressing the profound sentiments of the peoples of these Caribbean areas, this Committee declares that it is firmly and irrevocably opposed to any sale, transfer, mandate, trusteeship, or change of sovereignty of these peoples without the exercise of their inalienable human and democratic right of self-determination.

On behalf of the peoples of the West Indies and the adjacent Caribbean areas concerned, whose human aspirations and political interests it expresses, the Committee solemnly protests against any action on the part of Britain, France, and Holland or any other power that would in any way abridge or deny them their indefensible right to a dominant voice in the shaping of their own destiny. The Committee insists that the will of these peoples must be fully ascertained, in accordance with genuine democratic principles and processes, in respect to any change whatever in their political status.

Fully conscious of the fundamental justice of their cause and reposing confidence in the democratic sentiment of the Pan-American peoples, the peoples of the West Indies and the adjacent Caribbean territories involved openly proclaim their right to untrammeled self-determination. Any denial of this right to them will be opposed by every legitimate means and any attempt at such denial will constitute irrefutable evidence of imperialistic motives and designs on the part of every power involved in any change of sovereignty or establishment of military, naval, or aerial bases in these territories without the consent of the peoples immediately and most vitally concerned.

Moreover, any abridgement or denial of this fundamental democratic right of self-determination would be none other than a flagrant violation of the principles of democracy so long proclaimed by the nations of Pan-America. It is self-evident also that any such denial would weaken, undermine, and destroy the democratic structure which must underlie and sustain all Pan-American nationality and concert for defense. It is unquestionable, furthermore, that any refusal to recognize and to respect the national aspirations of the Caribbean peoples would be a clear denial and an unmistakable repudiation of the very principles of democracy and the rights of small nations for which the sympathies of the American and Latin American peoples are being solicited in the present crisis. This grave crisis in world affairs only raises most sharply the basic question of self-determination and self-government which had already been raised by the peoples of these territories.

The West Indies National Emergency Committee recognizes the imminent probability of changes of sovereignty in colonial territories in the New World and presents its case for the rights of the peoples, whose just cause it advocates, to autonomous national existence. The Committee draws attention to the fact that every nation in the New World developed from the status of a colony or colonies to its present position as an independent nation and declares that this historical circumstance should justly render every Pan-American nation sympathetic to the aspirations of the West Indian and Caribbean peoples for self-government.

The Committee points to the fact that the inhabitants in these areas have long since reached that stage in historical evolution where they have demonstrated their capacity for practical administration of government in accordance with modern democratic technique. West Indians participate in every department of government—legislative, executive, judicial—to such an extent that only a few posts are administered by Europeans solely because of the existing imperial connections. The Committee further points to the fact that the peoples of these areas exhibit all the characteristics of nationality and that vigorous movements for self-government have existed for a considerable period and have now reached a stage for full realization. Evidence of this is adduced in several instances and representations cited in the statement appended hereto.[8]

The recent world-shaking military events in Europe and the resulting critical situation for the West Indian peoples have heightened their insistent demand for self-determination and self-government. The declaration hereafter quoted, made by elected members of the Jamaica Legislative Council, as reported in the press of that country on 27 May 1940, is typical of the prevailing sentiment of the Caribbean peoples on this crucial question of sale, transfer, mandate, trusteeship, or change of sovereignty: "Should circumstances ever arise as to include the possibility of such a change then the people of this island would claim the right to determine their own destiny, and not be handed over as a piece of chattel to any foreign nation."

8. Not included here.

Such a realization of self-government has long been recognized as the goal towards which all Pan-American nations should inevitably move. In a message delivered to the Congress of the United States of America on 6 December 1869, President Ulysses S. Grant, speaking on the future of European colonies in the western hemisphere, declared: "These dependencies are no longer regarded as subject to transfer from one European power to another. When the present relation of colonies ceases, they are to become independent powers, exercising the right of choice and of self-control in the determination of the future condition and relations with other powers."[9]

At the recent Inter-American Conference held at Panama in September 1939, Foreign Secretary Eduardo Hay of Mexico presented the statement hereinafter quoted. "Because of the war some regions of America controlled by non-American states may cease depending on the authorities of those countries. That if it appears that some change in sovereignty is about to occur, a consultation meeting should be convoked in order to aid that region freely to determine its own political destiny. That it would be unjust to consider the American subjects of non-American nations simply as merchandise. That they should be given an opportunity to decide their own political destinies."

A resolution adopted by the official delegates of all the Pan-American nations at the American Scientific Congress held in Washington in May 1939 solemnly affirmed that the American republics were "all adherents to the principle of the right of each nation to determine its own destiny". In pursuit of this high purpose of self-determination, self-government, and the democratic concert of the peoples of the western hemisphere, the West Indies National Emergency Committee whole-heartedly subscribes to every sincere effort for the extirpation of all forces hostile to democratic institutions. It solemnly pledges its fullest cooperation with all the American nations in every action necessary to defend, to preserve, and to extend democracy in the western hemisphere and to uphold democratic principles throughout the world.

The Committee appeals to all who uphold democracy and to every true lover of liberty in all the Americas and indeed throughout the world to support the rightful claims and just cause of the peoples of the West Indies and the adjacent Caribbean areas to self-determination and self-government. Let the solemn warning of events be heeded and the inexorable logic of the present critical situation be squarely and fairly faced. Then the justice and wisdom of this earnest appeal will be acknowledged and support and recognition of these rightful claims will be duly accorded as absolutely essential to the mutual defense, security, welfare, peace, and progress of all the peoples of the Americas to the end "that government of the people by the people and for the people, shall not perish from the earth".

9. As usual, Domingo quotes meticulously: www.presidency.ucsb.edu/documents/first-annual-message-11 (accessed 26 January 2025).

23

Letter to Franklin D. Roosevelt

December 1940

Here Domingo shows that he is capable of writing in the language of diplomacy, although he doesn't hold back in his criticism of US policy. He received a quite detailed reply to this letter from Roosevelt's Secretary of State, Cordell Hull.[1]

NAACP Racial discrimination and political sovereignty in the British West Indies Folder 001432-002-0252. Found in Papers of the NAACP, Part 13 NAACP and Labor, Series A Subject Files on Labor Conditions and Employment Discrimination, pp. 33–34.

26 December 1940

Hon. Franklin D. Roosevelt
The White House
Washington, DC

Dear Mr President:

As you will doubtless recall, the West Indies National Council, acting in the interest of the peoples inhabiting the colonial possessions of France, Great Britain, and Holland in the Caribbean region, forwarded to you a copy of its "Declaration of Rights" which was presented to the Havana Conference of Foreign Ministers which was held last July.

Due to the activity of the Council, which was supported by the Jamaica Progressive League, the interests of the Caribbean peoples received the sympathetic support of Dr Leopoldo Melo, chief of the Argentine delegation to the Conference. As a result of the combined efforts of the friends of the West Indian peoples and the believers in fair dealings for all peoples of this continent, the Act of Havana was drawn up along lines of justice and democratic treatment for the people whose fate had been discussed at the Conference without their direct participation.

1. Letter from Cordell Hull to W. A. Domingo, 15 February 1941, WARA 2.3.5.

Shortly after the Conference, it was announced that the governments of Great Britain and the United States had successfully negotiated arrangements for the establishment of naval and air bases in the West Indies in exchange for 50 overage destroyers. Immediately our Council protested that such an agreement was violative of the rights of the inhabitants and contrary to the spirit of the Act of Havana which was based upon the theory of multi-lateral American action in all matters pertaining to hemispheric defense.

Since then steps have been taken to construct the bases. Our Council, representing the best interests of the peoples concerned, and desiring to preserve the good name of the United States, thus reducing continental suspicions and hostility, made certain suggestions to representative British West Indian organizations with respect to the conduct of Americans on the leased areas. These suggestions were embodied in a letter which the People's National Party of Jamaica sent to the Colonial Secretary of that island in September. For your information, I enclose a copy of the letter that was sent to the Colonial Secretary. You will note that in addition to the stipulations regarding the activities of Americans on the leased areas, the People's National Party draws attention to the Act of Havana as having a bearing on all such matters. Mr President, the question of the leases in the West Indies has become one of grave concern for the West Indian peoples.

The West Indian peoples, speaking through their truly representative organizations, are anxious to be assured that their fundamental human rights will be properly safeguarded in the lands of their birth. They have seen how on the Canal Zone in the Republic of Panama, under American control, West Indians have been subjected to every conceivable form of racial segregation and they are determined to do everything possible to prevent the introduction of similar Jim-Crow practices into their homelands. They fear, Sir, that the bases may become bases for the introduction of American racial prejudices.

Unknown to Americans, the West Indian peoples have for a long time been struggling for self-government. Due to their British traditions those efforts have been kept in strictly constitutional channels, but the history of the islands and British Guiana, as briefly shown in Appendix no. 2 of our "Declaration", should convince any fair-minded person that the West Indian peoples desire freedom to shape their destiny. During the past few weeks there has been a revival of the campaign for this country to acquire the islands from Great Britain in payment of war debts or in payment for credits or ammunition and ships. Such an act on the part of this country would be undemocratic and at variance with many of the expressions of this government on the right of all peoples, without exception, to control their own affairs. Such an act would be a violation of the rights of the West Indian peoples and in effect be a means for blocking their national development. It would be a thwarting of the aspirations of the inhabitants. But above all, in the terms of the interests of the United States, it would be a direct repudiation of the Act of Havana and calculated to stimulate the charge in Latin America of Yankee imperialism—a charge which your Good Neighbor policy has done much to offset.

Having in mind the best interests of the entire continent, our Council is anxious for you to make a statement on the two questions raised in this letter, namely, that the United States will observe the stipulations contained in the People's National Party [letter] and that this country has no intention of acquiring the West Indies by barter, purchase, satisfaction of debts, or by supplying Great Britain with credits in exchange.

I am confident that you, Mr President, are as anxious as our Council to see that democracy is extended to all parts of this continent, that the legitimate aspirations of the West Indian peoples are not thwarted; that the animosity of Latin America for this country is not revived; that the peoples of the Caribbean area are protected in their right to live their lives free from the galling humiliations which unfortunately exist on the Panama Canal Zone.

Respectfully yours,
W. A. Domingo
President
WEST INDIES NATIONAL COUNCIL

24

A Step in Advance—The Proposed New Constitution

March 1943

Domingo's release from detention coincided with Sir Arthur Richards's removal from office and with the announcement of a proposed new constitution for Jamaica, so he was in celebratory mood. Buoyed by the constitutional plans, Domingo remained sympathetic to Oliver Stanley, who visited Jamaica in January 1945, although he later became more suspicious about the sincerity of the Colonial Secretary's plans—and then, after the British general election, quickly disappointed by the new Labour government's actions.[1]

Public Opinion, 27 March 1943, p. 3

23 February 1943 marked the beginning of a new era in the political history of Jamaica, and it might well be the beginning of a new era in the entire British Colonial Empire. On that date the people of Jamaica and of the entire world were given the detail of the constitutional proposals offered to Jamaica by the Secretary of State for the Colonies, Colonel Stanley, grandson of Lord Derby, who had given to Jamaica its present constitution.[2] The new constitution envisaged in the proposals will mark a definite advance in the West Indies. It has features that are novel in the history of British imperialism. Hitherto it had been regarded as the fixed, if unwritten, policy of Downing Street not to live up to its oft-expressed declarations of encouraging the coloured colonial peoples to become self-governing.

Critics of British imperialism have always pointed to the fact that while sections of the Empire with a large white population (not necessarily a majority) had been given tangible means for the political control of their countries, no such means were given to portions of the Empire in which a majority of the population

1. W. A. Domingo, "Colonel Stanley's Speech—A Few Impressions", *Public Opinion*, 6 January 1945, p. 3; "Sparks from My Anvil", *Public Opinion*, 27 October 1945, p. 3.

2. The Conservative politician Oliver Stanley (1896–1950) held various ministerial positions before becoming Secretary of State for the Colonies in November 1942. Edward George Geoffrey Smith-Stanley, 14th Earl of Derby (1799–1869), known as Lord Stanley from 1834 to 1851, was a British statesman and Conservative politician who served three times as prime minister and was also secretary of state for war and the colonies from 1833 to 1834 and 1841 to 1845.

are not of European blood. And this despite repeated statements of a contrary nature from responsible representatives of the colonial government. This divergence between the manner in which white colonials are treated and the way in which non-Europeans are treated has caused much dissatisfaction and done more to embitter coloured colonials than any other single thing.

In the West Indies this has been especially marked. From 1865 until the last quarter of the last century there had been a progressive decline in the status of the West Indian colonies *vis-à-vis* Great Britain. During that time all the British West Indian colonies experienced a decline in the control of their own affairs, the only exception being the three B's—Barbados, the Bahamas, and Bermuda. Indeed, the process was halted in Barbados only because of the opposition of the local population which led to the famous Pope-Hennessy riots.[3] It must be noted that it is precisely the three colonies in which the white populations are proportionately highest that no decline of political power took place. This coincidence, coupled with the fact that Canada, Australia, New Zealand were advanced to the status of dominions, led many to believe that the withdrawal of political privilege in the West Indies was not altogether accidental.

This belief was strengthened by two important and revealing facts. There was the case of South Africa, which was given dominion status shortly after a bloody war in which the Boers had inflicted considerable casualties and humiliation on the British Army and had damaged the *amour propre* of the British government to an astounding degree. Then there was the frank and undisguised expression of British colonial policy by Mr Joseph Chamberlain, father of Neville Chamberlain.[4] Those two facts served to convince coloured Britishers that the British government was definitely committed to a policy of *ruling* the coloured sections of the Empire while other parts of it would be allowed a large degree of autonomy. Understanding this background and realising that the proposals of Colonel Stanley represent a big break with the prevailing policy, it is easier for us to appreciate the momentous character of the despatch which was read to the Legislative Council on 23 February.

The proposals came in consequence of joint representations made to the Colonial Office by the People's National Party, the Federation of Citizens' Associations and the members of the Legislative Council. Prior to the joint statement from these bodies, the British government had been in the happy position of being able to claim that Jamaicans did not seem to know just what they wanted. The statement blocked any such contention. The Colonial Office had to yield or stand revealed as being exposed to extending democracy in the Empire while

3. John Pope-Hennessy (1834–1891) had been made governor of Barbados in 1873 with a remit to bring about its federation with St Vincent, St Lucia, Grenada, and Tobago. Riots in 1876 caused the Colonial Office to back down, and Pope-Hennessy was quickly transferred to Hong Kong.

4. See above, p. 8.

fighting a war ostensibly for the securing of democracy for countries located outside of the Empire. The position was contradictory and full of dangerous implications. This was especially so because the British government, a signer of the Atlantic Charter, had explicitly stated that the Charter did not include the Empire. Freedom to British colonials was to be the private concern of the British government.

It was therefore very difficult for Colonel Stanley to have denied the united request to articulate representative bodies of the island. He was facilitated in making his decision by the fact that the demands contained in the joint statement were relatively mild even though they sought certain changes which are revolutionary in the British colonial system, although commonplace in the French and American colonial systems. Furthermore, the air was charged with the idea of freedom. Telling contrasts had been made between the behaviour of the Philippines and the people of the British East Indies when their respective territories were invaded by the conquering Japanese imperialists. The Filipinos had fought desperately against the invaders while Burmese and Malayans had in many instances aided the invaders. It was contended that this difference in behaviour was due to the difference in status in relation to the so-called mother country.

Those and other important facts contributed to the inevitability of far-reaching concessions being made by Colonel Stanley. Indeed, it was a good thing for him to do. He could then easily meet American pressure and criticism of the undemocratic attitude of the British Colonial Office by pointing to the fact that his government had conceded most of what had been asked for by the Jamaican people themselves. Certainly the British government could not be expected to thrust upon any people more than those people had themselves demanded.

Since the far-reaching features of the proposals have become public, many persons and organisations have flooded the press with letters of gratitude to this or that person for the proposals. Such an attitude is to be condemned. It shows a lack of understanding of international affairs and also reveals an almost dog-like attitude on public questions. After all, Colonel Stanley must be credited with having been in office when the concessions were made (and there can be no doubt but that he was sympathetic to them) but there is absolutely no necessity for being grateful to anyone for a long-withheld human right. That is not the way that really civilised and democratically inclined peoples act on public questions. They know their ordinary human rights and don't see any necessity for thanking anyone when those rights are at long last restored to them.

In any event the pages of Hansard give the facts. Asked by Mr Adams if he could hear the views of Jamaicans in England on the question of the constitution as "the Governor appears to be quite unable to make up his mind on the subject", Colonel Stanley replied, "It is not for the Governor to make up his mind: it is for me as the responsible minister to make up my mind."[5] That tells the whole story and should dispose of the question of gratitude for the constitutional proposals offered to the country. In subsequent articles I intend to deal with specific features of the proposed constitution. For the present it is enough to say that it constitutes a decided political advance and should prove of inestimable benefit to the people of Jamaica. It should improve their national morale and make them proud of their country. It should make them realise a sense of responsibility for the welfare of their native land. It should free their energies and bring to the surface qualities and capabilities which are only possible in an atmosphere of relative freedom.

The future of Jamaica is to a large degree in the hands of its people. Mr Manley has frequently asserted that the fitness of a people for self-government can best be gauged by the unanimity of their demand for it. Jamaicans have shown that unity. It is now their plain duty to unite to make the new constitution a success. It will not be easy. Mistakes will be made, but it is our task to reduce mistakes to the lowest possible minimum. Jamaica has not been offered self-government, but it has been given a fair enough start on the road, and what is more, the start is made up of practically all that we have demanded. Pending the final statement to be issued by the public bodies responsible for the gains made so far, it is the obligation of every lover of Jamaica to bend his energies to the patriotic labour of sinking differences in an effort to promote the general good through the new instrument that will soon be ours to use, abuse, or lose.

5. Domingo quotes the exchange accurately: https://hansard.parliament.uk/Commons/1943-02-17/debates/9b113648-652a-4f87-a113-4eeb1c09b7a8/Constitution (accessed 4 September 2024).

25

England's Debt to Jamaica

April 1943

The relationship between Empire and colony was at the heart of much of Domingo's writing. His reading of Marx gave him a basic economic analysis, spelled out in the title and content of this piece—which anticipates in brief compass Eric Williams's classic statement of his thesis that the profits from slavery helped finance the Industrial Revolution in Britain.[1] Indeed, two years after this piece Domingo reviewed Williams's *Capitalism & Slavery* and commended it for intervening in the popular "controversy" of Jamaica's indebtedness to Britain by providing the statistics to "prov[e] beyond doubt" how England's great families and industry had developed from African enslaved labour.[2] But Domingo also always sought to understand the psychology of what his French contemporary Octave Mannoni diagnosed as colonial dependence, one element of which was the widespread Jamaican view that the islanders ought to be grateful for Britain's benevolent attention.[3] Domingo was concerned to undermine that misperception.

Public Opinion, 10 April 1943, p. 4

In my article "The Proposed New Constitution—A Step in Advance", which appeared in *Public Opinion* of 27 March, I insisted that Jamaicans ought not to thank any particular individual for the political gains embodied in the proposals offered to this country by the Secretary of State for the Colonies. I insisted, instead, that what we gained was the result of our having fought manfully for them. Hence, if anybody is entitled to credit, it is not the Governor, who acted merely as Colonel Stanley's messenger, but those courageous leaders of the Jamaican people who had conducted an uncompromising and—in the light of the uses to which the Defence Regulations have been put—a dangerous fight for the few

1. Eric Williams, *Capitalism & Slavery*, Chapel Hill, NC: University of North Carolina Press, 1944. Eric Eustace Williams (1911–1981) was a writer and politician who served as prime minister of Trinidad and Tobago from 1962 to 1981. *Capitalism & Slavery* built on Williams's 1938 Oxford dissertation, but it also advanced new arguments not made in the thesis about the role of slavery in the emergence of capitalism: see Eric Williams, *The Economic Aspect of the Abolition of the West Indian Slave Trade and Slavery*, ed. Dale Tomich and William Darity, Jr, London: Rowman & Littlefield, 2014.
2. W. A. Domingo, "Capitalism and Slavery: A Review", *Public Opinion*, 26 April 1945, p. 2.
3. Octave Mannoni, *Psychologie de la colonisation*, Paris, France: Seuil, 1950.

democratic features contained in the famous despatch that was made public on 23 February.

Today I deal with another matter which, while not directly related to politics, has a very great influence on the thinking of Jamaicans as a whole. I refer to the widespread belief that Jamaicans owe to England a great debt of gratitude. This belief has been deliberately cultivated in recent years. Indeed, propagation of the belief bears all the earmarks of being inspired and organised. It has become a part of the psychology of Jamaicans to express their gratitude to England for a great variety of things. This feeling is quite widespread and assumes various forms. I propose to deal with a few of the most popular points.

1. We are told that we ought to be grateful that we are a part of the British Empire. I will not discuss the pros and cons of that contention, but I will say that just as Jamaicans are told that it is a great privilege to be a part of the British Empire, the people of the Virgin Islands are exhorted that in being American citizens they are fortunate to be a part of the world's greatest country. Martiniquans and Guadeloupians are similarly told that they are part and parcel of what was perhaps the world's most civilised nation—France. And so down the line all colonial peoples are imbued with the idea that the empire of which their country is a part is the best in the world. The whole thing boils down to what a people are taught and to the fact that they very often know nothing of other countries, which fact makes them incapable of making any critical comparisons between themselves and other peoples.

2. It is generally believed in Jamaica, just as it is believed in the colonies of every other West Indian country, that but for the naval and military power of their mother country the colonies would long ago have suffered the ravages of war. The fall of France debunked French West Indians on this score. Unquestionably the British and American navies have been the greatest barrier to invasion of the western hemisphere by Mr Hitler, but it must not be forgotten that the very fact that colonies exist and that their mother countries get involved in wars automatically brings the war in some of its forms to the colonies of those countries. This has been a sore point with Indian nationalists. They contend that being a part of the British Empire exposes them to attack even though they had no part in the preliminary diplomatic or economic manoeuvres which may have precipitated the conflict. The conclusion derivable is that while it is true that colonies are "protected" by their mother countries, it is also true that being colonies automatically exposes them to attacks from the enemies of their mother countries.

3. It is commonly believed that Jamaica owes a big debt to England for having emancipated our ancestors. Far be it from me to minimise the great and unselfish work of the abolitionists, but it must be kept in mind that Negro emancipation was only an act of justice. Millions of human beings had been torn from the

freedom of their own country and taken across the Middle Passage into the most degrading servitude imaginable. They toiled for centuries without compensation. The fruit of their labour was not theirs, but that of their masters, so emancipation was merely an act of imperfect justice. The truth is that instead of compensating the slaves for their years of toil, it was the masters who were compensated.

In 1939 I had a mild argument with a former elected member of the Legislative Council. The gentleman has since passed to his rest. He sought to convince me that I was ungrateful for demanding self-government, even though I had been careful to make it clear that I wanted no more for Jamaica than what had been accorded to New Zealand with a population about the same size as that of Jamaica. The gentleman became oratorical and to a degree insulting. He referred to the West Indian Emancipation [of] 1838 as an act of unparalleled British generosity and stated that we should be grateful to Englishmen for having brought us out of Africa to Jamaica, in which island we had been given an opportunity to absorb British civilisation and Christianity.

Without any display of heat I told him I could not be grateful to a man for having restored to me my freedom which he himself had deprived me of. In fact, the man ought to have paid me handsomely for the wrong he had done me. I suggested that I was not so sure that the British version of civilisation and Christianity was altogether a gain. I pointed out that the masses of China had their own language and culture and that their religion based on the writings of Confucius, Mencius, and other Eastern philosophers had developed in the Chinese many admirable human traits. Answering his angry charge of ingratitude (he had said that I was ungrateful as Englishmen had spilt blood for me and my race), I told him that I thought that we had spilt more of our blood for England than Englishmen had spilt for us. This seemed to leave him flabbergasted, so I had to explain just what I meant while he snorted with angry impatience.

I told him of what we had done for England during World War I, how our sons had volunteered by the hundreds in a war that was being waged thousands of miles from our shores, of how some had been frost-bitten in Halifax, of the thousands of pounds sterling we had contributed to Great Britain. He tried to belittle the value of the Jamaican blood shed in building up the British Empire, and I advised him to shock his mind a bit by reading the glorious military record of the British West India Regiment and learning of its exploits in Zululand and in various parts of West Africa.

I suggested that he should read Marx's *Capital* and learn something of the millions of pounds sterling that flowed from Jamaica to build up Bristol, Liverpool, and other English cities and of the thousands of pounds wrung from the muscles of Jamaicans only to be used riotously in England by various absentee landlords. I pointed to the vast squandering of Peter Beckford, who derived his wealth from

Jamaica and was at one time considered one of the richest men in England.[4] I added many more arguments, and I was pleased to discover that the eloquence of the M.L.C. [Member of the Legislative Council] began to limp when confronted by irrefutable historical facts.

Today certain local Bourbons who "neither learn nor forget" are repeating those discredited and hoary arguments.[5] We are being propagandised in an effort to convince us that we should not insist on our rights now. It is boldly suggested that such insistence is unpatriotic and constitutes some sort of impediment to the war effort. Fortunately, the British Colonial Office does not accept that view. Its granting of certain definite democratic rights must be in the opinion of certain "British Jamaicans" an act of treason.

No sane Jamaican should believe in national idolatry. We know that we are better off being British than if we were under a Fascist flag, but taking note of the lessons provided by history we are irrevocably convinced that improvement of our political status will make us better off spiritually and psychologically than if we remain a mere Crown Colony.

It is my contention that we gain in self-respect in proportion as we throw off the psychology of colonial serfs. The base of all this is political. Political power is the power to initiate and execute those acts which fundamentally influence the cultural, economic, and spiritual future of a people. If we owe a debt to England, then England owes an infinitely larger debt for the years of unrequited toil given to England by Jamaicans, for the millions of pounds derived from our sweat by absentee landlords, banks, insurance companies, steam-ship companies, and merchants, for the rivers of blood spilt by Jamaicans in wars declared or fought by England, for the long years of repression of our national spirit through the denial to us of our elementary democratic human rights. Let us hear no more of this patter about our owing a debt to any country for any of the reasons mentioned above. We are men and women, and as such we should not be on our knees to anyone or to any country. Let us stand up and be real human beings.

4. Peter Beckford (1672–1735) was a Jamaican-born planter, politician, and merchant, the son of one of the richest men in the colony of Jamaica. He sat in the House of Assembly of Jamaica for three decades and acquired a vast financial estate eventually worth around £300,000, which included 2,314 slaves. He was at the time the richest man in Jamaica and one of the wealthiest people in the world.

5. The phrase seems to have originated with the Scottish author David Masson (1822–1907) in his review of Lorenzo Benoni's *Passages in the Life of an Italian* (1853)' "Lorenzo Benoni", *Fraser's Magazine*, July 1853, pp. 87–94, at 93.

26

Two Human Bombshells

April 1943

Domingo here draws on a dramatic event reported in *The Gleaner*, when the Legislative Council was interrupted from the public gallery.[1] The newspaper identified the man as a Rastafarian, and certainly his main message was a demand for a return to Africa. Domingo is less interested in that message than in the shattering of the pompous ceremonial of the council, still presided over at this stage by his nemesis, Sir Arthur Richards, in one of the last sessions before his removal from the island.

Public Opinion, 17 April 1943, p. 4

Last Tuesday a bomb exploded in Jamaica. It exploded in the most unexpected of all places. It exploded in the seats of the mighty and made a mighty roar. It was not composed of TNT. It was made up of far more deadly and devastating material. It was composed of the dynamite of a long-repressed human yearning for freedom, that unquenchable urge for which men in all ages have risked and suffered much.

The bomb that shattered the stolid serenity of the Legislative Council and shook that august body out of its pompous punctility and respectability was in the persons of a humble black man and an equally humble black woman. They were simple people. They believed in democracy; that the rulers should sometimes hear directly from the ruled; that there should be direct contact between the governed and those who govern.

The appearance of Egbert Charles Smith and Rustel F. Bennett in the sepulchral hall where the laws of the land are ratified, if not made, created a mild sensation. They had dared to tread on sacred ground. They had injected themselves into the Council, unheralded and uninvited. They had disregarded the rules. They had violated all known concepts of respectability. They had smashed the drowsy dignity of the local parliament.

Undoubtedly they had taken the word parliament at its literal meaning. They went to talk, and talked. They did not say much. Most of their message was unde-

1. "Drama Grips Council as Man and Woman 'on a Mission' Halt Session", *The Gleaner*, 7 April 1943, p. 1.

livered, but they said enough to shock the Legislators out of their complacency. They delivered the message of a people who feel the urge for self-expression for national freedom. Those two simple people—one a plain man of the people, the woman so much like the vast majority of her sisters in this island.

She was dressed in a gaudy uniform of her own creation. No doubt the uniform inspired smirks and wisecracks from those who saw it or read about it, but those same smirkers would have gone into ecstasy if that uniform had been presented as a Paris creation or had adorned the back of a representative of a deservedly decaying aristocracy. But it is fashionable to laugh at things Jamaican. That is the true colonial psychology. It will not die in a hurry, because it is built out of an admitted consciousness of inherited inferiority. They have in them the dignity of human equality and they gave voice to that dignity in their simple and dramatic appearance at Headquarters House last Tuesday.

It may have been the first time in Jamaican history that such a scene was enacted, but similar scenes have frequently taken place in other countries. Time and again have the legislative halls of European and American countries been invaded by individuals who thought they had a mission to perform or a message to deliver. Usually those interruptions were regarded as the work of cranks or mad men. The invasion on Duke Street was, however, more than that. It was a brief but eloquent expression of the irrepressible desire of the people of African descent for a homeland. It was a plea for autonomy, a cry for freedom.

The religious beliefs of the bearers of the plea are unimportant. That they follow a "cult" of some sort is immaterial. No man rejects a message because its bearer is of a despised religious sect. Nearly all the dominant religions of today were at one time characterised as "cults". I make no apology for the religious beliefs of any people and I am not interested enough to set myself up as an expert on what is a good or a bad religious belief. I am not egotistic enough to assume that my beliefs are right and those of other people necessarily wrong.

Others, obsessed by their smug and death-like dignity, were no doubt shocked at the rude intrusion of the bold black man and his equally unafraid female companion. I was surprised, but not shocked. I would have been shocked, but their speech saved me from that. The drama may appear comic to others, but to me it has an element of tragedy. It is rich in human emotions.

Perhaps the Member for Manchester felt that here was visible proof of his contention that 5,000, not five, of his fellow-countrymen were deserving of being detained. The capital letters which adorn his name must have shivered at the indignity done to the august building. Hitler-like individuals no doubt felt that Hitler-like powers should have been exercised and the audacious and disrespectful couple consigned to the tender mercies of the Master of the Axe.

Smith may not be a wise man. Certainly he is not "educated". He has not been educated away from the strivings of his own people. But no one will deny his simple eloquence or challenge his sincerity. In a hall that has often reeked with insincerity and sonorous meaningless eloquence, this simple black man spoke with a passionate and sincere eloquence that everyone can understand. He looked authority in the face and said, "Honourable Gentlemen! I have come to ask for the freedom of my people .... We want national freedom."

Ponder the words. They must have sounded like a knell of doom to some of the Elected Members when they remembered that for the first time in about eight years they will soon be called upon by the people of this country to give an accounting of their stewardship. In an unexpected way the Elected Members were hearing from a section of their electorate.

That brief and interrupted speech contained a warning. It revealed that deep down in the consciousness of the masses there is a strong desire for freedom. It shows that even those who are the lowest down have been touched by the democratic currents of the age and that the fire that inspired the founders of the United States to struggle for national freedom is not out. It proved that that humble man and his woman companion are the spiritual relatives of the Djukas or Bush Negroes of Dutch Guiana, who centuries ago fought their way out of slavery and established in the wilds of South America what was perhaps the first group of free and independent people in the western world.

That speech was in the tradition of those illustrious haters of oppression, L'Ouverture, Pétion, Dessalines, Christophe, Boukman, who without aid from the outside, banished the curse of human slavery from the island of Haiti and established a nation of freemen.[2] That speech was in the tradition of the deeds of our own Maroons, who found in the fastnesses of the mountains the freedom denied them in the lowlands. That speech was in the spirit of those intrepid American and West Indian Negroes, who in the early part of the last century planted the flag of freedom on the west coast of Africa and created the Liberian nation.

The desire of that man and that woman and of their friends and followers is understandable. It is the same spirit that caused that so-little-known-of Jamaican mulatto, John B. Russwurm, to emigrate to Boston over 100 years ago, obtain a college education and become one of the founders of Liberia. That man and that woman who shocked the Legislative Council out of its deadening orderliness last Tuesday acted in the manner of those who truly love liberty and yearn for freedom. That speech was symptomatic. It told just what the masses are thinking. It limned their ambitions. The so-called educated will sneer at them and laugh at the "barbaric" and fantastic uniform of the woman, but no really civilised person will laugh at that brief and eloquent speech.

Today thousands of Jamaicans of all varieties share the desire for freedom. They have registered it by supporting the only political party in Jamaica that

2. Heroes of the Haitian Revolution: Toussaint Louverture, Jean-Jacques Dessalines, Alexandre Pétion, Henry Christophe, and Dutty Boukman.

fought for the attainment of self-government. Unlike the two unbidden, unelected and "temporary" members who addressed the Council to the astonishment and embarrassment of the regular members, most people in this island feel that the place for the establishment of national freedom is Jamaica. They feel that it can be done through constitutional fight rather than through flight. Already something has been gained. Our feet are on the threshold of freedom, and it is for us to march forward. The dawn of Jamaican nationhood is at hand.

> The toll may be heavy and the campaign long
> The road may be dreary, the barriers strong
> Our progress may falter and energies wane
> But steadfast in spirit our goal we will gain.

The above lines from our national song "Jamaica Arise" should stir every Jamaican to work without ceasing and without thought of self for those who will succeed us when we shall have passed on to the realm of dreamless sleep. Let us all join the chorus and repeat:

> Land of my birth I pledge to be
> Loyal and faithful, true to thee.[3]

3. The PNP song, written by Granville Campbell and William Seivwright.

27

Is There a Racial Minorities Question in Jamaica?

June 1943

This lengthy article sparked months of debate in the pages of *Public Opinion*. Domingo vociferously held to his firm principle for racial equality, without exception. In doing so, he rejected arguments for counterbalancing preferences for minorities and he admitted no consideration for varied positions of disadvantage. Below are the original article plus two further letters from Domingo.

Public Opinion, 12 June 1943, p. 3

Until a few years ago no one ever heard of the existence of a "racial minorities question" in Jamaica. Today with the exception of the demand of Chinese shopkeepers that they be permitted to arm themselves and the persistent and frequent protest of the East Indian Progressive Society for the removal of alleged racial discriminations and disabilities, practically nothing is said on the question publicly. The insistence of the organised East Indians in postulating the existence of the racial minorities problem in Jamaica, however, makes it necessary that the subject be examined.

What is a racial minority problem? A racial minority problem exists when a racial minority is oppressed by the majority racial group of that country or when the government of a country imposes disabilities upon a minority because of its race. A racial problem is distinct from a religious problem. A racial problem exists in South Africa, where the Africans are ruled by the white minority and made to suffer severe political, social, and economic disabilities because of their race. A racial problem exists in the United States where the Negro minority, 10 per cent of the population, is discriminated against politically, socially, and economically. In neither instance does the question of religion play a part. Whether a black South African or a coloured American is a Christian or not is immaterial. His personal behaviour is immaterial. It is his race, not his religion, wealth, education, or conduct, that fixes his status.

In Russia of the Czars and in many other countries racial and religious discriminations combined with and were buttressed by civil disabilities. The proscribed religion and the despised race were equally oppressed. This was the case of the

Jews generally. Theirs has always been a racial and religious question aggravated by the fact that they were usually a minority.

* * *

Conditions in Jamaica are different to those referred to above. In Jamaica people are free to practice their particular religious faith without fear of molestation by either the government or the majority population. Under ordinary circumstances the minority racial groups in Jamaica are never disturbed by the majority group because of racial antagonism. Whenever minorities were interfered with (and that has been so rare as to be hardly worth mentioning), it was not because of their race, but because of economic reasons incidental to the relations between employers and workers, traders and consumers.

The racial minorities of Jamaica suffer no legal disabilities because of their race and are not oppressed by the racial majority. On the contrary, looking on conditions in Jamaica honestly, it must be admitted that it is the racial majority that is at a disadvantage. Practically all the advantages in Jamaica are enjoyed by racial minorities. They have the best government jobs, they dominate the wholesale and retail business life of the country, they occupy a dominant position in the professions, they are to a large extent employers of labour. All this could not be if they were racially oppressed. It would not be if the racial majority had used its strength to monopolise for members of its group all the economic benefits of the country. Whatever else may be said to the contrary, this fact is proof that Negroes are very tolerant. Reverse the racial picture in Jamaica, and is it conceivable that any of the present minority races, if in the majority, would allow a Negro minority to control the economic and social life of the country? The present close and efficient organisation of the minorities gives us an idea of what could be expected if they were in the majority.

The extraordinary racial tolerance of the majority is exemplified not only by the success of the minorities in business, but by their success in the professions. If they had to depend on the support given them by clients and patients drawn exclusively from their own racial type, most of them would starve. It is therefore absolutely unfair to suggest that the racial majority oppresses the minorities, as is implied in the insistent assertion of the East Indian Society that there is a "racial minorities question" in Jamaica. The success of racial minorities proves conclusively that the racial majority of Jamaica is one of the most tolerant peoples of the entire world.

* * *

In the *Daily Gleaner* of 1 June there appeared a statement from the East Indian Progressive Society, of which Dr J. L. Varma is Secretary.[1] The statement purports to set forth the grievances of the East Indian community. It begins by claiming to speak "for the entire Indian community of Jamaica" and asserts that it "has a definite policy for the solution of the racial minorities question". It is not necessary to challenge the right of the Society to speak for all Indians, but in view of the fact that the statement refers to a "racial minorities question" it is necessary to ask if the Society by merely repeatedly postulating the existence of the question pretends to speak for the other racial minorities. The Society may, if it wishes, contend there is an Indian question in Jamaica, but it takes on too much territory when it includes the other racial minorities in its alleged "minorities" question. It is gratifying to learn from the statement that "East Indians in Jamaica consider themselves true Jamaicans and are prepared to make their contribution to the advancement of the country, and for the attainment of self-government for this country."

The authors of the statement affirm that the population of Jamaica is comprised of people of different racial stocks, coming as it does from four different continents, namely Africa, Asia, Europe, and America. This is a mis-statement, for there is absolutely no detectable inclusion of American aboriginal blood in Jamaica. But the addition of the mythical "American" racial stock serves to strengthen the contention of those who maintain that there is a "racial minorities question" in Jamaica. The more complex they make the population, the stronger they make the case for a "solution" of the "question".

The differences of "customs and languages" in Jamaica are infinitesimal and doomed to disappearance unless they are deliberately kept alive by those who find it profitable to stimulate the racial consciousness of minorities in Jamaica. If those "customs and languages" are perpetuated, we will in the future have a multi-lingual people. But fortunately the small total number of minorities in our midst, their dispersion in the island, and the tolerance of Jamaicans in matters of intermarriage tend to obviate any such calamity.

* * *

Self-determination is a term that was born during the First World War. It was political in its significance. It had primarily to do with the creation of new political entities. Race was concomitant, and politics dominant. Due to recognition of the political implications of the term, new political (not racial) states—Poland, Czecho-Slovakia, Jugo-Slavia, Finland—appeared. Some of them were old states, but they were now in the modern world. Self-determination does not mean, and

1. Dr Jia Lal Varma (1902–?). As a result of the disagreement, Dr Varma resigned from both the JPL and the PNP.

never was intended to mean, that every small racial or religious minority in a country was entitled to determine its own political future. It is an abuse of terms to imply that self-determination means political fragmentation.

It would be worse than impracticable in Jamaica. Indians are our largest minority. They are scattered over the country, although the bulk of the 30,000 of them are concentrated in two or three parishes. They are only about 2.5 per cent of the population and, as pointed out already, they and the other minorities are not oppressed by the majority, and local laws and practices do not give the majority racial group any advantages over the Indian minority. The statement refers to cultural self-determination. No one who really believes in democracy would advocate the suppression of the cultural heritage of the Indians, but it is obvious that were the Indians not stimulated to consider themselves as distinct from the rest of the population, they would in time assimilate and become average Jamaicans. Individual Indians themselves will decide the question.

RACIAL MINORITIES

Public Opinion, 24 July 1943, p. 2

Sir, In his letter to your issue of 17 July Mr I. N. Fyzullah accuses me of ignorance of local conditions and takes me to task for my criticism of the recent statement of the East Indian Progressive Society on the subject of local minorities. Even if, as Mr Fyzullah states, descendants of indentured Indians are classified as immigrants under the Immigration Law, is it not a fact that persons of Indian descent born in Jamaica enjoy equal political rights with other native-born Jamaicans? They vote, stand for elections, and have been elected to public offices. Only recently a prominent Indian announced that he intends to be a candidate for the House of Representatives in the coming election.

Mr Fyzullah asserts that "cases of discrimination against the racial minorities over a long period of time are obvious to anyone who has studied the problem". It must be noted that he uses the plural, "minorities", and affirms the existence of a "problem", but cites not a single case in support of his claim. It is on par with the statement that "long study of the moon makes it obvious that it is made of green cheese". That kind of argument is simply "begging the question".

My critic cites two instances of alleged "serious disabilities" suffered not by racial "minorities", but by the Indian minority alone. He objects to Indians being designated as "Asiatics". But the EIPS [East Indian Progressive Society] explicitly stated that the population of Jamaica is composed of racial stock from Africa, "Asia", Europe, and America. Obviously people whose ancestors came from Asia are of "Asiatic" origin just as the black people are of African origin and the local "Aryans" are of European origin. The term "Asiatic" is used racially, not nationally.

A person can be of an Asiatic race and of Jamaican nationality. Race is biological and "constant", nationality is political and subject to change.

So far as I know, the government of Jamaica has never prevented Jamaican-born Indians from emigrating because they are "Asiatics". If they cannot enter certain countries, it is not because of their Jamaican status, but because the country they desire to enter discriminates against "Asiatics". The fact that a Chinese or an Indian is born here does not prevent him from emigrating, but it does prevent him from immigrating into certain countries. The blame is not Jamaica's.

In my article which Mr Fyzullah objected to, I expressed my opposition to the alleged failure of the local government to place the marriage officers of all recognised religions on an equal basis, but it should be clear to Mr Fyzullah that "Hindu" and "Mohammedan" are religious not racial terms. A black African, a white Bulgarian, or a yellow Chinese Mohammedan would suffer in exactly the same way as the Indian Mohammedans are alleged to suffer in manners of marriage, so it is not a question of race. It is one of religion, I repeat. Mr Fyzullah resorts to the old and discredited practice of misquoting and distorting the views of one's opponent. He ascribes to me things I never wrote and takes delight in destroying the straw man of his own creation.

I never said that Indians "have the best government jobs, etc.". I did say the minorities do. Certainly the best jobs, etc. are not held by Jamaicans of the majority racial stock, so it is obvious that they are held by the minorities. That the Indian minority is not as prominent as the other minorities is due to the circumstances under which they came here. The Indians came as indentured agricultural labourers and the bulk of them are still labourers, but in that respect they are in no worse condition than other labourers. It is, however, to the great credit of the Indians that some of their number, in such a short time, under the unfavourable conditions incidental to their presence in the island, should have risen to the point that they have produced one of the leading law officers of the Crown, doctors, school teachers, etc. Many Indians are large landowners. Some of the largest property owners along the Spanish Town Road are Indians, and among their tenants are to be found Indians, and Jamaicans of the racial majority. Mr Fyzullah's challenge is meaningless since I never asserted the things he asked me to prove. I challenge him, in turn, to quote anywhere in my article that I had claimed what he alleged I claimed for the Indians.

The unusual and disconcerting method of argumentation adopted by Mr Fyzullah is best seen in his assertion that I objected to Chinese shopkeepers being allowed to arm themselves against "marauders" and to Chinese becoming Justices of the Peace. That is a disingenuous distortion of what I wrote. I will say, though, that I object, and every sensible Jamaican should object, to the Chinese or any other racial group being armed or appointed to any position because of their race. As I "truly believe in equality of privilege for all racial groups in this country",

I insist that no racial group be given special consideration by the Governor or anyone else. The racial minorities of Jamaica, without exception, must realise that if the population is to be given consideration on the basis of their race, the claim of the majority group should be paramount.

When the Governor deplored his past neglect of the Chinese, he disclosed, it appeared, an important feature of the policy of his administration—a policy which he most immodestly claimed had done more for the island than any other administration. Such a policy of recognition of racial groups, publicly revealed by its author and executor, perhaps explains why the racial minorities enjoy practically all of the advantages of the country. For the benefit of Mr Fyzullah and others I state that I favour recognition of people not on the basis of race, but solely on the basis of MERIT.

W. A. DOMINGO

P.S. It is interesting to observe that at present the entire population of Jamaica is paying an enormous tribute to the rice-growers of Jamaica who are principally Indians. It is significant that the government has turned a deaf ear to the pleas of the majority that the price of this "essential" commodity be regulated.

RACIAL MINORITIES AGAIN

Public Opinion, 7 August 1943, p. 2

Sir, Permit me to deal with a few loose ends in the controversy on the alleged "Racial Minorities (sic) Problem" in Jamaica.

In his letter in your issue of 31 July Mr I. N. Fyzullah tries to compare the situation of Indians in Jamaica (he makes no distinction between the immigrants who were brought to the island under specific conditions and their Jamaican-born de[sc]endents with the situation of Negroes in the United States. He refers to lynching and racial discrimination in the United States as they affect Negroes.

Lynching is mob murder and should never be condoned. It has been condemned by President Roosevelt and other prominent Americans. There are laws in America against murder by individuals or by groups. Similar laws exist in all civilised countries. But laws of themselves have not prevented murders by individuals in America, Jamaica, or India. Neither have laws prevented mob murders in America nor communal murders of Mohammedan and Hindu Indians by each other in their own country. Mob murder, whether lynching or communal killings, is not a normal feature of any country. But discrimination can be a normal feature of the life of a country. Contrary to Mr Fyzullah's belief, racial discrimination is legal in some parts of the United States. In those places it is almost as strong against Negroes as are the discriminatory practices of Hindus against the Untouchables of India.

Mr Fyzullah has not cited a single instance of legal discrimination in Jamaica against Indians or any other minority because of their race. He, however, asserts that in "times of disturbances", shops owned by Chinese and Indians are "chosen for attack". I do not know if this is true. It was not true in 1907 after the great earthquake. Shops were looted regardless of who owned them. But do we judge racial discrimination by the behaviour of a people in "times of disturbances" or by their behaviour in the long periods of normality between "times of disturbances"? The success of minorities in balance is a barometer of the behaviour of Jamaicans towards the minorities. The evidence seems to suggest that if there is any discrimination by the majority racial group, it is against businesses owned by their own people and in favour of the businesses operated by the minorities.

I am glad to see that Mr Fyzullah agrees that I am correct that the marriage disabilities suffered by Indians are religious, not racial. Mr Fyzullah asks if I object to people in Jamaica being allowed to arm themselves in self-protection. I do not. But I don't understand why Mr Fyzullah persists in trying to make it appear that I had objected to Chinese shop-keepers being armed in some of my writings on the subject or I at any time suggested that any people should not be allowed to defend themselves and their property from attack. Mr Fyzullah's attempt to "put words into my mouth" is an old but dishonest trick.

W. A. DOMINGO, Kingston, 2 August 1943

28

Are Negroes Men?

October 1943

Domingo joined the editorial team of the *New Negro Voice* some time in September or October 1943. He is listed as managing editor in January 1945, with T. A. Kitchener as business manager and publisher. There are several letters to the editor praising Domingo's contributions and his value as someone "widely known as a great writer and lecturer, with a brimful of knowledge on the Negro questions universally".[1]

New Negro Voice, 16 October 1943, pp. 1 and 4

A doctor cannot successfully treat a disease until he knows its symptoms. Concealment of symptoms is not in the interest of the patient. Negroes are the sick people of Jamaica. They are at the bottom of the social and economic life of the country. They are the poorest, least-educated, most underfed, worst-housed, worst clothed, and worst-treated section of the population. Their opportunities for advancement are cruelly circumscribed. Yet they are in the majority. They realise their condition, for they are the ones suffering. Neither prayer, slavish expressions of admiration for this or that individual, loyalty to this or that institution, senseless abuse of those who occupy more fortunate positions in local life, dreams of a glamorous afterlife in heaven, sentimental romancing about some ideal place outside Jamaica, nor self-pity will cure the ills of the Negroes of this country. The hard facts must be faced manfully and intelligently, which is simply another way of saying that Negroes of Jamaica must bestir themselves and struggle to achieve their salvation.

With few exceptions, the black people of Jamaica and their children's children are doomed to live their lives in this country. Only a few will emigrate. This elementary fact cannot be escaped. That being so, our task is to secure for Jamaican Negroes, men and women, the maximum amount of opportunity in Jamaica, their own country. There is no sense of dreaming about flight from Jamaica to some other country. Our destiny is right where we are, and it is largely in our own hands.

1. S. Williams, "Readers Glad to Have Mr Domingo", *New Negro Voice*, 23 October, 1943, p. 2.

Opportunities are not given; they are won. No oppressed people ever removed the burden from their shoulders by being on their knees. On our knees we are more easily kicked and more easily robbed. We must create opportunities, if not for ourselves, for our children. This requires an understanding of the odds against us and requires the formulation of plans for overcoming the odds.

The basic problems of the people in all countries revolve around work and wages. These in turn are determined by political action. Universal adult suffrage makes every Jamaican an equal politically. There are no colour line or class distinctions at the ballot box. There every man is a king and every woman a queen. No one is an inferior. It is there that Jamaicans of colour can strike the first and perhaps the most telling blow for improvement of their lot. Individuals voted into power should be individuals committed beforehand to supporting measures that will bring improvements in the social and economic fortunes of the majority of the population. THE MAJORITY OF JAMAICANS ARE NEGROES.

The prosperity of a country rests on the prosperity of the masses. The masses of Jamaica are black, and they must struggle to control and guide their future in this country in which Providence or history has placed them. Fight is far nobler than flight. By our own efforts we can cease being pariahs, almost unwelcome inmates of our own house. Improvement of the condition of black Jamaicans depends, in the long run, on black Jamaicans. We need to think clearly and stiffen our backbones. Wishful thinking must be converted into purposeful doing.

There will be no improvement in the lot of Jamaican Negroes until they obtain better jobs in their own country. The barriers to the economic progress of the masses are, to a large extent, connected with the limitations placed upon their earning power. Given a well-paying job, a man will live better. Severely kept from the better class of employment, a people must stagnate intellectually and socially. In Jamaica, Negroes, meaning people who are black, are excluded by all kinds of devices from obtaining some of the best kinds of employment in the country, although it is their labour and consuming power that make the country what it is.

Every obstacle in the way of black boys and especially black girls securing the better-paying and better class of work in this country must be removed. They are going to be removed if the people who are the victims of this type of boycott will discard their fears and meet job discrimination with the only kind of answer that can be understood by those who now refuse to employ dark-skinned clerks in stores and offices. That kind of discrimination must go. Removal of discrimination is not introduction of discrimination. The man who removes a source of grievance is a social benefactor. He is an agent of democracy. Removal of colour barriers in Jamaica is in the interest of the majority. It seeks to substitute injustice with justice, class, or colour exclusiveness with class and colour inclusiveness. Colour discrimination, especially in jobs, is an obstacle to national progress. It is an expression of the Nazi conception of superior and inferior peoples.

Governments which object to open discussion and public airing of existing grievances are Fascist in their outlook. Governments which persecute victims of colour prejudice when they protest against it are barefaced and vicious supporters of colour prejudice. Newspapers which refuse to discuss the facts of colour prejudice and colour discrimination in Jamaica approve of the prejudice and discrimination.

I am opposed to all forms of racial and colour discrimination. I oppose them because they are contrary to democracy. I oppose them because they affect me and my kind. I oppose them because I believe they are Fascist in conception and contrary to the principles of democracy for which the Allied Nations are professedly fighting. I believe black people are the inherent equals of white, brown, yellow, red, or "pink" people. History tells me I am right. Science confirms my belief. Because I am right, I fear no consequence. Race and colour discrimination in jobs, governmental and private, must go if black boys and black girls are to be the economic and social equals of other racial types in Jamaica. Equality of opportunity is the prerequisite of Negro improvement in Jamaica.

29
A Great African Leader
March 1944

Domingo here summarises the relationships he built with African students and professionals while in Harlem. He focuses on Nnamdi Azikiwe, expanding on a theme he frequently emphasised in his writing and editorial choices: the conjoined struggle of Africans and West Indians for self-government. In both cases he argued that "the trend of enlightened African thought" showed "that the problems of Nigeria" are "similar to the problems of the British West Indies".[1] In 1945 Domingo supported Azikiwe during the Nigerian General Strike, criticising his old foe, Governor Richards, for his treatment of Nigerian workers.[2] At Domingo's urging the PNP led protest meetings and demanded that the Colonial Office undertake an investigation. The Jamaican House of Representatives passed a unanimous motion expressing sympathy with the people of Nigeria.[3]

Public Opinion, 11 March 1944, p. 3

During my residence in the United States I had the privilege of meeting many Africans. I was glad to make contacts with these men for I had been curious to converse with people who came from the continent of my ancestors. The Africans I met varied as to education and the section of the continent they came from. The majority were from the West Coast—Liberia, Gold Coast, Sierra Leone, and Nigeria. The few East Africans in New York are mostly of Arab-Negro mixture and speak Swahili or Arabic. I remember two East African students. They were very black, tall, and straight. They had the reputation of being very good students, and one of them, after earning his master's degree at Columbia University, studied for his Doctor of Philosophy degree. He is now an instructor of anthropology in a reputable Western university.

---

1. Editor, "Africans Explain Their Problems", *New Negro Voice*, 24 February 1945, p. 1.
2. W. A. Domingo, "Futile and Dangerous", *Public Opinion*, 23 July 1945, pp. 3–4. For the importance of the General Strike and Azikiwe, see Oliver Coates, "'His Telegrams Appear to Be Hysterical, but He Is Very Astute': Azikiwe's Spectacular Self and the 1945 General Strike in Nigeria", *Journal of African Cultural Studies*, 30, no. 3 (2017), pp. 227–242, and Lisa Lindsay, "Domesticity and Difference: Male Breadwinners, Working Women, and Colonial Citizenship in the 1945 Nigerian General Strike", *American Historical Review*, 104, no. 3 (1999), pp. 783–812.
3. "PNP Asks Colonial Office to Probe Threatened Banishment of Azikiwe", *Public Opinion*, 16 July 1945, p. 1; "PNP Protest Meeting on Nigerian Crisis at Edelweiss Tonight", *Public Opinion*, 18 July 1945, p. 1.

Sol Plaatje, a very intelligent South African (a Basuto) visited the United States several years ago.[4] He was the author of a very valuable and informative book on South African conditions. Without being hysterical or radical, he succeeded in his calm way in delivering a blistering attack on the semi-slavery of coloured peoples in his native South Africa. He lifted the lid off imperialism so that all the sights could be seen and all the foul odours smelt.

I write the foregone as a preliminary to telling of a very great and coming African, a man who will be heard from and of as the years multiply. I refer to Nnamdi Azikiwe, MA, MSc.[5] Until I met "Zik", as he was better known in the United States, the most important African I had personally known was Dr Aggrey.[6] As a matter of fact, Dr Aggrey was more than an acquaintance of mine. I must have had over a dozen extended conversations with him and heard him speak at public meetings at least four times. Dr Aggrey was a very mild person, a sort of middle-of-the-roader. He was not a radical in his outlook on Africa. A believer in Christianity, he gave the impression of meekness personified, but he was unquestionably profoundly concerned over the future of his people and convinced that education and Christianity were the means to achieve their upliftment. He seemed never to be in a hurry. I remember chiding him for what seemed to be his patience and circumlocution of speech, and he retorted that he was an African and not a Westerner. Aggrey was fortunate, for he had as a friend, booster, and admirer a sincere and influential white educator, Dr Thomas Jesse Jones.[7] Based on their joint representations and the co-operation of the British government, Achimota College was founded in West Africa.[8] Aggrey is dead.

A REALISTIC THINKER

Less than ten years ago I attended a mass meeting in Harlem. The advertised speaker was to be Professor N. Azikiwe, an African. The meeting was well

4. Solomon Tshekisho Plaatje (1876–1932) was a South African intellectual, writer, and politician, and a founding member of the South African Native National Congress, which became the African National Congress. In New York in 1913 he met Marcus Garvey and W. E. B. Du Bois, as well as Domingo.

5. Nnamdi Benjamin Azikiwe (1904–1996) was a Nigerian statesman and political leader often referred to as the "father of Nigerian nationalism". In 1930 he obtained a BA in Political Science at Howard and Lincoln Universities, taking some courses with Alain Locke. He was a PhD candidate at Columbia University before returning to Nigeria in 1934.

6. James Emman Kwegyir Aggrey (1875–1927) was an intellectual, missionary, and teacher, born in the Gold Coast (later Ghana). A talented scholar, he graduated from Livingstone College in North Carolina with three degrees, and then took PhDs in theology and osteopathy before embarking at Columbia in 1915 in studies of sociology, psychology, and the Japanese language. During a long research trip to Africa in 1920 and 1921 he met and impressed future African leaders such as Hastings Banda, Nnamdi Azikiwe, and Kwame Nkrumah.

7. Thomas Jesse Jones (1873–1950) was a Welsh-American sociologist and educational administrator, bitterly criticised by W. E. B. Du Bois.

8. Achimota College is a co-educational boarding school in Ghana opened in 1927.

attended. Most of the audience appeared to be adherents of the Universal Negro Improvement Association. After the preliminaries the main speaker rose. He was a tall, lanky black man. There was nothing striking about his appearance. He might easily have passed for a Jamaican schoolmaster or any average well-dressed American Negro. To be truthful, I did not expect anything but the usual denunciations of white rule in Africa and trite statements that lacked practical content. I was, however, in for a shock. From the moment the speaker opened his lips I was convinced that I was listening to a man of considerable intellectual capacity. He spoke English with an accent that was neither American nor West Indian, but his language was precise and his words well-chosen. Unlike most of the Africans I had listened to, Dr Azikiwe went straight to the point. There was nothing of the tempo or character of the palaver. Absolutely no circumlocution. The speech was a revelation. It was packed with information regarding Africa, the prevailing currents of world thought in the field of education and politics, and permeated with a strong and incisive sense of realism. I was greatly impressed, and eagerly hastened to meet the young speaker at the close of the meeting. In conversation he impressed me as being modest and valid. The mildness was so opposite to his manner on the platform. He talked real sense. There was no ranting, no abuse, no romantic dreams, no nonsensical suggestions about revenge for what had been done to his country. Apparently the audience did not appreciate the cold, dispassionate, and eloquent discourse.

I learned that Zik was from Nigeria, and that after receiving his early education there, he had come to the United States for higher education. In that country he had piled up a creditable scholastic record and was a professor of sociology and economics at (I think) Lincoln University. I predicted a great future for the man, and was not surprised to learn later that he was the author of two or three books dealing with the political and economic aspects of the race question.

Years passed and I heard nothing of or from Zik until I read somewhere that he was editing a newspaper in his native Nigeria and had been sentenced to one year in prison for "criminal sedition" because he had reproduced an article which declared that despite all his talk about Christianity, the average white man's god seemed to be money.[9] Fugitive snatches came my way of the great fight made for

9. This refers to Azikiwe's time editing the *African Morning Post* in the Gold Coast. The article in question was "Has the African a God?" written by I. T. A. Wallace-Johnson. Azikiwe was initially convicted for sedition, but won his case in the West African Court of Appeal in March 1937 because his lawyers argued there was not sufficient evidence that Azikiwe was serving as the editor on the date the article appeared. Wallace-Johnson defended himself in court by refusing to answer to the public name associated with him on the court order, since the article was published pseudonymously. He was nevertheless convicted and sentenced, but the case gained much public attention in Britain and British colonies, prompting debate on the use of seditious laws in colonies. For a transcript of the court case, see Stephanie Newell, *The Power to Name: A History of Anonymity in Colonial West Africa*, Athens, OH: Ohio University Press, 2013, pp. 183–192.

his telling release by English liberals and Labourites, among them the late David Adams, MP. A lapse came, and I heard nothing more about Zik.

Several persons expressed sympathy for the poor Nigerians when it was announced that Sir Arthur Richards had been "kicked upstairs" from Jamaica to the well-paid post of the governorship of Nigeria. It seemed felt that the "untutored" Africans were in for a devil of a time with the one-time despot of Jamaica. I did not concur with this view. I knew that West Africans were fortunate in having as their leaders European- and American-educated men and women who had not, as is all too true in the British West Indies, divorced themselves from the masses of their countrymen. More than that, the Africans, intellectuals and masses had had no tradition of racial inferiority injected into them by having passed through a period of slavery to Europeans. The West Africans were in the country of their ancestors, and their traditions of manhood and independence were not sullied to any great degree. The history of the several countries had been transmitted to the people in writing and by word of mouth, and what is most important, the territories, for the most part, had come under British rule by treaty, not by conquest.

I freely predicted, and do so now, that if Richards should try any of his Hitlerian methods against the Nigerians, he will have a formidable antagonist in Zik, a man of courage and modern training, ideas, and impulses.[10] Since his return to Nigeria, Azikiwe launched four daily newspapers—the *West African Pilot* of Lagos, the *Eastern Nigeria Guardian* of Port Harcourt, the *Nigerian Spokesman* of Onitsha, and the *Southern Nigeria Defender* of Warri. He is the chief editor of his papers. Only recently he and seven African editors were chaperoned to England by the Colonial Office. Every effort was made to seduce them with nice treatment. They were wined and dined. But these men had a definite purpose from which they refused to be distracted by flattery or cajolery. Instead of giving press interviews lauding the marvellous time they were being given, or telling of the wonderful war efforts and sacrifices of the British people, the editors got together and prepared what must be regarded as one of the most devastating condemnations of British imperialism, and presented the British Colonial Office with a positive and detailed set of demands for self-government within a stated period.[11] The document criticised the undemocratic character of the British Colonial Office itself and slashed vigorously at the autocratic powers of governors and the undemocratic manner in which they are imposed upon the colonies without the consent of the governed.

10. "Sir Arthur Richards was a disastrous choice, who saw his task not as 'managing' nationalism, but of mastering and subduing it, despite clear instructions from London outlining his task as one of reform and political and constitutional progress"; John E. Flint, "'Managing Nationalism': The Colonial Office and Nnamdi Azikiwe, 1932–43", *Journal of Imperial and Commonwealth History*, 27, no. 2 (1999), pp. 143–158, at 155.

11. "Memorandum on the Atlantic Charter and British West Africa by the West African Press Delegation to the United Kingdom, 1 August 1943", CO 554/133/3, TNA.

The British press, as should have been expected, gave practically no publicity to the sensational and historical document, but its contents were broadcast to the outside world from London by competent and fearless representatives of the colonial peoples. The signature at the top of the list is that of Zik. I suspect that he is the driving force behind the movement that has united not only the chiefs and leaders of his country but also united the editors of the four West African colonies and protectorates. All of this strengthens my confidence that Sir Arthur Richards won't be able to browbeat or intimidate the Nigerians. They will take his measure and rate him at his true worth. The inflated values that surrounded him in Jamaica, and his reputation as a "strong man" may soon be tested, and when they are, I will not be the least bit surprised if he found his master in Zik.

A few months ago a writer discussed Azikiwe in the pages of the London *New Statesman and Nation* and pointed out that he is a growing power in West Africa that will have to be reckoned with. Zik is no fanatic, but he is an outspoken opponent of British imperialism. He is a great patriot and a lover of justice and democracy for all races and nations. His clear and informed mind and powerful pen make him a dangerous foreman, especially as he has engaged himself in the righteous cause of the national liberation of his people.

30

International Questions

May 1944

The range of Domingo's international interests was global. In his *Public Opinion* articles he touched upon the situations in Iran, the Middle East, Russia, Liberia, and Ethiopia, as well as the likely impact on the West Indies of US economic power after the war. From the British Empire he paid particular attention to India, Ceylon, and Nigeria, all clearly heading towards self-government or independence, and to New Zealand as an example to follow. The position of Canada within the American continent was given careful consideration. Thinking along the same lines, he emphasised that the Caribbean was part of the Americas, by geographical and historical logic, but with political consequences to eventually follow. It was in the same piece that he recognised that independence was the logical outcome of the movement for self-government.[1] This piece about the implication of colonial exclusions from the Conference of Dominion Premiers appeared under his regular title, "Sparks from My Anvil".

Public Opinion, 11 May 1944, p. 3

Most British West Indians are very unsuspicious where international questions are concerned. They act like innocents abroad in such matters. Their naivete is often childish. The tendency is for them to estimate men, measures, and events by broad ethical standards in blissful disregard of the actualities of human behaviour and the realities of a callous, selfish, and materialistic world.

For over a week a Conference of Dominion Premiers has been in progress in London. Important policies and plans are being formulated. These will directly or indirectly affect the colonial world. Indeed, it can be taken for granted that the future of British colonies is one of the most important topics of discussion. Next to nothing will be heard of the details of the talks. At the close of the Conference official statements will be issued, but there may also be secret understandings or agreements.

The complete exclusion of colonial peoples from British Imperial Councils is an ill omen. It should rouse their suspicions and excite their protests. Probably the most influential person attending the Conference is Field [Marshal] Jan Smuts of

1. W. A. Domingo, "Quo Vadis, Jamaica?", *Public Opinion*, 24 December 1943, pp. 3 and 6.

British South Africa.[2] He has an enormous prestige in the Anglo-Saxon world and his opinions are respected. He is regarded as an expert on Africa and Africans and by extension [o]n coloured peoples generally. West Indians have every reason to fear racial "experts". Nearly always they are committed to racial theories which postulate this or that "correct" treatment of coloured peoples. The Australian representative to the Conference may be a fine person. He might even be a professed Christian, but he is the head of a country that practises the exclusion of coloured people from a country originally belonging to a dark-skinned race. British subjects fare no better than others. Colour alone matters.

* * *

Canada, too, is represented. The dominion also practices of exclusion of British subjects of colour even though its banks and insurance companies earn millions annually out of the British West Indies. Just what these Prime Ministers are hatching for the so-called dependent Empire behind closed doors is not likely to be known in full. Deeds will doubtless tell the tale.

West Indians, because of the geographical position of their countries and America's interest in the region, may not be deeply affected, but there is no telling just what kind of economic plans will emerge from the Conference. As a people subject to the rule of the British, West Indians should keep their eyes on the Dominion and similar conferences and demand a full voice in all Imperial proceedings. Many writers on the colonial question have commented on the fact that the French allow their citizens from the West Indies to participate directly in the formulation of policies which affect the entire Empire. Martiniquans, Guadeloupans, and persons from French Guiana elected representatives to the French Chamber of Deputies and Senate. Many of these representatives rise to positions of eminence in the Empire. As was indicated in these columns a few days ago, there is to be even more complete incorporation of French colonials into the life of the Empire as a result of the conference held at Brazzaville last February. This will put the coloured Frenchman, whether he is black African or West Indian of any shade, and yellow Vietnamese (that is, presuming the old French Empire is reconstructed) on a much higher plane than coloured people in the British Empire.

The effect of such a revolutionary policy on the part of the French will in due time be felt in all parts of Africa. How the British will offset the force of this propaganda by example depends to a large extent on the attitude of the dominion of South Africa. Already the effects of the Russia solution of the colonial and race and national problem has excited the interest of Africans. One only has to

2. Jan Christiaan Smuts (1870–1950) was a South African statesman and military leader who served as prime minister of the Union of South Africa between 1939 and 1948.

read some of the recent declarations and copies of newspapers from British West Africa to realise that in that part of the world the educated classes are impressed by what has occurred in Turkestan and other parts of Central Asia.

The United States handles its colonial problem in a different way. In the case of the Philippines, complete independence had been promised on a fixed date, even before the Japanese conquest of the islands. But all along, the Filipinos, like the Puerto Ricans, had a Resident Commissioner at Washington who was consulted in Congress on matters affecting the territory he represented. No such system of real consultation for each colony exists in the British Empire. Theoretically, the colonies are consulted through the local government, but those governments are without exception merely the rubber stamps of the Colonial Office in London which appointed all the key officials.

* * *

It is a pity that the organised workers of Jamaica have no delegate attending the International Labour Organization Conference now in session at Philadelphia. If there was one such delegate in attendance, he would have been in a position to support the Panamanian delegates in their denunciation of the labour discrimination practised on the Canal Zone.

I have always felt that we in Jamaica don't realise the value of taking advantage of all the opportunities which present themselves to us to help ourselves and our kin in foreign lands. Tens of thousands of Jamaicans and their descendants are affected by racial discriminatory conditions which prevail in Panama, yet we seem indifferent. It is true that we sometimes complain feebly, but I have a suspicion that the complaints are made because they afford a chance to get rid of some anti-American bile. It is a pity that many of our progressives view public affairs through ideological spectacles. They think of movement, men, and measures in terms of the theories they espouse. Situated as we are, it is true that we must have definite objectives, but it is folly for us to be indissolubly wedded to any particular strategy. We must learn to be pragmatic.

A Jamaican delegate at the Philadelphia Conference would have come into contact with representatives of the various regional American labour movements and their leaders. These contacts could be used in the future to internationalise our case whenever necessary. A delegate from this country would have met delegates from American labour unions, some who might be Jamaicans. Ferdinand G. Smith, high official of the American Seamen's Union, is a Jamaican.[3] In addition to making these contacts, the Conference which is sponsored by numerous

3. Ferdinand Christopher Smith (1893–1961) was a black seaman and Communist labour leader: see Gerald Horne, *Red Seas: Ferdinand Smith and Radical Black Sailors in the United States and Jamaica*, New York: New York University Press, 2005.

governments had placed before it for consideration a very important document dealing with the social and economic future of the workers' in colonial countries. It might be a good idea even at this eleventh hour, for the organised workers of Jamaica to "crash" the Conference by sending a cablegram or an airmail letter to it supporting the stand of the Panama and other delegates on the discriminations practice on the Canal Zone. We need to be flexible. A Jamaican delegate to the Conference might have embraced the opportunity to support the Panama delegates in a speech in which he could have hinted [th]at the case presented by them would have been much stronger if the political disabilities suffered by coloured Panamanians of West Indian descent were removed. We need to wake up, I think.

31

Fight Our Internal Enemies As Well

May 1944

Domingo's journalism applied his conviction about racial equality to practical daily examples in Jamaica, including an emergent tourism industry. Prior to this piece, his arguments about racial minorities [#27] also included condemning the creation of a Chinese Platoon in the North Caribbean Forces of the military. "To separate a people is to isolate them and isolation must lead to misunderstanding and friction," he had argued. "Segregation is wrong. It is bad, whether it is voluntary or compulsory," because it sets groups up as distinctly different and must be opposed without exception for the precedent it may set.[1]

Public Opinion, 13 May 1944, pp. 3–4

I was very pleased to note that several Jamaicans of dark hue who attended the session of the Tourist Convention on Wednesday brought up the vital question of the type of publicity to be used to induce visitors to come to the island. I had made a similar suggestion in my article which appeared in *Public Opinion* the same day. In the discussion it was stressed that advertising in foreign countries should make it clear to intended tourists that the population of Jamaica is predominantly coloured. This should be a *sine qua non* of the publicity intended to bring travellers to this island.

However, I must confess that I was not particularly impressed with some of the arguments advanced by proponents of the idea as reported in Thursday's daily press. In our justified determination to protect ourselves from insult in our country and misrepresentation abroad, we must try to avoid being oversensitive. There is nothing to be gained from pretending that "black boys with holes in their trousers" do not climb coconut trees or that "higglers with large baskets on their heads" do not exist in Jamaica. We know that those are typical sights in our country, and there is nothing disgraceful about them. If we regard these sights as too numerous or as "bad", it is our task to try and change them, but while they exist we are simply wasting our time trying to conceal them.

1. W. A. Domingo, "Racial Segregation: Sir Arthur Richards' Legacy to Jamaica?", *Public Opinion*, 21 August 1943, p. 3; 28 August 1943, p. 4.

Jamaica needs and wants the tourist trade or "industry". Foreigners will only come to our shores if they are convinced that they will see strange, different, or picturesque scenes or people. Tourists visit Mexico and other countries because those countries provide them with conditions and sights which are unlike those they are accustomed to in their homelands. There would be no point in tourists leaving their country in order to see exactly the same things and types of people they are accustomed to seeing at home. Mexico attracts tourists because it has something different to offer them. They are told of these things in advance. The media employed are pictures and literature. Only the same appeals to curiosity will draw tourists to Jamaica, hence the necessity for showing and telling them just what they are likely to see. Naturally, there will be some extravagances of language. It is exactly that feature which stimulated objections. But we must not be hypersensitive. What we must insist on is that the portrayals presented to prospective tourists be factual; that they give a reasonably balanced, full, and complete picture. They should portray our country and people as they are, and not idealise or caricature them. The "boy" and the "higgler" must be shown, also pictures and descriptions of the other classes of Jamaicans.

* * *

I know and sympathise with our super-sensitiveness. I know its social and psychological roots. The vital point is that the advertising, written and pictorial, should prepare tourists for the kind of country they are about to visit. Tourists travel in the winter because they want to escape from the rigours of their climate. They come to the tropics to get away from snow and sleet. It would be no inducement to try and get them to go to a colder country at that time of the year.

It was unfortunate that the participants in the particular discussion did not find it convenient to consider the matter of the behaviour of local owners and managers of establishments which operate under public licence and cater to tourists. It is these owners and managers who very often humour the whims of colour-prejudiced Europeans and Americans. It is they who institute and enforce rules barring dark-skinned Jamaicans from their places. It is these owners and managers of clubs, etc. who sometimes inflict humiliation on their fellow-Jamaicans by ordering them out of places when some foreigner objects to their presence. We injure ourselves and our case when by our silence we appear to absolve or condone the reprehensible and pernicious conduct of our local exponents of colour prejudice. Nothing is gained by reserving all our venom for foreigners, especially Americans.

For instance, it is said that at present distinctly black Jamaicans are not denied service in the dining room and bar-room of Myrtle Bank Hotel; yet it is reported that not so long ago a black man was denied the use of the swimming pool solely because of the colour of his skin, although people of other shades, of his own or lower social standing in the community, were not similarly treated. It is the fundamental human right of every individual in a community to have access to the facilities of every place catering to the public, provided the individual conducts himself in a proper manner. These places operate under licences issued to them by the government—the theoretical representative and protector of all, not some, citizens. There should be no colour bar anywhere, but least of all in a country like Jamaica.

Once a man is barred from using a hotel pool because he is black, the next step may be to bar another man because he is brown, and so on *ad infinitum*. Prevent black people from using the pool and they will next be barred from drinking at the bar or eating in the dining room. Someone may even want to bar them from breathing the same air. The social rights of all the people in a community must be preserved and protected at all costs. This must be done even if the protected persons do not care to exercise their rights. It is for them to let their rights go by default, not for anyone to deprive them of their rights. That is the core of the matter. The fact that black people voluntarily abstain from going to certain places in Jamaica should not deprive them of their right to visit those places if they wish to do so.

I repeat what I wrote on Wednesday, namely, that the real menace to the enjoyment of decent treatment by dark-skinned Jamaicans in public places frequented by tourists will be most likely Jamaicans or residents in Jamaica who own or manage these establishments. Tourists could complain until they turn blue against the presence of one or two brown Jamaicans (black persons seldom visit these places), but the final decision in the matter will rest with the managers and, to an extent, on the manliness of the insulted individual.

Tourists of any nationality who visit Mexico or Cuba dare not ask for the ejection of a citizen of either country because he is black or brown with any hope of securing approval of his demand. It is true that there have been instances when such requests were made, but the local authorities protected the citizens and the makers of the insulting requests were the ones who suffered. President Battista [*sic*] of Cuba, it is said, personally intervened at a bathing beach in Havana and made it clear that Cubans of all colours were to have the freest use of public places regardless of whether tourists liked it or not. He laid down similar rules for night clubs, etc. I might add that Jamaica hasn't a single bathing beach to compare with Jones Beach, New York, yet black, brown, and white people use the facilities of the huge and ornate place on an equal basis. The races mingle on friendly terms with a minimum of friction.

In Jamaica the onus definitely rests on the "brown" people, since they are the ones most immediately affected, to fight the issue at all times and compel local owners and managers of establishments in which "incidents" occur to afford protection to Jamaicans of all shades. Nor must the serious and inescapable responsibility of our government be overlooked. No Mexican or Cuban government is ever likely to be indifferent to insults levelled at citizens of their respective country, nor should our government when Jamaicans are concerned.

Finally, there is no sense in our dodging the real issue by trying to transfer the major responsibility for conditions in this country from ourselves and our government to the tourists who come our way. It is our duty and interest to see that our guests behave in our country as they would have us behave in theirs. If they violate any of our laws, they should be punished, but first there must be laws to cover colour discrimination. No man should be above the law because he is white or is a foreigner spending money in our country. French, Cuban, and Mexican policemen arrest tourists of any nationality or colour when they break the laws of their country, and [our] own policemen should be encouraged to act in the same way under similar circumstances. There must be no condition in Jamaica such as is alleged to exist in Nassau, where a black or brown policeman may not arrest a white man. The only way a serious problem can develop in Jamaica is if we encourage or allow it.

32

Beware of Anti-Semitism

July 1944

Domingo's commitment to denouncing all forms of racism also emphasised a sense of allegiance among the victims of racial prejudice. One month before this article, he had written about the history of the Jewish diaspora's resistance to persecution. He argued that their story "reveals an almost unbroken faith in themselves, in their capacity to achieve, and in the justice of their cause" that should inspire "other oppressed and struggling peoples".[1] Here he specifically underlines the extent of antisemitism in all classes of Jamaican society.

New Negro Voice, 15 July 1944, pp. 1 and 3

It is a legal maxim that "those who come into court should have clean hands". Sufferers from disease should not try to infect others with it. Spreading a disease increases the difficulty of its eradication. There are people who denounce injustices done to them or theirs, while in turn they harshly oppress others. The victims of race or colour prejudice should be ever on their guard against perpetuating, spreading, or condoning those two evils. They should set their faces sternly against every form of race or colour discrimination. We must be consistent and not ask for ourselves more than we are willing to give to our neighbours.

In 1939 I was severely shocked in the way a certain young black businessman denounced Jews to me. He was bitterly anti-semitic. Today the same individual finds it profitable to attack those who openly discuss the inequalities of colour and race which bear down heavily on the black people of Jamaica. He claims that throwing the light of inquiry on the subject is equivalent to stirring up trouble. No doubt he prefers an undercover whispering campaign. I recall how he charged Jews with responsibility for the major part of the ills of black Jamaicans.

Since I have been out of detention I have talked with Jamaicans of every complexion and every walk of life and have been astounded at the amount of antisemitism I have met. I have heard people attempt to justify Hitler's barbarous treatment of Jews. I found it useless trying to reason with some of these individuals. Their speech was a veritable cloudburst of emotion, hatred, and ignorance.

1. W. A. Domingo, "A Lesson for Us", *New Negro Voice*, 6 May 1944, pp. 1 and 4.

I know that the disadvantaged are at times tempted to inveigh against those who are successful. There is an element of envy and jealousy in all of us. But Negroes should derive no satisfaction from the oppression inflicted on other races. Showing sympathy for oppressors and condoning injustice simply make matters worse for black people. Anti-semitism is the twin brother of Negrophobia. Any person who hates Jews will most surely hate Negroes. In America intelligent Jews and Negroes realise that they both suffer from race prejudice (although in different degrees), so they are seeking a common ground of understanding for joint self-defence. Conditions are different in Jamaica. There is no excuse for deep anti-semitism among Jamaicans. This sentiment is not confined to black or brown Jamaicans. It exists everywhere and in all classes. Jamaicans of any degree of Negro descent cannot afford to hate any people because of their race. No race deserves to be free if it enslaves or endorses the enslavement of another race. Let us go into court with clean hands.

33
A Traveller Returns
November 1944

Understandably, Domingo missed Harlem. He wrote nostalgically about it in several of his *Public Opinion* columns, and here seized on his friend William Seivright's visit to further educate Jamaicans about the quality of life there and the strength of interest among Harlem Jamaicans in what was going on in the homeland. The fly in the ointment was federation. With Domingo stuck in Jamaica, Roberts in New Orleans, O'Meally dead, and Brown increasingly close to Manley, there was no one in New York to put the case against federation, so it's unsurprising that Seivright found the federative tide running so strongly. Domingo's response is to affirm that federation has no support in Jamaica beyond an eccentric like E. E. A. Campbell who could be safely ignored. Unfortunately—as he must have known only too well—this was wishful thinking. Even *The Gleaner* had noted earlier in the year the shifting of sentiment towards co-operation of various kinds among the West Indian islands. Certainly, it opined, federation is "a far less fantastic idea than it would have been before the war; some would say that it is not fantastic at all".[1] More worrying from Domingo's perspective was Manley's growing enthusiasm for federation, an enthusiasm that would eventually cause an irrevocable estrangement.

Public Opinion, 10 November 1944, p. 3

HE SAW HARLEM

As can be understood, I was very anxious to have a talk with my genial friend, ex-Deputy Mayor William Seivright, on his return from my old stamping ground—New York City.[2] I have succeeded in having only a fleeting conversation with him regarding the Big City. The affable Alderman made it clear to me that he would not like to live in Harlem for long. The noise, tempo, and bustle of the place are not to his liking. It is a question of temperament and what one is accustomed to.

1. Editorial, *The Gleaner*, 4 July 1944, p. 6.
2. William McKenzie Seivright (1901–1969) was a businessman and prominent PNP politician.

Mr Seivright was in America for eight weeks. He lived at the Hotel Theresa in Harlem. He told me that the Jamaicans and other West Indians he met were not only hospitable but they were very solicitous of showing him as good a time as possible. I was thrilled when he told me of having met my old friends Dr Petioni, Osborne, Bowen, and others, and of the splendid manner in which they treated him.

I asked the Alderman what he thought of the great "slum" that Harlem is supposed to be, and he smilingly said that he had not seen any slum. When I suggested that according to New York City standards the area east of Fifth Avenue between 132nd and 135th Streets might be called a slum, the Alderman said he had seen the section but could hardly regard it as a slum. He was greatly impressed by the standard of living maintained by the coloured people of New York—not of a favoured few, but on the average, the entire people.

WE ARE BEING WATCHED

One thing [that] impressed Mr Seivright greatly was the amount of interest that the West Indians he had met were taking in their homelands. He assured me (and he made the same statement in two public speeches since his return) that West Indians in New York City, especially Jamaicans, are exhibiting a keen interest in developments in Jamaica. The new constitution and universal suffrage, for which the Jamaica Progressive League of New York had fought since 1936, were sources of great satisfaction, and the people in Harlem were keyed up over our elections. According to Mr Seivright, the PNP and its programme are well known and are approved by Harlemites who are expecting the voters of Jamaica to demonstrate their ability to appreciate the need for national political progress by supporting the Party's candidates in the election. The information is very inspiring and constitutes a challenge to our electorate not to let down their fellow countrymen abroad. It appears that Jamaicans in America, knowing what real labour unions are and how they function, look with disapproval on the abortion headed by "Blustermancy". They know that real labour unions are not merely sources of income for the leaders.

WEST INDIAN FEDERATION

Mr Seivright told me that West Indians in New York were very interested in West Indian federation. Jamaicans at home do not realise how strong the sentiment for this is among their kith and kin in Harlem. On the other hand, the people in Harlem do not understand that as far as Jamaica is concerned there is absolutely no sentiment for federation. It may seem strange to people of the other islands, but they must face the reality of the situation. The truth is that Jamaica is in sentiment isolated from the other islands. Great distances separate Jamaica from her British neighbours and there is very little contact between the peoples. In New York they are thrown willy nilly together and come to regard themselves as one. Federation may be a live political issue in Barbados, British Guiana, and the Leeward and Windward Islands, but it is a misreading of the facts for anyone to believe that Jamaicans have the slightest interest in it. And there are good reasons for this. The resolution of Hon. E. E. A. Campbell on the subject of federation which was passed in the Legislative Council has seemingly given a false impression to the outside world. Mr Campbell happens to be one of the most unpopular politicians in Jamaica, a man who lacks, and has long ago lacked, public confidence. His resolution was regarded in Jamaica as a mere gesture. It was a purely personal expression which could do no harm, so it was passed. It had, and now has, no mass support.

OUR IMMEDIATE OBJECTIVE

Apart from the geographical, commercial, and general isolation of Jamaica from the other islands, there is another powerful reason for Jamaica's indifference to federation. At this moment the island is struggling for self-government. It has made some slight gain in that direction. The people have their minds focused on obtaining the maximum amount of autonomy possible in the shortest time. It is, therefore, felt that there should be no diversion of public interest into controversial channels capable of distracting attention from the main goal of self-government. The feeling is that any absorption with federation now will befuddle the population and cause them to dissipate their energies in a direction not likely to bring them closer to their immediate objectives. There is fear that the present aim of Jamaica for Jamaicans, politically and in every way, may be sidetracked into discussions and campaigns that are of no current practical value to Jamaicans.

Mr Seivright's surprise at the clamour for federation in Harlem proves clearly and should convince West Indians in America that federation does not exist as a topic of political interest in Jamaica. For years I tried to explain the situation in Jamaica to West Indians in New York, but they stubbornly refused to understand. Theories won't help us, nor will wishful thinking. The reality is that at present there is no sentiment for federation in Jamaica, and any attempt to work up such a sentiment is doomed to failure and likely to injure the movement in Jamaica for national freedom.

34

Do You Know?

February and August 1945

Starting in 1943, a small semi-regular column appeared in *New Negro Voice*. Made up primarily of short historical bites of information, "Do You Know?" offered readers examples of black leadership and achievement. Under the pen-name "W.A.D.", Domingo published at least 25 of these columns. Readers praised the column in their letters, and offered advice for the types of leaders and innovators he should cover. In 1945 the column appeared in a new graphic format, with the busts of two black men in suits—one reading a magazine—flanking the title.

New Negro Voice, 24 February 1945, p. 2; 4 August 1945, p. 2

William Monroe Trotter was born in Boston. His father had been an officer in the Federal Army during the Civil War. Trotter was educated at Harvard University. Left a comfortable fortune by his father, he entered business and was on the road to success. Just at that time (the first decade of this century) Booker T. Washington was winning the support of influential whites. Trotter opposed what he considered the compromising policy of Washington. He gave up his business and devoted himself exclusively to fighting for the equal rights of Negroes. To this end he organised the National Equal Rights League.

Courageous and self-sacrificing, Trotter refused to compromise where human rights were concerned. He published the *Boston Guardian* at 21 Cornhill St, the address where William Lloyd Garrison had published his abolitionist newspaper the *Emancipator*. On a memorable occasion Trotter led a delegation of Negroes to the White House to interview President Wilson, whom they had supported at the polls. Wilson, a Southerner, had promised if elected to treat Negroes justly, but immediately after his election he inaugurated Jimcrowism in the government offices in Washington. Ushered into the presence of the President, Mr Trotter looked him squarely in the face and said: "Mr President, we come to you not as wards of the nation, but as full-fledged American citizens demanding our rights." He got no further. Mr Wilson backed out of the room, claiming that he had been insulted!

Trotter waged a ceaseless fight for his people. His last great effort was in connection with the Peace Conference of World War No. 1. He applied for a passport to go to France where the Conference was held. It was denied. Not daunted, although unaccustomed to physical hardship and well up in his forties, Trotter wore rough clothes, secured a job as a cook, and got to Paris. There he created an international sensation when he tried to present the case of American Negroes to the Conference. Naturally he was unsuccessful, but he had made the headlines and the United States was embarrassed. Trotter returned to America and continued his fight. Misunderstood by his people, he died of a broken heart about 15 years ago.

* * *

Prior to the advent of the radio, one of the most popular sources of musical entertainment was the automatic player piano. The instrument was to be found in many homes and public places in America and other countries. Despite the popularity of the radio, player pianos are still used considerably. It is not generally known that the development of this type of musical instrument was due largely to the inventions of Joseph H. Dickinson, a coloured American. From a crude beginning he brought the automatic player piano to its highest point of perfection. Mr Dickinson was until quite recently the active head of the largest enterprise manufacturing player pianos.[1]

* * *

It is a favourite contention of Negrophobists that Negroes contributed nothing of value to civilisation. Those who express this view are either ignorant or, knowing the truth, deliberately pervert it. Modern civilisation is based on iron. Without iron man would still be in the Stone Age. Not a few European writers have admitted that according to the best records available, iron was first smelted by natives of Central Africa; in other words, by black men. Said Dr Franz Boas, one of the greatest anthropologists who ever lived: "It seems likely that at a time when the European was still satisfied with crude stone tools, the Africans had invented the art of smelting iron. Neither Ancient Europe, nor Western Asia, nor Ancient China knew iron, and everything points to its introduction from Africa."[2] Indeed, Negroes have much to be proud of: humanity has benefited greatly from the contributions made by Africans to what is called civilisation.

1. Joseph Hunter Dickinson (1855–1936). Born in Canada, he moved to Detroit in 1870 and served two terms in the Michigan House of Representatives.
2. Quoted from W. E. B. Du Bois, *Black Folk Then and Now: An Essay in the History and Sociology of the Black Race*, New York: Holt, Rinehart and Winston, 1939, p. 99.

35

Our Forgotten Authors

January 1946

As well as demonstrating Domingo's nationalist impulses, this piece bears witness to his intellectual precociousness. Still a teenager in Kingston, he was reading English magazines, persuading the Institute of Jamaica to purchase Theophilus Scholes's *Glimpses of the Ages*, and reading the substantial volume. In addition, he was alert to the importance of the extraordinary Jamaican Isaac Edmeston Barnes, yet to be the subject of even a biographical sketch.

Public Opinion, 17 January 1946, p. 3

SERIOUS WRITERS

A few months ago I remarked that Trinidad, though smaller than Jamaica, had in recent years been more prolific than Jamaica in literary production. In making the statement I did not mean that more books, booklets, and similar material had been published. I confined myself largely to the fact that, so far as I knew, more Trinidadians than Jamaicans had essayed into the field of serious authorship. I cited J. J. Thomas, F. A. Durham, C. L. R. James, George Padmore, and Eric Williams.[1]

About the same time that the Trinidadians published their books, there were a few Jamaicans engaged in similar lines of intellectual activity but unfortunately, even among our cognoscenti, the writings of these men are absolutely unknown. How many Jamaicans who are interested in our literature know anything about Dr Louis Meikle, who was the earliest native West Indian advocate of West Indian federation? His book on the subject, though badly written and inaccurate in places, was first in the field and gave impetus to the movement for federation, not for administrative economy of purpose solely, but, as he conceived it, to enhance the social, political, and economic development of the people of the territories concerned.[2]

1. Frederick Alexander Durham, Trinidadian Pan-Africanist and author of *The Lone-Star of Liberia: Being the Outcome of Reflections on Our Own People* (1892). Cyril Lionel Robert James (1901–1989), Trinidadian political activist and historian.
2. See below, p. 305.

A SCHOLAR

Another Jamaican author of whom little is known in Jamaica is the late Dr Samuel E. Theophilus Scholes. I first learned of him a little over 30 years ago when I read an adverse criticism of his book *Glimpses of the Ages* in an English magazine. Mention of the fact that he was a Jamaican prompted me to induce the Institute to procure a copy of the volume. When the book arrived I read it in the Institute and found it a storehouse of information. It was then that I discovered that Dr Scholes had written *Chamberlain and Chamberlainism*, which dealt with the imperial policies of Joseph Chamberlain (father of Neville, of Munich fame), *The British Empire*, etc., all from the viewpoint of colonials.[3]

When I went to America I ran into a small group of Americans who literally worshipped Dr Scholes for his writings. I also learned something of the man. Mr Arthur Schomburg, a Puerto Rican mulatto who had the largest and most valuable collection in the world of literature of any sort written by or about Negroes, told me that if I went to the British Museum any day I would see an elderly black man poring over books and manuscripts and that the gentleman would be Dr Scholes, a learned and most self-sacrificing man.[4] A few years later, a friend of mine, acting on the description, located Dr Scholes in the Museum. He learned from the old man that he had had a tough time because of the revelations made in his writings that he was watched and dogged by the British police. Dr Scholes told my friend that not a single English publishing house would accept any more manuscripts from him. Dr Scholes's brother, who was for many years a chief accountant for one of the big railroads in America, lives here on pension.

FRIEND OF GREAT MEN

Another little-known Jamaican author was the late Dr J. Edmonestone Barnes.[5] Born in this island, he was educated as a civil engineer in England and Germany. He was a class-mate of the late Kaiser William of Germany, with whom he had corresponded for years. Dr Barnes did important scientific work for the British

3. Theophilus Edward Samuel Scholes (1856–1940), *The British Empire and Alliances, or, Britain's duty to her Colonies and Subject Races*, London: Elliot Stock, 1899; as Bartholomew Smith (pseudonym), *Chamberlain and Chamberlainism*, London: J. Long, 1903; *Glimpses of the Ages, or, the "Superior" and "Inferior" Races, So-Called, Discussed in the Light of Science and History*, 2 vols, London: J. Long, 1905–1908. See Patrick Bryan, "Black Perspectives in Late Nineteenth Century Jamaica: The Case of Theophilus E. S. Scholes", in *Garvey, His Work and Impact*, ed. Rupert Lewis and Patrick Bryan, Trenton, NJ: Africa World Press, 1991, pp. 47–63; Kim Blake, "T. E. S. Scholes: The Unknown Panafricanist", *Race & Class*, 49, no. 1 (2007), pp. 62–80; and Duncan Bell, *Dreamworlds of Race: Empire and the Utopian Destiny of Anglo-America*, Princeton, NJ: Princeton University Press, 2020, pp. 385–394.

4. Arturo Alfonso Schomburg (1874-1938) was a Puerto Rico-born historian and bibliophile.

5. Actually Isaac Edmeston Barnes (1857–1930), often mistakenly said to have been born in Barbados.

government in South Africa for some time, then he went to Liberia and settled. After a while he was made head of the Public Works Department of the Republic. For some time Liberia had been threatened by France and England. Slices of Liberian territory were allegedly incorporated into French and British colonies because of faulty frontiers.

To save the Republic more loss of land, Dr Barnes went to America at his own expense and put the case up to the late President Theodore Roosevelt. Liberia is a protégé of the United States. Mr Roosevelt was shocked at the barefaced theft of the land of the country, and he intervened and caused both England and France to stay their rapacious hands. As a result, the borders of Liberia were scientifically established. It was my good fortune to meet Dr Barnes and hear him lecture. Dr Barnes wrote some pamphlets. His most ambitious work, written when he was an old man, was entitled *The Economy of Life*.[6] The best thing in the book was the foreword by the famous English scholar, ex-Jesuit, and atheist Joseph McCabe, a life-long friend of Dr Barnes. The book itself was poorly constructed and rambling, but it contained a wealth of information.

It would be interesting if a complete bibliography of Jamaican authors were compiled. I suspect it would show much more serious literary efforts than most of us are aware.

6. J. Edmeston Barnes, *The Economy of Life: Some Suggestions for World Betterment*, Chorley, UK: Universal Publishing (Sidney R. Campion), 1921. Barnes was also the author of *The Economic Value of the Native Races of Africa in Relation to the Development of the Resources of That Continent*, London: Watts & Co., 1908. On Barnes's extraordinary career in South Africa, see L. Alan Eyre, "Isaac Edmestone Barnes in Kroonstad, Orange River Colony: The Troubled Life of a Black Jamaican Mining Executive 1903 to 1909", *Quarterly Bulletin of the National Library of South Africa*, 60, no. 4 (2006), pp. 105–127.

36

Jamaicans Eating Slop

April 1947

This piece appeared under Domingo's regular title, "Sparks from My Anvil". The newspaper article that he here refers to was dramatically entitled "Jamaicans Eating Slop, Says Report".[1] The report was based on a visit by medical and sanitary inspectors to Kingston Pen, and it told a story of homeless, starving, and diseased squatters driving crows off the Kingston garbage dump so they could collect scraps of decomposing food.

Public Opinion, 26 April 1947, p. 5

About three weeks ago I received a letter from a good friend who resides in Brooklyn informing me that Jamaicans in New York City and its environs were greatly upset over a news item which appeared in the *Amsterdam News*, a weekly newspaper published in Harlem. My friend did not send me the item in question, but made it clear that the report described certain deplorable conditions that were alleged to exist in Jamaica. As the news had caused consternation and embarrassment to my countrymen, and knowing their resentment at disclosure of bad conditions in their homeland being publicised in America, I concluded that the report dealt with the recent exposure of the appalling conditions that a fairly large number of our people are compelled to endure in the section of the Corporate Area known as Kingston Pen.

DISGRACEFUL

My assumption has been confirmed. I have since read the story which a local correspondent of the Associated Negro Press sent to America for publication in some 200 newspapers. Admittedly, the report is unpleasant reading but, while lurid, it was substantially what had appeared in the local press. Nobody in Jamaica can deny that the area on the eastern boundary of the May Pen cemetery is a collection of the most disgraceful and dilapidated shacks and hovels imaginable.

It should occasion no surprise that Jamaicans in America were embarrassed by the broadcasting of the report in that country. From my knowledge of the mental

1. Wilbert E. Hemming, "Jamaicans Eating Slop, Says Report", *New York Amsterdam News*, 22 March 1947, p. 4.

processes of Jamaicans and other West Indians in the United States, I would have been surprised if they had been undisturbed. I am convinced that most Jamaicans who read the report were less concerned about the miserable conditions under which some of their countrymen are forced to live than with the fact that coloured Americans should have read the story.

ROSY PICTURES

Generally speaking, West Indians in America paint rosy pictures of their countries. If they had been accustomed to telling the exact truth or to refraining from discussing the subject at all, they would not have been embarrassed. It is a case of chickens coming home to roost. The inordinate lies told by many Jamaicans abroad about social conditions in Jamaica were bound to act as boomerangs at some time.

In West Indian circles one can commit no greater sin than to give a photographic description of the conditions under which the vast majority of the population in these islands live, move, and have their being. Yet the facts were before their very eyes and statistics can easily be obtained from the report of the 1938 Royal Commission, from Handbooks, and, in the case of Jamaica, from the 1943 census. Why it should be considered unpatriotic to expose bad conditions in order to try and improve them is beyond my understanding.

HIGH TREASON

I have always thought that a knowledge of symptoms, of conditions, was a prerequisite to diagnosis and necessary for a proper prescription. But among West Indians in America, any such approach to the problems of their homelands is usually tantamount to high treason and a most mortal sin against their countries. Misrepresentations get us nowhere, nor will burying our heads in the sand. West Indians do not emigrate for the fun of it, as some of them try to make out in America, or to bestow the blessings of their superior presence on the benighted lands that give them domicile.

ITS FOLLY

The folly of this attitude should be obvious. In extenuation, it can be said, though, that some people do not really know their native country. They are romanticists and see Jamaica through rose-coloured spectacles. Invariably they argue from the point of view of the small minority who really live well or from the angle of the so-called middle class who enjoy a modicum of comfort, even though they are constantly in debt. Contrast this attitude on the part of West Indians with the behaviour of Puerto Ricans, coloured Americans, Indians, and similarly placed peoples. They make no bones about telling the exact truth in regard to their countries. Many of these people write books depicting the horrible conditions under which the majority of their compatriots exist. They see no necessity for exaggerating one way or the other. They present the photographic truth insofar as statistics and demonstrable facts reveal it.

FAR FROM CIVILISED

There can be no doubt whatsoever that conditions in western Kingston are far from civilised. Poverty, filth, ignorance, superstition, bad housing, hunger, and disease abound. Kingston Pen is undoubtedly the extreme expression of this evil condition, but Denham Town, Rose Town, and adjacent townships are little better. Providence Pen, the Hope Flats, Passmore Town, and other places are eyesores and incubators of disease, vice, and crime. Nor must it be thought that this condition is confined to the Corporate Area. It is endemic in the island. Travel anywhere and slum conditions are evident, with very few exceptions, in every town. Of course, there are some fine dwellings, but these are the exceptions rather than the rule.

THEIR OWN JUDGES

Most Jamaicans abroad prefer to have their country judged by the best rather than by its worst. This is natural, but there is no sense in denying the existence of the worst. The truth is (see the census reports on housing, income, and education) that the average Jamaican is badly housed, poorly paid, and semi-illiterate. Instead of denying these facts and deploring their exposure, Jamaicans in New York and elsewhere should be patriotically indignant that nearly 300 years of British colonial rule have brought the country no farther along the road to civilisation than this and pledge themselves to help the forces at home that are working for improvement.

IMPOSSIBLE TO HIDE

It is impossible today to hide the truth from the camera and the journalist. The conscience of the modern world will not endure this state of affairs. West Indians in America have earned much animosity from their American cousins because of their insensate pretence at being better than the people among whom they live and in whose country they were able to attain a far higher level of living and education than was possible for them in the lands of their origin. Nobody would suggest that Jamaicans should mount housetops and bellow about the evil economic and social conditions at home, but they should most certainly not pretend that conditions are better than honest people know them to be. By being discreet, truthful, and less bombastic about their country, our people abroad can save themselves much embarrassment and render a useful service to their countrymen who remain at home.

PART III

Securing Independence: New York, 1948–1964

Federation of Jamaica with the scattered far-distant islands, with their diverse populations, is artificial and sentimental. It is not based on any compelling Jamaican necessity. The peoples have different backgrounds, histories, cultures, traditions, and many conflicting political and economic interests. They compete in the same foreign markets with identical agricultural products.

Like his friend Adolphe Roberts in 1939, Domingo spurned the opportunity of a political career in Jamaica: there is little doubt that he could have become a leading light in the PNP.[1] Even after six (enforced) years on the island, he clearly felt that New York was now his home, and he returned as soon as he was allowed to. His send-off from Kingston was low-key, his arrival in New York unremarked. Within days, however, he reported coming to blows in a Harlem bookshop with his old antagonist Wendell Malliet. This, it turned out, would be a sign of things to come.

Domingo initially stayed with his son Karl in the Bronx. The FBI kept Domingo senior under surveillance, reporting in the autumn that he spent most of his time in the Schomburg Library while also frequenting the nearby Calypso Club: he was clearly living a perfectly balanced life.[2] Interviewed ten years later by the US Immigration and Naturalization Service, Domingo said—according to the FBI report—that when he got back to the USA, "I had a fair amount of funds and was over 60 [in fact he was 58]. I was thinking of retiring, but I decided to go into the importing business with which I was familiar."[3] During his six years in Jamaica Domingo had received a small PNP salary and presumably been paid a pittance for his *Public Opinion* columns, but he had still managed to accumulate property in Kingston.[4] It's possible that Norman Manley, who clearly felt responsible for

1. On Roberts's spurning of a possible political career in Jamaica, see Peter Hulme, "W. Adolphe Roberts and Jamaica", *Jamaica Journal*, 34, no. 3 (August 2013), pp. 14–23, at 16.
2. Letter from Director of FBI J. Edgar Hoover to Assistant Attorney General, T. Vincent Quinn, 6 October 1947, FBIWAD.
3. FBI file 65-35099 "Wilfred Adolphus Domingo", 14 January 1963, referring to INS file A3252158, FBIWAD. The interview took place on 17 September 1957.
4. In a letter to Amy Jacques Garvey, Domingo writes of still having a "place on West Street" and "lots ... on Elspeth Road" (20 April 1954), AJGP.

Domingo's predicament, had lent him money which Domingo put to good use. In New York he now established the Wildom Distributing Agency, based at 913 Jackson Avenue in the Bronx.

* * *

Preparatory activity for the Caribbean Labour Congress and Closer Union Commission conferences took place in New York just before Domingo's return. A meeting at the Abyssinian Baptist Church in June 1947 saw Manley, Adams, and others, including Nnamdi Azikiwe, discussing federation, and in the same month a meeting at the NAACP offices of a special committee of the West Indian-American group set up for the promotion of better relations between the Caribbean and the United States was attended by Manley, Adams, Augustine A. Austin, Hope Stevens, and Bindley Cyrus, along with NAACP officials Walter White and Channing Tobias.[5] It established an organisation to finance the movement for West Indian self-government, specifically, in the first instance, to raise $10,000 to defray the costs of the CLC meeting.[6] This fundraising was in the hands of Austin, who probably provided most of the money himself. A follow-up meeting on 11 July, with just Austin, Tobias, and White present (and so Austin the only West Indian), agreed that the group's name should be the American Association for Caribbean Advancement (AACE), although this was soon changed to the American Committee for West Indian Federation (ACWIF). The committee on objectives consisted of Austin, Ethelred Brown, Rayford Logan, and W. E. B. Du Bois, Brown's presence indicating the JPL(NY)'s willingness to work towards federation despite its two chief founders' adamant opposition.[7]

By the time the ACWIF presented a memorandum to the CLC Jamaica conference in September 1947, Austin was chairman and Richard B. Moore secretary.[8] This long memorandum—clearly Moore's work—includes as appendices copies of three documents attesting to the lively interest New York West Indians had taken in their homelands: the Declaration of Rights of the Caribbean Peoples to Self-Determination and Self-Government presented to the Pan-American Foreign Ministers' Conference in Havana in July 1940 [#22]; the Statement of

5. "Call for West Indian Unity", Report from the British Consulate General in New York, forwarded to the Colonial Office by E. E. Sabben-Clare of the British Embassy in Washington, DC, CO 537/2259, TNA. Except in quotations, in the text we follow a broad distinction between the general idea of "federation" and the official project of "Federation". Real-estate and insurance mogul, Antiguan-born Augustine Alexander Austin (1880-1959), owned the Antillean Holding Company. Bindley Charles Cyrus (1894–1976), Barbados-born Chicago attorney. Channing Heggie Tobias (1882–1961), Georgia-born YMCA official.

6. NAACPACWIF, pp. 72–73.

7. NAACPACWIF, pp. 80–82.

8. "Memorandum of Federation and Self-Government of the West Indies", NAACPACWIF, pp. 85–117.

the West Indies National Emergency Committee to that Havana conference in response to Cordell Hull's address; and the Appeal to the World Security Conference of the United Nations on behalf of the Caribbean Peoples made in San Francisco in May–June 1945. The first two were chiefly Domingo's work, with some input from Moore; the third was exclusively Moore's work.[9]

The main text of the ACWIF memorandum was firm in its support for a West Indian federation, but equally adamant that "Federation is the union of independent sovereign states, hence there can be no federation worthy of the name where there is no recognition of actual independence and sovereignty."[10] In this connection the document quoted Algernon Aspinall—for many years secretary to The West India Committee in London—to the effect that "The terms 'confederation' and 'federation' are strictly only applicable to the federal union of independent sovereign states."[11] This was always Domingo's point: independence for the individual units should come *first*, then—if agreed—federation. To agree to federation first was to surrender a sovereignty you didn't actually possess. Moore finally seemed on board with this argument, though still deeply committed to making federation work. He clearly thought—mistakenly—that in British eyes federation was the *sine qua non* for self-government. As John Mordecai puts it, "part of the emotion attached to the idea of federation was due to its being seen as a necessary prelude to self-government".[12]

Austin and Moore were steaming ahead, but in the process risked alienating their African-American colleagues. Walter White wrote to Channing Tobias

9. These documents are included in the section "The Pan-Caribbean Movement in Harlem" in Richard B. Moore, *Caribbean Militant in Harlem: Collected Writings 1920–1972*, ed. W. Burghardt Turner and Joyce Moore Turner, Bloomington, IN: Indiana University Press, 1988, pp. 262–290.

10. "Memorandum of Federation", p. 89.

11. Algernon Aspinall, *Handbook of the British West Indies, British Guiana and British Honduras, 1926–27*, London: West India Committee, 1926, quoted in "Memorandum of Federation", p. 89.

12. John Mordecai, *The West Indies: The Federal Negotiations*, London: Allen & Unwin, 1968, p. 32. Sir John Stanley Mordecai (1903–1986) was a Jamaican civil servant who became secretary to the West Indies Federation and then deputy governor-general of Jamaica. His is the most comprehensive and generally fair-minded account of Federation's troubled life and eventual demise, with the advantages and disadvantages of being written by an administrative participant. On this period, the best studies of West Indian politics within the context of decolonisation are: Gordon K. Lewis, *The Growth of the Modern West Indies*, New York: Monthly Review Press, 1968; Gerald C. Horne, *Cold War in a Hot Zone: The United States Confronts Labor and Independence Struggles in the British West Indies*, Philadelphia, PA: Temple University Press, 2007; Jason C. Parker, *Brother's Keeper: The United States, Race, and Empire in the British Caribbean, 1937–1962*, New York: Oxford University Press, 2008; and Spencer Mawby, *Ordering Independence: The End of Empire in the Anglophone Caribbean, 1947–1969*, Basingstoke, UK: Palgrave Macmillan, 2012. Specifically on Federation, see the essays in *Social and Economic Studies*, 6, no. 2 (June 1957), and Jason C. Parker, "The Failure of the West Indies Federation", in *Ultimate Adventures with Britannia: Personalities, Politics and Culture in Britain*, ed. William Roger Louis, London: I. B. Tauris, 2009, pp. 235–245.

complaining about the lack of consultation: "Certainly I cannot afford to involve the Association [NAACP] if Austin is going to act in this manner." He also noted that "there is another West Indian faction led by Wendell Malliet which is bitterly opposed to Austin and his group".[13] White informed Austin of his displeasure, Austin apologised, and the contretemps was seemingly put behind them.[14] White was certainly right about Wendell Malliet's objection to the AACE. Malliet was, of course, a strong proponent of federation; indeed, as he modestly put it, "We have been the strongest voice in the United States for thirty years in favor of the federation of the British Caribbean" (with Malliet the "we" is always royal). His "grave misgivings" about the new organisation, Malliet explained in his newspaper column, were because in this same group "are the men who piloted the West Indies National Council to ill-fame and disaster", further characterised as "a small band of unprincipled men, of willful and deliberate intentions, whose only purpose is to do their damnedest to get Communist ideas and all that Communism means into the West Indies".[15] He named no names, but the likely suspects would include Richard B. Moore, still vice-president of the WINC and still, just, a member of the CPUSA, and the WINC's former president, W. A. Domingo, shortly to return to New York from his enforced sojourn in Jamaica. The following week Malliet waded, if tentatively, into Jamaican national politics, implying—though he was careful not to state it—that this new organisation would end up financing the PNP in its political and labour union struggles with the JLP. Malliet's sympathies clearly lay with Bustamante ("a man in whom we have great confidence, and for whom we have the deepest affection and respect"), but he offered himself as an honest broker "when we arrive in Jamaica in the near future".[16] A meeting of the AACE on 17 July consolidated the planning: Austin was able to report that the funding target had almost been reached. Despite his reservations, Malliet supported Moore's resolution in favour of the importance of the CLC.[17]

In June 1946 a testimonial dinner was offered to Malliet at the Hotel Pennsylvania. Many of the names attending were familiar: Savory, Petioni, Morris, Stevens, as well as a scattering of the great and good from the east of the region—Grantley Adams of Barbados, T. Albert Marryshow from Grenada. But the JPL

13. Letter from Walter White to Channing H. Tobias, 15 September 1947, NAACPACWIF, pp. 108–109. White references the report of Austin's speech in the *Pittsburgh Courier*. Although Austin was supposedly just an observer, he clearly played a significant part in the conference: see "Labour Conference Opens with Stirring Speeches", *The Gleaner*, 3 September 1947, p. 22; "Speakers Declare in Favour of Federation at 'Torch' Meeting", *The Gleaner*, 10 September 1947, p. 14; and the lengthy report written by Richard B. Moore, "West Indians Seek Free Commonwealth", *People's Voice*, 27 September 1947, p. 8.

14. See the exchange of correspondence between White and Austin ("Memorandum of Federation", pp. 110–117).

15. A. M. Wendell Malliet, "World Fronts", *New York Amsterdam News*, 14 June 1947, p. 10.

16. A. M. Wendell Malliet, "World Fronts", *New York Amsterdam News*, 5 July 1947, p. 8.

17. "Destiny of Peoples of the Caribbean", *The Gleaner*, 23 July 1947, p. 10.

was also well represented through Ethelred Brown, Richard S. Trew, and Theo Burrell. And also present was the now single again Eulalie Domingo.[18] On his return to New York, Domingo perhaps felt a degree of frustration or resentment that Wendell Malliet had used the years of Domingo's absence to cement his own position within the New York West Indian community, helped by his commitment to the federal idea that was animating those with an Eastern Caribbean origin. When Domingo and Malliet met in Richard B. Moore's book centre, words were evidently spoken and fists flew.[19]

* * *

The 1947 CLC meeting had greater political significance than its forerunners because it immediately preceded and laid some of the groundwork for the Montego Bay conference later that month, although the difficulty delegates had in getting to Jamaica was some indication of one of the drawbacks to the idea of federation. Opening the meeting, Manley made it clear what he meant by federation:

> I reject totally any sort of mis-marriage between colonial rule and federation and I would predict for such a marriage such an abortion as politics has never seen, and I say that a federated West Indies cannot aim at any smaller immediate objective than dominion status (applause). I cannot imagine what we should be federating about if it is not to achieve the beginning of nationhood.[20]

The metaphor may have been unfortunate, but the sentiment was clear, as was Manley's understanding that federation would come first and would lead to West Indian nationhood.

The meeting ended on the evening of Monday 8 September in a torchlit march through the city and a public gathering at Kingston Race Course with a crowd of 30,000 in attendance.[21] The CLC spokesmen were unanimous in their expressions of unity and brotherhood, and uniformly vituperative about Alexander Bustamante, who, as leader of the party that had won the 1944 election, was the unofficial prime minister. It was clearly a fly in the ointment of Caribbean labour solidarity that the most popular political party and the largest trade union in the territory hosting the congress should be standing aloof from proceedings. An even greater problem, one cannot help but feel, was being stoked by the lan-

18. "Plan Testimonial to Honor Malliet", *New York Amsterdam News*, 25 May 1946, p. 25.
19. W. A. Domingo, Letter to Norman Manley, 15 August 1947, NMP. It was called the Frederick Douglass Book Center, 141 West 125th Street, New York.
20. "Labour Conference Opens with Stirring Speeches", *The Gleaner*, 3 September 1947, pp. 1 and 22, at 22.
21. "Speakers Declare in Favour of Federation at 'Torch' Meeting", *The Gleaner*, 10 September 1947, p. 14.

guage used to describe Bustamante by these partisans of federation: Busta (as he was universally known in Jamaica) had a good memory for slights. Adams kicked things off by telling the crowd that they were "keeping back the cause of West Indian progress" as long as they kept Bustamante as prime minister. They should have chosen Manley, he openly declared. Albert Gomes then stuck the knife in. He had gone to reason with Bustamante, he reported, only to be greeted by "an extraordinary display of maniacal glee … a display of buffoonery such as I have never seen in my life".[22] Austin restricted himself to a note of sorrow that he would have to report back to New York on the "dissenting voice from Jamaica".

Despite this splendid display of Caribbean unity (Bustamante excepted), it's a moot point whether, in the rush towards federation, the members of the CLC grasped the distinction that Moore had made in his memorandum. In any case, the federative momentum generated in Kingston ground to a halt on the north coast when Creech Jones, generally regarded as among the most sympathetic of British politicians to West Indian interests, declared that the subject of a *self-governing* federation was outside the immediate terms of reference, the Colonial Office having opined that the CLC's proposals were "precipitate and unfeasible".[23]

Reporting back to New York, Richard Moore put a positive spin on proceedings in an article headed "West Indians Federate for Nationhood". The agreement reached, Moore reported, "gives official recognition to the popular demand for a united West Indian nation". His gloss was triumphalist:

> To a keen observer of the Caribbean scene, nothing less than these decisions was to be expected in view of the preceding Kingston conference of the Caribbean Labor Congress. The age-old demand of the West Indian people for voluntary federation with full self-government attained to such clear expression and challenging power at that epoch-making conference that the results of the Montego Bay conference were almost a foregone conclusion. The senile restraining fetters of empire were compelled to yield to the lusty forward thrust of the emerging Caribbean Commonwealth.[24]

If the British were interested in federation with eventual self-government and the CLC wanted federation with immediate self-government, then—irony of ironies—Domingo's position was voiced in Montego Bay by his old adversary Alexander Bustamante. As one newspaper report put it: "West Indians Demand Complete Independence". The Colonial Secretary had warned, as the report has

22. Albert Maria Gomes (1911–1978) was a union leader and writer; he founded and edited *The Beacon* (1931–33). A prominent figure in discussions of federation, his political star was eclipsed by the rise of Eric Williams in the mid-1950s.
23. Quoted in Mordecai, *The West Indies*, p. 38.
24. Richard B. Moore, "West Indians Federate for Nationhood". *New York Amsterdam News*, 27 September 1947, p. 11.

it, "that federation under the British crown was the quickest road to self-rule". Bustamante attacked Creech Jones for, in Bustamante's own words, "attempting to intimidate delegates by predicting calamity if they failed to organize a federation". Disagreeing with this prophecy, Bustamante announced that "The time has come after 200 years of British rule not just for federation but for self-government." Turning to Creech Jones, he added "Your government is helping to retard the progress of our country. We are willing to face the dangers of independence."[25] Moore's gloss on Bustamante's words, few of which he actually quoted, was: "Playing upon insular prejudice in the manner of an accomplished demagogue, Bustamante assumed the role of champion of Jamaica alone, thus conveniently furnishing that division which is all that imperialist oppressors need to destroy the people's struggle for liberation." Having voiced his objections, Bustamante uncharacteristically swallowed them and supported the final set of resolutions which saw the establishment of a Standing Closer Association Committee (SCAC) to draft a federal constitution in favour of closer union.[26] He was probably assuaged by the compromise in which the basic principle was recognised as being that "each unit retains complete control over all matters except those specifically assigned to the federal government".[27] A cynic might suggest he was hedging his bets. In any case, this compromise, according to Mordecai, "trammelled the Federation from its birth".[28]

The disintegration of the CLC as an organisation followed Adams's defence of British colonial policy at the United Nations General Assembly in Paris in October 1948, causing Richard Hart to denounce the CLC's own president in the *CLC Monthly Bulletin*: "The President of the Caribbean Labour Congress has, on one of the most important issues of all time, thrown away the golden opportunity to be the champion of the cause of colonial peoples everywhere struggling for freedom."[29] Moore also weighed in. "Every intelligent native of the Caribbean," he wrote, "and every thinking, liberty-loving person, devoted to the freeing of millions of colonial and semi-colonial peoples from the yoke of imperialist oppression, must repudiate and condemn the statement of Grantley H. Adams."[30]

25. "West Indians Demand Complete Independence", *Atlanta Daily World*, 18 September 1947, p. 1.
26. In his postmortem on the West Indies Federation, Moore suggested that Bustamante's "temporary espousal of federation" was due to the influence of Wendell Malliet ("Caribbean Freedom and Nationhood", in Moore, *Caribbean Militant in Harlem*, p. 297.
27. *Conference on the Closer Association of the British West Indian Colonies (11th–19th September, 1947): (Montego Bay, Jamaica), Colonial no. 218*, London: HMSO, 1948, quoted in Mordecai, *The West Indies*, p. 37.
28. Mordecai, *The West Indies*, p. 38.
29. *CLC Monthly Bulletin*, September–October 1948, quoted in Bolland, "Democracy and Authoritarianism", p. 104.
30. "Statement from the Pan-African Federation", *Barbados Observer*, 13 November 1948, quoted in F. A. Hoyos, *Grantley Adams and the Social Revolution*, London: Macmillan, 1974, p. 141.

A lot of bad blood was beginning to flow. Bustamante was one thing, but Hart, Moore, and Adams were all supposed to be on the same side, the side of federation. It did not bode well, and the Caribbean labour movement soon split on ideological grounds. Meanwhile, the BITU went its own merry way, happily unaffiliated with anybody else and so spared the trials and tribulations that come with association. Bustamante had also won the 1949 election, though with a reduced majority. Whatever his disagreements with Manley over federation, at this stage Domingo clearly still saw himself as a PNP cadre in New York [#38]. Meanwhile, as always, he kept a close eye on what people were writing about Jamaica, in this case the poet Langston Hughes [#37].

The SCAC established in Montego Bay had a series of meetings across the region under the chairmanship of Sir Hubert Rance, Governor of Trinidad, but Bustamante kept the JLP well away from proceedings. Recommendations for slow and modest progress towards Federation were presented in October 1949 and published the following year. Three particularly tricky issues were touched upon, all of which would return to haunt the federal project. Rance recommended that population should not be the basis for representation, a move solely aimed at preventing Jamaica having a built-in majority since more than 50 per cent of the total population of the federal units lived on that one island. In addition, it was recommended that dual membership of unit and federal bodies should not be permitted and that Trinidad should be the capital seat.[31]

As the recommendations were discussed across the region, further splits emerged. With the governor-general due to have extensive reserved powers, Grantley Adams called the plan "not much more than a glorified Crown Colony"— and he predictably wasn't happy with Trinidad being the capital.[32] Opposition parties in Trinidad and Grenada showed sympathy with Adams's view, although they were outvoted. The two main Jamaican parties agreed to support the proposals, although Bustamante felt that considerable financial assistance from the UK would be necessary for economic development. This was a view that Wendell Malliet was also pushing in New York. In 1951 Malliet had spent five months in Jamaica, where, in his own words, he "took an active part in the discussions and plans which led to the favorable action taken by both houses of the Jamaica Legislature in accepting federation in principle".[33] However, by the end of 1952 one could sense the seeds of doubt in Malliet's writing on the subject. He still pronounced himself a federalist and praised the *New York Times* for support-

31. *Report of the British Caribbean Standing Closer Association Committee, 1948–49*, London: HMSO, 1950.

32. Quoted in Mordecai, *The West Indies*, p. 41.

33. A. M. Wendell Malliet, "Caribbean Federation", *New York Times*, 24 November 1952, p. 22. The JLP member of the House of Representatives Donald Sangster said at the time: "Federation in some form or the other is inevitable and necessary .... There is no division at all in this country on the necessity for federation" (quoted in Edward Seaga, *My Life and Leadership. Volume 1: Clash of Ideologies, 1930–1980*, Oxford, UK: Macmillan Education, 2009, p. 64).

ing the idea, but at the same time he issued a note of caution, echoing Adams's reservations:

> It should be emphasized, however, that responsible opinion in Jamaica, a cornerstone in any federal structure in the area, is not likely to go along with what appears to be the British idea that federation is to bring about a union of geographical areas of poverty, backwardness, unemployment and frustration under a glorified system of Crown Colony government with some rather high-sounding name or title.[34]

With federation so central to the post-war agenda, it was difficult for Domingo to fulfil his promise to be the PNP's point man in New York. Instead, Manley's main contact became Ethelred Brown, still JPL(NY) secretary. Wendell Malliet took up the equivalent position for the JPL and Bustamante. Manoeuvring was complicated since both parties were now in favour, at least in general terms, of a movement towards federation with dominion status, though Malliet had been much more consistent in his backing of this position than had Bustamante, and he therefore needed to keep prodding his leader. As support for the recommendations of the SCAC was expressed in several island legislatures, Malliet sought stronger Jamaican backing through a meeting he called at the offices of *New York Amsterdam News*, establishing a temporary committee called the West Indies Emergency Committee for Federation, with himself as chairman, Norman Procope as vice-chairman, and Reginald Pierrepointe as secretary. Malliet stressed the need for federation to be backed by a reconstruction loan of $1 billion.[35]

However, with plans for Federation taking shape, Malliet grew less and less enamoured of the kind of federation it was turning out to be. As early as August 1953 he was writing that "Jamaica cannot afford to become a part of the kind of Federation that has been proposed .... She is really moving into a union that would delay her own development and progress"; and in November 1956 he was no more sanguine, given the absence of any funded plan for economic development. That $1 billion was not going to be forthcoming—and he was doubtless naive to ever believe it a possibility.[36]

By this point, British Guiana, British Honduras, and the British Virgin Islands had all opted out, but the federal train continued its stately progress, the next stop being London in April 1953, where the Rance proposals were modified, though their principles remained uncontested, and a concrete plan for Federation was produced and returned to the participating West Indian governments for approv-

34. Malliet, "Caribbean Federation".

35. "Meet Seeks Jamaica Federation Backing", *New York Amsterdam News*, 20 January 1951, p. 4. Norman Fitz-Roy Procope (Trinidad, 1900–2000).

36. Wendell Malliet, "This Is Our Time to Think", *The Gleaner*, 29 November 1956, p. 10. The words from 1953 are a self-quotation from an unknown original.

al.[37] During the ensuing months, all agreed to the plan. With Bustamante now seemingly on board, all was temporarily sweetness and light in Jamaica.

At this point the Roberts/Domingo alliance swung back into action: after five years without contact, the old friends reconnected in August 1952 [#39]. First Roberts wrote to *The Gleaner* about what he called the "mirage" of federation, outlining all the practical reasons why it would never work.[38] Domingo wrote a letter in support, underlining what Jamaica stood to lose, and then a further letter responding to editorial disagreement with his position.[39] If there was a difference between the two of them, then it would be that Roberts was slightly more willing to discuss how—if it was definitely going to happen—a federation might be made to work. So, as part of a *Gleaner* forum in September 1955, he focused on the proposed composition of the senate which, with the Windward and Leeward Islands becoming seven units, would give the small islands 14 out of the 20 senators. All seven units, Roberts pointed out, would fit into three Jamaican parishes. The conclusion proved prophetic: "I regard it as sure that if Jamaica accepts a foolish structure, she will some day secede from the Federation in disgust."[40]

In June 1954 Bustamante and other JLP leaders visited New York, previously regarded as a PNP fiefdom despite the best efforts of Wendell Malliet. They gave a talk in Harlem, which led to an ill-natured exchange in the letters page of the *New York Amsterdam News* between William Ricketts, who offered a withering critique of Bustamante's speech ("almost inarticulate"), and Ben Burrell—once of *The Crusader* and the JPL, but now a JLP supporter.[41] The exchange spilled over into *The Gleaner*, with Burrell suggesting that Ricketts was actually a pseudonym for W. A. Domingo, and Domingo—denying the accusation—doubling down on his critique of Bustamante and letting rip at Burrell ("an excellent example of stupidity, recklessness, and irresponsibility").[42]

By the time of the next SCAC conference, in February 1956, Manley had replaced Bustamante as chief minister in Jamaica and was keen to put his own

37. *The Plan for a British Caribbean Federation Agreed by the Conference on West Indian Federation Held in London in April 1953, Cmd. 8895*, London: HMSO, 1953.

38. W. Adolphe Roberts, "West Indian Federation: It Is a Mirage!", *The Gleaner*, 29 April 1953, p. 8.

39. W. A. Domingo, "Federation and Patriotism", *The Gleaner*, 7 May 1953, p. 8; "Federation Challenged", *The Gleaner*, 29 May 1953, p. 8.

40. W. Adolphe Roberts, "I Have Never Been Enthusiastic", *The Gleaner*, 7 September 1955, p. 8.

41. William Ricketts, [title illegible], *New York Amsterdam* News, 10 July 1954, p. 14; Ben Burrell, "Bustamante Critic 'Childish' He Says", *New York Amsterdam News*, 24 July 1954, p. 14.

42. W. A. Domingo, "JLP Leaders in New York", *The Gleaner*, 26 August, p. 7; Ben Burrell, "Jamaicans Abroad", *The Gleaner*, 24 October 1954, p. 8; W. A. Domingo, "Jamaicans in New York", *The Gleaner*, 3 November 1954, p. 6. Domingo wrote in similar terms to Amy Jacques Garvey, particularly noting the speech of Mrs Leon ("dangerous and effective"). On Mrs Leon, see Courtney Desiree Morris, "Becoming Creole, Becoming Black: Migration, Diasporic Self-Making, and the Many Lives of Madame Maymie Leona Turpeau de Mena", *Women, Gender, and Families of Color*, 4, no. 2 (Fall 2016), pp. 171–195.

mark on proceedings, while in Trinidad Eric Williams, though not yet a member of the legislature, had been mounting a vigorous campaign against the 1953 plan. In a pattern that would recur until the final derailment, no decision was ever regarded as binding, with every meeting dedicating itself to reopening decisions taken at the previous meeting. And now that fleshly detail had to be put on the agreed bones, further sticking points emerged, notably over customs union, income tax, and freedom of movement.

The train may have moved slowly and the rails ahead had yet to be laid, but nobody wanted to stop. Britain wanted to be rid of what was increasingly seen as a political problem and a financial burden, and the Caribbean countries saw no other available route to full self-government. Gordon Lewis sums up the situation:

> Both as an idea and as a set of institutions [Federation] was British inspired throughout, even British imposed, imposed, that is to say, in the special British sense in which the colonials were presented with imperial proposals which, they were politely assured, they could accept or not but which were so conditioned that in effect the dependent peoples had no alternative but to accept, the acceptance then in turn being advertised by the colonial officialdom as evidence that federation was the "free choice" of the governed.[43]

At this stage, however, without agreement on fundamental matters, the plan—whatever its title—looked more like a loose confederation than a true federation, entered into with fingers crossed that the intractable problems could be solved over the initial five-year period. A Standing Federation Committee now began to meet, with the choice of a capital seat the subject of much unseemly wrangling. Trinidad finally won the vote. The agreement was signed in London on 23 February 1956, and parliament passed the British Caribbean Act on 2 August 1956. Although he hadn't been part of that earlier *Gleaner* forum, Domingo had not taken a vow of silence on the issue: his pamphlet *British West Indian Federation: A Critique* [#40], his longest published piece of writing, was a last-minute attempt to influence what was now close to being a *fait accompli*. In fact, he realised the cause was lost. He had it on good authority, he told Amy Jacques Garvey, that many top PNP figures disagreed with Manley, but that they "hadn't enough guts to oppose him". The situation left him bereft: "My dear Mrs Garvey, I am a disappointed person. Jamaica has no particular attraction for me any more. I dreamed of a free country, but that dream is now a nightmare."[44] There was a final letter

43. Lewis, *The Growth of the Modern West Indies*, p. 354.

44. W. A. Domingo, Letter to Amy Jacques Garvey, 5 September 1956, AJGP. Bustamante had tried to pitch himself as a successor to Marcus Garvey, but Domingo recalls that Amy Jacques had supported Norman Manley on public platforms (W. A. Domingo, Letter to Amy Jacques Garvey, 16 June 1954, AJGP). Amy Euphemia Jacques Garvey (1895–1973) was a Jamaican-born journalist and activist, and the second wife of Marcus Garvey. Despite that relationship, she and Domingo had a warm correspondence: see #47.

too, on the irrational distribution of seats in the Federal parliament. By November, even Wendell Malliet was backing away: "This is not the kind of Federation that we in the U.S. laboured and sacrificed so much over the years to achieve. We are accepting the shadow and not the substance of what we believe should be of practical and material benefit to an under-developed area and people."[45]

The British parliamentary model having prevailed, political parties were needed to contest the Federal elections. In February 1956, while meeting in London, a number of the leaders had agreed to form a West Indian-wide party with a socialist agenda: Manley (Jamaica), Adams (Barbados), Bradshaw (St Kitts), Bird (Antigua), Eric Gairy (Grenada), and Karl La Corbiniere (St Lucia).[46] Manley was elected president, Adams first vice-president. The West Indian Federal Labour Party (WIFLP) proved a more than adequate forum for internecine squabbling over the five years of its existence. The first difficulty it faced was that member parties had to be *declared* socialist parties. Eric Williams's People's National Movement in Trinidad was not so declared, despite its policies being in some respects considerably more radical than those of some of the member parties. Williams was not amused. The following year associate membership was introduced so that the People's National Movement could be signed up. Williams was barely placated. The next and considerably larger crisis the WIFLP had to face was Manley's announcement that he wasn't going to stand for the Federal parliament, which would assuredly have led to him becoming Federal prime minister. As a result Jamaica was left as a dangerously underinvested outlier. The champion of the federative principle in the Caribbean was now a *Jamaican* protagonist, however loudly he proclaimed his commitment to Federation.

With Federation up and running, after a fashion, Domingo broadened his range, writing to *The Gleaner* on the occasion of Ghana's independence to celebrate the man hailed by the country's president as its "father", W. E. B. Du Bois.[47] This paean elicited a curious response from Amy Jacques Garvey, which consisted almost entirely of quotations from Du Bois's writing in the 1920s critical of Marcus Garvey, as if such remarks were themselves somehow proof that Du Bois *couldn't* rightly be regarded as the "father" of the newly independent state.[48] Domingo was obviously puzzled too, which didn't stop him taking the opportunity to analyse Kwame Nkrumah's remarks about Garvey in his recently published autobiography. Recognising that Nkrumah had been enthused by Garvey's *Philosophy and Opinions*. Domingo pointed out that Nkrumah committed himself to

45. Wendell Malliet, "Federation Presents a Challenge", *The Gleaner*, 15 November 1956, p. 12; "This is our time to think ...", *The Gleaner*, 29 November 1956, p. 10.

46. Robert Llewellyn Bradshaw (1916–1978), labour activist and first premier of St Kitts. Eric Matthew Gairy (1922–1997), trade union leader and first prime minister of Grenada until his overthrow in a coup in 1979 by Maurice Bishop. Karl Donald George La Corbiniere (1908–1992), ophthalmologist and parliamentarian.

47. W. A. Domingo, "'Father' of Ghana", *The Gleaner*, 25 April 1957, p. 8.

48. Amy Jacques Garvey, "Du Bois and Garvey", *The Gleaner*, 1 May 1957, p. 10.

African nationalism, as distinct from Garvey's *black* nationalism ("not the kind of philosophy Marcus Garvey preached").[49]

If Manley was founding a Federal Labour Party, then Bustamante had to have one too: the Democratic Labour Party (DLP) included the opposition party in Trinidad and the governing party in St Vincent. Like Manley, Bustamante was not going to run for Federal office. Unlike Manley, he never even considered the possibility. He was content to put all his eggs in the Jamaican basket, with an election due in 1959. Both Federal parties were the product of expediency and both were run from Jamaica, a country whose commitment to Federation was already looking less than solid before the parliament had even met.

Domingo's last-ditch opposition was to no avail: Federation formally came into being on 3 January 1958, consisting of ten territories covering 8,000 square miles and with a population of three and a quarter million. Jamaica had more than half the area and more than half the population. The West Indies Federation was hailed in the *New York Times* as a "tribute to the political genius of Britain" under the less than felicitous headline "Birth of a Nation".[50] Fortunately for Domingo, that was not the end of the story. The March 1958 elections produced a surprise, with the WIFLP only just winning most seats but not a majority, and three independents from Grenada and Barbados holding the balance of power. Adams became Federal prime minister by default, not an outcome that was warmly welcomed even by most of his allies.

In a personal blow to Manley, 12 of the 17 seats in Jamaica went to the DLP. Critics of Federation took new heart. Domingo's new pamphlet appeared in April 1958, restating his earlier arguments, but with the title, *Jamaica's Folly*, making his position crystal clear.[51] Now sensing that the tide was running in his favour, Domingo kept hammering away in further letters to *The Gleaner*, often taking issue with Federation's supporters, including Gordon Lewis.[52] Even some of the strongest proponents of Federation had been slowly but increasingly disillusioned by the form it was taking. Richard B. Moore, for example, wrote an anguished account of Norman Manley's less than triumphant visit to New York in September 1958 when he fielded questions about Federation from Harlem residents.[53] To the first question, as to what prevented Caribbean leaders from pushing for independence at the recent London conference instead of accepting a federal structure with no sovereignty, Manley replied "Perhaps the timidity of West

49. W. A. Domingo, "Father of Ghana", *The Gleaner*, 7 June 1957, p. 10, quoting *Ghana: The Autobiography of Kwame Nkrumah*, New York: Nelson, 1957, p. 183.
50. "Birth of a Nation", *New York Times*, 24 April 1958, p. 30.
51. W. A. Domingo, *Federation—Jamaica's Folly*, Kingston, Jamaica: The Gleaner, 1958.
52. W. A. Domingo, "Federation", *The Gleaner*, 5 February 1959, p. 10; "Federation", *The Gleaner*, 28 February 1958, p. 15; "Federation", *The Gleaner*, 5 March 1959, p. 10; "Federation", *The Gleaner*, 14 July 1959, p. 8; "PNP Policies", *The Gleaner*, 10 August 1959, p. 12.
53. Richard B. Moore, "Revelations and Reflections on West Indies Federation", *New York Amsterdam News*, 2 November 1958, p. 8.

Indians!" Moore characterised the answer as "somewhat surprising and hardly serious". Moore's follow-up question pulled no punches: "Since what has been established as a federal structure for the Caribbean Federation is obviously totally inadequate, being a temporary hodge-podge makeshift which if maintained can only discredit the very idea of genuine federation and self-government, when will a serious drive be made to achieve full Commonwealth status and to build a free united Caribbean nation?" Manley demurred from Moore's premise. From New York, Domingo talked openly about secession [#41].

On the defensive, Manley began to talk about Federation as a five-year experiment. The Jamaican general election campaign was gearing up to be fought on the grounds of who could present themselves as the better nationalist, with Federation seen as the inevitable enemy of Jamaican national interests. Although his strategy worked insofar as he won the 1959 election, Manley had backed himself into a corner from which he could never find a way out. Then at the PNP's annual conference in October 1959 Manley tried to identify a specifically PNP policy on Federation: "We conceive that in the long run there are real and great advantages in federation but those advantages cannot be accepted at the price of anything that would destroy or injure us in a fundamental respect."[54] Not exactly a ringing endorsement.

A series of inter-governmental conferences (September 1959 and May 1961, with ministerial committees in between) gradually dug Federation into a deeper and deeper hole as positions became further entrenched and personal relationships increasingly bitter. In Jamaica the JLP abandoned any pretence of being in favour in principle of Federation and just argued that if Jamaica couldn't get its way it needed to go it alone. Domingo inserted a large paid advertisement in *The Gleaner* on 29 October 1959 asking "Do You Want Jamaica To Remain in the Federation?" and calling for a referendum [#43]. He kept up his letter-writing too, correcting PNP minister Wills Isaacs for suggesting that he had "abused" Federation and responding to arguments by supporters of Federation such as Frank Hill.[55] He was also not above pointing out the contradiction between the Federationists' motto about "dwelling in unity" and the insults traded by Grantley Adams and Eric Williams.[56] And then, in late 1959, he managed to make a truly significant mark on the proceedings, as seen in #42 and #44, after attending a talk given by Adams in New York.

* * *

54. "Advantages in Federation", *The Gleaner*, 26 October 1959, p. 1.

55. W. A. Domingo, "Abusing Federation", *The Gleaner*, 28 November 1959, p. 10; "Federal Status", *The Gleaner*, 2 January 1960, p. 6: "I even taxed my patience to wade through the series of articles on the subject by Mr Frank Hill in your columns. The articles represented a Niagara of words and a Sahara of thought despite the effort to appear learned."

56. W. A. Domingo, "Dwelling Together", *The Gleaner*, 2 April 1960, p. 6.

The ante was considerably upped in January 1960 when Manley took some of his ministers to London to ascertain from the British government its attitude should Jamaica, finding it impossible to settle its differences with its partners, demand to be allowed to leave the Federation and seek dominion status on its own. After some hesitation, a "potential permit to secede" was granted and Manley could announce on his return home that "If we cannot reach early agreement, Jamaica will leave Federation and will seek independence on her own."[57] Once again Manley had narrowed the gap between himself and Bustamante—while weakening the Federal foundations. And once again Manley found himself immediately outflanked when Bustamante refused to nominate a JLP candidate for a vacant Federal seat and announced the JLP's irrevocable decision to oppose Federation and to campaign to take Jamaica out, thus providing a clear dividing line between the two parties.[58] Blindsided, Manley rashly announced a referendum on whether Jamaica should stay or leave, a decision which served to worsen his already deteriorating relationships with Adams and Williams, the very people he needed to negotiate with in order to reach a deal that he could present to the Jamaican people. It was a tall order and probably doomed to failure, particularly since, while those negotiations were taking place—inevitably fractious, inevitably reported in detail in the Jamaican press—Bustamante was out on the campaign trail, a full year ahead of the PNP.

Returning from a Lancaster House meeting where the details for a revised Federation had been hammered out into a White Paper, Manley laid a motion to accept them before the Jamaican House of Representatives on 6 July 1961. After an acrimonious debate lasting four days, the JLP sprung another surprise when one of its members proposed an amendment "rejecting the London report and requesting HMG to take the necessary steps to introduce legislation to grant Jamaica independence on May 23, 1962, and to seek admission for Jamaica in the British Commonwealth as a Dominion". The amendment was always going to be rejected, but it had the great electoral advantage of enshrining Bustamante as the first leader to call for immediate independence, an enshrinement particularly galling for Manley, whose call for *eventual* independence (scorned at the time by Bustamante) had been seen as seditious by the British authorities 20 years previously. Bustamante's masterstroke turned the negative of opposing Federation into the positive of promoting Jamaican independence: "It is universally known that I am opposed to Jamaica continuing in the Federation, and I invite all those who agree with me, regardless of party affiliation, to join in this movement, which is intended to protect Jamaica."[59] PNP members and supporters—such as Domingo and Roberts—were thereby licensed to park their party loyalty until the referendum had taken place, even if they had to hold their nose to do so.

57. "Early Agreement, or Out Goes Jamaica", *The Gleaner*, 19 January 1960, p. 1.
58. See the account in Seaga, *My Life and Leadership. Volume 1*, pp. 58–59.
59. "JLP Move: Jamaica as Dominion", *The Gleaner*, 12 July 1961, p. 1.

Only now was the referendum date announced: 19 September 1961. Domingo campaigned hard. Since the PNP was backing a "yes" vote, he had little option but to take issue with their propaganda, so his letters to *The Gleaner* continued apace.[60] The JLP fought a hard and disciplined campaign, whereas the PNP provided only lukewarm support for Manley. On a 60.87 per cent turnout, "no" received 54.1per cent of the votes, "yes" 45.9 per cent. The West Indies Federation was dissolved on 23 May 1962. Jamaica became independent on 6 August 1962. The JLP had won the general election on 10 April, so Bustamante became the first prime minister of independent Jamaica. Domingo was among the first to analyse the situation.[61]

Although Roberts and Domingo were both present in Kingston on 6 August 1962, even Manley's biographer notes that the independence celebrations, and Manley's speech at them, "deliberately excluded the patriots", such as Domingo, Roberts, Brown, O'Meally, and Cox: "Instead the ceremonies were characterized by a narrow parochialism and a continuing colonial reverence."[62] It was left for Domingo to honour Roberts after his friend died soon after independence [#48] and for him to offer a final summary of the significance of the JPL.[63]

* * *

Over his last years there can be seen in some of Domingo's letters a concern with establishing the genealogy of Jamaican independence, a concern that begins to overlap with the idea of national heroism. As could be anticipated, it was the pre-eminence of Marcus Garvey that Domingo wished to contest. The modern discussion of national heroes was given its impetus by a book published in 1952 by Domingo's JPL colleague W. Adolphe Roberts, although in fact the idea has a long history in Jamaica, going back at least as far as 1899 (during the childhood of both Domingo and Roberts), when *The Gleaner* ran a prize competition to identify Jamaica's greatest men (prize: 5s).[64] Part of Frank Cundall's work at the Institute of Jamaica involved his production of the *Biographical Annals of Jamaica*, another early example of the importance of significant lives to the writing of Jamaican history, later supplemented by a member of black middle class, Rev. C. A. Wilson's *Men of Vision*, "written from the Negro standpoint", with its early recognition of Garvey.[65]

60. For example, "Comments on PNP Pamphlet", *The Gleaner*, 22 August 1961, p. 12, and "Independent Nation Only Outside the Federation", *The Gleaner*, 2 September 1961, p. 4.
61. W. A. Domingo, "PNP Defeat", Letter to *The Gleaner*, 25 April 1962, p. 15.
62. Arnold Bertram, *N. W. Manley and the Making of Modern Jamaica*, Kingston, Jamaica: Arawak, 2016, p. 33.
63. W. A. Domingo, "The Jamaica Progressive League: Jamaica's Outpost of Goodwill and Friendship in the United States", *Souvenir Journal: 2nd Anniversary Celebration of Jamaica Independence*, New York: Jamaica Progressive League (of New York), 1964, p. 11.
64. "Jamaica's Greatest Men", *The Gleaner*, 23 December 1899, p. 11.
65. Frank Cundall, *Biographical Annals of Jamaica: A Brief History of the Colony Arranged*

From its beginnings the JPL had a strong cultural dimension—inevitable with Roberts at the helm: one of its announced aims was to encourage the study of the history, geography, and literature of Jamaica. Once the JPL(K) was up and running it established a cultural programme called "Jamaicanizing Jamaica", which aimed to show public honour to a group of distinguished islanders. Edward Jordon was first up. In December 1938, celebrating the founding of the PNP, Domingo proclaimed that "The spirit of Jordon, whose statue adorns East Parade, is not dead", associating that pioneer with contemporary nationalist politics on the island.[66] Research was undertaken, a pamphlet was prepared, and a wreath was laid on his statue on 8 February 1940 with Norman Manley as principal speaker.[67] And it was indeed in front of this statue that Manley delivered several of his early speeches as leader of the PNP.[68] Paul Bogle was second in line, but Governor Richards's Emergency Regulation Act put to a stop to all that kind of nonsense, so the programme shuddered to a halt, only resuming in earnest after Roberts's return to Jamaica in October 1949 and his publication in 1952 of *Six Great Jamaicans: Biographical Sketches*.[69] Roberts's six were Edward Jordon, George William Gordon, Robert Love, Bishop Enos Nuttall, Thomas Henry MacDermot, and Herbert George de Lisser. We've encountered five of them already. The other, Enos Nuttall, was a Lancastrian who had come to Jamaica in 1862 as a lay missionary but was ordained into the Anglican church, of which he eventually became an archbishop, acting as a figure of huge moral authority on the island.

Probably the most significant of these six for this postwar period was Gordon, the only one who had given his life for the cause, and so a genuine martyr as well as a patriot. Gordon's reputation had been boosted in the mid-1930s by Sydney Olivier's revisionist work, which laid the blame for the Morant Bay killings at the door of Governor Eyre.[70] It perhaps wouldn't be too fanciful to see Jordon and Gordon (the two "great Jamaicans" of Roberts's six who had died before his birth) as the chosen JPL ancestors—though presumably Roberts didn't wish Gordon's fate on his friend Domingo. Roberts chose no living figures, which effectively ruled out all participants in contemporary Jamaican politics, although his

as a Guide to the Jamaica Portrait Gallery, Kingston, Jamaica: Institute of Jamaica, 1904. This included several free coloured men, including Edward Jordon. C. A. Wilson, *Men of Vision: A Series of Biographical Sketches of Men Who Have Made Their Mark upon Our Time*, Kingston, Jamaica: *The Gleaner*, 1928.

66. "League Group Study Life of Edward Jordon", *The Gleaner*, 30 October 1939, p. 4.

67. "City Folk Pause to Pay Tribute to Great Jamaican", *The Gleaner*, 9 February 1940, p. 1. In May, Roberts and J. E. Clare McFarlane talked about Jordon at a meeting of the JPL ("News in Brief", *The Gleaner*, 23 May 1939, p. 6).

68. Matthew J. Smith, "Introduction", in W. Adolphe Roberts, *Six Great Jamaicans: Biographical Sketches* [1952], Kingston, Jamaica: Ian Randle, 2018, pp. xi–xvi, at xiii.

69. On the context in which Roberts's book was published, see ibid., pp. xi–xvi.

70. Sydney Olivier, *The Myth of Governor Eyre*, London: L. & V. Woolf, 1933. See Howard Johnson, "From Pariah to Patriot: The Posthumous Career of George William Gordon", *New West Indian Guide*, 81, nos 3/4 (2007), pp. 197–218.

postscript does mention relatively recently deceased figures who had made "noteworthy" contributions, among them S. A. G. Cox, J. A. G. Smith, and Marcus Garvey. In addition, as a historian and a liberal nationalist, Adolphe Roberts had a regional and ecumenical notion of "greatness". In the early 1950s he lectured extensively, often in small towns and villages, about the history of Jamaica and the Caribbean region, with Toussaint, Bolívar, and Martí as his lodestars, about whom he'd published essays in 1949.[71]

The publication of *Six Great Jamaicans* in March 1952 seems to have sparked the PNP member Fred L. B. Evans to institute a debate in the Jamaican House of Representatives on his resolution to recommend that the birthdays of J. A. G. Smith and Marcus Garvey be observed as public holidays.[72] Norman Manley spoke warmly in favour of the two individuals, but proposed an extension of the idea:

> I wonder whether some method cannot be devised, that a holiday can be created for national figures in Jamaica—in honour of more men than one; that a roll of fame which might depend on two conditions, one, that they are dead and two, their elevation to that historical roll of fame is made by resolution in this House, something perpetually remembered by succeeding generations.[73]

That year *The Gleaner* ran a series of articles under the heading "National Heroes", many of which defended or attacked the idea that Marcus Garvey offered the pre-eminent exemplar.[74] In his long August 1952 letter to Adolphe Roberts, Domingo opined that the work of Garvey and Smith "was transient" with respect to Jamaica and in comparison with that of Love, Cox, Jordon, Gordon, and Sam Sharpe [#39].

As early as September 1948 Ken Hill, then mayor of Kingston, had proposed the erection of a statue of Marcus Garvey. The reasoning read, in part: "WHEREAS THE LATE MARCUS GARVEY, through his teaching and his work first fired the souls of the negroes of the British Caribbean with racial pride and national con-

71. See Roberts, *These Many Years*, pp. 322–323.

72. "Garvey, Smith Memorial Decision by House", *The Gleaner*, 9 July 1952, pp. 1, 3, and 5. Frederick L'Overture Barca Evans (1908–1985). Both Smith and Garvey had died relatively recently (in 1942 and 1940 respectively) and so were perhaps more prominent in people's minds than Roberts's examples; but they were also both darker-skinned than all apart, perhaps, from Love, so Evans may have been making a point. Evans (who styled himself "Slave-Boy" and was notorious for his multiple suspensions from the House) soon resigned from the PNP in protest against the expulsion of the 4 Hs and (re-)formed the United Negro Party, which had been started in 1943 by H. C. Buchanan.

73. "The Past and Nation-Building" [1952], in *Norman Washington Manley and the New Jamaica: Selected Speeches and Writings, 1938–68*, edited with notes and introduction by Rex Nettleford, Kingston, Jamaica: Longman Caribbean, 1971, pp. 113–115, at 115.

74. For example, Ranny Williams, "Selection a Very Intimate Matter", *The Gleaner*, 30 July 1952, p. 8; and Peter Simple, "It Seems to Me", *The Gleaner*, 28 July 1952, p. 8.

sciousness and thereby assisted greatly in laying the foundations of the national movements now striving for self-determination for the people of this area ...".[75] The following year, during a discussion in the Legislative Council on his motion for legislation to preserve the island's historical buildings and monuments, P. M. Sherlock, secretary of the Institute of Jamaica, spoke, in the context of the importance of a sense of history for creating national unity, in favour of the erection of a Garvey statue, noting his achievement in "giving the Negro a sense of pride in himself and his forefathers": it was right, therefore, that "his memory should be perpetuated".[76] All this was well and good, but financial support was not forthcoming: the public subscription proved meagre, while Bustamante was reluctant to provide any funds, perhaps because Hill, the prime mover, was still a prominent member of the PNP. Nonetheless, Hill's motion was probably the first articulation of two misconceptions about Garvey: that he fired the people of the West Indies with national consciousness, and that he had thereby helped lay the foundations for the national movements (such as the PNP) currently striving for self-determination.

In July 1954 the JLP government again turned down a request from the Kingston Corporation for funding for a statue, prompting the English journalist Gordon St Clair Scotter to ask, "what did Marcus Garvey ever do for this country, beyond taking a great deal of money out of it, and then going to live in England?"[77] Outrage was relatively sparse, though Edna Manley—writing in support of her fellow sculptor Alvin Marriot, who had a bust of Garvey looking for a site—spoke of him as "a great pioneer of his people".[78] Eventually funds were granted for the bust of Marcus Garvey to be erected in King George VI Memorial Park, and it was unveiled on 4 November 1956 amid no controversy whatsoever. The governor, Sir Hugh Foot, attended, as did the Bishop of Kingston, politicians of all stripes (including Bustamante), a delegation of the UNIA from the USA, and the second wife, Amy Jacques Garvey. Norman Manley (now chief minister after the PNP had won the 1954 elections) read an address; Edna Manley unveiled the bust.[79] Ironically, it was as if Garvey were being inducted *post mortem* into the Jamaican establishment.

During the late 1950s and early 1960s the JLP's disenchantment with Federation had the consequence of making it a more nationalist party, with its cultural policies not obviously distinguishable from those of the PNP, and so for a few years a cultural moratorium prevailed. The Jamaica National Trust Commission

75. "Statue of Marcus Garvey Proposed", *The Gleaner*, 10 September 1948. p. 5.
76. "Monuments: Bishop Gibson Urges Govt. Money Aid", *The Gleaner*, 11 November 1955, pp. 1 and 7, at 7.
77. G. St C. Scotter, "Today", *The Gleaner*, 6 July 1954, p. 8.
78. Edna Manley, "A Head of Garvey", *The Gleaner*, 8 July 1954, p. 8.
79. "Garvey Bust Unveiled", *The Gleaner*, 5 November 1956, p. 14; "CM: Garvey Liberated Spirit of Freedom", *The Gleaner*, 8 November 1956, p. 12.

was established in 1958 (renamed Jamaica National Heritage Trust in 1985), with the bill to establish it receiving warm support from both political parties.[80]

In these years Garvey did not feature largely in public debates, but Domingo was drawn into further discussions of his long-time antagonist by epistolary exchanges with the English businessman Christopher Hills [#45 and #46] and with Garvey's widow Amy Jacques Garvey [#47]. The game-changing move came in 1964 when Garvey's remains were returned to Jamaica from England and re-interred in a new monument in King George VI Memorial Park, which was renamed National Heroes Park. In his last piece of published writing, Domingo urged "sane, dispassionate" reflection before Jamaica committed itself to turning Marcus Garvey into Jamaica's first and pre-eminent national hero [#49], but his words were ignored.

* * *

Figure 10 W. A. Domingo in later life. (*The Gleaner*, 21 August 2011, p. F10)

Domingo's second marriage had taken place in 1957 to Mabel Hunte, a nurse. A son, Wilfred B. Domingo, was born the following year. One last campaign remained, against the US quota system pertaining to Jamaican immigration, which Domingo thought should be lifted once Jamaica became independent.[81] As his daughter Yolanda explained, the JPL led the fight and Domingo wrote the

80. "National Trust Bill Passed", *The Gleaner*, 12 December 1958, p. 14.
81. See the account "Notes and Jottings on the League's Struggle with Immigration", in *Souvenir Journal: 2nd Anniversary Celebration of Jamaica Independence*, New York: Jamaica Progressive League (of New York), 1964, p. 16.

case that was eventually accepted by the US senate, although she blamed the exertions of the campaign for the stroke which incapacitated him in 1964.[82] He died on 14 February 1968, and was buried five days later in Woodlawn Cemetery in the Bronx.[83] His death was reported on the front page of *The Gleaner*.[84] Norman Manley's warm tribute followed a few days later, along with reports of Domingo's well-attended funeral in New York, where the eulogy was delivered by the Jamaican ambassador to the USA.[85] W. A. Domingo was awarded the Jamaican Order of Distinction on 17 October 1977.

82. Yolanda Domingo, "U. S. Immigration Visas", Letter to *The Gleaner*, 13 September 1966, p. 10.
83. Woodlawn Cemetery, 4199 Webster Avenue, The Bronx, New York 10470, Cliff plot, range 23, grave 36.
84. "W. A. Domingo Dies in New York", *The Gleaner*, 16 February 1968, p. 1.
85. Norman Manley, "One of the Dedicated Men", *The Gleaner*, 22 February 1968, p. 3; "Jamaica Still Needs Courage, Faith of Wilfred Domingo", *The Gleaner*, 23 February 1968, p. 19. "W. A. Domingo: A Eulogy by Ambassador Johnson", in Noel White, *The Contribution of West Indian Immigrants to the Negro Community of the United States*, MA dissertation, Teachers College, Columbia University, 1968, pp. 101–104. Anthony Johnson (1938–2021), JLP senator and Jamaican ambassador to the USA.

37

The Truth about Jamaica

January 1949

In the autumn of 1948 the African-American magazine *Ebony*—in an attempt to boost its income from travel companies—sent the eminent black poet Langston Hughes to enjoy a holiday in Jamaica and to become the latest in a long line of northern black visitors to Jamaica to decide on brief acquaintance that the island was free of the colour prejudice that stained the life of the USA.[1] Domingo put him right.[2]

Ebony, 4, no. 3 (January 1949), pp. 7–8

It was with mixed feelings that I read Langston Hughes's article on "Jamaica" in your November issue. As a native Jamaican who lived in this country for a generation and who spent six years in Jamaica, only returning to the United States 14 months ago, I think I am qualified to discuss some of the social conditions which exist in the island.

With everything Mr Hughes says about the beauty of the island, I agree. There is perhaps no more beautiful spot on earth. It is when Mr Hughes attempts to discuss the existence or non-existence of color prejudice that I find myself in total disagreement with him. There is color prejudice in Jamaica. To the average American of color, the color line in Jamaica is not obvious, to use Mr Hughes's word. But that does not preclude the existence of a color line. Nor does the fact that Mr Hughes did not *run into a color line* make convincing proof that there is none. Surely, it should not be strange to find the immigration officials, doctor, and health nurse at the airport colored in a country with 98 percent of its people of some degree of African blood.

Mr Hughes remarked about the large swimming pool at Myrtle Bank Hotel in which "tan-skinned youngsters from the 'better families' disported themselves". I know a story about that pool. I will gamble that Mr Hughes did not see a single *black* individual in the pool. About three years ago, a black man, who edits a

1. Langston Hughes, "Jamaica: Easy-to-Reach Paradise Offers Perfect Prejudice-Free Vacation Spot", *Ebony*, 4, no. 1 (November 1948), pp. 44–48.
2. The Hughes/Domingo exchange is discussed in Tiffany M. Gill, "The Precarities of International Travel", *Modern American History*, 4 (2021), pp. 213–218.

leading publication in Jamaica, knowing that his European advertising man swam in the pool regularly, attempted to do likewise and was barred. As he told me the story, he got a lot of explanations after he had protested and was finally told that he could swim in the pool, but it was clear that the concession was made only because the editor was in a position to give adverse publicity to the occurrence.[3]

It is clear that Mr Hughes in his brief stay in Jamaica did not hear stories of vicious discrimination based solely on color which took place in some of the night clubs he named—Morgan's Cove, Springfield, Glass Bucket, and Wickie Wackie. Recently, four American Negroes, three light-brown skin and one black (the latter a woman), went to Morgan's Cove, which by the way was owned by a black man. The three lighter persons were admitted without question, but the woman was denied admittance. In regard to the Wickie Wackie, about a month ago, the Jamaican *Gleaner* published an item which revealed that some dark-skinned Jamaicans of the "better class", one of them a medical student, were denied admittance to the club. The manager of the club had the audacity to publish a letter in the *Gleaner* in which he admitted that discrimination exists, but he tries, like so many Jamaicans, to pretend that it is a matter of "class". May I ask how can the class of a person be known if he is dressed suitably and has the money to pay his entrance?

I repeat. There is color prejudice in Jamaica. It is not only the whites who show prejudice but the people of mixed blood exert it against those who are darker in complexion. An American Negro, if he is not black or very dark, if well-dressed and possessed of money, can go anywhere the visibly mixed Jamaican can go. In fact, he is welcomed. But the dark-skinned American Negro (especially a woman) is likely to run into embarrassing situations. In America a person who is known to be a Negro (which means he may be as dark as Schuyler or as fair-skinned as Walter White) may go to social gatherings of his people without feeling he is not wanted on account of his color.[4]

What I have written must not be taken to mean that American Negroes of all shades of complexion cannot have a really good time in Jamaica, but they must not go there believing there is no color line. A whole lot will depend on the complexion of the individual.

W. A. DOMINGO
New York, NY

---

3. See Krista Thompson, "Diving into the Racial Waters of Beach Space in Jamaica: Tropical Modernity and the Myrtle Bank Hotel's Pool", in her *An Eye For The Tropics: Tourism, Photography, and Framing the Caribbean Picturesque*, Durham, NC: Duke University Press, 2006, pp. 204–251.

4. A good friend of Domingo's, George Samuel Schuyler (1895–1977), was a black writer, journalist, and social commentator. He and Domingo were both socialists in the 1920s, but Schuyler later became known his outspoken political conservatism.

38
PNP Plan
November 1949

Domingo's loyalty to the PNP showed no immediate sign of waning as the 1949 elections approached. He continued to use the letter columns of *The Gleaner* to press the view from New York in favour of Norman Manley. His belief, however, that the PNP was "on the threshold of a sweeping victory" was way off the mark as the JLP achieved its second election success, albeit with a reduced majority.

The Gleaner, 29 November 1949, p. 12

THE EDITOR. Sir:—Along with thousands of other Jamaicans in New York City I have been following the progress of the campaign of the People's National Party and the Bustamante Party in the elections which will take place in a month's time. Having to depend on reports from friends in the homeland, the opinions of acquaintances recently arrived here from there, and on what appears in your columns and other publications in Jamaica, I am heartened to believe that the PNP is on the threshold of a sweeping victory which will relegate the present regime into a long-deserved oblivion.

Naturally, I am a partisan of the PNP. Indeed, most Jamaicans here who take any interest in the politics of their native country are supporting Mr Manley and his associates. Jamaicans in this country usually feel chagrined and embarrassed over the fact that the first government under the new constitution was of the type which they now ardently and prayerfully hope will be decisively beaten at the polls on 20 December.

I have been privileged to read the pamphlet *Plan for Progress* which the PNP has issued as its campaign document. It is a masterpiece of sane, purposeful, and moderate thinking. The Plan is splendidly thought out and each part dovetails into the rest with the sole object of producing conditions which will increase the productivity of the country and enhance the well-being of its inhabitants. The Plan is in striking contrast to the wild and misleading statements contained in the advertisements of the Labour Party which appear in your columns so frequently. The latter deal in generalities and emphasise the alleged fear of its authors of what they call "Communism" and "Socialism". Unless the average voter is to be influenced by slogans, it is difficult to believe that such an individual will follow the unchartered, unspecific lead of Mr Bustamante. What has Mr Bustamante to offer in a detailed and specific way as an alternative to the Plan of the PNP? Mere denunciation is not enough. Simply calling names is not enough. This has been illustrated in America.

The late President F. D. Roosevelt was denounced by practically all of the American press. He was called "Socialist" and "Communist" by his political opponents because he put the interests of the masses above those of the few, and he was elected to office four times—a record in US history! His successor, President Truman, a year ago was opposed by the same forces. He was denounced as supporting what is derisively referred to as the "Welfare State", and he confounded everybody by winning the election. Only a couple of weeks ago, the majority of the New York press supported John Foster Dulles for the Senate against ex-Governor Lehman and the voters disregarded the charges of "Socialism", "Communism", and "Welfare State" and voted Mr Lehman into office! In England, despite the howlings of Winston Churchill and his aristocratic friends and all the attacks on the Labour government for nationalising industry, it is significant that the Labour Party has not lost a single by-election—this despite austerity and the rest of it in England.

The lesson to be derived from the instances cited in the last paragraph seems clear. The people are not concerned about name-calling. They are interested in improving their condition of life. Jamaicans are no different. They made the mistake of voting Bustamante and his crew into power, and now they have the opportunity to undo the harm they unwittingly did to themselves and their country by putting power into the hands of men who are totally unfitted by training to handle the affairs of state in a modern age.

Returning to the programme of the PNP, it seems to me that anyone who reads it objectively, without prejudice one way or the other, but who has the welfare of the country at heart, must confess that the Plan is a carefully considered, co-ordinated blueprint designed to improve the lot of the majority of the population. The issues of the campaign are joined. Name-calling, distortions of truth, violence, beclouding of issues, none of these must be allowed to sway the electorate from its duty of sending to office men who are trained, men with a comprehensive and co-ordinated plan, men who are not interested in seeking glory, self, and power, men whose sole interest is devotion to the uplift of their countrymen, who are animated by the ideal of the "greatest good for the greatest number".

I am, etc.,
W. A. DOMINGO
913 Jackson Avenue
New York 56, NY
21 November

39

Reconnecting with Roberts

August 1952

After Domingo had returned to New York in August 1947, it was Roberts's turn to spend a considerable amount of time on the island: two short visits in 1946 and 1948 were followed by his permanent move back to Kingston in October 1949. In his autobiography Roberts says that he was asked by many people to form a new political party to fight the general election of 1949. He had certainly been unimpressed by the growing socialist tendencies apparent in the PNP and by Manley's prevarication on the push for self-government. But he knew that any party he led would only take votes from the PNP, allowing Bustamante an easy ride. His relationship with Manley cooled, especially when the PNP fell into line with the British push for federation. Instead, Roberts threw himself into his role as a cultural nationalist, succeeding Una Marson as editor of the Pioneer Press, to which he contributed *Six Great Jamaicans*, to which Domingo refers. Domingo and Roberts had clearly not been in touch for more than five years before this letter of reconnection, which raises issues of federation, national heroes, and immigration, three recurring themes in Domingo's writing over the next ten years. It also demonstrates Domingo's generosity of spirit, both to a colleague like Roberts and to a political opponent such as De Lisser.

Letter to W. Adolphe Roberts, 21 August 1952, WARA 2.3.5 [WARA = W. Adolphe Roberts Archive (MS 353), National Library of Jamaica]

615 East 168th St.
New York 56, NY
21 August 1952

Dear Roberts,

On several occasions since I returned to New York five years ago I planned to write to you, but for one reason or another deferred doing so until now. It would be impossible for me to remember all the important things which have occurred in or about Jamaica since my return, but I would be remiss in my duty as a Jamaican and one who is deeply interested in the future of the country if I did not refer to a few matters in which we are mutually interested, matters which are of current moment to the island.

Before entering the main subjects of this letter, I must congratulate you on your booklet *Six Great Jamaicans*. I bought several copies of the book and of some of the others, principally *Tales of Old Jamaica*, which I gave to friends.[1] I also gave the Schomburg Collection of the 135th Street Public Library a set of the books, for I feel that in any collection of Negro or West Indian literature Jamaica should be adequately represented. I should like to make a present to the Library of a copy of Arthur Nicholas's poems, but my friend in Jamaica who bought several copies for me told me that he cannot obtain any more.[2]

In regard to the booklet you wrote, I must congratulate you on the concise and interesting way in which you treated your subjects. Above all, the material was handled not from the English or imperial point of view but from that of Jamaica, as should always be. I feel sure that with enough circulation in the island and among Jamaicans everywhere a healthy national spirit will be developed and maintained. There is one thing I don't understand, namely, why the Pioneer Press has made no effort to tap the big colonies of Jamaicans in Panama and New York, especially the latter. Properly handled there should be a good market for the books.

I was particularly pleased that you included Dr J. Robert Love. I heard him speak when I was a boy. At that time he was losing his memory, but it was obvious that he was a man of great learning, enormous energy, and gifted with outstanding oratorical powers. That he was a patriot, maybe racial, it is true, is undeniable. You state that you did not know if he was married. I remember quite clearly that he was. I understood that his wife was a white woman, but I am not sure if she was American, although I assumed so. He had a son who returned to Florida after the death of his father.

Many years ago, I was with a group of colored Americans. Among them was a man named Kinloch who could not be told from a Caucasian. When he learnt that I was from Jamaica he told me that he was from Charleston, SC and that his grandmother was from Kingston. He asked me if I knew "Joe" Love in Jamaica, and when he told me that he meant Dr Love I said yes. Kinloch said that in his youth in the South Love was regarded as one of the finest theologians, pulpit orators, and race champions in Florida and Alabama. Another thing, McMillan of the Colony Club told me when I was in Jamaica that a relative of his had all the papers of Dr Love, so you may be able to get some more data on the Dr from that source.

1. W. Adolphe Roberts, *Six Great Jamaicans: Biographical Sketches*, Kingston, Jamaica: Pioneer Press, 1952; rpt, Kingston Jamaica: Ian Randle, 2018; Clinton V. Black, *Tales of Old Jamaica*, Kingston Jamaica: Pioneer Press, 1952.

2. Arthur Edward Nicholas (1875–1934), *Arcadia*, London: Books For Today, 1949.

I have had to defend your choice of De Lisser as a great Jamaican. Jamaicans here judge him not by his talents and industry but by the use that he put them to in relation to the masses of his country. I tell the people that whether or not we like his views, De Lisser was a man of considerable literary talent and that he loved Jamaica in his own way. That he had industry is beyond dispute. His novels, as I recall, *Jane* and *Susan Proudleigh*, were true pictures of the strata of Jamaican society that he set out to depict. His reporting on the US and on Panama in *The Gleaner* when I was a boy were, I believe, authentic. I enjoyed his *In Cuba and Jamaica*. We must recognize talent and ability for what they are and give due credit, regardless of our own prejudices.[3]

Your treatment of Gordon and Jordon is excellent, though brief in compass due to space limitations. The Anglo-Irish historian Justin McCarthy gives a short but informative account of the Morant Bay affair.[4] I hope that some day someone with the ability and properly armed with data will write the life of S. A. G. Cox. In all this pother over holidays for our so-called "patriots" I wonder why Sandy Cox has been left out. Here was a man of the upper middle class championing the cause of the lowly, oppressed, and despised black masses. I pay no attention to his motive. All I know is that he did a good job stirring up the national consciousness of Jamaicans; that he organized the Jamaica Club, the first island-wide political party in modern Jamaica; that he broke through the apathy of the black people, the backwardness of the peasants, and the supercilious opposition of the other classes and caused the election of Fred Evans to the Legislative Council; that he fought the evils of coolie labor; that he published a little paper, *Our Own*, modeled after the Irish Sinn Fein; that he sacrificed himself and his family for Jamaicans, and doing all these things, he made young Jamaic[ans] of the day think nationally and pointed out to them the value and true meaning of political power. I know all this for as a youngster Garvey and I were junior secretaries of the National Club.

I saw in the *Pittsburgh Courier*, a colored newspaper, that you had an article on the proposal to have a holiday specially dedicated to the memory of Garvey and Smith. I could write plenty on the subject, but I know people will say I am prejudiced, so I remain silent. But I agree with your thesis, which I understand is that holidays should be for men of really great stature, men who have contributed very definitely in measurable ways to the progress of their country. Mere local popularity of a period should not be enough. The work done by Jordon for Jamaican civil liberties entitles him to live forever in our history. So is the work of Cox and Gordon. A statue should be erected to the memory of Sam Sharpe who led the abortive slave rebellion in 1831, which uprising for human freedom quickened

3. Herbert G. de Lisser, *Jane: A Story of Jamaica*, London: Methuen, 1914; *Susan Proudleigh*, London: Methuen, 1915; *In Cuba and Jamaica*, Kingston, Jamaica: *The Gleaner*, 1910.

4. Probably referring to Justin McCarthy, *A History of Our Own Times*, New York: Harper & Brothers, 1880, vol. 2, pp. 307–325.

the freedom of our fathers.[5] We must be realistic and not be swayed by every passing sentiment. I know it is not expedient in the present political and racial climate of Jamaica to be outspoken on certain matters, but history should not be distorted or sacrificed on the altar of sentimentalism. (For personal reasons, please do not quote me on the subject of the holiday.) I believe that the work of Smith and Garvey was transient and not of such as to be regarded as having contributed anything of permanent value to Jamaica; but one must make concessions to emotions and sometimes to ignorance.

I come now to what I think should be regarded by you as the crowning event of your political career —the passage unanimously recently of a resolution in the House to set up a Constitutional Committee to prepare a self-government constitution for Jamaica for submission to the British government. That was an historic event. I will always give you the credit you deserve for the turn of events in Jamaican politics. A few of us, O'Meally, Burrell, and I, in particular, had for years bemoaned the colonial status of Jamaica with its humiliating connotations. I had written about the matter in the Negro press as early as about 1914, but it was left to you to give our discontent and dreams body and form by organizing the League. You it was who travelled to Jamaica at your own expense and converted Manley and today the fruits of your efforts are seen, even if you and those of us here who supported and aided you get no credit. It is enough that Jamaicans in so short a time should have been transformed from a docile, empire-loving, and unnationalistic people into a national community. I know, of course, that economic pressure, frustration with Britain, returned emigrants, and the great and self-sacrificing work of Manley and others contributed considerably to the new spirit. The events of 1938 hastened the growth of our consciousness, but the JPL, founded by us in New York, deserves the credit for giving the movement political direction.

Since I read about the unwonted and certainly welcome unity achieved by the House on such a basic issue as a new constitution, I have bombarded Jamaica with letters on the subject. I have written to the *Gleaner* (although I don't think the letter was published, for I oppose federation on general principles or as a condition previous for Jamaican freedom), Manley, Allen, Ken Hill, Nethersole, setting forth my views.[6] As yet none of those gentlemen has answered me, but I am hopeful as they are busy.

I don't know your present views but I think you used to be cold on the question of federation. You certainly put Jamaica's case and cause first in your thinking. If I am correct in this, you and I are in complete agreement. In the letters I wrote to Jamaica I implored the gentlemen not to allow the ideal of federation, whether its

5. Samuel Sharpe (1801–1832) was an enslaved Jamaican who led the 1831–32 Baptist War slave rebellion. He was proclaimed a National Hero of Jamaica in 1975.

6. Probably Edward V. Allen (1897–1966), PNP stalwart and member of the House of Representatives from 1949 to 1959.

realization for Jamaica will be good or bad, to interfere with our forward march to full autonomy. I maintain that the freedom of the country should not be conditioned by or rest on federation; that the moth-eaten arguments about poverty, size of territory and population, weakness, lack of experience, illiteracy, etc., should not interfere with our indefeasible right to be autonomous, just as are Israel (a desert), an artificially created nation, Iceland, a frozen wilderness, Lebanon, and other "small", "weak", "inexperienced", and "poor" countries.

To me federation may be of value to Jamaica in a different world, perhaps a Socialist world, but to waste time over such a controversial matter, especially with the two continental colonies opposed and with our people on the threshold of their national freedom, is to be poor strategists and poor Jamaicans, too. West Indies, I point out, is a geographical or regional term. There are several nations in the area, each with its particular history, customs, and interests. Only British Caribbeans, because of their British connections, argue for federation and become passionate about it. Dutch-, French-, and Spanish-speaking Caribbeans have no such movements among them. These people are realistic and have no foolish dreams on the subject. How much better it would be for British West Indians as a whole if instead of trying to make *one* nation they took the British classification of seven or six colonies in the area and each one fight for full freedom. The British are in the mood and cannot long deny any colonial people the right to be a dominion. All that is necessary is the will on the part of the colonial peoples, which means that they must be united. We in Jamaica are and should use the fact to gain *our* freedom now.

We should confront the British government with a fact. A constitution that demands not less than Puerto Rico and even more since we should as a dominion have control of our fiscal affairs and over our foreign relations would embarrass the British, and the Labor Party would have to support us. Now is the time to be audacious and more audacious. We have the necessary unity among ourselves.

But I am fearful that the PNP with its incomprehensible adherence to federation may, without sufficient thought or patriotism, allow federation to delay *our own* political progress. This will be bad, for even if we federate, Jamaica will be in the position of being tied to peoples with whom we have little or no contact in any way. The result will be that it will be like a convoy with Jamaica, the fastest ship, the pace-maker of the BWI [British West Indies], having its speed limited to that of the slowest ship in the convoy.

I know that Jamaica has rejected the Rance Committee recommendations. But when I was in Jamaica I noticed a tendency on the part of the PNP, because of its acceptance of federation, to make concessions which no sensible people should ever make. I refer to the basis of representation in the federal parliament in case federation becomes a fact. Rance proposed that Jamaica should have 16 of the 50 seats in the parliament although Jamaica has 40 percent of the population. On a proportional population basis we could be entitled to 20 seats. Why this generosity at our expense? Why penalize us for having the largest population? Why penalize us for our fecundity? Only fools would agree to making any concessions where representation is concerned.

Finally, a strong reason why we should have a genuine self-governing constitution is that by losing our colonial status we will be able to circumvent the McCarran Bill which limits us to a mere 100 persons per year to immigrate into the US. Colonial peoples are the only ones in this hemisphere who have quotas. The self-governing areas have no quotas, so if we become a dominion we automatically benefit by being able to emigrate to the US. At the very least the *status quo ante* of approximately 1,000 annually will be restored, but it might be quite possible to increase the number as we would have no quota and the number of immigrants admitted yearly is governed by the overall total which has never been used up.

This last matter is vital to Jamaica with some 24,000 seeking visas. You, Busta, Norman Sinclair, and thousands of Jamaicans have been immigrants.[7] America has meant much to us and to our dependents at home. It seems to me that we should do everything to re-open the door to America which led to opportunities and superior living for thousands and thousands of Jamaicans and which made it possible for hundreds of our people to acquire professions, wealth, education, and a standard of living not possible of attainment by them in any part of the British Empire.

I have discussed many subjects and done so with frankness. I would like your reactions and criticisms. By the way, if it is convenient, please send me your article on the Garvey-Smith holiday which I understand appeared in the Sunday *Gleaner*.

My health is none too good. X-rays have disclosed that I have a stomach ulcer. Age is taking its toll. I manage to get around just the same and people tell me I look well. Through the Jamaican papers I read of some of your local activities. I am sorry that this letter should be so lengthy, but I think the matters dealt with required some kind of detailed treatment. Give my regards to our mutual acquaintances.

Yours sincerely,
W. A. Domingo

I sent *Public Opinion* an article on Jamaica's right to self-government. I hope Fairclough will publish it. I was a bit mild, knowing his and the paper's attitude on federation.

---

7. Norman Sinclair (1900–1966), PNP member of the House of Representatives from 1944 to 1955.

40

British West Indian Federation: A Critique

August 1956

This pamphlet appeared in August 1956 with a preface by W. Adolphe Roberts. Domingo had 1,000 copies printed and sent 250 to Jamaica, 50 intended for politicians and prominent people, including members of the press corps, others for sale in bookshops. He asked Amy Jacques Garvey to help him find somebody to distribute them, while confessing that he was fighting a lost cause: "I harbor no illusions."[1] He also sent the pamphlet to W. E. B. Du Bois, asking if he would review it in the *National Guardian*. Du Bois didn't, eventually explaining that he was in favour of Federation and didn't want to write a negative review, to which Domingo's response was that he was all in favour of robust debate and wouldn't have taken it personally. He also mentions in this letter that he had sent copies of the pamphlet to both Forbes Burnham and Cheddi Jagan in British Guiana, which was just about to vote—and which rejected the opportunity to join the West Indies Federation.[2] The significance of Domingo's arguments in this pamphlet was underlined by the essay's reproduction in the autopsy on Federation edited by David Lowenthal and Lambrinos Comitas.[3] Domingo's old friend Richard B. Moore came close to blaming Domingo for the referendum result when he wrote in his own postmortem on Federation: "One of the worst things that happened was the distribution in Jamaica of two pamphlets written and sent from here [New York] by W. A. Domingo. In these pamphlets this former progressive advocate of federation now opposed it by appealing to the worst reactionary narrow, insular, and base passions of the most backward people of Jamaica."[4] In fact, of course, Domingo had *always* opposed federation.

---

1. W. A. Domingo, Letter to Amy Jacques Garvey, 17 August 1956, AJGP.
2. W. A. Domingo, Letter to W. E. B. Du Bois, 28 November 1956; W. E. B. Du Bois, Letter to W. A. Domingo, 11 June 1957; W. A. Domingo, Letter to W. E. B. Du Bois, 11 August 1957. All in W. E. B. Du Bois Papers, MS 312, Special Collections and University Archives, University of Massachusetts Amherst Libraries.
3. *The Aftermath of Sovereignty: West Indian Perspectives*, ed. David Lowenthal and Lambrinos Comitas, New York: Anchor, 1973, pp. 163–187.
4. "Caribbean Freedom and Nationhood", in Richard B. Moore, *Caribbean Militant in Harlem: Collected Writings 1920–1972*, ed. W. Burghardt Turner and Joyce Moore Turner, Bloomington, IN: Indiana University Press, 1988, pp. 292–305, at 298. Moore Turner repeats the error herself (p. 85).

British West Indian Federation: A Critique, Kingston, Jamaica: *The Gleaner*, 1956

With practically no opposition in the territories concerned, the British Caribbean islands, with the exception of the Virgin Islands, will be federated in 1958. The conditions under which this result was accomplished hampered the emergence of an informed opposition. Public discussion, the necessary prerequisite of political action in democratic communities, was virtually absent when the question of Federation was considered. Supporters of Federation had the "dice loaded in their favour" and refused or appeared unwilling to challenge dissident views. They assumed an attitude of lofty disdain for any opinion not in harmony with their own and ignored the mutterings of dissent which arose at a late stage. From the start the Federationists had the press and other media of publicity and propaganda on their side. These were either controlled by them or were generally favourable to the proposition that it was imperative for the British Caribbean territories to form some sort of a political union. In one instance, the Federationists went so far as to characterise some feeble last-minute questionings as communistic, implying that arguments and ideas are not to be assayed for their intrinsic worth but on the basis of their source.

Writing in his column in *Public Opinion*, a Jamaican weekly newspaper, a few months before the signing of the document which committed the islands to federate, Mr Michael Manley, journalist and prominent trade union organiser, son of Chief Minister Manley of Jamaica, admitted with what seemed to be a touch of doubt as to the wisdom of Federation, that the demand for a Federal union had no mass basis, that it was sponsored by politicians, and when finalised, will have been imposed by them. He deplored the fact that the bulk of the people to be affected knew very little about the subject and were indifferent. In effect, the inhabitants of the islands were being led, or driven, like sheep.[5]

Because of these circumstances the British West Indian population has been confronted with a *fait accompli*. How serious the result may be to them in the years ahead is shown by the reply given by Chief Minister Manley, as reported in *Public Opinion* of 28 April 1956. Asked if a unit could secede if it became dissatisfied with the workings of the Federation, Mr Manley answered, "I think not." In other words, the principal architect of Federation, an able and experienced lawyer, regarded the union as indissoluble. No provision is made for a trial period of even 25 years to test the value of the union to each of its disparate units.

Although the die has been cast, final ratification is yet to be made by the various legislatures, so an *ante mortem* should be in order. It might be possible even at this late date for some of the legislators who accepted the idea without appearing to have given it any critical study or to have made an appraisal of its possible

5. Michael Manley (1924–1997) was a later leader of the PNP and Prime Minister from 1972 to 1980 and from 1989 to 1992.

effects to stop and take that "sober second thought" considered important in personal affairs. Nothing is perfect and above critical examination. It should never be too late to correct a mistake.

West Indian proponents of Federation at no time, in Jamaica at any rate, courted or engaged in any full dress discussions in which the pros and cons of the subject were carefully assessed and the full play of controversy brought into operation. There was no careful, selfish, if you will, scrutiny or evaluation of the question from the point of view of the special interests of each colony. Public debate on the desirability or wisdom of Jamaica entering the Federation was discouraged and even resisted. The pros had a field day. Seemingly having long decided that some sort of union must *ipso facto* be beneficial to every unit, including their own, they proceeded with what was evidently their pre-determined plan.

From an unknown source this writer received a copy of *Freedom News Letter* from Jamaica by mail. In it is reported what purports to be the exact answer given by the Chief Minister of Jamaica to the question: "Don't you believe your government enjoys sufficient prestige and goodwill to allow the people to decide by referendum whether we join such a federation without achieving independence first?" Mr Manley is quoted as saying, "We can do anything but will not permit a referendum."

The quoted reply was made at a public lecture by Mr Manley under the auspices of the Jamaica Manufacturers' Association at the Carib Theatre in Kingston on 22 April 1956. It leaves no conclusion but that it was his irrevocable intention to foist Federation on Jamaica. Implicit in the answer to the question, which challenged the wisdom of Jamaica subordinating its own struggle for the fullest self-government in favour of Federation, is the fear that public discussion, the necessary, salutary, and inevitable concomitant of a referendum, might upset plans that already had been formulated. It is a sad, disheartening, and revealing commentary on the trend of Jamaican politics.

From time to time this writer persistently, but vainly, tried in the Jamaican press to lure Jamaican Federationists into a debate on the topic. Apparently ventilation of the subject was tabooed by them. It was not to be publicly examined in all its aspects, least of all from Jamaica's special point of view. It appears to be a case of, "We have spoken; there is no further discussion; the case is closed." Failure to provoke open discussion leaves one alternative—analyse the arguments and try to discover the motives and influences which appear to have induced Jamaican Federationists to include their country in the nascent union.

At the outset it must be made crystal clear that there is no intention of imputing or ascribing self-serving or ignoble motives to anyone. Nor is there any purpose [in] applying opprobrious terms, such as "tory", "traitor", "Communist", "reactionary", etc., to the defenders of Federation. Cold war epithets will find no place in this critique; but cold, dispassionate arguments will. It is only fair to assume that everyone acted and is acting in good faith.

The attitude of Jamaican Federationists, in the light of available evidence, cannot be regarded as based on a respect for and acceptance of the generally observed principles governing the adoption of a programme or a course of action likely to profoundly affect a country and its future population. Facts, logic, and the conclusions legitimately derivable from them appear not to be considered of the highest importance. This was demonstrated when Mr Manley declared to a group of Jamaicans in New York last winter, shortly after he had signed the document in London which committed Jamaica to be a member of the burgeoning Federation, that opponents of his action had "logic, arguments, and common sense" on their side, but lacked "faith". The inescapable inference is that Mr Manley and his supporters possess an abundance of "faith", but are perhaps destitute of sound logic and good argument for their cause. "Faith" is said to be necessary in matters of religion, but it is hardly a safe guide for political action of the sort envisaged by Federation. A famous American orator defined faith as "belief without evidence".[6]

The more West Indian Federationists, especially Jamaicans, defend their position for an overall Federation, the less convincing their arguments become. These questions naturally arise: Why should the islands federate? Should Jamaica and British Honduras, situated as they are geographically, be part of the Federation? Should Federation of a sort, even if considered desirable, take precedence over the attainment of self-government by each political unit of the British Caribbean? Should Federation, at best a dubious political grouping, be equated with or linked to self-government, a fundamental political and human right?

The usual glib answer is that unity means strength; that the units are each too small in area or population to be important in world affairs; that the inhabitants are "one people". It is not true that unity necessarily increases strength. It can seriously weaken some of its components. A chain, as is known, is as "strong as its weakest link". It does not become stronger by adding some "strong" links. The argument about size is indeed novel and will be dealt with later.

Is it true that West Indians are one people? The majority of them are of Negro ancestry with varying degrees of admixture with other races. Among these diverse peoples exist many sharp and ominous cleavages of class, colour, and race. It is impossible to wish this fact away. But even if the population was homogeneous to the ultimate degree in each colony, or in the colonies as a whole, that would not be a convincing reason for them federating with their far and near, insular and continental, neighbours in the area.

6. Ambrose Bierce: "Faith, n. Belief without evidence in what is told by one who speaks without knowledge, of things without parallel". First published in 1911, *The Devil's Dictionary* had been republished in 1957, which is perhaps when Domingo had read it or seen reviews.

The French, Germans, Italians, Poles, and Spaniards occupy the same European land mass and are of the same race, meaning that by and large their observable physical resemblances are greater than their dissimilarities, but this "oneness" is not regarded by Europeans as a compelling reason for federating their nations. Similarly, the inhabitants of China, Mongolia, and several Asian countries occupy the same land mass and look so much alike physically as to be virtually indistinguishable from one another, but neither geographical proximity nor physical alikeness is regarded as constituting a substantial basis for uniting the several nations into one nation. Geographical contiguity and similarity of language and customs, in the cases of Canada and the United States, and Mexico and Guatemala, not to mention many countries of South America, are not rational grounds for individual nations agreeing to obliterate their independent national existence.

If being of Negro descent in the Caribbean is justification for federation, Haiti and the French West Indies, with their heavy Negro populations, eminently qualify for inclusion in any such union! The patent absurdity and unreality of this type of argument condemn it completely. Race is not a legitimate ground for federating nations or territories. The British and American Virgin Islands are in the Caribbean and the inhabitants are mostly English-speaking Negroes, but they will not be in the Federation, the former, although British, as a result of their own free choice. To insist that race or language should be the basis of a federation is to accept the dangerous and discredited Hitlerian doctrine of "race and nation", a Nazi concept which repudiated the principles of democracy and was itself repudiated in a bloody holocaust. It is unbelievable that any sane person, cognisant of the history of Latin America, whose oneness of religion also exists, would seriously suggest that these nations sink their national individualities and federate. As a matter of history, be it noted, the Central American Republics were politically united in their early existence, but national characteristics and conflicting interests developed, resulting in defederation.

What, then, is the discernible driving force that actuates West Indian politicians? That force seems to be the long connection of the territories with Great Britain. It is significant that of all the Caribbean peoples, it is only among the British-controlled ones that there is any agitation for regional federation. Limitation of the agitation to one segment of peoples of the area excludes any other conclusion than that the special attitude is primarily due to their peculiar conditioning.

An understanding of the psychological aspects of the question offers the only feasible explanation why colonies as far apart as 1,000 miles, separated by water, as are Jamaica and Trinidad, were urged by their leaders and encouraged by the British government to federate. The motivation could not be cultural or historical for there is no uniform culture, if any special culture at all, in the British West Indies. As for a common history, there is none except insofar as the islands are the colonial possessions of England. Dominica, St Lucia, and Grenada have been under French rule and until this day the inhabitants, as well as of Trinidad, speak a French *patois* and retain vestiges of French culture and customs. Every island or colony has its own history with which the inhabitants are naturally familiar; but only a few outside scholars—specialists—are likely to be interested enough to study individual insular histories. Ignorance of Jamaica is as profound among Trinidadians as is ignorance of Trinidad among Jamaicans.

Identity of economic interests does not exist among the units. On the contrary, they produce practically the same primary agricultural commodities and seek the same foreign markets; thus in reality they are competitors. Each wants, because of understandable internal reasons, to increase its production. Competition, or the effort of each unit to sell more goods to the same customers, is likely to be intensified. It is the natural aim of each colony to industrialise to the limit of its resources; but this normal and laudable objective will pose severe problems which must ultimately lead to friction inside the union. It seems, therefore, that the urge for federation which will soon be effectuated by West Indian politicians rests on no firmer foundation than the fact that the colonies have been tied to Britain, their political "motherland", for a long period of time.

There are several federations extant. The United States, Canada, Australia, Switzerland are notable examples of such political arrangements. In each of these cases the component units occupy the same landmass and are contiguous. There is no separation by water. Wherever islands are or were federated, the distance between one island and its nearest neighbour in the union is relatively insignificant. This is true of the Windward and Leeward Islands in the British West Indies. For centuries there has been considerable inter-island trade and travel between the two island-federations. Movement of peoples in between the two groups of islands and, for that matter, in the eastern sector of the British West Indies, has been practically unhindered. On the other hand, Jamaica and British Honduras, situated far to the west, are virtually isolated from the eastern colonies, continental and insular. There is little travel or communication between the two sectors, consequently few family ties exist between the peoples of the two areas—east and west. Because of their proximity to each other, and the movement of peoples within the eastern colonies, numerous family connections exist. Thus a Barbadian may have close relatives who were born in Trinidad, St Lucia, and British Guiana. Jamaican family ties are with Cuba, Central America, and the United States.

The British government realistically recognised the ineluctable fact of geography when it federated the Leeward and Windward Islands separately, although at one time they were federated together. The federation had the distinction of being logical and practical. It was not synthetic. It facilitated, as was doubtless intended, administration. The second realistic recognition of the physical facts of the area was when Colonel Oliver Stanley, then Secretary of State for the Colonies, sent a despatch to the West Indies on 14 March 1945, stating the willingness of the Imperial government to support some sort of federation. In the document, the Colonial Office suggested consideration of one Federation to include all the colonies or two Federations—one, western, presumably composed of British Honduras and Jamaica, the other, obviously consisting of the colonies in the east, including the mainland territory of British Guiana.[7]

By advancing the idea of two federations the British government clearly suggested that an overall federation might not be desirable or be the best means of achieving unity. Obviously the British government is not likely to sanction, unless compelled by the determined action of the inhabitants of an area, any type of political union likely to weaken the economic grip of England on her colonies. England's policy, motivated by intelligent self-interest, most naturally is to make concessions when they are inevitable, with the objective of reducing as much of the financial responsibility as possible, while retaining the maximum economic and political advantages.

It is significant that West Indians at home and abroad completely ignored the suggestion for the creation of two federations. They argued with disarming simplicity that the "bigger the area, the better". They contended, and still contend, that a "new nation" of approximately 3,000,000 people is capable of cutting a more important figure in world affairs than two "new nations", each with a population of less than 2,000,000. Only an incorrigible optimist who is oblivious of the realities of the present-day world can exaggerate into a faith the future of any small and weak nation, whether it has ten or three million people. The irrefragable fact is that a small nation can hope to make an impression on world affairs only through the skill of its statesmen or if its territory contains products vitally needed by mankind.

Evidently the leaders, and perhaps the peoples, of the two mainland colonies have not been impressed by the logic or wisdom of joining the Federation. Neither race, language, culture, nor political attachment to England has, up to now, had much weight in deciding the conduct of British Guiana and British Honduras. How long this aloofness will continue is problematical, for the British government and the units to be federated are exerting maximum pressures on the two recalcitrant colonies in an effort to have them reverse their position.

Nothing better illustrates the indifference of West Indians in America regarding the political future of their islands than the damning fact that apart from the Jamaica Progressive League of New York, there is no organisation of West Indians in the metropolis dedicated solely to the task of securing self-government for any section of the British Caribbean. There are cricket, literary, and social clubs, religious and fraternal groups a-plenty, but only one political organisation in a population of over 200,000 West Indians in the United States. The Jamaica Progressive League was founded in 1936 by a group of Jamaicans in New York at the

7. *Closer Association of the British West Indian Colonies*, London: HMSO, 1947.

instance of W. Adolphe Roberts, poet, historian, and novelist, a Jamaican by birth. The objective of the League was clearly stated in its Declaration:

> Firmly believing that any people that has seen its generation come and go on the same soil for centuries is, in fact, a nation, the Jamaica Progressive League pledges itself to work for the attainment of self-government for Jamaica, so that the country may take its rightful place as a member of the British Commonwealth of Nations.

Nothing is said about federating with any other colony or island in the Caribbean. The Declaration is a forthright statement of intention. Nothing in it is opportunistic, equivocal, apologetic, or conditional. The establishment of Jamaica as a self-governing dominion with all its attributes was the aim. For this purpose the League worked and sacrificed. Its many early drives for funds to help the People's National Party in Jamaica were unconnected with anything not contained in the Declaration. Campaign and organisational funds were collected and sent to Jamaica for that specific purpose.

At this point it should be instructive and profitable to examine the ideas of West Indians in the United States who favour Federation—one Federation. The subject was not new in the eastern islands. It had often been bandied about. Discussion and advocacy of federation was a distinguishing feature of the politics of the area. That this should be so is understandable. The existence of the already-federated islands made the subject a foremost part of the political thinking of the sector. Jamaica manifested little interest in the controversy. Relative remoteness gave no urgency to the matter in the two western colonies, so they took no active part in it.

Paradoxically, one of the high priests of federation was a Jamaican, Dr Louis Meikle, who wrote a rambling and incoherent book on the subject some 50 years ago.[8] Dr Meikle had spent part of his early life in the United States at a time when annexations of the islands to the United States was being mooted for American strategic reasons. Appalled by the prevailing racial situation in the United States, he expressed his opposition to annexation by advocating federation. Dr Meikle spent the last years of his life in Trinidad.

The question of federation was for the first time definitely projected on the Jamaican political scene by Hon. T. Albert Marryshow of Grenada as part of a speech he delivered in Kingston in 1945.[9] An accomplished orator, Mr Marry-

8. Louis Meikle, *Confederation of the British West Indies vs. Annexation to the United States of America*, London: Sampson Low, 1912. On Meikle, see Eric D. Duke, "The Diasporic Dimensions of British Caribbean Federation in the Early Twentieth Century", *New West Indian Guide*, 83, nos 3 and 4 (2009), pp. 219–248, at 27–28.

9. On 23 November 1945. Marryshow was visiting Jamaica at the invitation of the PNP, so Domingo was presumably present: see "Mayor Gives Cocktail Party for Hon. Marryshow", *The Gleaner*, 24 November 1945, p. 16.

show's speech, couched in sentimental terms, evoked some emotional response, but local indifference soon reasserted itself. Mr Marryshow had long crusaded for federation in the columns of his weekly newspaper, *The West Indian*, which circulated almost entirely in the eastern islands. He had also frequently toured those islands and British Guiana to lecture on his favourite topic. The few Jamaicans who heard of federation in their island did so only in a vague manner. To them it was remote and unrelated to their destiny.

It is beyond successful contradiction that in the islands the inhabitants, as a general rule, regard themselves as Trinidadians, Barbadians, Jamaicans, Antiguans, etc., not as West Indians. This is particularly true of Jamaicans. Separated from the other colonies under the Union Jack by relatively large stretches of water, as are Jamaica and British Honduras, development of a genuine regional national feeling was next to impossible. At best the term "West Indian", even when restricted to the British insular possessions, is geographical, not national.

British Caribbean immigrants in the United States, as well as Bahamians, Bermudans, Guianese, and Hondurans are called West Indians. The last four groups of immigrants protest the designation as inaccurate, but the American majority fixed the pattern, so most of the immigrants sensibly accept the term, even though they know that Puerto Ricans, Haitians, and Dutch and French Caribbeans are, geographically speaking, West Indians.

This lumping together of all English-speaking Caribbeans in the United States has had the effect of creating a loose, superficial unity—an artificial oneness. The new-born and synthetic oneness generated an emotional support of Federation. Many Jamaicans, who never heard of Federation in their island, becoming "West Indians" in the United States, have been psychologised into accepting the new political concept without scrutiny. They seem to reason, if they reason at all, that since they are "West Indians", not Jamaicans, in America, it would be ideal if all the islands were united under one government.

Leadership of New York federationists is in the control of individuals from the eastern islands where the issue has been alive for generations. Many of these leaders hail from an existing federation. For the most part their islands are small (even in West Indian terms) and without any significant mineral resources. Only Trinidad, largest of the group, has any mineral wealth. Smallness of territory and lack of mineral potentialities tend to imbue the people with a sense of frustration and hopelessness. They can see no future for their countries unless they are attached to richer and larger units—hence their vehement advocacy of federating not only their closely situated islands, but all the British Caribbean colonies, seems necessary and logical to them. They see in Federation a source of borrowed strength and the means of easing population pressures through emigration to the other islands, thereby effecting their own insular improvement and salvation.

A British Colonial Office-sponsored conference met at Montego Bay, Jamaica in 1947 to discuss West Indian federation. Representatives from all the Caribbean colonies attended. New York federationists sent a statement to the gathering setting forth their views on the question at issue. The document contained the theory, aims, and strategy of its sponsors. The gist of the thesis is that federation and self-government are indivisible. According to its authors, federation and complete self-government—dominion status—are inseparable and should be achieved *simultaneously*. Federation is defined as the political union of several units with the federal government enjoying independence. Without independence, it is argued, federation is a cruel and obvious fraud.

An examination of this view is in order. It is idealistic, but fallacious. Federation does not operate in a vacuum and is not determined by a special or strained definition. In the world of actuality, federation means the organic combining of several units for common purposes which, it is believed, will be mutually advantageous. To this end, each unit loses some of its sovereignty to the federal government. Independence is neither connoted nor inherent.

Federations are either voluntary or imposed. The United States, Canada, Australia, and Switzerland are examples of federations which were created more or less voluntarily. The units of each nation have previously enjoyed sovereign rights to a great degree. Malaya and the Leeward Islands, on the other hand, were federated by the British Imperial government for colonial administrative purposes. Both types of federation are functioning realities regardless of how they came into being. It is manifestly ridiculous to contend that the Leeward Islands are not federated because they are a Crown Colony and therefore not independent. Such an argument belongs to the limbo of illogicality and is an egotistical disregard of reality. It is a patent *reductio ad absurdum*.

The present writer, a Jamaican, passionately believes in self-government and democracy. He regards them as synonymous. He strongly disapproves Jamaica's inclusion in an overall federation as artificial and fraught with the possibility of disaster for the island, especially when it is recognised that with 59 per cent of the territory and 53 per cent of the population, Jamaica is to have only 38 per cent of the seats in the Federal parliament! In other words, with over half the area and the population, Jamaica will have less than two-fifths of the representation! Jamaica is penalised, it seems, because of its size and the fecundity of the population!

Few Jamaicans visit or migrate to the eastern colonies. There is nothing to attract them to those territories. Most important, considering the politics of the area, it must not be forgotten that Jamaicans successfully, through hard work and personal and financial sacrifices, led the fight for British West Indian democracy as expressed in universal suffrage and unitary self-government. History, honestly written, will show what part the writer played in the political drama in shaping policies suggesting the raising of badly needed organisational and campaign funds in the United States (funds without which, as leaders of the People's National Party have frequently publicly testified, victory would have been impossible or long-delayed); besides speaking and writing for years in Jamaica and the United States for the cause nearest to his heart—the extension of democracy in the British West Indies through winning complete autonomy for Jamaica.

Without federating with any country, Jamaica single-handedly secured an advanced constitution. It is no exaggeration to claim that the success of Jamaica in wresting political concessions from Great Britain inspired other British colonies, even in far-off Africa, to accelerate or make demands for national freedom. After the 1944 Jamaican constitution was won and published, members of the British parliament, as well as the English press, frequently stated that the results achieved in Jamaica would have important effects on the future of the British colonial empire. They did.

It is generally conceded by observers of the British Caribbean scene that Jamaicans are politically more advanced, alert, aggressive, and progressive than their fellow-islanders. Existence of robust political parties in Jamaica in contrast to the absence of such a phenomenon in the other colonies, is striking proof of the vitality of Jamaican politics. But for the forensic skill and deft negotiating of Mr Manley at the conferences in Trinidad and London, federation would have been a dead issue. Conflict of interests—customs union, inter-island immigration, tariff, etc.—was very much to the fore. Mr Manley succeeded in having settlement of some of the most vital and controversial issues that will affect individual units of the "new nation" postponed. These important matters are to be decided AFTER the union has been in existence for FIVE years.

A heavy responsibility rests on Mr Manley. The future of the country has been largely determined by him. It is true that the Jamaica Labour Party, led by Alexander Bustamante, eventually endorsed Federation, but nobody who knows the glaring limitations of the erratic labour leader would credit him with the ability to negotiate anything requiring first-class intellectual resource. However, it must not be forgotten that Mr Bustamante's support of Federation was not consistent. At one time he was against it, later he changed his mind, seemingly as he was moved by the spirit. At first he described Federation as the federating of poverty and conditionally opposed it. Subsequently, with the announced ambition of becoming the first Federal "Governor General", a dream he boastfully expressed, he supported the idea.

Mr Manley's influence on Jamaica has been powerful and largely benign. His countrymen look to him for leadership. Few care to disagree with him or to criticise him publicly. A prominent coloured American, Rev. G. Hawkins, who visited Jamaica recently, stated from a platform at a mass meeting also addressed by Mr Manley in New York City in April 1956 that he had noticed in Jamaica that Jamaicans mentioned Mr Manley's name with "awe". Unquestionably Jamaica owes a debt of gratitude to Mr Manley and the devoted army of humble organisers of the People's National Party. They roused the people out of political apathy and passivity.

The programme of social, political, and economic reforms for Jamaica initiated by the People's National Party should prove of lasting benefit to the island. Its rehabilitation should be quickened. The devotion, integrity, patriotism, and experience of Mr Manley and his associates in the government should result in an improvement of the conditions of the masses. For the first time since the 1944 Constitution Jamaica has a "clean" government. So far, unlike its predecessor, it has been untouched by scandals of graft or ineptitude. No longer are Jamaicans embarrassed or chagrined by acts of official buffoonery and venality. Jamaicans can now be proud of their young nation.

The attitude of this writer on West Indian affairs has never been one of "narrow, insular chauvinism". On the question of federation, he has endeavoured to be realistic and sensible. He believes it is naïve and absurd, to use polite terms, for anyone to have thought that the British Tory government would grant independence and favour federation simultaneously. The uneven political development and status of the units provided the Imperial government with an ideal excuse for blocking or delaying autonomy. Any demand for both objectives to be obtained together invited failure and revealed a lack of elementary political sagacity. Experience has shown that only when pressed by more than mere words has the British government been willing to make far-reaching concessions to any colonial possession.

The British government, naturally thinking in terms of its national interests, can be expected always to act in a manner consistent with the protection of those interests. Federation of any sort, especially among peoples of diverse political levels and experiences, will be used to bind the area to the British as long as self-government is withheld. Once that is understood, it should be obvious, to use a much-abused word, that the twin goals of federation and self-government were not likely to have been attained at the same time.

It might well be asked: If you oppose Jamaica's inclusion in the Federation, do you oppose Federation as such? What is your alternative for Jamaica? Reasons of a general character answering the first question have already been presented. The first goal of every colony should be to obtain maximum self-government for itself, whether it is called dominion status or some other name. Terms are immaterial.

The primary democratic and national desideratum is that each unit control all of its own affairs. On this there should be no compromise. Self-government is the essence of democracy. It should never be conditioned by or linked to a demand for federation. It is the peak of unreality to make the dual demand, even assuming federation to be the panacea some people appear to think it will be. Freedom, independence, or autonomy is the prescriptive and indefeasible right of all peoples, whether their territory or population is large or small.

As they are now governed, the British Caribbean colonies consist of seven units, including two on the mainland. Geography and history determined this arrangement. However, being under British control it was inevitable that several types of united regional activities would be encouraged or imposed. The important fact to bear in mind is that each colony is *administered separately*.

Some of the islands are semi-feudal and this condition is reflected in their politics. As a consequence, some of the colonies, even some of the islands in a colony, are more advanced than others. For administrative efficiency, as already stated, the Imperial government at some time federated the Leeward and Windward Islands. It did more, it attached the Cayman and Turks and Caicos Islands to Jamaica, and Tobago to Trinidad. Proximity influenced this procedure, which can be regarded as an example of British realism.

Considering the foregoing facts and the relative remoteness of Jamaica and British Honduras from the nearest islands of the eastern sector, it does not appear to be in the best interests of the western colonies to enter the Federation. Such an important step should follow presentation of the most convincing arguments and evidence demonstrating that joining the union would be advantageous to them. At any rate it should not be capable of adversely affecting the units politically or economically or of retarding their individual forward march towards complete autonomy—the goal of all virile peoples. If union there be, it should be probationary, not virtually indissoluble. Federation is no cure-all. Its most enthusiastic champions admit this. Even the most ideal federation can offer no guarantee of prosperity. Sir Hilary Blood, former Governor of Barbados, made this clear in a public statement in England.[10]

The fallacy of the thoughtless optimism that Federation will bring inter-island and big commercial benefits to Jamaica was neatly illustrated by Mr Vere Johns in his column in the Jamaica *Star*.[11] The official figures for the first three months of 1956 showed that Jamaica bought £227,000 of goods from the other islands while they bought only some £2,000 odd from Jamaica. In other words, Jamaica spent with them roughly £100 to every £1 she sold to them. Federation should not be based on emotion. Nothing but cold, hard facts and logical arguments showing the definite unitary advantages possible should influence the adoption of any such policy. Searching scrutiny should precede decision. There should be no sentimental or romantic approach about helping "small brothers". Only the really rich can afford to be philanthropic in international affairs, not the poor.

Historically, federation was unpopular in some of the eastern islands. In 1876 the attempt of the British government to federate Barbados with the Windward Islands caused the "Federation Riots" during the regime of Governor Sir John

10. Sir Hilary Rudolph Robert Blood (1893–1967) was the governor of Barbados from 1947 to 1949.

11. Joseph Vere Everette Johns (1893–1966) was a Jamaican journalist, actor, and radio personality.

Pope Hennessy.[12] The loss of life and property was great. Observing how other British colonies obtained their independence, West Indians, if they are a virile people seeking what some of the most backward and illiterate peoples of Asia, Europe, and Africa have gained or are about to gain, should not imagine that through some peculiar undemonstrated superiority they can evolve a new technique or tactic for becoming free—if they really desire freedom.

The experience of former colonies and the geographical realities of the British Caribbean suggest the practical strategy of forthrightly struggling, without deviation, for the major goal of self-government. With each colony enjoying self-government federation, if shown to be necessary and capable of promoting general improvement, could be considered seriously. Concentrating on obtaining federation or equating it with self-government obscures the real issue—the right of every colonial people to seek and win control of their political life. Juxtaposing the two ideas or goals is bad or self-defeating strategy for it balances a fundamental national and moral right with what is at best an artificial and dubious political grouping. Self-government is not dependent on federation. Each can exist alone. One is fundamental; the other adventitious—synthetic.

Acting on the principle of fighting for the basic rights of their countrymen, the Jamaica Progressive League of New York, in 1936, initiated the propaganda that mushroomed into a mass movement in the island and brought great changes in its constitution. The campaign conducted in Jamaica by the People's National Party from 1938 to 1943, considered daring and fantastic at first (and opposed vigorously by Alexander Bustamante, who formed his Labour Party after the New Constitution was proclaimed) caught the imagination of the people, and today it would be impossible easily to deprive them of any of their hard-won rights. As a result of the struggle, with its sacrifices of time and money and the imprisonment of some of its active participants, Jamaica made significant democratic gains. The example acted like a catalyst and spurred other colonies to seek for themselves a similar relationship with Great Britain. The friendly competition among the Caribbean units proved beneficial and should be given credit for their recent rapid political progress. It is fair to assume that if Jamaica had continued its battle for full self-government and had not been lured or thrust into the extraneous issue of federation, using the past as a guide, the island would in a short period of time have won dominion status (the goal set by the Jamaica Progressive League) and furnished another example of political progress for the sister colonies to emulate.

On the point of each colonial unit obtaining self-government some exponents of putting federation before or along with self-government make much of the size of some of the islands. They persistently misrepresent the arguments of their opponents by claiming that the demand for self-government of each colony is tantamount to asking that every island or islet in the British Caribbean become

12. See above, p. 219.

a dominion or an independent political entity. Such a manifestly distorted presentation of the views of their opponents is naked dishonesty. No responsible person interested in the future of the islands has ever made such a demand. There is an obvious difference between a "colony" and an "island". A colony, as in the case of the Leeward Islands Federation, may consist of several islands.

Failure to grasp the simple difference between colony and island, the first a political status subject to change, the second a permanent geographical fact, should be attributed to obtuseness, confusion of mind, or a deliberate attempt to befuddle the issue by making a straw man and claiming a great forensic victory by destroying it with senseless epithets and laboured sarcasm. The size of a country has nothing to do with its right to be self-governing. Singapore is demonstrating this truism by demanding dominion status. It sent a delegation to London for that purpose at about the same time the West Indian delegation was there negotiating for federation, not for political freedom. Singapore is only 225 square miles in area (about one-twentieth the size of Jamaica) and a half mile distant from the Malay Federation, but neither fact deterred the population from aiming at a separate political existence for their island. It is conceivable that a self-governing Singapore, guided by national or regional self-interest, might later decide to be organically linked to Malaya. The negotiations failed, but it is significant that the British Colonial Office did not repudiate the right of Singapore to be self-governed because of its size. The reason given was that the territory is needed for British Imperial security and as a vital part of Western military defence. Implicitly the British government recognised the inherent right of Singapore to have an independent political existence.

When it comes to Jamaica and the other Caribbean colonies, there can be no legitimate objection based on military necessity. The islands are far removed from the centres of Communist ferment. The difference between the attitudes of the people of Singapore and those of the West Indies lies in the nature of their conditioning and their history and traditions. West Indians have no traditions or ideal of independence. Emancipation a little over 100 years ago is not calculated to inspire them with a strong desire for colonial liberation. Long colonial subjection and indoctrination have developed in them a feeling of dependency on outsiders. In the main they seldom look to themselves for leadership and representation in their relations with the world. This is so because of no innate reason. It is the result of their conditioning.

The argument has been made with pontifical finality that it would be difficult, if not impossible, for each colony separately to win self-government. The contention ignores the spirit of the age and the lessons of history. Within the last three decades, especially during World War II, several new nations have come into being, large in area but small in population; others are relatively large in population but small in area. Some are rich in natural resources while others are poor.

Some are largely illiterate; others fairly literate. Size of population or area, wealth or poverty, education or illiteracy, is no criterion for denying self-government to a people demanding it.

The United Nations created Libya, a huge and desperately poor desert-nation. It created Israel, which lives to a large extent off the largesse of Jews in other parts of the world. Iceland, until recently linked to Denmark, has a comparatively large area, very little cultivable land, and a population of 155,200 in 1954. Tiny Luxembourg has long been a nation. Soon Somaliland, another sparsely populated desert, will be given its independence. Mention need not be made of the other new and old, small and poor, nations in existence.

When Hitler threatened England with defeat in 1940, the United States government prepared and circulated a document which foreshadowed the independence of each European colony in the New World in ten years in the event of a Nazi conquest of England, then the one undefeated belligerent European colonial power. Nothing in the document hinted that federation of the Caribbean colonies should be a condition of their becoming free nations. That kind of stipulation seems to be peculiarly West Indian in concept. If Jamaica or any other colony, through struggle or negotiation, had first gained dominion status, it would have inspired the other colonies to demand a similar status for themselves. England gave freedom to rich Burma, India, and Pakistan and is in process of conceding dominion status to Nigeria and Gold Coast.

It is a gross repudiation of the rules of logic, an affront to common sense, an ignoring of recent history, and a cynical disbelief in the proclaimed official British policy to grant independence to colonies, to suggest that Great Britain, having relinquished control of its rich Asian possessions and about to concede independence to Nigeria and Gold Coast, both abounding in natural resources, would deny self-government to West Indian colonies. These territories have been often described by the British themselves as financial liabilities, so it is to be assumed that England would be more than happy to rid herself of the burden.

The West Indian islands are of no strategic value to England today. Whatever protection they may need from foreign attack will be provided by the United States—the most powerful nation in the world—through the Monroe Doctrine and subsequent inter-American declarations which obligate the 21 American nations to defend the entire continent. Latin America has frequently gone on record supporting the liquidation of colonialism in the Western hemisphere, so there already exist powerful influences in favour of autonomy for the colonies. As independent nations in the Western hemisphere, the West Indian peoples would be able to by-pass the racial inequities of the McCarran Immigration Law which do not affect the citizens of the autonomous nations of the American continent.

Many islanders support Federation because they believe it will facilitate emigration from the densely populated islands into British Guiana and British

Honduras. Apart from the indisputable right of the continental colonies to control their demographic character, it should be clear that mass migration will not be easy and may be fraught with misunderstandings, friction, and disappointments. Large numbers of people do not voluntarily move into less developed areas (even of their own country) unless it is to escape religious, racial, or political oppression. They do not go into strange and undeveloped countries and endure hardships unless they are attracted by exceptionally high economic rewards. The belief and hope that the total British Caribbean Federation will provide outlets in the mainland for "surplus" portions may well be illusory—a chimera. Conceivably, the Federation of 1958 may result in flooding less densely populated islands, like Jamaica, with immigrants from the more popular areas. Trinidad realised this and baulked at unrestricted inter-island migration at the Trinidad Conference.

The glorious and inspiring struggle of Jamaica to rid itself of the humiliating bonds of colonialism indicates what can be done in the West Indies by determined and courageous indigenous nationalists. By deviating from the goal of self-government fixed by the Jamaica Progressive League and becoming entangled with Federation, Jamaica has retarded not accelerated Caribbean freedom. Internal self-government of Jamaica is, admittedly, a long step in advance of what existed until recently, but the objective of colonials this century should be for complete autonomy—control of every aspect of national activity. Less than this shows moral weakness and cowardice and reveals a sense of dependency, if not of inferiority.

The French North African possessions of Morocco, Algeria, and Tunisia are contiguous. Their populations are more or less similar in race, religion, language and culture. At no time have the peoples of the region based their right to freedom on federation of their territories. Each nation fought for its own liberation. Economic considerations, no matter how alluring, have never induced North Africans to give second place to their human dignity and rights. Imbued with the ideal to be men among men in a world of really "free nations", they fought, still fight and sacrifice, to secure their individual national autonomy and complete control of all their affairs.

Ceylon, the model of some federationists, has shown the way. Only about 50 miles from India, the Ceylonese people never agitated for union with their racial and religious brothers of the sub-continent, never compromised their right to a free political existence. Today they are a completely independent state. Federation will hamstring or make more difficult the fight of the more progressive West Indian colonies for full control of their affairs—domestic and foreign.

Federation plays into the hands of the metropolitan power. The union may benefit some of the eastern islands, but this does not necessarily make it politically and economically desirable for Jamaica, British Honduras, or British Guiana. Inclusion of Jamaica is a great disservice to the country. Federation fosters an illusion of greatness, size, wealth, importance, and freedom. Sooner or later it will intensify insular jealousies and differences. Friction seems inescapable. "Big brother" Jamaica can easily be out-voted with only 17 out of 45 seats, although on the basis of population and area it is entitled to at least 22 seats in the Lower House of the Federal Parliament. Obviously the Jamaican delegates to the London Conference, in accepting the arbitrary and unfair distribution of voting power were concerned more about Federation than about their own country. With them it was Federation, not Jamaica, first. Federation, not colonial liberation, was their obsession, hence the amazing, dangerous, and unwarranted voting concessions.

West Indian delegates apparently went to the conferences on Federation not primarily to secure extension of the national and democratic rights of their countries, but to ensure continuation of ephemeral advantages now enjoyed in the British market. For some time the agricultural exports of the islands, especially Jamaica, have cost more to produce than similar articles in competing countries. As a consequence, British West Indian sugar, bananas, and citrus fruits have had to depend on British subsidies, direct and indirect.

This fact seems largely responsible for the decision of the Jamaican delegation to join the strange and unnatural Federation. Economic opportunism, not moral principles, was the dominating motive. Markets, not human rights, were the incentive. West Indians have the unfortunate habit of mixing political and economic questions in their relations with England. They attach greater importance to economic questions, even though the arrangements are subject to change, than to eternal moral and political principles; hence they subordinate the basic human rights of their people to be autonomous and temporise with open or veiled colonialism. Seemingly they find it difficult to differentiate between moral values and opportunism. Freedom should be the uncompromising goal of subject peoples. Gained, national freedom provides its possessors with the indispensable tools for effecting their economic rehabilitation.

In concluding this analysis of the theory and possible effect of Federation on Jamaica, it should be useful to quote from the *New York Times* editorial of 22 February 1956, entitled "Caribbean Federation":

> A new nation is taking form on our doorstep, one of the strangest nations, geographically speaking, in the world .... It will be a remarkable nation, stretching over 1,000 miles of water, which is the distance that divides Jamaica and Trinidad, the two main units .... The islands compete against each other with the same products—rum, sugar, bananas, citrus fruits, tobacco and spices.

There can be little disagreement with the terms "strangest" and "remarkable".

41
Secession
December 1958

In the very first session of the Federal parliament, Ken Hill, previously a leading member of the PNP but now of the DLP, caused a ruckus by tabling a motion calling for a review of the constitution with the idea of moving immediately to dominion status. The review was supposedly not due, under an earlier agreement, until the fifth year of Federation, although careless wording ("not later" than the fifth year) had left the door open.[1] This move had much more to do with Jamaican politics than it did with Federation itself, but, on the back foot, Grantley Adams agreed to a review conference not later than June 1959, just postponing the issue for a year, at which point Hill declared that if the Federal government continued to annoy Jamaican public opinion, "the government would in fact be negotiating the secession of Jamaica from the Federation", the first mention of the S word.[2] A series of contentious issues—whether the capital seat should be built at Chaguaramas, currently a US military base; whether a planned Jamaican oil refinery needed special protection; what kind of tax revenue the Federation might collect—served to damage the relationships between Federation's three principal proponents, Manley, Adams, and Williams. Personal relationships, previously warm, became strained and then broken. By October 1958 Manley was flirting himself with the S word. In response to Adams's remarks about Federal taxation, he sent a statement to *The Gleaner* on 31 October, printed the following day under the headline "Jamaica May Leave Federation".[3] That is, if its best economic interests were threatened. Federation's difficulties over Chaguaramas and the Jamaican oil refinery fractured the unified front that Adams, Williams, and Manley had initially presented. Bustamante, sensing an opportunity for domestic advantage, seized on the issue of Federal income tax to demand in a newspaper advertisement "A New Constitution—for the W. I. … or Secession".[4] Domingo was not slow to take advantage of the suggestion that Jamaica might secede.

---

1. Mordecai, *The West Indies*, pp. 101–102.
2. *WIHR* Debates, 26 June 1958, vol. 1, col. 706, quoted in Mordecai, *The West Indies*, p. 105.
3. "Jamaica May Leave Federation", *The Gleaner*, 1 November 1958, p. 1.
4. Alexander Bustamante, "Statement of Policy on Federation", *The Gleaner*, 5 November 1958, p. 16.

Letter to *The Gleaner*, 29 December 1958, p. 15

THE EDITOR. Sir:— In his broadcast to the people of Jamaica on 28 November, which later appeared in your paper as an advertisement, Chief Minister, N. W. Manley, the most potent influence in Jamaica to include the island in the West Indian Federation, admitted that his country was facing a crisis. No one can deny this.

The frank and threatening statements of Prime Minister Sir Grantley Adams that a retroactive Federal income tax could be imposed on the units brought into the open some of the dangers and contradictions inherent in the Federation, as it stands. It is a pity that Mr Manley and other Jamaican politicians did not foresee what was inevitable.

Under the sub-head, "My Advice", in the broadcast Mr Manley makes it clear that he led Jamaica into the Federation because of purely sentimental reasons. That the Federation should so soon be on the verge, so to speak, of disintegration, is to be deplored. Foresight should have controlled those who advocated entry of Jamaica into the union. Mr Manley correctly indicts his arch-rival Sir Alexander Bustamante as being also responsible for Jamaica being in the so-called "new nation". Mr Manley warns that if Federation is to continue, "we must do some new thinking". With this every Jamaican should agree. There should be no fanatical determination to maintain a bad position, one that is now proving to be unwise as far as Jamaica is concerned.

I believe Jamaica should not have joined the Federation. Too many factors were against Jamaica. Distance, conflicting interests that meant rivalry, unfamiliarity with the other units, and the fact that politically Jamaica was far in advance of the others. What should be the nature of the "new thinking"? First, it should give Jamaica's interests—economical, political and national—major consideration. Sentiment should not intrude itself. Second, answering Mr Manley's appeal that "all Jamaica join in a united front" in order to protect Jamaican interests, I believe that there can be no doubt that the central issue when the Federal Constitution is to be revised is that Jamaica should have seats in the Federal House in proportion to the population of the island. There should be no retreat from this demand. Sir Alexander Bustamante has made that one of his main points and the weekly organ of the PNP, Mr Manley's party, has made the same demand twice, editorially. Proportional representation will be the principal means by which Jamaican interests can be protected. I hope that Mr Manley will declare himself on that crucial point, even as Sir Alexander has done.

Prof. Gordon Lewis recently treated your readers to a learned article in which he tried to prove that a federation is indissoluble. Theoretically this may be so, but it will be a practical impossibility for the lesser units of the Federation to prevent Jamaica from seceding. How will they be able to compel Jamaica, the largest unit, to remain in the union? Mr W. Adolphe Roberts some time ago in your columns remarked that he never heard of a junior partner being able to compel the senior partner to maintain an undesired partnership. Mr Manley has repeatedly stated that "no one can compel us to stay in if we wish to leave". A writer in your columns not long ago humorously remarked he could not conceive of a fleet of Grenadian fishing boats enforcing an unwanted and unwise federation on Jamaica.

A last word: From all I can gather, Jamaicans are now awake to the menace that Federation is to their future. The advisers of Sir Alexander Bustamante see the vote-catching value of organising and responding to this Jamaican attitude. If Mr Manley is to win the coming elections, he had better take heed and show himself no less a good Jamaican than his rival. He may use more subtle methods and more dignified language, but he cannot, if he hopes to win, give the impression that he is opposed to what is today the seemingly unanimous feeling of Jamaicans. That feeling is, I think, that Jamaica should get out of the Federation as soon as possible.

I am, etc.
W. A. Domingo
New York City
NY, USA
14 Dec. 1958

42

Adams and Federation

October 1959

With feelings already running high about how Federation was shaping up, Grantley Adams stopped in New York in October on his way to Australia for a meeting of the Commonwealth Parliamentary Association and gave a speech to a group of West Indians at the Little Carnegie Theatre, a gathering organised by the Caribbean League of America.[1] No verbatim report of the speech exists but, piecing the event together from various accounts, it seems to have passed off amicably enough until the question period.[2] According to a Federal Information Office release reported in *The Gleaner*, Adams outlined developments that had taken place in the Federation over the previous 21 months, explained some recent difficulties such as Chaguaramas, and asked the New York West Indian community for their moral support.[3] After his speech, emollient comments were made by Hope Stevens, head of the CLA, and Hulan Jack, Borough President of Manhattan, and messages of greeting were read out from Norman Manley and Hugh Cummins, respectively premiers of Jamaica and Barbados.[4] On the platform behind Adams, according to the FIA, were Richard B. Moore, W. A. Domingo, Reginald Pierrepointe, and Herman P. Osborne (though Domingo points out that they were in fact scattered at different points throughout the auditorium). Pierrepointe's own report for the West Indies News Service added some details, such as the fact that Adams's remarks had been smattered with his usual off-the-cuff quips about the superiority of Barbadians to other islanders and that Stevens had made flattering mentions of various individuals who had helped the West Indies along the road towards self-government, such as Moore and Domingo.[5]

---

1. The Caribbean League of America was basically the New York branch of the PNP, set up by Norman Manley with the help of Daisy Brooks-Johnson and Reginald Pierrepointe; Reginald Pierrepointe, "Prime Minister Adams' Address in New York" (26 October 1959), RBMP, Box 10, folder 2, p. 5.
2. See the accounts in Mordecai, *The West Indies*, p. 187, and Duke, *Building a Nation*, pp. 1–3.
3. The FIO release was picked up by the *Gleaner*'s Federal Bureau in Port of Spain and immediately transmitted to Kingston, where the report appeared as "Adams: No Danger of Federation Breaking Up", *The Gleaner*, 20 October 1959, p. 1.
4. Hulan Edwin Jack (1906–1986), born in St Lucia, raised in British Guiana, was a powerful figure in New York municipal politics. Hugh Gordon Hylvestra Cummins (1891–1970), a fellow member of the Barbados Labour Party, took over as premier of Barbados when Adams became Federal prime minister.
5. It's unclear whether Pierrepointe's report was ever published, but there is a copy of it in

Written questions were read out. Moore asked why West Indian political leaders had not secured independence, commonwealth status, and "all the other essentials of genuine nationhood", and also offered critical remarks about the stereotypes that Adams was peddling. Adams had also previously suggested that Jamaica was unsuited to a large number of seats in the Federal parliament because it had an illiteracy rate of 50 per cent, a slanderous remark that Domingo corrected. On the platform Adams first said that he had got the figures from something written by Esther Chapman (which would hardly have assuaged Domingo) and then tried to pass his remarks off as light-hearted banter. Decorum seems to have been maintained, but Domingo was not prepared to let matters rest and, in response to the *Gleaner* report, fired off this letter to correct some misapprehensions and to give a more accurate rendering of the speech and the discussion that followed. See #44 for further developments.

Letter to *The Gleaner*, 26 October 1959, p. 10

THE EDITOR. Sir:—I have just read the news item on the front page of your issue of the 20th under the heading "Adams: No Danger of Federation Breaking Up", which was relayed to you from Port of Spain, Trinidad. The news dispatch emanated from the Federal Information Office and purports to be a report on the meeting in New York which was addressed by Sir Grantley Adams, Prime Minister of the West Indian Federation. As one who was present, I am forced, in the interest of truth, to assure you that the release of the Information Office is misleading. Furthermore, it said nothing of the offensive remarks made by the inept Sir Grantley to the audience of West Indians from different islands. It is a pity that Mr Manley, whose message to the meeting was read, was not present to hear his protégé denigrate Jamaica and laud Barbados. If there was a tape recording made (I did not see a machine), it should be instructive to hear the words that fell from the lips of the Prime Minister, not of Barbados alone, but of all the units of the Federation.

In the first place it is not true that Mr Osbourne [*sic*], Mr Moore, Mr Pierrepointe, and I were on the dais. We sat in different parts of the audience. On the dais were Judge and Mrs Herman Stoute, Hon. Hulan Jack, Attorney Hope Stevens, a Mr Walker, W. I. [unreadable], Sir Grantley, and a Mr Richardson, who were introduced [unreadable]. Mr Jack and Mr Stevens spoke. Sir Grantley was

---

Richard B. Moore's papers at the Schomburg: "Prime Minister Adams' Address in New York" (26 October 1959), RBMP, Box 10, folder 10. Pierrepointe also wrote an unpublished reply to a flattering profile of Adams that had appeared in the London *Observer*: "Open Letter to the London Sunday Observer on its Profile of Sir Herbert Grantley Adams" (22 May 1959), same folder, responding to "Top West Indian", *Observer*, 26 April 1959, p. 8. It was significant—and must have given succour to Domingo—that prominent federalists such as Moore and Pierrepointe, and to boot countrymen of Adams, were offering such trenchant criticisms of the form that Federation was taking under his leadership.

the main speaker. The Prime Minister did say that Federation had formidable obstacles to face, such as Customs Union and the freedom to pursue their own economic course. He referred to the question of Federal taxation.

The Federal Information Office did not tell West Indians that Sir Grantley said that the average Trinidadian "prefers calypso to working", and when rebuked in a question, seriously asked if anyone knew a Trinidadian who did. Sir Grantley said in the course of his address, which was a laudation of the superiority and virtue of Barbadians, that Barbados has an illiteracy of only 1 per cent in contrast to Jamaica's 50 per cent. He said too that Barbadians are "the most industrious and the most intelligent of West Indians". This did not take well with the audience, so when questions were permitted, Mr Richard Moore, a Barbadian federationalist, asked the speaker if he did not realise that making offensive and invidious comparisons was a bad way to promote West Indian unity. Sir Grantley said he had been joking, but from the fact that his speech was interlarded throughout with praise, many of them unsubtle, of his fellow Barbadians, it was obvious that his explanation convinced nobody.

I asked Sir Grantley if it is not true that the 1943 census of Jamaica showed an illiteracy of less than 28 per cent and if he meant to convey the idea that Jamaican illiteracy had nearly doubled in 16 years. The answer was that the 50 per cent increase had been derived from [two unreadable lines] that many illiterate persons concealed their illiteracy. Of course this latter applied as well to all countries of the world, not only to Jamaica. I corrected the Prime Minister by showing that Mr Manley did not ask for 34 but for 32 seats in a House of 65 Representatives. Sir Grantley admitted that I was right. The clear impression that any individual could gain from the claims of Adams was that Jamaicans, though the most illiterate, had asked through Mr Manley for the most power in the Federation. I am immodest enough to believe that I punctured the statements of Sir Grantley regarding Jamaica.

Today, suspecting that there was no truth in the claim that Barbados has only 1 per cent illiteracy, I contacted the British Information Service for definitive figures. I was referred to the Non-Self-Governing Section of the United Nations and got this information. The latest official figures that give a breakdown of illiteracy in the Eastern British West Indies are for 1946. Here they are: Barbados for people over 15 years of age 9 per cent; Leeward Islands 19 per cent; Windward Islands 34 per cent; Trinidad and Tobago 26 per cent. I checked the Jamaica Census for 1943 and on page lviii found the illiteracy rate to be 25.6 per cent, not the slanderous 50 per cent of Sir Grantley.

It is more than strange that Sir Grantley, a trained barrister who should appreciate the need for referring to official statistics, is neglecting this, the only dependable source when discussing a question like illiteracy and making [two unreadable lines] did he minimise Barbadian illiteracy and magnify that of Jamaica? Why? I wonder how Jamaican Federationists feel after learning the low opinion of Jamaican intelligence held by Mr Manley's protégé, Sir Grantley Adams, Prime Minister of the Federation.

Lest anyone think I have exaggerated anything, I suggest that you or anyone else contact Mrs Johnson and other members of the Jamaica Progressive League who were present at the meeting. Finally, I am surprised that the Federal Information Office should be guilty of sending out such a misleading and inadequate report. Was it to conceal the tactlessness and indiscretion of Sir Grantley? I wonder.

I am etc.,
W. A. DOMINGO
615 West 168th St
New York 56, NY
22 Oct. 1959

43

"Do You Want Jamaica to Remain in the Federation?"

October 1959

The possibility of a referendum on Federation had first been raised by the JLP minister Robert Lightbourne in January 1958.[1] Although *The Gleaner* usually published Domingo's letters, he perhaps felt that in a paid advertisement he could speak even more forcefully and directly.

Advert in *The Gleaner*, 29 October 1959, p. 11

Now is the time for a Referendum!

Fellow Jamaicans,

Our country is at the crossroads of its destiny. The recent Federal Conference in Trinidad must have been an eyeopener to you. The open hostility of the other islanders to the just demands of Jamaica, and their undistinguished aim of using the Federation as a means of exploiting Jamaican resources for their benefit, must have shocked you.

It was no surprise to me. For over three years, through the publication of two pamphlets and numerous letters in the Jamaican press, I warned our leaders that Jamaica had nothing to gain but much to lose by being in this unnatural Federation. They ignored my warnings and refused to heed the obvious. They ranted sentimentally about our being "one people" and about helping our "little brothers".

The British government wanted the Federation, even as it had forced Federation upon the helpless native peoples of Central Africa. As you know, these African victims of a Federation are now in rebellion against it. Our leaders, despite our revealing experiences, stubbornly persist in trying to keep Jamaica in a Federation—an unholy alliance—that is against our best interests and which has only served to engender bad feelings between us and the other units.

Faced with a situation that is fraught with future danger for us, what should be our next step? Obviously we should not remain in a partnership in which we do

1. Robert Lightbourne, "Federal Conspiracy", Letter to *The Gleaner*, 30 January 1958, p. 10.

not enjoy our full rights. It is not our fault that our population is more than half of the total population of the Federation. It is not our fault that our vital interests conflict with those of Trinidad and her satellites. It is not our fault that we are politically progressive.

Jamaicans have had, have, and will always have little personal and commercial contact with the Eastern Caribbean. Our only ties are regional (which we share with the non-British territories, as well) and the fact that we and they (the Easterners) are colonies of Great Britain. How many of you have ever seen or spoken to a St Lucian, a Trinidadian, an Antiguan, a Kittisian, or a Monserratan in Jamaica? How many of you have friends or relatives in those islands? Jamaica joined the Federation at the dictation of its political leaders, who did not consult the people. They acted without study or understanding and solely because of sentiment. Responsible statesmen do not allow their emotions to dominate them. When mistakes are made every effort should be made to correct them before their consequences are beyond repair.

What, then, should be our next move? A democratically conducted PLEBISCITE should be undertaken without delay to ascertain the feelings of the majority of Jamaicans on the paramount question: DO YOU WANT JAMAICA TO REMAIN IN THE FEDERATION? I am confident the answer would be resounding "NO."

And after this, what? Let us reason together. Alone, without help from any outside source, without federating with any other Caribbean colony, Jamaicans from 1938 sacrificed time, money, prestige, and life itself, and won self-government for their NATION. Several Jamaicans, including myself, suffered loss of liberty in this noble cause. Today we are internally self-governed. Are we an inferior people that we should be satisfied with partial control of our destiny, or should we not prove ourselves real men and women and move on to COMPLETE NATIONAL FREEDOM?

Federation proved to be a snare and a delusion. The argument that for Jamaica to be recognised as a NATION it is necessary to be in a Federation is an obvious fallacy. Lurking behind this attitude is a fear of the Jamaican people or a belief that they are inherently inferior and incapable of conducting their own affairs. Are you inferior?

Study the world of today. Lebanon, Israel, Iceland, Luxembourg, Ghana, to mention only a few, are small and weak NATIONS. Yet they are independent. Soon, other small, weak, and poor NATIONS, including Somalia, the Cameroons, and Western Samoa, will be independent. None of them is part of a federation. The argument that Jamaica cannot afford a diplomatic service is worse than fallacious. Poorer NATIONS maintain diplomatic representatives wherever necessary. Besides, the money contributed to the Federal treasury and the funds spent to maintain an army, could be put to better use in securing genuine "international recognition" for Jamaica.

Think, my countrymen, what membership in the United Nations will mean for Jamaica? Think what complete self-government will achieve for us with respect to the McCarran Immigration Act. Jamaican immigrants into the USA, because they are not citizens of an independent country, are limited to a quota of 100 per year. If we became independent—DOMINION OR REPUBLIC as you choose—Jamaica will bypass this restriction on our immigrants since independent NATIONS in the western hemisphere are exempt from quota restrictions.

My fellow countrymen, I appeal to you as one who fought and sacrificed 20 months of his freedom for his country and countrymen, to agitate for a REFERENDUM. You flooded your delegation in Trinidad with cablegrams. Now is the time to make yourselves decisively heard as to whether or not you want your country to remain in the Federation.

Our delegates fought in Trinidad for democratic representation in the Federal parliament. Let them be consistent and democratic enough to seek YOUR OPINION, in a REFERENDUM, on this most momentous question. You, your children and their children will be affected. Do not leave the decision to any one man, no matter how righteous or brilliant he may be. YOU SHOULD AND MUST DECIDE.

I firmly believe that Jamaica's best interests will be served by our country voting to LEAVE THE FEDERATION. Such a vote will be a MANDATE for Jamaica to continue its fight for FULL FREEDOM. Let "the voice of the people be the voice of God" in truth and in fact. Let there be government of the People, by the People, for the People.

W. A. Domingo
615 East 168th Street
New York 56, NY

44

"Padmore, Zik—Not I—Criticised UN Speech": Challenge to Adams

December 1959

In Barbados, Domingo and Moore's criticism of Grantley Adams's New York speech ([#42]) was read as criticism of Barbados, so the *Barbados Recorder* struck back, suggesting that Moore had been away from the region too long to understand what was going on and that "West Indians in America" should concentrate more on charity and less on politics.[1] Moore responded aggressively, defending the right of West Indians in the USA to offer counsel, although the newspaper didn't publish his letter.[2] Back from Australia, Adams took up the cudgels once more with Domingo in his sights. In an address to the Federal parliament on 18 November 1959, he defended his New York speech, suggesting that there was a conspiracy to get rid of him and speculating about Domingo's and Pierrepointe's links with Communism. Pierrepointe responded in the *Barbados Recorder*, accusing Adams of using smear tactics behind the curtain of parliamentary privilege.[3] Domingo also responded vigorously in this letter. It was undoubtedly his highest-profile epistolary exchange, one from which he emerged victorious, leaving Adams's reputation in tatters.

Trinidad Guardian, 20 December 1959, p. 8

Editor "Sunday Guardian":—I have just read in your issue of 2 December an account of the speech Sir Grantley Adams, Prime Minister of the West Indies Federation, delivered in the Federal Parliament in defence and explanation of statements he made in a public address in New York last October in which he made certain offensive and divisive references to Jamaicans, Trinidadians, and other non-Barbadian members of the Federation.

In his defence, Sir Grantley does not deny having made the slanderous statements, but tries to minimise them by claiming he was joking. He further resorts to the thread-worn and discredited device of dragging a red herring across the trail by calling me, along with two other West Indians, "Reds". Sir Grantley is

1. "Dear Mr Moore", *Barbados Recorder*, 2 November 1959, p. 4.
2. "An Open Letter to the Editor of the Barbados Recorder," RBMP, Box 10, folder 2.
3. Reginald Pierrepointe, "Reply to P. M.", *Barbados Recorder*, 17 December 1959, p. 4.

alleged to have said that there is "a conspiracy to fire" him. Obviously, if such a conspiracy exists, it must be among those in a position to 'fire' him, and certainly West Indians living in far away New York are not capable of achieving this result.

As to my being an enemy of the Premier because of statements he made in Paris eleven years ago, all I can say is that it is sheer invention. I remember reading press dispatches of his speech, but I never wrote a word or had anything to say about it. The people who denounced Sir Grantley at the time, as far as I can remember, were Nnamdi Azikiwe of Nigeria, other prominent African leaders, and the late George Padmore, who scathingly referred to the incident in his book *Africa: Britain's Third Empire*.[4]

I am not a personal enemy of Sir Grantley Adams. I never met the man until the evening of his New York meeting when, as an act of respect for his position, I joined the line of people who shook his hand. In accusing me of being a Communist, the Premier descended to a level that reveals his true stature. Caught in a trap of his own making, revealed as a narrow-minded Barbadian chauvinist, he could find no better defence than to drag a red herring across the trail. Let him deny that he made the statement.

As for myself, I have never been a member of any Communist organisation in my life. I charge Sir Grantley, in addition to being a slanderer, with being a cowardly violator of the truth. Doubtless he enjoyed parliamentary immunity in the House, but I challenge him to discard his parliamentary protection and make the categorical statement that I am a Communist. Let him be a man and risk my suing him for slander and for appropriate damages. That is my challenge.

Finally, West Indians can judge the truthfulness of Sir Grantley about joking by bearing in mind that he has repeatedly claimed that Jamaicans are 50 per cent illiterate, and the indisputable fact that he was visibly embarrassed when I challenged his statistics. The question from Mr Moore, a Barbadian, as to the odiousness of comparisons evoked considerable approval from the audience. It was only after the Prime Minister had spoken that questions were permitted and asked.

I suggest that Sir Grantley learn to adhere to the truth; that he refrain from making statistical affirmations until he has verified them; that he lift himself above the level of denouncing those who faithfully report his remarks; that he conduct himself abroad in a manner capable of reflecting credit on his high office.

W. A. DOMINGO
New York

4. George Padmore, *Africa: Britain's Third Empire*, London: Dobson, 1949.

45
Federation
July 1960

These are the final two letters in an increasingly bad-tempered exchange that Domingo had in the pages of *The Gleaner* with Christopher Hills.[1] Hills had replied immediately to Domingo's letter of 16 June; Domingo responded; Hills replied; Domingo responded; Hills replied; Domingo's "final word", below, provoked a further letter from Hills, introducing Marcus Garvey into the argument, a red rag to the bullish Domingo, who finally got the "last" word.[2] Except it didn't turn out to be quite the last word, since Hills wrote again to *The Gleaner* after Domingo's radio broadcast from New York urging a "no" vote in the referendum on Federation. Domingo responded in even more trenchant terms.[3]

Letter in *The Gleaner*, 23 July 1960, p. 8

THE EDITOR, Sir:—Permit me this final word in the controversy which Mr Christopher Hills precipitated in your columns with me. I had hoped that the exchange between us in which I exposed so many of his inaccuracies and false reasons would have induced him to act wisely and retire as gracefully as possible. But he is, as the saying goes, a "hog for punishment".

In his latest effusion in your issue of 14 July he continues to put words in my mouth and to make absolutely inaccurate statements. I list a few of them.

1. It was he who attacked me and introduced the subject of birds. I countered by showing that wings are not always useful for flying and cited dodoes and penguins.

---

1. English-born businessman Christopher Brian Hills (Grimbsy, 1926–Santa Cruz, California, 1997) had moved to Jamaica in 1947. He became prominent in insurance and export as well as running a furniture shop and later an art gallery, in which capacity he was close to Edna Manley and her husband. His export business specialised in spices, and he became a proponent of the food supplement spirulina, starting a foundation which survives him. He left Jamaica in September 1961 to take up a research appointment in the Bahamas, later moving to California.
2. Christopher Hills, "Federation", *The Gleaner*, 17 June 1960, p. 10; W. A. Domingo "Federation", *The Gleaner*, 25 June 1960, p. 8; Christopher Hills, "Federation", *The Gleaner*, 29 June 1960, p. 10; W. A. Domingo, "Federation", *The Gleaner*, 13 July 1960, p. 10; Christopher Hills, "Federation", *The Gleaner*, 14 July 1960, p. 12; Christopher Hills, "Federation", *The Gleaner*, 10 August 1960, p. 10.
3. Christopher Hills, "Domingo's False Light", *The Gleaner*, 30 August 1961, p. 8; W. A. Domingo, "Penchant For Lying", *The Gleaner*, 18 September 1961, p. 8.

2. Mr Hills claims that I admit "the principle that federation is good for the rest of the world but not good for Jamaica". I wrote nothing of the kind. I said, as I have always said, that federation seems desirable for the Eastern West Indies because of the inescapable fact of geography, family ties, and trade relations, but it is not good or necessary for Jamaica. Federation is a political union. Col. Stanley, then Secretary of State for the Colonies, in his famous dispatch on a "Closer Union", suggested that two West Indian federations might be more practical than a single one. He hinted that the eastern territories might join up together and that Jamaica might unite with British Honduras. Our West Indian leaders, moved by illusions of grandeur and without clear thought (as I see it) preferred a single federation with all its anomalies and difficulties. In my opinion Jamaica stands to lose in the setup. Mr Morris Cargill, like a growing number of Jamaicans, believes, as he broadcasted recently, that Jamaica stands to lose, not gain by remaining in the incongruous conglomeration which Mr Manley and Mr Bustamante dragged our country into.

3. I did not put words in the mouth of Mr Philip Sherlock or anyone else. I quoted from a public report made by the panel of federalists after a tour of Jamaica some two years ago. Mr Sherlock was a leader of the panel.

4. Mr Hills has a knack of introducing irrelevancies into an argument, which probably explains his references to Hitler, Nasser, and Castro. I believe in sticking to a point and not beclouding issues.

5. A shining example of how reliable are the statements and arguments of Mr Hills is shown when he claims that I keep "trotting out the fact that Mr Manley himself called it 'the most improbable federation ever conceived', but this was years ago". The statement of Mr Manley was quoted in *The Gleaner* of 29 January 1960. By the magic of his arithmetic, Mr Hills transformed a bare six months into "years". Nuf sed.

6. Mr Hills mentions possession of a degree (I presume he means a college degree). I respect academic attainments but do not worship them. Some of the best informed and brainiest men that ever lived never possessed a college degree while some big fools do. Herbert Spencer, one of England's greatest thinkers, a man who dominated the intellectual world of England to a great extent in the fields of political science, philosophy, and the social sciences in the nineteenth century, did not have a college degree.

7. Regarding Mr Manley, I have the highest respect and regard for him personally and think him a man of great intellect, one who would be near the top in any field in any country, but like all of us he is fallible. I am convinced that he would not want me or anyone to think him infallible. A careful reading of his many statements on Federation and on Jamaica's right and ability to be an independent nation by herself, leaves no doubt that Mr Manley has done a lot of soul-searching on the subject and that but for his stubborn refusal to yield to some of his

own inescapable conclusions he would long ago have taken Jamaica out of his "improbable federation". I agree that legal training helps the mind to ferret out relevant facts and to argue with skill, but this facility of the mind is not the exclusive possession of legal practitioners.

8. Mr Hills wants me to list the names of prominent Europeans who are not in agreement with the ideas he attributes to M. Debre.[4] I will not bother to do this. Implicit in the request is the assumption that M. Debre's views are shared unanimously by all prominent Europeans. This is obviously not so.

This is, Mr Editor, my last word in the controversy with Mr Hills. Your readers are the best judges of the value of his contributions on the subject of Federation.

I am, etc.,
W. A. DOMINGO
New York 56, NY, 17 July 1960

P.S. Next month Cyprus, less populous, smaller in size than Jamaica, will become an independent nation.

4. Michel Jean-Pierre Debré (1912–1996) was the first prime minister of the French Fifth Republic (1959–62).

46

Garvey, Domingo, and Hills

August 1960

Letter to *The Gleaner*, 25 August 1960, p. 10

THE EDITOR. Sir —I had decided to ignore Mr Christopher B. Hills, but he has forced me to answer his reckless and semi-illiterate letter in your issue of 10 August. Stung by my exposure of his ignorance of natural history by giving the habitat of penguins as the North Pole and his massacre of arithmetic by characterising a six-month-ago statement of Mr Manley as having been made "years" before, Mr Hills, like the poor controversialist he is, resorts to the coward's tactic of personal defamation. Instead of arguing the points at issue regarding Federation he introduces matters not in the least bit related to the discussion.

If he is nasty-minded and stupid I did not have to say so: his letters spoke most eloquently for him. I have never tried to appear as a "martyr". When I was detained in Jamaica in 1942 by Governor Sir Arthur Richards the case caused such a furore and international concern that both the Jamaican and British governments were flooded with protests from all parts of the world. Jamaica was aroused and a local Civil Liberties Committee was formed by Mr N. W. Manley, Mr Leslie Ashenheim, and others. Jamaicans were shocked at the obvious injustice when I was taken off the ship at Port Royal and held for 20 months for, as Mr Ashenheim wrote, no crime known to the law. Shortly after my arrest the British government had the local Emergency Law changed to conform with the British Law. All this is a matter of record.

My case created a big stir in England itself, and Mr Adams, a Labour MP, raised the question regularly in the House of Commons. The late George Padmore worked like a Trojan on my behalf. Several MPs championed my case and worked for my release. Ultimately President Roosevelt intervened, as many persons in Jamaica know, and under American pressure the British government released me a few days before Jamaica got its new Constitution.[1] I have never claimed to be a martyr and have no hankering to be one. I make my public contributions, however small, in the interest of what I conceive to be justice and best for humanity.

Mr Hills has indulged in "exposing" me or doing what Jamaicans call "tracing". To do this he resurrects the case of the late Mr Marcus Garvey and tries to prove

1. See above, pp. 171–2.

by garbled quotations from Mr Garvey's book that because I disagree with the author I was some sort of a "traitor". Mr Hills is free to regard Mr Garvey as the "greatest of Jamaicans". Personally, I think of Richard Hill, George William Gordon, S. A. G. Cox, N. W. Manley as among the truly great Jamaicans.[2] These men did not talk and present the country with impractical schemes and a lot of foolish bombast. They achieved definite and tangible things for Jamaicans.

Mr Hills quotes copiously from Mr Garvey's *Philosophy and Opinions*. The book was written to prove its author as guiltless as an infant and his opponents the vilest sinners imaginable. The book is self-serving—an apologia. At the beginning I want to state these principles. I concede to every individual the right to disagree with me, and insist on my corresponding right to disagree with anyone. I consider Mr Manley my friend and I am sure he would not want me to agree with everything he does or says simply because I have the highest personal regard for him. I do not have to agree with all my friends or disagree with all my opponents as to their political and religious beliefs.

I am sure Mr Hills does not break with his friends, assuming he has some, because they do not admire or approve his style of argumentation or because he thinks Mr Garvey the greatest of Jamaicans. I hardly think he shuns his friends because they do not endorse his views on politics, religion, or Federation. Friendship does not mean uncritical agreement. Many of the world's leaders in all fields have friends with whom they differ violently in politics and religion. I hold it my duty, my right, to express myself on public questions regardless of whom I disagree with. In my lifetime I have publicly disagreed with men like the late Dr Kelly Miller, Dr W. E. B. Du Bois, Sir Alexander Bustamante, Mr Marcus Garvey, and now with Mr Manley. I have tried always to avoid personalities.

Mr Hills makes an alleged quotation from Mr Garvey's book. I checked and found no such quotation on page 240 as claimed by Mr Hills. Instead I found that he picked out a paragraph here and another there and put them together. That is another example of the scrupulous methods of argumentation practiced by Mr Hills! Mr Hills is a careless reader. Seemingly he wanted to show me up and defame me. As the history of Africa is unfolding itself before our eyes, the ideal or dream of a united Africa appears utopian. Look at the Congo and the multitude of new states, large and small, rich and poor, that have emerged on the continent.

Because I openly disagreed with Mr Garvey, Mr Hills calls me a "betrayer." This is a vicious word to use in characterising anyone. But let us see. Mr Garvey's book is clearly self-serving. The author was out to prove all his opponent crooks and enemies of the Negro race. Only Mr Garvey and those who supported his views were honest. This is obvious nonsense. Mr Garvey attacked nearly every

2. Richard Hill (1795–1872) was a Jamaican lawyer and leader of the free people of colour when they campaigned for equal rights in the early nineteenth century. In addition to his legal practice, Hill was also a naturalist, a poet, and an educator.

outstanding American Negro leader, and when they counterattacked he whined and called them traitors. It is significant that at the time there were over 300 Negro newspapers published in the United States and probably less than five supported the Garvey programme. None of the big papers like the *Chicago Defender*, *Amsterdam News*, *Baltimore Afro-American*, *Pittsburgh Courier* supported him.

Mr Hills wrote that I was editing *The Emancipator* during Mr Garvey's trial. This is false. The pieced-together quotation taken from the books is, as far as I am concerned, mostly a tissue of lies. I knew Amos, the former bodyguard of President Roosevelt, casually. The fact that Mr Amos [was] entrusted with such an important and responsible duty proves, it seems to me, that he must have been a man of the very highest character. As for what Mr Amos is alleged to have done against Mr Garvey, I have no knowledge but I can hardly believe he acted "unconstitutionally".[3] At this point I want to make it clear that discussing Mr Garvey is unwelcome and distasteful to me. It has been thrust on me by Mr Hills, who apparently believed that the best way to prove his case for Federation is to besmear his opponent rather than counteract their arguments. I prefer Mr Garvey to rest in peace.

Mr Garvey wrote his book, as is evident from its contents, to justify his conduct. To do this he made wild, unfounded, and unprovable charges against his opponents. He offered no evidence except his "beliefs". There is no proof. The internal evidence in the book reveals Mr Garvey to be a most unreliable witness against me. Perhaps the similarity of their forensic methods endeared Mr Garvey to Mr Hills. He seems to regard the kind of "proof" in the book as incontrovertible. It is a recognised legal principle that it is the duty of the accuser to prove his charges. This applies to even Mr Hills's "greatest of all Jamaicans".

Mr Garvey said I was a "draft evader". This is a lie. I went to the British Military Mission at 110 West 42nd Street, New York City, and after a physical examination was "exempt" from military services. Mr Garvey wrote that he "believed" I concocted the "promulgation" of certain threatening letters sent to the Federal Judge. Since when has "belief" become proof? Calling me an arch-plotter means exactly nothing. I can call Mr Hills any name I want, but that will not be proof. For a charge to stand it requires outside support. Mr Hills quotes Mr Garvey as saying I signed a petition to Mr Harry M. Daugherty, US Attorney General. This is a most stupid lie. On pages 294–300 of the *Philosophy and Opinions* the petition is published in full and the names and addresses of the signers given, and my name is not among them. That shows how reliable was the statement that I "plotted" against Mr Garvey.

I wonder if Mr Hills knows this fact. Mr Garvey's case lasted for nearly a month. He dismissed his coloured American counsel, Mr Henry L. Johnson, early in the

3. James Edward Amos (1874–1953) was Theodore Roosevelt's personal attendant and bodyguard before working for the FBI as a firearms instructor.

trial and conducted his own defence. There is an old adage that "he who acts as his own lawyer has a fool for a client". There was the curious and comical spectacle of the counsel questioning himself as a witness. But the climax came when he called the late Bishop Collins to the stand to testify for him. The Bishop had been the head of the Roman Catholic Church in Jamaica, and was then President of Fordham University.[4] Mr Garvey asked the Bishop if he knew the defendant in the case and he replied, yes. The next question was this: "What is the reputation of the defendant Marcus Garvey for veracity and honesty?" The Bishop answered "Doubtful."

Mr Hills stated that I opposed Mr Garvey "openly". This does not look like plotting. It is not widely known in Jamaica that during the period when Mr Garvey was in America he met violent opposition from American and West Indian Negroes. There were several near riots in Harlem and other parts of the country. Very few American Negroes of prominence or education supported Garvey. They regarded him as an ignorant loud-mouthed upstart. A few did join up with him, apparently lured by the fantastic salaries he promised and never paid. The most outstanding was the late Prof. William Pickens, who turned against Garvey in a short time.

I did not want to stir up cold ashes but Mr Hills compelled me to defend myself and tell the truth. I submit that neither he nor his witness is to be trusted. I doubt that many Jamaicans know that Mr Garvey, because of his practice of libelling his opponents, had to make public apologies six times after he was successfully sued for libel. He was found guilty of libelling Robert S. Abbott and apologised in his paper; he had to apologise and retract in the *Negro World* statements he had made against Edgar Grey, Richard Warner, and Edwin Kilroe; he had to apologise for and retract libellous statements he made against Cyril V. Briggs; and in Jamaica he had to apologise in court for statements he made regarding the Judiciary of the island. There is Mr Hills's witness for you.

I am, etc.,
W. A. DOMINGO
New York, NY
14 August 1960

4. John J. Collins, SJ (1856–1934).

47

Your Late Husband

January 1961

After Domingo returned to New York, one of his main sources of information for what was happening on the ground in Jamaica was Marcus Garvey's widow, Amy Jacques Garvey. The two exchanged frequent letters, Amy sending Domingo newspaper cuttings and even packets of his favourite cerasee bush, from which he'd make tea. They were Kingstonians of the same generation and shared many interests. Their correspondence was warm, but stayed clear of the subject of Marcus Garvey until early 1961. This letter from Domingo is one of his longest to Amy, responding to a number of issues she had raised in her letter to him of 12 January 1961. We include here just the second half of Domingo's letter.

Letter to Amy Jacques Garvey, 15 January 1961, AJGP [AJGP = Amy Jacques Garvey Papers, Box 1, file 7, Fisk University, Nashville, Tennessee

Dear Mrs Garvey, …

Your late husband: This is a very delicate matter. Indeed, I would never have touched it but for your statement that "I know you hate M.G." I have never written publicly about him except in relation to absolute facts and only in defense of myself. For example, Mr Christopher Hills, in his foolish and ill-informed letter in the *Gleaner*, tried to destroy me in Jamaica. I had no alternative but to defend myself.[1]

My attitude towards M.G. was conditioned by two things: his attitude towards me and his public statements and behavior. As to the first, I knew him from Jamaica. We were friends. When we met, he was a stranger to Kingston. He attended Coke Guild. He was a staunch British subject. Although younger, I had read extensively and hated British imperialism. We clashed in a debate in which he favored annexation of Jamaica to Canada rather than to the US. I took the

---

1. See #46. Despite Domingo's recognition of the "delicacy" of the issue, it seems that Amy Jacques Garvey had never held Domingo's view of her husband against him. In 1945, for example, she wrote to Domingo to ask if he would consider joining the UNIA delegation to the Fifth Pan African Congress where his "knowledge of world affairs", "ability as a journalist", and "contacts in America and West Africa" would fit him as "a representative of our race and the nationalist movement". Amy Jacques Garvey, Letter to W. A. Domingo, 28 July 1945, AJGP.

opposite side and his side won. I won't go into our relations in Kingston after that. He had made sacrifices in the printers' strike. As a foreman at Benjamin's plant he did not have to go on strike, but he did. I won't mention the elocution contests he promoted in Jamaica and the results. Nor will I refer in detail to a pamphlet which, in a sense, we both wrote in Kingston and he published. I came to [the] US in 1910 and wrote him as promised. He never answered. I read of his activities in Jamaica, the founding there of the UNIA, his troubles in Costa Rica, his trip to England, etc. About 1915 I received a letter from him telling me he had been invited to visit the US by Booker T. Washington. At this point I will mention that I had read practically every book in the Institute dealing with the Negro. I had read Booker T.'s *Up From Slavery* and interpreted the US race problem in terms of our Jamaican shade problem. I told M.G. of the books I had read and recommended that he read Blyden's *Christianity, Islam, and the Negro Race*.[2] The book had changed me and it changed Garvey.

On his arrival in New York mine was the second house he visited. I gave him advice and introduced him to many people. His first meeting was a complete failure. It was at St Mark's Hall and he was catcalled by the audience. How it happened I do not know, but he fell from the platform. He stayed in Harlem for some time collecting funds for the establishment of a Tuskegee in Jamaica.[3] That was his avowed reason for coming to America. He toured the US after the East St Louis riots of 1916 or 1917.[4] On his return to New York he joined Hubert Harrison's Liberty League of Negro Americans. Harrison's movement failed, and from the failure Garvey started his UNIA in the US. He promoted many things—African Communities League, etc. His organization had a tough time. I was never a member but I attended and helped in matters of parliamentary procedure of which he was at the time ignorant. There were times when he had fist fights with his officers.

In 1918 he started the *N. World*. He asked me to edit the paper. I took him to the printers, and helped all I could then. I started the slogan of "Africa's Redemption" in its columns, but not in the religious sense. By this time I had come to see that the American Negro problem was not to be evaluated in terms of blacks versus mulattoes as was the case in Jamaica. Apparently Garvey did not. He attacked Negro leaders and when they replied he accused them of attacking him. I was never a member of the movement.

We disagreed because he openly stated that he believed in capitalism and I was a Socialist. After we parted company, I opposed his views (which was my right) by

2. Born on St Thomas, Edward Wilmot Blyden (1832–1912) was primarily active in Sierra Leone and Liberia. *Christianity, Islam, and the Negro Race* (1887) was his most influential book.

3. Founded in 1881, the Tuskegee Normal School (now Tuskegee University) was the historically black college led by Booker T. Washington.

4. A series of violent attacks on African-Americans by whites between late May and early July 1917.

publishing *The Emancipator*. Garvey by this time had started the Black Star Line. After he was shot, not for the reason he gave and most of his followers believed and which story has passed into history, the company gained great popularity. Millions of dollars flowed in.

We had our controversy. He gave me blows and I returned them. He sought my vulnerable points and I his. I never counseled people to assassinate him or anyone. I heard him tell crowds that Negroes unlike Italians did not have a country of their own, but they could do like the Italians did with their "traitors". He told crowds that Randolph, Owen, Bridges, Briggs, and Domingo ought to be under six feet of earth.[5] My wife was terrified for my safety.

I will not go into his legal troubles. His side is amply stated in the second volume of his book.[6] In it I am mentioned 22 times. He singled me out for abuse and misrepresentation. He even sought, from the way he stated it, to have me dubbed a communist. You know he claimed I was a draft dodger, etc. That is one of the points made by Hills. M.G., without offering a scintilla of proof, accused me of treachery, etc., and that I conspired with Samuel Duncan in doing certain things.[7] These things were all false, pure inventions.

I have been most careful in seeing that I said or wrote nothing untrue about him. I could have told much. His book is most scurrilous of me. He had offered me any job in his organizations that I would accept. I cite the foregoing so that you can understand my attitude. Any time anyone quotes from the book as evidence against me, I will be forced to use the book itself in my defense. Proof of the falsity of much he said about me is in the book itself.

I come now to my present attitude. In the first place I do not believe that he made a single original contribution to the solution of the Negro or African problem. Every idea he put out had been expressed over and over again by American Negro leaders, Douglass, Du Bois, Washington, etc. The Pan-African movement which led to the liberation of Africa was started in the early 1900s by a Trinidadian, Sylvester Williams, and continued by Du Bois, who is today regarded in Africa as the "father" of Pan-Africa. He was an honored guest in both Ghana and Nigeria. Garvey did much to popularize and dramatize the idea of African freedom from colonialism. His contribution was great, but it lacked a theoretical basis. Every young African leader who has been in the forefront of African freedom has been influenced by Socialism, Du Bois, and Garvey. West Indians think or know only of Garvey. They know nothing of the great and basic contribution of Du Bois.

5. William Bridges (1891–1963), editor of *Challenge Magazine* and a well-known stepladder orator in Harlem.

6. See above, p. 37, n. 93.

7. On Duncan, see above, p. 38, n. 99.

I enclose a letter from Prof. Skinner who lectured over the TV on Africa.[8] It speaks for itself. I have tried to be honest and frank on this delicate subject. I hope I have not hurt you. That is far from my intention. Your statement prompted me to set the record straight.

Best wishes for you and your family. Kindly return Dr Skinner's letter.
Sincerely yours,
W. A. Domingo

8. Possibly Elliot Percival Skinner (1924–2007), Trinidad-born anthropologist who later became the first African-American department chair at Columbia.

48

W. Adolphe Roberts

October 1962

Domingo and Roberts consistently wrote supportive pieces about the work and travails of each other. Domingo had already written one long and angry piece about the refusal—which he laid at Bustamante's door—to allow Roberts back into Jamaica in 1945, and another letter in 1955 suggesting that Jamaica should honour Roberts.[1] Here he mourns the loss of his friend.

Letter to *The Gleaner*, 10 October 1962, p. 16

THE EDITOR, Sir:—Jamaica suffered a great loss in the death of W. Adolphe Roberts. I first met Mr Roberts at the house of the late James S. Watson in 1936. Prior to that I had heard a Jamaican writer had made for himself quite a name as a journalist, poet, historian, and novelist in New York City. At the time of the party at Judge Watson's home, where the conversation revolved largely around Jamaican conditions, Roberts approached me and said he wanted to meet me again regarding some serious action relating to Jamaica. Among the guests present were the late Claude McKay and Mr Wendell Malliet.

The outcome of the future meeting with Mr Roberts was the organisation of the Jamaica Progressive League. Others had individually dreamed of achieving self-government for Jamaica, but it was left to Roberts to organise the first effective attempt for this purpose since the unsuccessful efforts of the late S. A. G. Cox, who organised the Jamaica National Club in 1905 and struggled for six years to win the goal of Home Rule. The literary contributions of Roberts were considerable. He wrote many books and edited several American magazines. His writings are distinguished for clarity of style and gracefulness of diction. He was not a great writer, but he added considerably to the output of Jamaican literature. His range was wide.

My own association with Roberts was in connection with his political activities on Jamaica's behalf. Many persons have been hailed as the "father" of Jamaican self-government, but, if we are to measure accomplishment rightly, we should

1. W. A. Domingo, "The Barring of W. Adolphe Roberts", *Public Opinion*, 2 May 1945, p. 3; 3 May 1945, p. 3; 4 May 1945, pp. 2–4; W. A. Domingo, "A True Patriot", *The Gleaner*, 17 February 1955, p. 8.

concede that the first practical effort, after Cox, aimed at gaining for Jamaicans control of their government must go to the man who ORGANISED that effort. Roberts did not dream dreams and remain in an ivory tower. At his own expense he returned to Jamaica from New York in 1937 and sowed the seeds of his liberal ideas on Jamaica, which seeds developed into the mighty tree that became the Dominion of Jamaica on 6 August 1962.

Jamaicans seem not to realise the benefits that became theirs as a direct result of the founding of the League in 1936. One of the first measures advocated by the League, under Roberts, was a reform of the conditions governing entry into the Civil Service. Before then it was almost impossible for the average Jamaican youth to enter the Service. It was hedged around with conditions cunningly devised to make the Service an exclusive club, so to speak. The League wrote every member of the Legislative Council indicating the injustices in the system. With the exception of the late C. A. Reid of Manchester not a single member of the Council replied. Not even the late J. A. G. Smith. Undaunted, the League corresponded with Mr Reid and at its instance he introduced a bill for the restoration of competitive Civil Service examinations. Today when one goes into a government office—the Savings Bank or any other office—the clerical staff is a true cross-section of the Jamaican population. This reform was a direct result of the work of the League under the leadership of Mr Roberts.

Roberts also wrote a pamphlet which was distributed in Jamaica. In this pamphlet he advocated, without compromise, Jamaica's right to be a self-governing dominion. He often told the story of his encounter with the late Mr H. G. de Lisser, editor of the *Gleaner*. Roberts outlined his plans for Jamaican constitutional reforms to the editor who was then "government-maker" of the island. According to Roberts, Mr de Lisser roared that Jamaica would become a dominion only over his dead body. Roberts lived to see an independent Jamaica. The *New York Times* of 17 September wrote this of Mr Roberts in its long obituary of him. "The achievement of independence of Jamaica this summer was a source of pride to him, and perhaps represented his greatest contribution to his time."[2] To this I add my humble amen. My great fear is that Jamaicans, especially their "historians", will fail to see Jamaican history in its proper perspective. So many people imbue their thinking with their egos and their prejudices that the great contribution of Roberts and of his brainchild the Jamaica Progressive League to the freedom of Jamaica may be obscured, even ignored. We should learn to give credit where credit is due.

As for the man Roberts, I found him a very democratic person of great personal charm, and simplicity personified. He had no airs. He was just another human being from whom exuded warmth, thoughtfulness, courtesy, and from whom one could always learn something. He had great learning and much expe-

2. "W. A. Roberts, 75, Author, Is Dead", *New York Times*, 17 September 1962, p. 31.

rience as a man of the world. He loved humanity and believed in the equality of all mankind. Had he chosen, he could have forgotten Jamaica and been just another American of distinction in his chosen fields. His talents would never have added to the lustre of his native land. But he was above all a JAMAICAN.

While we mourn the loss of this great man, this humble man, our greatest tribute to him can well be a dedicated determination to make his dream-child—an independent Jamaica—become a beacon of progress and freedom in the Caribbean area.

I am, etc.
W. A. DOMINGO
New York
2 October 1962

49
Evaluating Garvey
September 1964

With Jamaica independent and a JLP government at the helm, the Kingston auctioneer and UNIA member J. Leslie Alexander took the initiative to seek the repatriation of Marcus Garvey's remains from their burial site in London. Kwame Nkrumah, a great admirer of Garvey, had been looking to move the remains to Ghana and had the support of Garvey's second wife, Amy Jacques Garvey. Alexander enlisted the support of the first wife, Amy Ashwood Garvey, and Edward Seaga moved quickly to throw the weight of the Jamaican government behind Alexander's quest by appointing him as a government envoy and by announcing plans for a national shrine in George VI Park where a Garvey mausoleum could be created.[1] Making this announcement, Seaga linked the plan to a Cultural Development Programme, which also included the restoration of the birthplaces of Bustamante and Manley, a major feature of which was "the commemoration and enshrinement of national heroes".[2] The decision to enshrine Marcus Garvey as a national hero did not go unquestioned. The Kingston lawyer Bruce Barker wrote a dry letter to *The Gleaner* outlining the facts of Garvey's life, as drawn from the only book about him in the Kingston public library, and suggesting that the facts "do not appear to support the claim to be a Jamaican National Hero".[3] Inevitably, Domingo weighed in, his last words on the subject.

The Gleaner, 12 October 1964, p. 18

THE EDITOR, Sir:—At the risk of being one of those who "rush in where angels fear to tread", and the added risk of being misunderstood, I should like to discuss a question that is prominently before the Jamaican public. The subject is so charged with sentiment that many leading Jamaicans, regardless of what they know or really think, are not likely to touch it with a nine-foot pole. I refer to the proposal to bring the remains of Mr Marcus Garvey from England to Jamaica for interment in a national mausoleum that is to be built for the purpose. No one

1. Seaga's own account is in Seaga, *My Life and Leadership, Volume 1*, pp. 127–34.
2. See "Garvey Mausoleum to be Built Here", *The Gleaner*, 13 August 1964, pp. 1 and 25.
3. Bruce Barker, "Marcus Garvey", *The Gleaner*, 10 September 1964, p. 8. Bruce Beacroft Barker (1921–1989). The book was likely Len S. Nembhard, *Trials and Triumphs of Marcus Garvey* [1940], rev. edn, Kingston, Jamaica: Jamaica Times, 1953.

can object to the return of the body of any individual to his native country for its final burial; but when the individual is apotheosised as a "national hero" a careful, informed, and impartial study should be made of his life, deeds, preachings, and accomplishments. History imposes this duty on every people or nation.

It appears that the government of Jamaica is deeply involved in the movement to honour Mr Garvey. This being so, the government owes it to itself, Jamaica, the world, and posterity to ascertain the facts in relation to what is proposed. There should be no sentimental or legendary approach. Facts, reason, and fidelity to truth should be the guiding principles. There should be no catering to or placating of any section of the population. All Jamaicans should insist that the matter in hand, being of national, not racial or sectional importance, be historically correct and well-based and not likely to be adversely reviewed and be a source of future national embarrassment. There should be no creation or perpetuation of legend or a myth.

Some years ago a prominent Jamaican in discussing Mr Garvey's place in Jamaican history said to me: "You cannot fight a myth with facts and reason." With this I agree. But when a nation builds a great monument, in this case a mausoleum, for someone, the matter should be given the most exacting examination. The monument should be on a historical foundation as solid as those to Dessalines and Toussaint L'Overture of Haiti, Antonio Maceo and Marti of Cuba, Simon Bolivar of Venezuela, George Washington and Abraham Lincoln of the United States, etc. are based.

What is the basis of some Jamaicans' belief that Mr Garvey should be presented as Jamaica's No. 1 national hero? Jamaicans should ask themselves these pertinent questions. What lasting good has Mr Garvey done for Jamaica intellectually, politically, economically, or socially? What concrete thing has he done to free Africa from colonialism? What enduring good has his philosophy, whatever it is, done for the Negro race? Truthful, factual answers to these questions can help fix his place in history; and by history I do not mean what some Jamaicans believe, but what the facts reveal.

As far as I know, Mr Garvey did not at any time advocate the self-government or independence of Jamaica. There is no record of him initiating or leading a movement in or out of Jamaica for the national freedom of the island. Those who claim he did should cite proof from his writing and reported speeches in support of their claim and not deal in speculation or vague generalities. I recall hearing him described as "great" because he once asked the British government for several million pounds for the rehabilitation of Jamaica. Asking for money for a nebulous, undefined scheme means absolutely nothing.

Not even the most ardent supporter of the "national hero" movement can point to a single concrete or tangible thing done by Mr Garvey to rid Africa of colonialism. On the contrary, during the Italy–Ethiopian conflict, when Negroes of the world were enthusiastically supporting Ethiopia, Mr Garvey was chased out of Hyde Park, London by African and West Indian students when he attacked Haile Selassie, thereby giving objective support to Italy. The incident was reported from London in the Negro press in the United States by the late George Padmore of Trinidad, who became one of the principal advisers of Kwame Nkrumah when Ghana won its independence. Ghana gratefully honoured Padmore's memory for his services to the first African colony to be liberated from colonialism.

There are some people who regard Mr Garvey's advocacy of "Back to Africa" as a great and original philosophical contribution to his race. The *Daily Gleaner* of 17 September 1960 published a brief review written by me of the "Back to Africa" movement, giving irrefutable proof that it was an old American concept dating back to 1816.[4] I showed, too, that in 1912, four years before Mr Garvey's arrival in the United States and six years before he launched his ill-conceived Black Star Line, a West Indian, "Chief Sam", raised funds in America, bought a ship and took several hundred American Negroes to West Africa. I cited other instances of Negro emigration en masse from the United States. So the "Back to Africa" ideas [were] no original creation of Mr Garvey; he merely copied the idea and gave it international publicity. The movement has been a colossal failure. Most of the liberated African nations, controlled by patriotic, educated, and practical men, sanely limit the number and type of immigrants into their countries. There is no shortage of unskilled labour in Africa. Free Africa needs and welcomes carefully selected immigrants who have skill, education, or capital.

Generally speaking, Jamaicans of colour are ignorant of facts regarding their race. They are either ashamed of their racial type because of so-called aesthetic reasons or because they ignorantly believe it has no creditable past. In this respect American Negroes are far ahead of their racial brethren in other parts of the world. They have a [illegible] graph. During the last hundred years they have probably made more worthwhile creative contributions to the world in the fields of art, literature, science, music, and invention than all the other Negroes of the world combined.

Most of the ideas promulgated by Mr Garvey were current in the United States from before emancipation in 1863. He learnt about them in this country and gave them great publicity. It is said that he gave his race "inspiration". The word needs defining. In this country there have been outstanding Negro leaders like Frederick Douglass, Booker T. Washington, J. C. Price, Mrs Mary Bethune, Monroe Trotter, and W. E. B. Du Bois, who provided their people with sane, intelligent, practical programmes suited to the social, economic, and political milieu of their country.[5] They did not indulge in sensational statements or launch impractical schemes.

4. W. A. Domingo, "It Started All Back in 1816", *The Gleaner*, 17 September 1960, p. 8.
5. Joseph Charles Price (1854–1893), educator and orator; Mary McLeod Bethune (1875–1955), educator and civil rights activist.

About 25 years ago the leader of the UNIA in Jamaica expressed his disagreement with my views on his organisation. I challenged him to show me a group of Negroes anywhere in the world who have progressed intellectually, socially, economically, or politically by adopting the philosophy of his organisation. He failed to do so. This same gentleman later launched a great business and insurance scheme in Jamaica that was a dismal and costly fiasco. The Black Star Line was a monumental failure because of mismanagement and ignorance, and the "Back to Africa" idea was and is an unrealistic, impractical dream.

The role of the critic is neither pleasant nor rewarding, especially when one's motives are likely to be misunderstood. Therefore, because of the involvement of the Jamaican government and the importance of the subject, I make the following suggestion. Before final action is taken, a committee of historians, scholars, and others, including some members of the faculty of the West Indies University, be appointed to study and evaluate the question. The committee should be instructed not to rely on "beliefs" or unsubstantiated statements from any source, least of all the self-serving propaganda that used to emanate from Mr Garvey, now from his present-day supporters. Efforts should be made to consult the American Negro and white press of the period, also books by responsible authors. It must be remembered that Mr Garvey did all of his important work in the United States. He never set his foot on African soil.

Jamaica cannot afford to be the laughing stock of the world by creating a fragile image or perpetuating a historical myth. A sane, dispassionate, objective analysis is necessary. History does not forgive or condone ignorance. Claims that are not supported by unimpeachable evidence cannot survive the test of time. Important conclusions and decisions require intelligent assessment. Sentiment is no substitute for knowledge. Wilful ignorance is criminal. Legend is not history. Stop! Look! Think!

I am, etc.,
W. A. DOMINGO
New York City
NY, USA
23 Sept. 1964

Conclusion
A Man of Conviction

no one, and I repeat, no one in the world made greater sacrifices or suffered more for the cause he believed in—the cause of freedom for Jamaica and our escape from the bonds and fetters of British Imperialism.[1]

After Domingo's death, the national heroes' project took narrative shape in the capable hands of Sylvia Wynter, with George William Gordon and Paul Bogle taking their places as forerunners of Garvey, the three of them providing a context for Bustamante and Manley.[2] Her main task was to explain how the two traditions of parliamentary revolt and labour revolt were fused together in the conjoined figures of Gordon and Bogle—prefiguring the analogous fusion of the two cousins. She offered a masterfully even-handed account of Bustamante and Manley in which cousinly rivalry spurred each to both emulate and complement the other: "Each one began to obsess the other with something of his obsession. Bustamante set out to found a Union, and in order to strengthen his Union, founded a political party. Manley set out to found a political party and to strengthen his party founded a Union."[3] In order to link the national heroes together in an unbroken narrative, Garvey's somewhat chaotic seven years back in Jamaica (1927–35) have to be presented as having sown the seeds for both self-government and the protection of labour, in other words foreshadowing the obsessions of both Manley and Bustamante, a description that enshrines Garvey as the one national hero who embodied the qualities elsewhere shared between two (Gordon/Bogle, Manley/Bustamante). With this narrative hegemonic, twentieth-century Jamaican historiography has been dominated by the perspectives of the two main political parties, founded by Norman Manley and Alexander Bustamante, with Marcus Garvey positioned as the original national hero who transcends party politics.

The prevailing story, particularly where it is concerned with creating heroes, leaves little room for a person such as Domingo. A man of distinctive views, he had relationships with all three of his "national hero" contemporaries, all of which

1. Norman Manley, "One of the Dedicated Men", *The Gleaner*, 22 February 1968, pp. 3–4, at 3.
2. Frank Hill, "Preface", in Sylvia Wynter, *Jamaica's National Heroes*, Kingston, Jamaica: Jamaica National Trust Commission, 1971, p. i. See Howard B. D. Johnson, *The Politics of the Past: National Heroes in Post-Colonial Jamaica*, 2003 Elsa Goveia Memorial Lecture, Kingston, Jamaica: Department of History, University of the West Indies Mona, 2003.
3. Wynter, *Jamaica's National Heroes*, p. 31.

ended in profound disagreements. As the selection of writings in this volume shows, Domingo was at the epicentre of the most productive political debates of his era. He was remarkably prolific for a man who made his living primarily as a businessperson, but only a fraction of his writing appeared in the books and magazines prioritised by scholars. Since he never took up political office, his political commitments have been misapprehended or even overlooked entirely. His commitments to labour and left politics did not result in significant union activity, so he does not appear in these annals. As a stalwart thinker and analyst, he was never classed as a literary writer nor gained any association with emergent universities. In other words, Domingo became affiliated with none of the institutions that provide historical narratives and house memorials.

In September 1936, just as Domingo was signing up to the platform Adolphe Roberts had composed for the Jamaica Progressive League ("Firmly believing that any people that has seen its generations come and go on the same soil for centuries is in fact a nation"), Marcus Garvey was expressing praise for Hitler for wanting the Germans to keep their blood pure, "just as we want to keep ours pure".[4] It might appear as if Domingo was on the right side of history: his vision of a self-governing Jamaican nation came to pass in 1962 in a constitution that doesn't mention race, while Garvey's "pure blood" fantasies were soon just a discredited facet of Nazi ideology. It's therefore ironic, to put it mildly, that Garvey is memorialised and lionised in twenty-first-century Jamaica while Domingo is entirely forgotten.[5]

Indeed, to the extent that he does have a public profile, Domingo most frequently appears—no doubt to his posthumous chagrin—through the distorting lens provided by Marcus Garvey. So, for example, in his influential biography of Garvey, *Negro with a Hat*, Colin Grant characterises Domingo as "a fast-thinking chameleon with an equally fast-twitching smile".[6] Domingo is turned into an untrustworthy Harlem wide boy—very much the image that Garvey himself wanted to convey of his erstwhile friend after their falling out. Domingo's politics were those—Grant suggests—of someone who "cultivated political alliances without fully signing up to any one group", ignoring Domingo's membership of the Socialist Party of America and the African Blood Brotherhood for African Liberation and Redemption, his co-founding the JPL, of which he was a life-long member, and his membership of the PNP between 1938 and 1947.[7] Margaret Stevens's assessment picks up on Grant's word, calling Domingo a "political

4. *Black Man*, 2, no. 3 (September–December 1936), pp. 1–2, quoted in *MGP*, 7, p. 568.

5. The Jamaican journalist Ken Jones was almost unique in calling Domingo and Roberts "the two real pioneers of Jamaican Independence" ("Remembering Wilfred Domingo: A Pioneer of Our Independence Movement", *The Gleaner*, 21 August 2011, p. F10).

6. Colin Grant, *Negro with A Hat: The Rise and Fall of Marcus Garvey*, London: Vintage, 2009, p. 107.

7. Ibid., p. 140.

chameleon", a description that does less than justice to Domingo's political consistency in navigating the choppy waters through which he lived.[8] In fact, the overwhelming impression of his political career seen whole is of somebody who stuck to his views and principles through thick and thin from 1917 until his death half a century later. He was always a man of conviction.

* * *

Domingo's views could be summed up as socialist, anti-imperialist, nationalist, internationalist, anti-racist, anti-fascist, and Africanist. He belonged to that colonial generation galvanised by the Soviet Revolution of 1917. He never joined the CPUSA, but could certainly be thought of as a "fellow-traveller" in the 1930s and 1940s, usually sympathetic to Third International positions and to the intermittent anti-fascism of the Soviet Union. His socialism then became urgent when, following the strikes and labour protests in Jamaica in 1938, he joined other educated Jamaicans who sought to shift middle-class opinion about their poorer compatriots by broadcasting the appalling living and working conditions of peasants and urban labourers. His interventions contained no bleeding-heart paternalism. Instead, his starting point was to celebrate the "industry and ingenuity" of the peddlers in Kingston's iconic Coronation Market who turned old car tyres into sandals despite being forced to work in "vile" unsanitary conditions.[9]

On his own account, Domingo's unwavering anti-imperialism dated from his teenage years in Kingston and quickly found confirmation and theoretical support in New York. He had no time for the flim-flam of Empire. For all their desire for self-government, Adams, Manley, and Williams—all educated at Oxford—suffered, as Gordon Lewis puts it, "from the social religion of Anglolatry and so could not break, psychologically, the umbilical cord that tied them to British values".[10] It is no coincidence that those who most strongly spoke against federation—Domingo, Roberts, and eventually Bustamante—had no such British connections.

The nationalism was also in place by the time Domingo left Jamaica in 1910, cemented by his education in Sandy Cox's National Club. In his early years in

8. Margaret Stevens, "The Early Political History of Wilfred A. Domingo, 1919–39", in *Caribbean Political Activism: Essays in Honour of Richard Hart*, ed. Rupert Lewis, Kingston, Jamaica: Ian Randle, 2012, pp. 118–143.

9. Ognimod [W. A. Domingo], "Make the Coronation Market Sanitary", *Public Opinion*, 14 December 1946, p. 15. An early venture of Domingo's had involved importing scrap rubber from Jamaica into New York (see above, p. 15, n. 1).

10. Lewis, *The Growth of the West Indies*, p. 359. Harold Cruse's accusation that Domingo was an "Afro-Britisher" was way off the mark, as Winston James demonstrated (*Holding Aloft the Banner of Ethiopia: Caribbean Radicalism in Early Twentieth-Century America*, London: Verso, 1998, pp. 268–269 and 274–284, commenting on Harold Cruse, *The Crisis of the Negro Intellectual: From Its Origins to the Present*, New York: William Morrow, 1967, p. 127).

Harlem there were three kinds of nationalism that Domingo had no time for. He was—as he remained all his life—a British citizen, but he gave that nationality no kind of attention. Stuart Hall's idea of "familiar strangeness" just wouldn't apply to Domingo: a British West Indian who never visited the UK and took no particular interest in the country, and yet who never took out US citizenship—as he could have done—and so never really engaged with issues of African-American identity in the USA.[11] The other kind of nationalism that Domingo rejected was Marcus Garvey's so-called black nationalism. There were personal reasons for this: Domingo basically thought that Garvey was a charlatan. But Domingo also never had any sympathy for the fantasy of a separate African nation which Garvey began pushing for in 1920.[12] For Garvey nationhood meant the African nation, a totally unrealistic prospect based—as Domingo often pointed out—on his ignorance of the continent and of the desires and interests of its inhabitants. Nor, despite his very decisive anti-racist interventions, did Domingo want a politics ultimately *based* on race.

The charge most often made against Domingo's nationalism is that of "islandism". Those who still think favourably of the federal idea (such as Eric D. Duke and Earl Gooding) speak of "islandism" to denigrate the supposedly "narrow" thinking of Jamaican or other island nationalists as opposed to the "broad" regionalism favoured by advocates of federation.[13] Sometimes this becomes "insularity", with its even clearer connotations of solipsism.[14] Although it was only briefly and never satisfactorily achieved, the idea of West Indian nationalism is often naturalised in such a way that Jamaican or Trinidadian nationalisms are seen as "fragmentary insular nationalisms".[15] To which Domingo's response would be that the very idea of internationalism—to which he was committed—suggests relationships between nations: in other words, you need a nation before you can be international.

Domingo was also one of the foremost analysts of fascism, his writings, along with those of the likes of Jawaharlal Nehru and George Padmore, consistently

11. Stuart Hall, *Familiar Stranger: A Life Between Two Islands*, London: Allen Lane, 2017.
12. *MGP*, 11, p. lxxxiii.
13. Eric D. Duke, *Building a Nation: Caribbean Federation in the Black Diaspora*, Gainesville, FL: University Press of Florida, 2016; Earl Gooding, *The West Indies at the Crossroads*, Cambridge, MA: Schenkman, 1981.
14. "[T]he triumph of the sentiments of insularity over those of nationalism"; Lloyd Braithwaite, "Progress Toward Federation, 1938–1956", *Social and Economic Studies*, 6, no. 2 (June 1957), pp. 133–184. The two generations of Caribbean intellectuals following Domingo's were almost all committed to the idea of federation (Braithwaite, Norman Girwan, Franklin Knight, and Walter Rodney), and these have been the ones to write the histories of Caribbean thought.
15. "There was a distinct contrast between a unifying regional West Indian nationalism and the fragmentary insular nationalisms in each colony"; O. Nigel Bolland, "Democracy and Authoritarianism in the Struggle for National Liberation: The Caribbean Labour Congress and the Cold War, 1945–1952", *Comparative Studies of South Asia, Africa and the Middle East*, 17, no. 1 (1997), pp. 99–117, at 114.

demonstrating what he called in 1938 the "essential kinship of imperialism with fascism" [#19]. In 1943, after emerging from his detention, he reminded readers that governments who "object to open discussion" are "Fascist in their outlook" and that "all forms of racial and colour discrimination" are "Fascist in conception and opposed to the principles of democracy for which the Allied Nations are professedly fighting" [#28]. Far from simply mobilising support for the Allied war effort, Domingo was pinpointing the affinity between imperialism and fascism, therefore demonstrating the need for *new* democratic projects that will break with the past.

Domingo's interests and proclivities have often made it difficult to pigeonhole him. A left-wing socialist of Leninist sympathies who never joined the Communist Party. A committed anti-colonialist who resisted the siren call of federation embraced by almost all of his contemporaries. Nowhere is this difficulty more evident than in Domingo's Africanism. Despite his unrelenting opposition to Marcus Garvey, Domingo took great pride in black achievements, showed consistent interest in events in Nigeria, and publicised the Fifth Pan-African Congress in Manchester in 1945, highlighting the role of his friend Amy Jacques Garvey as a lynchpin in its organisation.[16] Always slightly aslant to mainstream ideas, Domingo contributed to all these areas, even if his contributions are often downplayed or misunderstood precisely because his ideas cannot be easily confined to any one of them.

* * *

Figure 11 W. A. Domingo's grave site in the Woodlawn Cemetery, New York. (Photograph by Peter Hulme)

16. See Myles Osborne, "Africa in Jamaica: George Padmore, W. A. Domingo, and *Public Opinion*", in *The Edinburgh Companion to British Colonial Periodicals*, ed. David Finkelstein, David Johnson, and Caroline Davis, Edinburgh, UK: Edinburgh University Press, 2024, pp. 519–530.

The last words belong to one of the men who knew Domingo best and who appreciated his character even after political disagreements had caused a rift between them:

> He had a sound knowledge of history and a keen insight into the future and how it was likely to shape itself. As a public speaker he had a great range of rhetorical fire, but as a writer he was cool, logical, unrelenting, and one of the shrewdest controversialists I have ever known. And he was a most lovable and simple person who demanded little for himself as to be free to demand all for his causes. Those of us who knew him well will never forget this unforgettable man.[17]

17. Manley, "One of the Dedicated Men", p. 4.

Index